CliffsAP®

English Language and Composition

3RD EDITION

by

Barbara V. Swovelin

WILEY

Wiley Publishing, Inc.

About the Author

Barbara Swovelin has taught AP and Honors classes since 1982. She serves as an AP English Exam Reader and a College Board Consultant. Mrs. Swovelin has also taught graduate-level test preparation classes at California universities since 1986. She currently teaches at Torrey Pines High School in Del Mar, California.

Publisher's Acknowledgments

Editorial

Acquisitions Editor: Greg Tubach

Project Editor: Donna Wright

Copy Editor: Elizabeth Kuball

Composition

Proofreader: Melissa D. Buddendeck

Wiley Publishing Composition Services

CliffsAP® English Language and Composition, 3rd Edition

Published by:
Wiley Publishing, Inc.
111 River Street
Hoboken, NJ 07030-5774
www.wiley.com

Copyright © 2006 Wiley, Hoboken, NJ

Published by Wiley, Hoboken, NJ
Published simultaneously in Canada

Library of Congress Cataloging-in-Publication data is available from the publisher upon request.

ISBN-13: 978-0-471-93368-7

ISBN-10: 0-471-93368-6

3O/RV/QV/QY/IN

Printed in the United States of America

10 9

WILEY

Text Permissions

Art Credits

Author Acknowledgments

This book is dedicated to my husband, Jerry, who assisted and inspired me when I needed it most. I want to thank Dr. Jerry Bobrow for always believing in me, and I want to recognize Dr. Allan Casson, in memoriam, for his invaluable technical assistance in the first two editions of this book. Finally, I would like to thank all of my students and acknowledge Carrie Cunningham, Bill Danielson, Jessica Grossman, Tim Hong, Vincent Liang, Oliver Miao, Cindy Mong, Cheya Pope, Kelley Schiffman, and Derek Southern for their invaluable help with the essays.

Table of Contents

PART I: INTRODUCTION

PART II: ANALYSIS OF EXAM AREAS

PART III: DIAGNOSTIC MINI-TEST

PART IV: PAST AP ENGLISH LANGUAGE ESSAYS

PART V: GLOSSARY OF IMPORTANT TERMS FOR THE AP ENGLISH LANGUAGE AND COMPOSITION EXAM

PART VI: SIX FULL-LENGTH PRACTICE TESTS

PART VII: SUGGESTED READING LIST

Study Guide Checklist

❑ Become familiar with the test format, page 3.

❑ Familiarize yourself with the answer to Questions Commonly Asked About the AP English Language Exams, page 5.

❑ Carefully read Part II: Analysis of Exam Areas, beginning on page 11.

❑ Take the Mini-Test section by section by section, strictly observing the time allotments, beginning on page 45.

❑ Check your answers, analyze your results, and read the sample essays and analysis, beginning on page 50.

❑ Familiarize yourself with the AP exam terminology by carefully reading Part V: Glossary of Important Terms for the AP English Language and Composition Exam, beginning on page 63.

❑ Take Practice Test 1 section by section, strictly observing time allotments, beginning on page 79.

❑ Check your answers and analyze your results, beginning on page 99.

❑ While referring to each item of Practice Test 1, study ALL of the answers and explanations, including the student essays and analysis, beginning on page 103.

❑ Take Practice Test 2 section by section, strictly observing time allotments, beginning on page 121.

❑ Check your answers and analyze your results, beginning on page 144.

❑ While referring to each item of Practice Test 2, study ALL of the answers and explanations, including the student essays and analysis, beginning on page 147.

❑ Take Practice Test 3 section by section, strictly observing time allotments, beginning on page 165.

❑ Check your answers and analyze your results, beginning on page 187.

❑ While referring to each item of Practice Test 3, study ALL of the answers and explanations, including the student essays and analysis, beginning on page 191.

❑ Take Practice Test 4 section by section, strictly observing time allotments, beginning on page 209.

❑ Check your answers and analyze your results, beginning on page 231.

❑ While referring to each item of Practice Test 4, study ALL of the answers and explanations, including the student essays and analysis, beginning on page 235.

❑ Take Practice Test 5 section by section, strictly observing time allotments, beginning on page 253.

❑ Check your answers and analyze your results, beginning on page 274.

❑ While referring to each item of Practice Test 5, study ALL of the answers and explanations, including the student essays and analysis, beginning on page 277.

❑ Take Practice Test 6 section by section, strictly observing time allotments, beginning on page 295.

❑ Check your answers and analyze your results, beginning on page 316.

❑ While referring to each item of Practice Test 6, study ALL of the answers and explanations, including the student essays and analysis, beginning on page 319.

INTRODUCTION

Format and Scoring of a Recent AP Language and Composition Exam

Format	
Section I: Multiple-choice questions (approximately 55)	60 minutes
Section II: Free-response sections (3 essays)	135 minutes
Total time	195 minutes

Scoring

1. In the multiple-choice section, you earn 1 point for each correct answer. To eliminate random guessing, 0.25 point is deducted from the total for each wrong answer. Unanswered questions do not count for or against your score. The multiple-choice section equals 45% of the total exam score.

2. The three essays are each scored holistically; the scores range from 1 to 9 (or 0 for a blank paper or one that does not attempt to answer the question). These scores are then calculated to equal 55% of the total exam score. You can read more detailed information on the scoring of the essays in the "Introduction to the Essay Section," later in this book.

3. The multiple-choice section score is added to the free-response section score to produce a composite (or total) score. Finally, this composite is translated into a 5-point scale that is reported in July to you, your secondary school, and any college designated by you.

4. AP final scores are reported as follows:
   5 = extremely well qualified
   4 = well qualified
   3 = qualified
   2 = possibly qualified
   1 = no recommendation

General Description

The AP English Language and Composition Exam is used by colleges to assess your ability to perform college-level work. Actual college credit (either for one semester or for an entire year) may be offered by colleges and universities. The test lasts 3 hours and 15 minutes and consists of two major sections. The multiple-choice section includes approximately 55 questions that address four reading passages. All the questions in this section have equal value. The second portion of the test is called the free-response section. You are given three essay topics, and you must write an essay on each of the three topics in 2 hours and 15 minutes. The suggested time allotment for each essay is 40 minutes, and an extra 15 minutes is added for reading the essay prompts. Each of the essays is of equal value in your final score.

The multiple-choice questions are designed to test your ability in analyzing prose passages. These passages are drawn from a variety of sources, rhetorical modes, historical or literary periods, and disciplines. You will be asked questions about the passages' style, content, and rhetoric. Expect four reading passages with between 12 and 15 questions per passage. However, do not be surprised if you receive five reading passages, which occasionally happens. If this is the case, the number of questions for each passage will be reduced accordingly. The multiple-choice questions are carefully written and screened by the AP Test Development Committee and the Educational Testing Service (ETS). The committee is ethnically and geographically balanced, and its members represent public and private high schools, as well as colleges and universities. The committee is responsible for choosing the passages for both the multiple-choice section and the essay portion of the exam. All of the multiple-choice questions are pretested in college classes before they are used on AP examinations.

The essays test your writing ability in a variety of modes and for a variety of purposes. These timed essays measure your expository and analytical writing skills, skills that are essential to success in many college exams. In general, expect that the three different essays will give you an opportunity to demonstrate that you can do the following:

1. Analyze how an author's rhetoric and style create meaning, based on one given reading passage.
2. Analyze an author's key point(s) in a given passage and create an argument essay that discusses the validity of the author's message.
3. Synthesize an argument of your own, based on multiple given passages, all dealing with similar subject matter.

The essay examinations are read and scored during a 7-day period in early June. In 2000, more than 300 readers representing the United States, Canada, and other foreign countries read more than 115,000 AP English Language exams; by 2005, more than 700 readers scored essays from 240,000 test-takers. More than half of the AP readers are college or university instructors; less than half are high school teachers. Each reader is assigned to score only one essay question during the reading session; therefore, each student's work is read by at least three different readers. Some essays are read and chosen as samples to be examined by all the readers, while others are checked by the table leaders and question leaders after an individual reader has scored the essay. You can trust that the essay scoring is as professional and accurate as possible. All readers are thoroughly trained and retrained throughout the week of scoring.

Each essay is scored on a scale from 0 to 9. After reading a large number of randomly selected essays, a committee creates a scoring guide that differentiates between the numerical scores for each of the three essay questions. Therefore, the scoring guide is based on the students' *actual performance* in writing the essays, not how the question writers *anticipate* they should perform.

Overall, the entire exam is designed to show student awareness of how an author creates meaning through language use, genre conventions, and rhetorical choices. A qualifying score demonstrates your ability to perform college-level work.

Questions Commonly Asked About the AP English Exams

Q. Who administers the test?

A. The Advanced Placement exams are sponsored by the College Board. The test is administered through the Educational Testing Service (ETS).

Q. What materials may I bring to the test?

A. Bring your identification card, as well as plenty of pens for the essays and pencils for the multiple-choice questions. You may not bring a dictionary, a thesaurus, or any other reference book.

Q. May I cancel my score following the exam?

A. Yes. You always have this option. Check the current AP Bulletin for procedures and deadlines.

Q. Is there a penalty for a wrong answer?

A. Yes. To discourage random guessing, 0.25 point is deducted for each wrong answer. You should make only educated guesses.

Q. How can I prepare?

A. Practice! Become comfortable with the test and its format. Take several practice exams to work on your timing. Learn new or unfamiliar terms that you might be expected to know for the exam. Practice your essay planning and timed writing. Practice paraphrasing what you read so that this skill becomes second nature before the exam.

Q. How do I register for an AP exam?

A. See your school counseling office for registration information. Most schools register candidates in March for the upcoming May AP exams.

Q. Is paper provided for the essays?

A. Yes. In fact, you'll write all of your essays in a special book that conceals your identity from the readers who score it.

Q. How many students take the AP English exams every year?

A. Each year, the number of students taking the test increases. In 2000, more than 115,000 students took the AP English Language and Composition Exam, while more than 189,000 took the AP English Literature and Composition Exam. By 2005, 240,000 students took the AP Language and Composition Exam, while 287,000 took the AP Literature and Composition Exam.

Q. Why are there two English exams?

A. Because not all colleges offer the same curriculum for freshman English. The two separate exams—AP English Language and Composition and AP English Literature and Composition—permit each college to designate the exam that best reflects its curriculum.

Q. What's the difference between the two English exams?

A. The two exams are similar; both test your ability to analyze the written word and to prove that you can communicate intelligent ideas on a given subject. However, the AP Language and Composition Exam asks more questions about nonfiction; there is no poetry on the language exam. The language exam also places more emphasis on rhetorical analysis and the study of *how* language works. Expect to write argumentative essays and rhetorical/style analysis essays, and synthesis essays that explore various authors' positions. In contrast, the literature exam places greater emphasis on literary analysis; it includes poetry, fiction, and drama. You should expect to analyze several poems on the literature test.

Q. Which exam should I take?

A. The best way to decide which exam to take is to ask the college that you plan to attend. A college may offer either one or two semesters of credit depending on its freshman English curriculum. Generally, a school that has a literary component combined with expository writing skills in its freshman English course gives up to a full year's course credit for the literature exam. Conversely, a school that has a full year of freshman writing in various rhetorical modes may give up to a full year's credit for the language exam. In addition, you must know your own strengths and weaknesses, your likes and dislikes. If you enjoy prose reading and persuasive, analytical writing, then the language exam is for you. If you have a strong literary background, especially in American and British literature and poetic analysis, then the literature exam will be a better fit.

Q. Is one exam easier than the other?

A. They are equally rigorous.

Q. What is an average score?

A. To earn an average score of 3, you must answer approximately 50% to 60% of the questions correctly on the multiple-choice section and also write three adequate essays. At a typical test administration, two-thirds of all test-takers receive a score of 3 or higher.

Q. Can I take both the literature exam and the language exam in the same school year?

A. Yes, they are administered on different days.

Q. How can I find out how much college credit I'll get if I pass the test?

A. Contact the college and ask the admissions office for a clear, written response. Do not be surprised to find that this is a somewhat confusing issue, compounded by the fact that two English exams exist. Additionally, some colleges and universities consider an overall score of 3 as passing, while other colleges require a 4 or even a 5. Some colleges do require that all freshmen take their freshman English class, usually a composition course. In addition, some schools or programs within a college have different requirements.

Q. Do colleges get separate scores for my multiple-choice and essay sections? May I get the two separate scores?

A. No to both questions. Only your overall score, based on a scale of 1 to 5, will be released to you or to any college.

Q. What if my school does not offer an AP course or I did not enroll in the course? May I take the test anyway?

A. Sure! Although an AP course is theoretically designed to prepare students for the test, much of that "preparation" consists of reading quality literature—both fiction and nonfiction—and practicing analysis, critical thinking, and close reading in addition to taking practice AP exams and understanding the format of the exam. You can do this on your own, especially if you have disciplined study habits. However, I do strongly recommend that you read this test-preparation book carefully, and, if you can, also explore the College Board website (www.collegeboard.com/ap).

Q. When will I receive my AP exam scores?

A. You will receive your scores at about the same time as the colleges do, in early July.

Q. How can I obtain previous exams to use for practice?

A. You may order previously released exams directly from the College Board at the Advanced Placement Program, P.O. Box 6670, Princeton, NJ 08541-6670. You may also order materials online; the AP section of College Board information can be found at the College Board's online store at www.collegeboard.com/ap.

Q. How often are previous exams released to the public?

A. Multiple-choice exams are released every 5 years; essay topics are released every year.

Q. **If I am not certain of the correct answer, should I guess on a multiple-choice question?**

A. Don't be afraid to make an educated guess if you can eliminate at least two of the answer choices. Remember that you get no credit for a question you skip, but you do lose 0.25 point for a wrong answer. If a question seems really hard for you, or if you know from your pretesting practice that it is a question type that tends to stump you, let it go and skip it. Don't forget to leave that answer space blank on your answer sheet when you do fill in the next answer. You will find more information on guessing and eliminating answers in the "Introduction to the Multiple-Choice Section," later in this book.

Q. **Can I still pass the test even if I don't finish all the multiple-choice questions in time?**

A. Yes! Many students don't finish all the questions and still receive a passing score. Naturally, if you don't finish, you need to exhibit good accuracy on the questions you do complete and write three good essays. If you are running out of time, do not randomly fill in multiple-choice answers; the chances are you'll get too many wrong and lose 0.25 point for each wrong answer.

Q. **Should I take the multiple-choice passages in the order they appear on the exam?**

A. Many students choose to answer the multiple-choice passages in the order they appear on the exam, as it is a very systematic and logical approach. However, keep a steady pace and do not let one passage eat up too much of your time, subsequently causing you to slight your time on the last passage(s). Overall, remember that your score is determined by the total number of questions you answer correctly, minus 0.25 point for wrong answers.

Q. **What score will I get for a right answer, a wrong answer, and no answer in the multiple-choice section?**

A. For each correct response, you receive 1 point; a wrong answer deducts 0.25 point from your score; and an omitted answer earns 0. If you get every multiple-choice answer correct, the total score will equal 45% of 150, or 67.5 points. You will find more explanation on converting raw scores to scaled scores on page 8.

Q. **Does the scoring give extra weight to one of the essays?**

A. No, all three essays are counted equally. Because the essay portion of the test is 55% of your total score, each essay equals 18.3% of your essay score.

Q. **Should I plan my essay in advance?**

A. In general, yes, planning your essay in advance is a good strategy. An outline is never required and will never be seen by the readers anyway, but clear and logical organization is, indeed, an important criterion on which your essay is scored. You need to at least organize what points you intend to make and the order in which you plan to present them.

Q. **How many paragraphs should I write for each essay?**

A. As many paragraphs as you need to fully develop and present your ideas. Although the introduction-body-conclusion format is most frequently used, the number of body paragraphs presented varies from student to student and topic to topic. An introductory paragraph that contains a thesis is understandably an appropriate beginning, but don't worry if you don't get to the conclusion. Read more about essay organization and development in the "Introduction to the Essay Section," later in this book.

Q. **How many pages should each essay be?**

A. No set length is required; however, most high-scoring essays are at least 1½ pages long. Naturally, some essays are shorter and some are longer. Instead of worrying about length, concentrate on addressing all of the tasks of the topic and developing your ideas thoroughly. Be aware that very short essays, such as those that are only about half a page in length, are considered "unacceptably brief" and score very low; they simply do not demonstrate enough development of ideas to receive a passing score. You can read sample student essays in the "Introduction to the Essay Section," later in this book, and get a feel for length.

Q. **How much should I worry about grammar and spelling?**

A. Good news! You don't have to worry too much about your spelling. If you can spell reasonably well, no reader will dock your score. When you read any of the scoring guides for essays, you will notice that the word "spelling" is never mentioned. The readers are remarkably tolerant; they want to read your words. Grammar and punctuation can be another issue, though. The readers are always willing to overlook what they call "minor errors" or "honest mistakes" that are made under timed pressure. They understand that what you have produced is a first draft that is likely to have a few flaws. However, if your errors are persistent and serious, the reader will have to lower your score. In fact, the scoring guide states that no essay that is particularly poorly written—one with errors so severe that they distract the reader's attention from the student's ideas—may receive a score higher than a 2.

Q. **Should I write my essays in cursive or should I print?**

A. You need to write as legibly as you can, so use whatever method is easiest to read. The readers want to be able to reward you for your essay; to do so, they have to read the words. Please don't forget to use a nice black or blue pen; avoid ones that bleed through paper, because you'll want to write on the back of the page.

Q. **Do the essays need a title?**

A. Not at all. It will never affect your score. I can guarantee that readers are bored by dull titles anyway. Why not just get started on the essay itself?

Q. **May I be creative in my essay writing?**

A. The number-one rule is that you must address the essay question; if you can do so in a creative fashion, you may be rewarded, as long as it works well. However, writing something as far-fetched as a poem or short story would be unacceptable. Again, when you read some sample scoring guides, you'll notice that creativity is never mentioned as a specific criterion for scoring. The basic tenets are that your essay must be focused on the topic, organized, and well developed. Accomplish all of that in a creative style with a strong voice and the reader may be pleasantly surprised. I've read essays with a creative approach that received a 9 because they covered all the necessary points and presented ideas in such a refreshing style.

Q. **How much of the essay passage should I quote?**

A. No set, formulaic answer exists. Yes, you do need to refer to the passage appropriately in order to support your ideas, and many of those examples should take the form of quotations. However, a string of irrelevant quotations, glued together with a few of your own words will not help your score at all. Read the many sample essays in this text to get a feel for what's appropriate.

Q. **Can I pass the test if I don't finish an essay?**

A. Of course! Understandably, a radically unfinished essay will receive a very low score, so try to pace yourself accordingly, devoting approximately 40 minutes to each essay. Doing so should allow you time to finish each essay. Also, practice your pacing many times before the test. I also advise practicing the planning period over and over. If, within approximately 10 to 12 minutes, you can organize what you're going to say and the order in which you're going to present it, you should have enough time to actually write the words and sentences. Finally, if you find yourself in a time crunch on the day of the test, remember that body paragraphs are much more important than concluding paragraphs—especially conclusions that merely summarize. You should devote your time to getting your ideas down on paper. The readers' constant motto is: "Reward the writers for what they do well."

Q. **Can you tell me how to approximate my score from my practice tests into an AP scaled score of 1 through 5?**

A. Approximating your score is a bit more complicated than merely counting your numbers right and numbers wrong, but follow these directions and use the chart that follows. Additionally, you will find a sample scoring worksheet located in this text after each full-length sample exam (on the page before the answers and explanations).

The total score on the exam is 150. Because the essay and multiple-choice parts are weighted 55% to 45%, there are 82.5 points for the essays and 67.5 points for the multiple-choice questions. Because the three essays are graded on a 9-point scale, each point on your essay raw score will be multiplied by 3.0556. Three 9s would total 27, and 27×3.0556 would total 82.5. If there are 55 multiple-choice questions, each point in the raw score would be multiplied by 1.2272 to equal 67.5, Remember that the raw score in the multiple-choice section is determined by the number of correct answers minus 0.25 point for each wrong answer. A test with 30 right, 20 wrong, and 5 omitted would have a raw score of $30 - 5$, or 25. This raw score converts to a total of 30.68 (25×1.2272).

The total number of points required for a final score of 3, 4, or 5 varies each year, but a very reasonable assumption is approximately 104 to 150 for a score of 5, 92 to 103 for a score of 4, and 76 to 91 for a score of 3. The following chart gives you an idea of the combined scores you need on the essay and the multiple-choice sections in order to receive final scores of 3, 4, or 5. The chart assumes that there are 55 multiple-choice questions and 3 essay questions graded from 0 to 9.

If a student received 5s on all three essays, in order to receive a final score of 3, he or she would need a raw score (the number correct minus 0.25 times the number wrong) of at least 18 on the multiple-choice section. To receive a final score of 5, that student would need a raw score of at least 46 in the multiple-choice section.

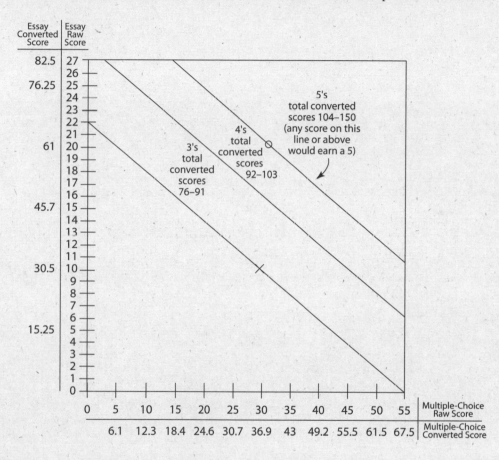

Some Successful Testing Strategies

1. Increase your awareness of the test structure. Know how many questions you'll be asked, how much time you'll have, what basic skills you'll need, and so forth. Of course, these preliminaries are all covered in this book.

2. Understand the thought process behind the exam. If you understand what the test-makers have in mind when they write questions and answers, you'll avoid fighting the test, and your elimination of wrong answers will go faster.

3. Read the test directions carefully! Become familiar with the wording of the directions in advance so that you'll be as comfortable as possible on the day of your AP exam.

4. Mark your answer sheet carefully. If you skip an answer, mark it in your test book, and then carefully enter the next answer on your answer sheet.

5. Practice your pacing and timing skills. For multiple-choice questions, complete the easiest ones first; in essay writing, follow your preplanned strategy.

6. Overall, be prepared! Become familiar with the test. Remember that increased comfort builds confidence and relieves anxiety. These skills can all be improved by practicing frequently.

PART II

ANALYSIS OF EXAM AREAS

This section is designed to introduce you to each AP area by carefully reviewing the

1. ability tested
2. basic skills necessary
3. directions
4. analysis of directions
5. suggested approaches and strategies

Introduction to the Multiple-Choice Section

The multiple-choice section is normally 60 minutes long and consists of about 55 questions. You should expect four reading passages that represent a variety of rhetorical modes (for example, narration, argumentation, persuasion, description). The passages may vary in length from about 300 to about 800 words. Each passage is followed by 10 to 15 questions based on its content. These questions are not ordered by level of difficulty. Occasionally, a multiple-choice section of the exam may have five passages, rather than four, with fewer questions per passage. The total number of questions is approximately the same on every exam.

Remember that you're not expected to be familiar with the passage or its specific content. Consider this section akin to a scavenger hunt; the passage will give you everything you need, it's just up to you to find it and think about it accurately. Any technical information crucial to comprehending the passage, as well as unusual or foreign phrases, will be defined for you.

You will be more comfortable with both the essay and multiple-choice sections if you are adept at reading works from many genres and time periods. For instance, the test can cover works from autobiographies or biographies, historical writing, essays and literary criticism, journalism, political writing, nature writing, and scientific writing. The test passages can be up to about 400 years old, so you'll need to practice comprehending and appreciating the styles of older pieces as well as contemporary ones. A student who only practices with modern-day authors will not be as relaxed or efficient during the exam as one who has been exposed to John Milton or Dr. Johnson.

Beginning in 2007, at least one multiple-choice passage will contain documentation of some sort, such as footnotes. Expect some questions about this documentation, such as what inferences you can draw from the source in a footnote. The questions that deal with documentation will focus on what a reader can infer from such information as footnotes, but you will *not* be asked about proper citation form or punctuation. The reading passage that has documentation will, of course, ask questions about the passage's content; only a few questions will concentrate on the documentation.

Ability Tested

This section tests your ability to analyze the linguistic and rhetorical choices of an author. You are expected to show an awareness of the stylistic effects created by specific word choices and syntactic decisions. These questions also test your ability to examine prose passages critically; to understand the author's meaning and purpose; to comprehend structural organization; to recognize rhetorical modes; and to analyze syntax, figurative language, style, and tone. The level of difficulty reflects college-level study.

Basic Skills Necessary

In general, you need an adequate background in grammar plus skills in literary and rhetorical analysis. Although the questions don't specifically ask for definitions of terms (such as *subordinate clause* or *syntax*), you should be familiar with terms that may show up in the question stems or as answer choices. See the "Terms for the Multiple Choice and Essay Sections," later in this book, for a review of the terms you're likely to encounter on the test. In addition, you need to have developed proficiency in careful reading for your analysis and interpretation of the passages. You can gain this proficiency by using active, visual reading.

Directions

Directions: This section contains selections from prose works and questions on their content, form, and style. Read each selection carefully. Choose the best answer of the five choices to each question.

Questions 1– . Read the following passage carefully before you begin to answer the questions.

Analysis of Directions

- Use self-discipline to manage your time effectively during the test. You can develop this skill through practice. You should divide your time for each passage accordingly. Do not let yourself fall further and further behind as the test progresses.

- Answer all the questions to the best of your ability before going on to the next passage. This strategy prevents you from having to return to any given passage at the end of the test just to answer a few skipped questions. If you put yourself in the position of returning to a passage, you'll have to reread it and that process is too time-consuming.

- Read each passage carefully and critically. First, paraphrase the author's ideas as you read; then, concentrate on the author's effective word choices. Avoid getting bogged down in diction, whether it's a word you don't know or the structure of a sentence that's confusing. Simply keep trying to get the main point and then let the questions guide what you need to know.

- Read all the answer choices. Remember that the directions ask for the *best* answer choice, which means there can be more than one reasonable choice for each question. Eliminate wrong answer choices. Never forget that the wrong answer is wrong for a reason. The correct response will not have a single wrong word in it. You can become more proficient at eliminating wrong answers by practicing spotting the wrong word or phrase in the incorrect responses.

Suggested Strategies for Reading Passages and Questions

1. **First, skim the question to find out what you should concentrate on.** Skimming the questions before reading the passage helps you focus on what the test-writers found important. Skimming involves a very fast reading speed—approximately 1,000 words per minute—so be aware that during this skimming, you are really just glancing at the questions. Ignore any "generic" questions, such as ones that ask you the author's main purpose or main point; instead, try to find approximately five specific ideas that you can look for while you read the passage. Do not try to memorize the questions; you're just glancing at them to help you focus on the passage while you read.

   This technique works well, but you must practice it frequently enough before the test for it to become second nature. You should look for the specific content of each question. For example, don't merely note that a question asks you to draw an inference. You must also focus upon the specific content included in the inference. Prior practice is essential for you to become comfortable with the strategy of skimming the questions prior to reading the passage.

2. **Read each passage *actively* and *visually*.** Active reading means that you should underline and mark key words and ideas (just the few most important ones) as you read. Don't sit passively and merely let your eyes move across the page. Scientific studies support the idea that active readers gain higher immediate retention than do passive readers, and immediate retention is all you need in this case. You won't be concerned at all with long-term memory on the day of the exam.

   Visual reading means that you should picture any action of the passage in your mind; create a movie, if you will. Visual reading is a most valuable tool for eliminating distractions while reading. It gives your brain a task to perform and helps keep your mind on the content of the passage. Most people are visual learners; they remember more after they have "seen" something, even if it's in their imagination. Both of these strategies enhance your immediate retention and concentration—just what you need the most on this test. Practice these skills daily and watch them become more effective with continued use.

3. **Paraphrase while you're reading.** This technique also helps your immediate retention and understanding of the author's ideas. By definition, paraphrasing means that you can articulate the author's ideas in your own words.

This is an essential skill for comprehension, and, like visual reading, it gives your brain something to do that is on task while you read. Every question that asks about a passage's main ideas or an author's point can be answered correctly if you paraphrase accurately. For any given passage, paraphrase each paragraph as a unit, and then paraphrase the author's overall point that covers all of the paragraphs. Practice by writing down your concise statement of an author's point immediately after reading a paragraph or a whole passage. Later, you can develop this skill to the point that it's internalized, and you can paraphrase very quickly. You'll find that, eventually, you can paraphrase effectively while you're reading.

4. **Read the question carefully after you've read the passage.** Don't assume from an earlier skimming that you know each question well. You must understand exactly what you're being asked. Students frequently choose the wrong answer because they have misread the question, either by reading too quickly or by not being sure what's actually being asked.

5. **Read all the answer choices carefully.** Eliminate a wrong answer choice as you read it by crossing out that letter in the test book. Never waste time rereading the wrong answers. Make sure that your answer choice is accurate according to the passage and that it answers the question.

6. **Leave the most difficult questions until the end of each section.** From your practice on the test, you can learn to recognize which questions are harder for you and which ones you can do accurately and quickly. Then use this knowledge as part of your personal strategy to get the most correct answers you possibly can. Remember to treat each passage as a unit and try to answer all the questions you can for that passage within your time limit before going on to the next passage.

7. **One way to increase your score is to always analyze the questions that you get wrong on the practice tests.** Try to identify the specific reason why you selected each incorrect answer choice. Did you misread the question? Did you misread the answer? Did you work too quickly? Try to detect any trends; for example, a certain question type may always be the hardest for you. Then you can study, analyze, and understand why the correct answer is better than your choice. This analysis will help you to stop repeating the same mistakes.

8. **Practice!** With extensive practice, you'll increase your familiarity with the question types. Thus, you'll begin to think like the test-makers, not the test-takers, and your score will improve.

Reasons Answers May Be Wrong

Understanding how to eliminate incorrect answer choices saves time and increases accuracy. Of course, the test-writers are trying to mislead you. If you understand the tricks they frequently throw at you, you'll work faster to eliminate wrong answers and you'll be less likely to be deceived by them. When trying to eliminate wrong answers, remember to think like a test-writer, not a test-taker. Remember to cross out each wrong answer in the test booklet; don't waste time rereading these wrong answers. Wrong answers can be:

1. Contradictory to the passage: If you read the passage carefully and paraphrase accurately you won't be tricked into the time-consuming process of rereading it to decide if the answer is consistent with the passage.

2. Irrelevant or not addressed in the passage: Again, poor readers are tricked into rereading to look for ideas that weren't there in the first place. Readers who are accurate at paraphrasing can quickly eliminate the irrelevant or "never addressed" answer choice.

3. Unreasonable: If the answer makes you shake your head and ask, "Where did they get that idea?", it's unreasonable. You can learn to spot unreasonable answer choices quickly.

4. Too general or too specific for the question. Understand the degree of specificity that you need for a correct answer. For instance, if the question asks for the best title of a passage, you need a general answer, one that encompasses the content of the entire passage. On the other hand, if you're asked about the author's use of a certain quotation, the correct answer is likely to be quite specific.

Finally, never forget that the wrong answer is wrong for a specific reason and will *always* have an inaccurate word or phrase. Practice crossing out the exact word or phrase that is wrong and you'll find you can perform faster and with greater confidence. The correct answer will not have a single word that is inaccurate.

Question Categories to Expect

In general, the test questions tend to fall into just a few categories. By becoming familiar with these areas, you can more quickly understand what you're being asked. Also, you'll be more comfortable with the test format and able to work faster. As with all testing strategies, it is essential to practice recognizing the question types *before* the test.

A brief analysis of these questions types follows.

Questions About Rhetoric

Most of the questions on the test are of this type and test your ability to understand *how* language works in each passage. These questions ask you to analyze the *syntax* (sentence structure and word order), *diction* (word choice), point of view, and figurative language and its effects. Your mere recognition of these elements is not enough; you must be able to understand precisely how and why the devices of rhetoric produce particular effects.

Here are some of the ways this question type may be worded on the test:

- The shift in point of view has the effect of . . .
- The syntax of lines _____ to _____ serves to . . .
- Which of the following choices best describes what "_____" symbolizes?
- The second sentence is unified by metaphorical references to . . .
- As lines _____ and _____ are constructed, "_____" is parallel to which of the following?
- The antecedent for "_____" is . . .
- The third sentence remains coherent because of the use of . . .
- The phrase "_____" has the effect of . . .
- The style of the passage can best be characterized as . . .
- The sentence "_____" is chiefly remarkable for its . . .

Questions About the Author's Meaning and Purpose

These question types also appear frequently on the test. They measure your ability to interpret the author's theme, meaning, or purpose. As with the rhetorical questions, these questions are closely tied to specific word choices; however, now you must determine *why* the author chooses the wording, not what effect it produces. These questions demonstrate the understanding of the author's thematic reason for choosing certain phrases.

Here are some of the ways this question type may be worded:

- Which of the following best identifies the meaning of "_____"?
- Which of the following best describes the author's purpose in the last sentence?
- The main purpose of "_____" is to make clear . . .
- The author emphasizes "_____" in order to . . .
- The sympathy referred to in line _____ is called "_____" because it . . .
- What is the function of _____ ?
- By "_____," the author most probably means . . .
- In context, which of the following meanings are contained in "_____"?
- In the commentary in the second footnote, the author's primary purpose is most likely . . .

Questions About the Main Idea

These questions also appear quite frequently; they test your understanding of the author's ideas, attitude, and tone. To prepare for these questions, paraphrase everything that you read. First, make yourself practice this skill in writing—literally write down an author's point in a sentence or two. After such practice, you'll be able to do it internally while you read, and you'll have greater comprehension.

Here are some of the ways these questions may be worded:

- The theme of the second paragraph is . . .
- The speaker's attitude is best described as one of . . .
- The speaker interests the audience by stressing the idea that . . .
- It can be inferred from the description of _____ that which of the following qualities are valued by the author?
- In context, the sentence "_____" is best interpreted as which of the following?
- The atmosphere is one of . . .
- Which of the following would the author be LEAST likely to encourage?
- Which of the following is true about the various assertions made in the passage?
- All of the following ideas may be found in the passage EXCEPT . . .
- Which of the following can be inferred from the author's documentation?

Questions About Organization and Structure

Appearing less frequently than the first three question types, these questions test your ability to perceive how the passage is organized. For example, you need to know if the passage follows a compare/contrast structure or if it gives a definition followed by examples. Other passages may be organized around descriptive statements that then lead to a generalization. These methods are just a few of the ones an author may use to organize ideas. You also need to understand how the structure of the passage works. For example, you must know how one paragraph relates to another paragraph or how a single sentence works within a paragraph.

Here are some of the ways this question type may be worded:

- The quotation "_____" signals a shift from . . .
- The speaker's mention of "_____" is appropriate to the development of her argument by . . .
- The type of argument employed by the author is most similar to which of the following?
- The speaker describes _____ in an order best described as moving from . . .
- The relationship between _____ and _____ is explained primarily by the use of which of the following?
- The author's discussion depends on which of the following structures?
- Which of the following best describes the function of the third paragraph in relation to the preceding two?

Questions About Rhetorical Modes

You should expect only a few questions of this type on the test. These questions ask you to identify and recognize the various rhetorical modes that authors use. You must know the difference between narration, description, argumentation, and exposition. Understanding *why* a particular mode is effective for the author's ideas is also helpful.

Here are some of the ways these questions may be worded:

- The pattern of exposition exemplified in the passage can best be described as . . .
- The author's use of description is appropriate because . . .
- Which of the following best describes the author's method?
- Because the author uses expository format, he is able to . . .
- The speaker's rhetorical strategy is to . . .

Other Possibilities

Be aware that these question types do not constitute a complete list. You will encounter questions that don't seem to fit into a category. However, by understanding what question types are asked most frequently, you will increase your familiarity with the test and improve your understanding of how to find correct answers. Don't be thrown off balance by questions that don't seem to fall into set categories.

Examples of Multiple-Choice Passages and Questions

This section contains two passages that are typical of the ones chosen for the multiple-choice section of the exam, followed by sample questions. Read the passage(s) carefully, and attempt to find the correct answer to each question. The answers and their explanations follow.

Set 1

Directions: The following excerpt, from the 20th-century writer Ellen Meloy, is typical of the difficulty of the passages you will encounter on the actual AP English Language and Composition Exam. Read it carefully and then answer the 15 multiple-choice questions that follow. Choose the *best* answer of the five options. Answers and explanations for the questions immediately follow. Then, you will find another sample passage with its questions, answers, and explanations.

The morning sun, already burning an eighty-degree day, tops a cliff cut with fine strata of red rock and broken at its foot by emerald cottonwoods and a silt-gold river. I don a khaki uniform shirt, shorts,
(5) ninety-seven-cent hot pink thongs and, clipboard in hand, walk from the trailer to a boat ramp plunked down in nearly a million acres of sparsely inhabited desert. This is an act of courage. Courage to face the violation of isolation rather than isolation itself, for I
(10) savor the remoteness and the rare times I'm alone on this muscular river in southern Utah, a precious ribbon of wild water between reservoirs and the suck holes of industry and agriculture.

Officially, I'm here to have my peace disturbed.
(15) Floaters must have a permit to run this stretch of river. During the peak season a ranger checks lottery-drawn launch dates and a short list of gear related to safety and environmental protection. The permit system allows the federal agency in charge
(20) to hold numbers of floaters to a maximum of about 10,000 a year, set in 1979, when use increased 250 percent in just three seasons. Each year since, the actual number of people down the river has hovered close to this ceiling, which the agency believes is
(25) the river's capacity for a "quality wilderness experience." Socially, if not physically, however, "wilderness experience" seems to have become an illusion if not irrelevant. Right now I'm the voluntary ranger managing both the illusion and the irrelevance.
(30) Most people accept the permit system as a panacea for the explosion in numbers of river runners and the consequences for a fragile riparian corridor. Others find regulation about as painless as an

IRS audit. They see the Southwest as a region of
(35) federally neutered rivers where a person is no longer free to kill himself in a four-foot rubber ducky pulling an inner tube piled with beans, testosterone, and a small machete. Instead, some geek rangerette at the put-in asks to see his bilge pump.
(40) The boat ramp is swarming with people and vehicles to be shuttled to the take-out. Someone's dog is throwing up what appears to be rabbit parts. I'm approached by a pickup driven by a man waving a spray nozzle and hose hooked to a large barrel of
(45) allegedly lethal chemicals. He's from county weed control, he says. Have I seen the loathsome pepperweed? Not a leaf, I lie.

Cheerfully I sign the permit of the outfitter who specializes in theme river trips—stress management
(50) seminars, outings for the crystal fondlers or fingernail technicians of East Jesus, New Jersey, overcoming, at last, their irrational fear of Nature. Today's load is priests troubled by a lapsed faith—pale, anxious, overweight fellows in the early stages of heat-
(55) stroke. I also check gear and answer questions about bugs, snakes, scorpions, camps, rapids and Indians (one side of the river is reservation land). Do I live here full-time? they ask. No, I respond, except for an occasional shift at the put-in, I'm on the river eight
(60) days out of sixteen, six months a year.
Would I please call their mother in Provo to tell her they forgot to turn off the oven? Am I afraid of being alone when the ax murderer shows up? Did Ed Abbey live in that trailer over there?
(65) Some rafts look as if they barely survived World War II.

Others are outfitted with turbodynamic chrome-plated throw lines, heat-welded vinyl dry-bags, cargo nets spun from the fibers of dew-fed arachnids from Borneo, horseshoes, volleyball sets, sauna tents, cof-
(70) fin-sized coolers stuffed with sushi, a small fleet of squirt boats, whining packs of androgynous progeny who prefer to be at home fulfilling their needs electronically. All of this gear is color-coordinated

(75) with SPF 14 sunscreen and owned by business majors in Styrofoam pith helmets and Lycra body gloves, in which they were placed at birth. Once loaded, their boats are pieces of personal architecture, stunning but nevertheless stuck on the sandbar six feet out from the boat ramp after a dramatic
(80) send-off.

1. The speaker of the passage is best described as a

- **A.** chronicler of events of the past
- **B.** dispassionate eyewitness of the scene
- **C.** commentator on contemporary American mores
- **D.** concerned and angry ecologist
- **E.** fictional persona describing imaginary events

2. In the first paragraph, the author uses the reference to her "ninety-seven-cent hot pink thongs" in order to

- I. set a tone of casual and humorous informality.
- II. show the speaker's unconcern for the expected ranger uniform
- III. exemplify man's desecration of the natural world

- **A.** I only
- **B.** I and II only
- **C.** I and III only
- **D.** II and III only
- **E.** I, II, and III

3. The move from the first paragraph (lines 1–13) to the second (lines 14–29) can best be described as a shift from

- **A.** personal reminiscence to impersonal inquiry
- **B.** poetic description to dispassionate reasoning
- **C.** philosophical meditation to satiric argument
- **D.** minute description to explanatory generalization
- **E.** personal expression to objective exposition

4. In lines 25–26, the author puts the phrase "quality wilderness experience" in quotation marks in order to

- **A.** draw special attention to a phrase that sums up the meaning of the whole passage
- **B.** give proper credit for a felicitous phrase that is not her own
- **C.** help the reader to remember the phrase
- **D.** disassociate herself from the language of the federal agency
- **E.** encourage wider participation in "wilderness experience"

5. The third paragraph of the passage (lines 30–39) employs all of the following EXCEPT

- **A.** pun
- **B.** simile
- **C.** metaphor
- **D.** hyperbole
- **E.** slang

6. All of the following words or phrases are examples of the author's use of colloquialism EXCEPT

- **A.** "plunked down," lines 6–7
- **B.** "muscular river," line 11
- **C.** "rubber ducky," lines 36–37
- **D.** "geek rangerette," lines 38–39
- **E.** "East Jesus, New Jersey," line 51

7. In the fourth and fifth paragraphs (lines 40–65), the author characterizes the rafters by describing all of the following EXCEPT their

- **A.** possessions
- **B.** physical appearance
- **C.** occupations
- **D.** responses to nature
- **E.** dialogue

8. In the final paragraph, all of the following are probably fanciful comic details EXCEPT

    A.   "turbodynamic chrome-plated throw lines," lines 66–67

    B.   "heat-welded vinyl dry-bags," line 67

    C.   "the fibers of dew-fed arachnids from Borneo," lines 68–69

    D.   "sauna tents," lines 69

    E.   "progeny who prefer to be at home," lines 71–72

9. In lines 71–73, the phrase "androgynous progeny who prefer to be at home fulfilling their needs electronically" refers to

    A.   discontented house pets unaccustomed to outdoor life

    B.   children who would rather be watching television or using their computer

    C.   elaborate radio equipment carried by the rafters

    D.   expensive refrigeration units that are slowly defrosting

    E.   electric motors for propelling the river rafts

10. The effect of the last sentence of the passage (lines 77–80) can be best described as a(n)

    A.   comic anticlimax

    B.   resolution of an argument

    C.   symbolic metaphor

    D.   deliberate understatement

    E.   allegorical conclusion

11. In the course of the passage, the speaker suggests her disapproval of all of the following EXCEPT

    A.   rafters hostile to government regulations

    B.   industry and agriculture

    C.   stress management seminars

    D.   conspicuous consumers

    E.   government regulation of the wild rivers

12. In which paragraph is the speaker's feeling for the landscape revealed most clearly?

    A.   the first

    B.   the second

    C.   the third

    D.   the fourth

    E.   the sixth

13. A primary rhetorical strategy in the passage is to

    A.   use the experience of an individual's life to generalize about life in general

    B.   stimulate the reader's interest by withholding important information

    C.   convince the reader of the speaker's objectivity by presenting an opposing viewpoint

    D.   make its point by an accumulation of carefully observed details

    E.   imply support of a position that is later to be withdrawn

14. In the course of the passage, the speaker uses all of the following tones of voice EXCEPT

    A.   amused

    B.   annoyed

    C.   arrogant

    D.   satiric

    E.   cheerful

15. The primary rhetorical purpose of the passage is to

    A.   describe an idyllic scene in nature

    B.   protest against the loss of the isolated wilderness

    C.   comment upon a popular misconception

    D.   satirize aspects of the back-to-nature movement

    E.   reveal the personality of the speaker

Answers and Explanations for Set 1

This passage is from Ellen Meloy's essay "Communiqué from the Vortex of Gravity Sports."

1. **C.** The passage is written in the present tense, and describes events of the present time. Though it sometimes employs overstatement for comic effect, the passage is apparently a factual, not a fictional, account. Though the speaker is mindful of ecology, she is neither angry nor dispassionate; she is an amused and amusing commentator on this scene that reveals some contemporary American mores.

2. **B.** The speaker's hot-pink thongs reveal her humorous informality and her unconventional notion of a uniform. To read a "desecration" of the natural world into this detail is to miss the tone, to take the passage far too seriously. Because it is the speaker who is wearing the thongs, it is unlikely that they carry such dire significance.

3. **E.** The first paragraph places the speaker in the scene, and tells us something of her feelings. The second paragraph gives an explanation of why she is here. Of the five answers, E is the best choice, because it avoids the outright errors of "reminiscence" and "inquiry," of "reasoning," of "meditation" and "argument," and of "minute description" and "generalization."

4. **D.** Because the speaker has serious doubts about the accuracy of this phrase, she disassociates herself from it by using quotation marks. It may be that she objects to the trite and ungrammatical use of "quality" as an adjective; she certainly questions the use of the word "wilderness" to describe this situation.

5. **A.** The paragraph does not use a pun, but it does employ a simile ("painless as an IRS audit"), metaphor ("explosion," "neutered"), hyperbole or overstatement ("four-foot rubber ducky"), and slang ("geek").

6. **B.** The phrase "muscular river" is figurative, a personification of the river, but it is not colloquial diction. The other four phrases are examples of the effective use of colloquialism in the passage.

7. **D.** These paragraphs describe the rafters' equipment and appearance, the jobs of some of them, and, in indirect discourse, their dialogue. We are not told about their responses to nature.

8. **E.** The "progeny who prefer to be at home" are, no doubt, all too real. The other details are more likely to be comic inventions.

9. **B.** The phrase is a circumlocutionary way of describing the children who prefer television or computers to wild rivers.

10. **A.** Words and phrases like "architecture," "stunning," and "dramatic send-off" suggest some big event, but the reality is the anticlimax of "stuck on the sandbar six feet out from the boat ramp."

11. **E.** The second and third paragraphs suggest that the speaker approves of government regulation of the rivers as a way to protect the "fragile riparian corridor." Her disapproval of the macho rafters who object to the permit system underlies the comedy of the third paragraph. Paragraphs five and six make fun of trendy stress management seminars and the conspicuous consumption of the too-well-equipped rafters, while the first paragraph speaks of the "precious ribbon of wild water between reservoirs and the suck holes of industry and agriculture."

12. **A.** The speaker reveals her own feelings about the wilderness in the first paragraph of the passage.

13. **D.** Of the five rhetorical strategies proposed, only the use of observed details is relevant to this prose.

14. **C.** At one time or another, the speaker sounds amused, annoyed, satiric, and cheerful, but she is never arrogant.

15. **D.** Though the passage does reveal the speaker's regret at the loss of isolated wilderness in the first paragraph, the subject is not developed. Most of the passage is concerned with the presentation of the rafters seeking a "quality wilderness experience."

Set 2

Directions: This second sample passage was written by Frederick Douglass. Read it carefully and answer the 11 questions that follow. As always, select the best answer choice.

Very soon after I went to live with Mr. and Mrs. Auld, she very kindly commenced to teach me the ABCs. After I had learned this, she assisted me in learning to spell words of three or four letters. Just (5) at this point of my progress, Mr. Auld found out what was going on, and at once forbade Mrs. Auld to instruct me further, telling her, among other things, that it was unlawful, as well as unsafe, to teach a slave to read. It would forever unfit him to (10) be a slave. He would at once become unmanageable, and of no value to his master. As to himself, it could do him no good, but a great deal of harm. It would make him discontented and unhappy. These words sank deep into my heart, stirred up senti- (15) ments within that lay slumbering, and called into existence an entirely new train of thought. It was a new and special revelation, explaining dark and mysterious things, with which my youthful understanding had struggled, but struggled in vain. I now (20) understood what had been to me a most perplexing difficulty—to wit, the white man's power to enslave the black man. It was a grand achievement, and I prized it highly. From that moment, I understood the pathway from slavery to freedom. It was (25) just what I wanted, and I got it at a time when I

least expected it. Whilst I was saddened by the thought of losing the aid of my kind mistress, I was gladdened by the invaluable instruction which, by the merest accident, I had gained from my master. (30) Though conscious of the difficulty of learning without a teacher, I set out with high hope, and a fixed purpose, at whatever cost of trouble, to learn how to read.

The very decided manner with which he spoke, (35) and strove to impress his wife with the evil consequences of giving me instruction, served to convince me that he was deeply sensible of the truths he was uttering. It gave me the best assurance that I might rely with the utmost confidence on the results (40) which, he said, would flow from teaching me how to read. What he most dreaded, that I most desired. What he most loved, that I most hated. That which to him was a great evil, to be carefully shunned, was to me a great good, to be diligently sought; and the (45) argument which he so warmly urged, against my learning to read, only served to inspire me with a desire and determination to learn. In learning to read, I owe almost as much to the bitter opposition of my master, as to the kindly aid of my mistress. I (50) acknowledge the benefit of both.

1. From its content, we can infer that the passage was written by a(n)

   A. 19th-century white narrator hostile to slavery

   B. modern historian

   C. ex-slave looking back on his past

   D. modern autobiographer

   E. white narrator sympathetic to slavery

2. From the report of Mr. Auld's words in lines 8–13, we can infer that he believed that the illiterate slave was

   I. a valuable legal property

   II. incapable of learning

   III. content with his or her position

   A. III only

   B. I and II only

   C. I and III only

   D. II and III only

   E. I, II, and III

3. Of the following, which are figurative rather than literal?

   I. "sentiments within that lay slumbering," lines 14–15

   II. "an entirely new train of thought," line 16

   III. "the pathway from slavery to freedom," line 24

   A. I only

   B. I and II only

   C. I and III only

   D. II and III only

   E. I, II, and III

4. The antecedent of both uses of the pronoun "it" in lines 22 and 24 is

A. "revelation," line 17
B. "things," line 18
C. "understanding," lines 18–19
D. "difficulty," line 21
E. "power," line 21

5. In line 34, the word "decided" can be best defined as

A. judgmental
B. definite
C. inclusive
D. stentorian
E. patriarchal

6. In lines 41–42 ("What he most . . . I most hated"), the author employs

I. two sentences in a parallel structure
II. a parallel structure in the first sentence (line 41)
III. a parallel structure in the second sentence (line 42)

A. I only
B. I and II only
C. I and III only
D. II and III only
E. I, II, and III

7. In lines 42–44 ("That which to him . . . to be diligently sought"), all of the following are balanced against each other EXCEPT

A. "that which . . . was to me"
B. "him . . . me"
C. "great . . . great"
D. "evil . . . good"
E. "carefully . . . diligently"

8. In line 50, if the word "benefit," which can mean "a kindly act" or "anything contributing to improvement," is used to denote the first of these meanings, the final line of the passage is an example of

A. paradox
B. overstatement
C. metaphor
D. irony
E. personification

9. The passage could be used to support effectively a general argument about

A. the kinder treatment of slaves by women than by men
B. the importance of motivation to learning
C. the physical cruelty in the treatment of slaves
D. the dangers of education
E. the corruption that results from power

10. All of the following describe the style of the passage EXCEPT

A. the use of carefully balanced sentences
B. the occasional use of short, loose sentences
C. the use of the first-person pronoun
D. the use of original metaphors and similes
E. the use of indirect discourse

11. The passage illustrates the truth of the paradox that

A. learning may be power
B. slavery may be freedom
C. a foe may be an ally
D. poverty may be wealth
E. a falsehood may be truth

Answers and Explanations for Set 2

The passage is from the autobiography, *Narrative of the Life of Frederick Douglass, an American Slave* (1845).

1. **C.** The first 20 lines of the passage reveal that the speaker had been a slave, and that he learned that literacy is the "pathway from slavery to freedom." The passage itself is evidence of achievement of that literacy.

2. **C.** We can infer the value of the illiterate slave from the slave owner's fear that the literate slave will have "no value." We see his willed belief in the contentedness of the slave from his saying that the literate slave would be "discontented and unhappy." Because Mr. Auld takes pains to withhold education from his slave, he cannot believe that slaves are incapable of learning.

3. **C.** The first quotation personifies "sentiments," and the third compares literacy and a "pathway." The word "train" has as one of its several literal meanings "series" or "sequence," and the use of the word here is literal, not a reference to Amtrak.

4. **A.** It is tempting to see the whole clause "I now understood . . . the most perplexing difficulty" as the antecedent of "it"; if the pronouns refer to a single word, it must be "revelation" (line 17) rather than "understanding" (lines 18–19) because this "understanding" is "in vain." The antecedent must be an "achievement" of the speaker.

5. **B.** As it is used here, "decided" is an adjective meaning "definite" or "unhesitatingly."

6. **E.** There are three parallels here. Both short sentences balance the "What he . . ." clause with the "that I . . ." clause, and the two sentences use the same parallel structures.

7. **A.** The phrase "that which" is not repeated or balanced. It is the subject of both parts of this compound sentence.

8. **D.** If "benefit" is used with its associations of kindness, it is ironic in this context, because Mr. Auld's real purpose was to maintain his power over his slave. That his attempt to prevent his slave from learning to read motivates him to do so is also an example of dramatic irony.

9. **B.** The passage is essentially about Frederick Douglass's learning to read, and he gives much of the credit for this achievement to his motivation, his "fixed purpose, at whatever cost or trouble." The other topics are perhaps true, but none is really an issue in this passage.

10. **D.** There are no similes and only a few commonplace metaphors in the passage. Lines 26–29 are carefully balanced. The last sentence of the passage is a good example of a short, simple sentence. Lines 8–11 use indirect discourse, and the whole passage employs a first-person speaker.

11. **C.** The paradox central to the passage is Mr. Auld's double role of oppressor and benefactor.

A Successful Approach to the Multiple-Choice Section

Many who take the AP exam don't achieve their best scores because they spend too much time dwelling on hard questions, leaving insufficient time to answer the easy questions they can get right. Don't let this happen to you. Use the following system to mark your answer sheet.

For each passage and its set of questions:

1. Answer easy questions immediately.
2. On more difficult questions, take advantage of being able to mark in your test booklet. As you eliminate an incorrect answer choice from consideration, mark it out in your question booklet as follows:

    A̸.
    ?B.
    C̸.
    D̸.
    ?E.

Notice that some choices are marked with question marks, signifying that they may be possible answers. This technique will help you avoid reconsidering those choices you've already eliminated and will help you narrow the possible answers. If you've managed to eliminate two or more answers from consideration but still are not sure of the answer, mark a guess answer at this point. If you wish to reconsider these guess answers before you go on to the next set, you'll be able to identify them from the marks you've made eliminating wrong answers.

3. On questions you find very difficult—those on which you cannot eliminate wrong answers, leave the answer blank (but be careful to mark your next answer in the right place on the answer sheet), put a checkmark in the margin next to the question, and go on. Sometimes, consideration of other questions in the set suddenly sheds light on the questions you left blank, and you can then quickly return to it and choose an answer.

Note: You don't have to erase the marks you make in your test booklet. However, don't make extraneous marks on your answer sheet because in machine scoring, such marks can be counted as wrong answers.

A Patterned Plan of Attack

Multiple-Choice Section

Follow this procedure for each passage and set of questions.

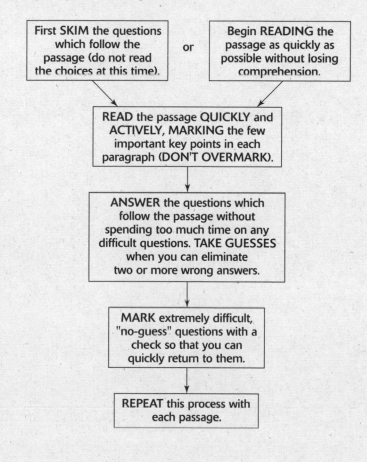

Introduction to the Essay Section

This section of the AP exam, also called the free-response section, requires you to write three essays. Beginning in 2007, you will be given 2 hours and 15 minutes to complete the essays. (This includes an extra 15 minutes exclusively for reading the passages for the synthesis essay.) The suggested time for writing each essay is 40 minutes. You must complete all three essays within the 2-hour writing time limit. You must write an essay on each of the three essay topics; you will have no alternative choices. Each of the three essays is equally weighted at one-third of the total essay score, and the total for the essay portion equals 55% of the entire AP test score. (A more detailed explanation of the essay scoring follows.) You will be given an essay-writing booklet in which to write your essays; the actual test booklet includes some blank space to plan your essays.

A variation of the argument essay, the synthesis essay, will debut in 2007. For this essay, you will be given six or seven passages. Each passage will be approximately 200 to 350 words in length; however, one of the passages is likely to be a visual document, such as a picture, an editorial cartoon, a graph or chart, and so on. Because of the increased amount of reading, the test development committee has added 15 minutes to the essay section. You will be instructed to read the passages for this essay first, and *then* open your test booklet to read the essay questions. In other words, you get 15 additional minutes to do the extra reading that the synthesis essay presents, then, when you open your test book, you still have 2 hours to read the other essay prompts and write all three essays. In the synthesis essay, your task will be to present an argument that synthesizes information from at least half of the given sources and explores your position on the issues, using appropriate evidence to back up your ideas. In the second argument essay you will have only one source to analyze.

A second essay type will give you just a single passage and ask you to form an argument on the validity of the passage's ideas. This topic is similar to the synthesis essay in that it asks you to present an argument, but it differs by having only one source to read, instead of the multiple passages in the synthesis essay. Therefore, these two essays are classified as "argument" essays. You will want to support your position with examples and ideas from the passage, and add appropriate evidence from your education and knowledge of the world's events.

The third essay type requires you to analyze the rhetoric of a passage and understand an author's rhetorical purpose. You'll want to discuss both the author's point and what the author intends the reader to do with it. Although style analysis is indeed one component of this rhetorical analysis, this essay requires that you go beyond style alone and explore the author's ideas in greater depth. You'll want to analyze the breadth of rhetorical strategies the author uses.

Ability Tested

This section tests your ability to demonstrate an understanding of *how* language works while simultaneously demonstrating your ability to communicate intelligent ideas in essay form. You should read the prose passages very carefully and then quickly articulate ideas, because each essay should be written in approximately 40 minutes. Your discussion of such literary aspects as tone, attitude, and persuasion is essential to earning a good score.

Basic Skills Necessary

The basic skill you need for the essay section is the ability to articulate and prove a thesis through concrete examples. You must be able to write on any assigned subject. Your paragraphs should be well developed, your overall essay organization should make sense, and your writing should demonstrate college-level thinking and style. The basic writing format of presenting an introduction, body, and conclusion is helpful, but to achieve a high score, you *must* demonstrate *depth of thought*. Overall, you must show that you can read the question (and any subsequent passages) carefully, plan an intelligent thesis, organize and present valid and sufficient evidence while connecting such evidence to the thesis, and demonstrate college-level skill with your own language.

Directions

Each essay topic has its own wording and, therefore, its own directions, but general instructions similar to the following are printed on the cover of the essay booklet:

Directions: Three essay questions are printed in this booklet. Use this booklet to make your notes. You will be told when to open the essay-writing booklet and begin. Suggested writing time is given for each question.

Analysis of Directions

Although each essay topic has its own specific requirements, use these general suggestions for all of your essays:

- Use the test booklet to plan your essay. A poorly planned or an unplanned essay frequently reveals problems in organization and development.
- Practice frequently so that you're comfortable with the timing.
- Become familiar with the types of topics and comfortable with writing in a variety of modes.
- Organize your ideas logically, and be careful to stay on the topic.
- Write as legibly as possible; the readers want to be able to read your essay.

Suggested Strategies for Essays

Remember the following as you practice writing the essay:

- Use the standard format with an introduction, body, and conclusion, but do not force a formulaic and overly predictable five-paragraph essay.
- Clearly divide ideas into separate paragraphs; clearly indent the paragraphs.
- Stay on topic; avoid irrelevant comments or ideas.
- Use sophisticated diction and sentences with syntactic variety.
- Be organized and logical in your presentation.
- Be sure to address all of the tasks the essay question requires.

Essay Scoring

Each of the three essays equals one-third of the total essay score, and the entire essay (free-response) section equals 55% of the total exam score.

Each essay is read by experienced, well-trained high school AP teachers or college professors. The essay is given a holistic score from 1 to 9. (A score of 0 is recorded for a student who writes completely off the topic—for example, "Why I think this test is a waste of money." A student who doesn't even attempt an essay, who leaves a blank page, will receive the equivalent of a 0 score, but it is noted as a dash [—] on the reader's scoring sheet.) The reader assigns a score based on the essay's merits as a whole, on what the essay does well; the readers don't simply count errors. Although each essay topic has its own scoring rubric (or guide) based on that topic's specific information, a general scoring guide for rhetorical analysis and argumentation essays follows. Notice that, on the whole, essay-scoring guides encompass four essential points; AP readers want your essay to be (1) on topic, (2) well organized, (3) thoroughly developed, and (4) correct in mechanics and sophisticated in style.

High Score (8–9)

High-scoring essays thoroughly address all the tasks of the essay prompt in well-organized responses. The writing demonstrates stylistic sophistication and control over the elements of effective writing, although it is not necessarily faultless. Overall, high-scoring essays present thoroughly developed, intelligent ideas; sound and logical organization; strong evidence; and articulate diction.

- *Rhetorical analysis essays* demonstrate significant understanding of the passage, its intent, and the rhetorical strategies the author employs.
- *Argument essays* demonstrate the ability to construct a compelling argument, observing the author's underlying assumptions, (addressing multiple authors in the synthesis essay) and discussing many sides of the issues with appropriate evidence.

Medium-High Score (6–7)

Medium-scoring essays complete the tasks of the essay topic well—they show some insight but usually with less precision and clarity than high-scoring essays. There may be lapses in correct diction or sophisticated language, but the essay is generally well written.

- *Rhetorical analysis essays* demonstrate sufficient examination of the author's point and the rhetorical strategies he uses to enhance the central idea.
- *Argument essays* demonstrate the ability to construct an adequate argument, understand the author's point, and discuss its implications with suitable evidence. The synthesis argument will address at least three of the sources.

Medium Score (5)

Essays that earn a medium score complete the essay task, but with no special insights; the analysis lacks depth and merely states the obvious. Frequently, the ideas are predictable and the paragraph development weak. Although the writing conveys the writer's ideas, they are presented simplistically and often contain lapses in diction or syntax.

- *Rhetorical analysis essays* demonstrate uneven or insufficient understanding of how rhetorical strategies create an author's point. Often, the writer merely lists what he or she observes in the passage instead of analyzing effect.
- *Argument essays* demonstrate the ability to present an argument, but they frequently provide limited and inadequate discussion, explanation, or evidence for the writer's ideas. The writer may not address enough of the sources in the synthesis essay. Oversimplification of the issue(s) minimizes the essay's effectiveness.

Medium-Low Score (3–4)

These essays are weaker than the 5 score because the writer overlooks or perhaps misreads important ideas in the passage. The student may summarize the passage's ideas instead of analyzing them. Although the writer's ideas are generally understandable, the control of language is often immature.

- *Rhetorical analysis essays* demonstrate little discussion of rhetorical strategies or incorrect identification and/or analysis of those strategies.
- *Argument essays* demonstrate little ability to construct an argument. They may not clearly identify the author's point, may not present multiple authors' points of view in the synthesis essay, and may offer little evidence for the student's position.

Low Score (1–2)

These essays demonstrate minimal understanding of the topic or the passage. Perhaps unfinished, these essays offer no analysis of the passage and little or no evidence for the student's ideas. Incorrect assertions may be made about the passage. Stylistically, these essays may show consistent grammatical problems, and sentence structure is usually simple and unimaginative.

- *Rhetorical analysis essays* demonstrate little ability to identify or analyze rhetorical strategies. Sometimes these essays misread the prompt and replace it with easier tasks, such as paraphrasing the passage or listing some strategies the author uses.

- *Argument essays* demonstrate little ability to understand the author's point (or multiple authors in the synthesis essay) and then construct an argument that analyzes it. Minimal or nonexistent evidence hurts the essay's effectiveness. Some students may substitute an easier task by presenting tangential or irrelevant ideas, evidence, or explanation.

Types of Essay Topics

Although the wording varies, the exam essentially presents three types of essays: the synthesis essay, the argument essay, and the rhetorical analysis essay. Become familiar with each type so that you can efficiently and quickly plan your essays on the day of the exam and stay on topic.

1. **The Synthesis Essay:** This essay type presents six or seven passages on the same subject; one of these documents will likely be a visual one (such as a chart, photograph, or political cartoon). You need to read all the documents carefully and then, using at least half of them, synthesize the various authors' points, while intelligently discussing their validity. Therefore, this essay is like the argument essay; it just asks you to incorporate more viewpoints from more sources. Incorporate explicit and implicit evidence from the documents plus your own ideas based on your knowledge of the world and its history. Your purpose is to present an intelligent and thoughtful discussion on a subject, acknowledging various viewpoints from the authors while bringing in your awareness of the world.

2. **The Argument Essay:** This essay presents one passage; read it carefully and formulate an essay discussing the extent with which you agree or disagree with the author's points. Like the synthesis essay, you will be well served if you intelligently address multiple sides of the issue and persuasively explore evidence from the passage and your understanding of the world.

3. **The Rhetorical Analysis Essay:** This essay presents a passage and asks you to analyze the rhetorical and literary strategies the author uses to create effect or meaning. Accurately identify the devices the author uses and evaluate *how* these devices create meaning. Be sure that you understand the effect and author's meaning before you begin writing. Uncertainty results in muddled ideas. Refer to the passage liberally, incorporating quotations into your own ideas.

Pacing the Essay

With an average time of only 40 minutes per essay, you should divide your time as follows.

Spend about 10 minutes reading the topic and the passage carefully and planning your essay.

This organizational time is crucial to producing a high-scoring essay. In the first 10 minutes, you need to follow these steps. Do it efficiently, and you'll know what you want to write and the order in which you'll present your ideas.

1. Read the topic's question carefully so that you know exactly what you're being asked to do.
2. Read the passage carefully, noting what ideas, evidence, and rhetorical devices are relevant to the specific essay prompt.

3. Conceive your thesis statement, which will go in your introductory paragraph.

4. Organize your body paragraphs, deciding what evidence from the passage you'll include (using multiple passages in the synthesis essay) or what appropriate examples you'll use from your knowledge of the world. Know what relevant remarks you'll make about the evidence. Understand your body paragraph divisions—when you'll begin a new paragraph and what idea unifies each paragraph.

The importance of this planning phase cannot be overemphasized. When your essay has been planned well, your writing flows faster, your essay stays on topic and is well organized, and the paragraphs are well developed. You must practice this essential planning step several times before you take the actual AP exam.

Take about 25 minutes to write the essay.

If you've planned well, your writing should be fluent and continuous; avoid stopping to reread what you've written. Twenty-five minutes is sufficient time to produce all of the writing needed for a good score. In general, most high-scoring essays are at least two full pages of writing.

Save about 5 minutes to proofread your essay.

Reserving a few minutes to proofread allows you time to catch the "honest mistakes" that can be corrected easily, such as a misspelled word or punctuation error. In addition, this time lets you set the essay to rest, knowing what you've written, so that you can go on to the next topic and give it your full attention.

Planning the Essay

Your planning and organizing should be done in the test booklet, which provides space for that purpose. Begin by reading the essay question carefully. Underline the key words and phrases of the prompt so that you *thoroughly* understand what your tasks are. Then read any accompanying passage analytically, always keeping the essay question in mind. As you read, underline important ideas and phrases that relate to the topic. Your goals while reading are to:

- Understand and critique the author's point.
- Relate the passage to the essay question.
- Begin gathering evidence to support the points of your essay.
- Look for nuances of diction and syntax (for rhetorical analysis essay topics).

After you've read both the question and the passage carefully, you're ready to plan and organize your essay. Again, use the space provided in the test booklet. Organize your thoughts using whatever method you're most comfortable with—outlining, clustering, listing, and so forth. Planning at this stage is crucial to producing a well-written essay and should provide the following:

1. Your thesis statement
2. A list of supporting evidence
3. The order of presentation of that evidence
4. A list of logical paragraph units
5. Notes on analysis or commentary to be added regarding the evidence (analysis which connects your evidence both to your thesis and to the essay question)

Be careful to manage your time during the planning stage. If you overplan, you may run out of time to commit all your ideas to paper; if you fail to plan sufficiently, you're likely to produce an unorganized essay or one that's not as thorough as it should be. Remember that you do not have time to write out full sentences for everything that is in the preceding list, with the possible exception of the thesis. Simply jot down phrases and ideas quickly. Your goal here is only to plan the essay; if you do that well, your writing will go much faster. You'll then need only to put it all down on paper, in complete sentences, and you'll have produced a well-written essay.

Writing the Essay

A convenient format for essay writing uses the standard structure of introduction, body, and conclusion. The body should be made up of several paragraphs, but the introduction and conclusion require only one paragraph each.

In your introduction, make sure that you include a strong, analytical thesis statement, a sentence that explains your paper's idea and defines the scope of your essay. Also, be sure that the introduction lets the reader know that you're on topic; use key phrases from the question if necessary. The introductory paragraph should be brief—only a few sentences are necessary to state your thesis. Definitely try to avoid merely repeating the topic in your thesis; instead, let the thesis present what it is that you will specifically analyze. Imagine, for instance, that the topic asks you to "analyze the ways in which the author re-creates his experience, perhaps considering such devices as diction, imagery, pacing, and contrast." A bland, repetitive thesis might read, "The author uses diction, imagery, and contrast to re-create his experience." A more effective thesis might state, "The author's terrifying experience is vividly reconstructed through fast-paced diction, darkly menacing imagery, and stark contrasts in pacing." Although this second thesis still uses the structure of the topic, it at least identifies the thrust of the student's ideas.

The body paragraphs are the heart of the essay. Each should be guided by a topic sentence that is a relevant part of the introductory thesis statement. For rhetorical analysis essays, always supply a *great deal* of relevant evidence from the passage to support your ideas; feel free to quote the passage liberally. In your argument essays, provide appropriate and sufficient evidence from the passage(s) and your knowledge of the world. Prove that you are capable of intelligent "civil discourse," a discussion of important ideas. However, always be sure to connect your ideas to the thesis. Explain exactly how the evidence presented leads to your thesis. Avoid obvious commentary. A medium- to low-scoring paper merely reports what's in the passage. A high-scoring paper makes relevant, insightful, analytical points about the passage. Remember to stay on topic. (More specific advice for developing your body paragraphs follows.)

Your conclusion, like your introduction, shouldn't be longwinded or elaborate. Do attempt, however, to provide more than mere summary; try to make a point beyond the obvious, which will indicate your essay's superiority. In other words, try to address the essay's greater importance in your conclusion. As one AP reader remarked, "I ask my students to get *global and noble*." Of course, you should also keep in mind that a conclusion is not absolutely necessary in order to receive a high score. Never forget that your body paragraphs are more important than the conclusion, so don't slight them merely to add a conclusion.

Remember to save a few minutes to proofread and to correct misspelled words, revise punctuation errors, and replace an occasional word or phrase with a more dynamic one. Do not make major editing changes at this time. Trust your original planning of organization and ideas, and only correct any obvious errors that you spot.

Developing Strong Body Paragraphs

AP readers give high scores to essays that thoroughly develop intelligent ideas. Students who notice more details and concepts in the prompt and present their relevant ideas in articulate, thoughtful prose receive higher scores than those who only see a few ideas to comment on and do so with simplicity. Therefore, strive to make your body paragraphs strong. Generously use examples from the prompt, both implicitly and explicitly. In other words, sometimes weave direct quotations and phrases from the prompt into your own sentences and sometimes refer to the author's ideas in your own words. But be sure to quote the text liberally and use it to develop and present your ideas on the topic. Thoroughly explore and explain the relationship between the text examples you present and your ideas; do not assume the reader can also read your mind.

Additionally, understanding the writer's rhetorical appeal will help you analyze the persuasive tools the writer uses to sway an audience's response. Three appeals are possible:

- An appeal to **logos** employs logical reasoning, combining a clear idea (or multiple ideas) with well-thought-out and appropriate examples and details. These examples are logically presented and rationally lead to the writer's conclusion.

- An appeal to **ethos** establishes credibility in the speaker. Since by definition "ethos" means the common attitudes, beliefs, and characteristics of a group or time period, this appeal sets up believability in the writer. He or she becomes someone who is trusted and concerned with the readers' best interests.

- An appeal to **pathos** plays on the reader's emotions and interests. A sympathetic audience is more likely to accept a writer's assertions, so this appeal draws upon that understanding and uses it to the writer's advantage.

Now let's look at some specific advice for the different essay types.

In your argumentation essays, which include the synthesis essay based on multiple passages and argument essay based on one passage, you want to show that you understand the author's point(s) and can respond intelligently. Comprehending the author's point involves a three-step process: (1) clarifying the claim the author makes, (2) examining the data and evidence the author uses, and (3) understanding the underlying assumptions behind the argument. The first two steps are usually directly stated or clearly implied; understanding what the author must believe, or what the author thinks the audience believes, is a bit harder but is a skill that can easily be practiced. To intelligently respond to the author's ideas, keep in mind that the AP readers and college professors are impressed by the student who can conduct "civil discourse," a discussion that fully understands all sides before taking a stand. Avoid oversimplification and remember that, as the current chief faculty consultant put it, "Judgment stops discussion." Let the reader watch your ideas develop instead of jumping to a conclusion and then spending the whole essay trying to justify it. Also be aware that you don't have to take only one side in an issue. Frequently, a very good essay demonstrates understanding of multiple sides of an issue and presents a "qualifying argument" that appreciates these many sides. Show awareness of culture, history, philosophy, and politics. Prove that you are in touch with your society and the world around you. The topics give you the opportunity to intelligently discuss issues; seize that opportunity and take advantage of it.

In your rhetorical analysis essays, be sure to accurately identify rhetorical and literary devices the author employs, and then examine *how* they create effects and help build the author's point. In your AP English classes, you will likely be introduced to terminology appropriate to rhetorical analysis; this book also offers a glossary of terms you can use. High-scoring essays never merely list such devices, however. Instead, intelligent analysis explores the depth of the author's ideas and how the author's presentation enhances those ideas. Be sure you understand the author's rhetorical purpose: Is it to persuade? to satirize some fault in society? to express ideas? Then dive into the depth of the author's thoughts and enjoy how good writing enhances interesting ideas. Like the argument essays, you'll want to liberally use the text, both implicitly and explicitly. A sophisticated writer embeds phrases from the text into his or her own sentences during discussion. Avoid copying complete sentences from the text; choose just the exact word or phrase that suits your purpose and analyze it within your own sentences.

A Few Words About Satire

Recent language and literature exams have sometimes included prompts that are from satiric and/or comedic works. Students who are not practiced in writing about satire and recognizing the devices of the satirist may be at a disadvantage over those who are comfortable with such tools. The subtlety and nuances of satire can sometimes go unnoticed; some students may find it hard to know how to analyze the rhetorical strategies that satirists use. Although, of course, satirists can employ all of the devices of rhetoric, quite often they make use of caricature, hyperbole, understatement, irony, wit, sarcasm, allusion, and juxtaposition. (These terms are defined in "Terms for the Multiple-Choice and Essay Sections," later in this book.)

Frequently satire is characterized as one of two types: *Horatian satire* is gentle, urbane, smiling; it aims to correct with broadly sympathetic laughter. Based on the Roman lyrical poet Horace, its purpose may be "to hold up a mirror" so readers can see themselves and their world honestly. The vices and follies satirized are not destructive; however, they reflect the foolishness of people, the superficiality and meaninglessness of their lives, and the barrenness of their values. *Juvenalian satire* is biting, bitter, and angry; it points out the corruption of human beings and institutions with contempt, using *saeva indignation,* a savage outrage based on the style of the Roman poet Juvenal. Sometimes perceived as enraged, Juvenalian satire sees the vices and follies in the world as intolerable. Juvenalian satirists use large doses of sarcasm and irony. If you do receive a piece of satire to discuss in your essay topics, be aware of the rhetorical devices of the satirist and use them to your advantage.

Some Suggestions About Style

On the actual exam, you won't have enough time during your proofreading to make major adjustments to your style. However, as you practice, you can experiment with some stylistic devices that you can easily incorporate into your writing. Remember that top-scoring essays are stylistically mature and that your goal is to produce college-level writing. By answering the following questions and then practicing these suggestions, you'll improve your writing.

- How long are your sentences? You should try for some variety in sentence length. Remember that the occasional concise, simple sentence can pack a punch and grab a reader's attention when it's placed among a series of longer sentences. If an essay's sentences are all of the same length, none of them stands out.

- What words do you use to begin your sentences? Again, variety is desirable. Try to avoid "there is" or "there are" (or any other dull wording). Also avoid beginning every sentence with the subject. For variety, try such grammatical constructions as a participial phrase, adverbial clause, and so on.

- Does every word you use help your essay? Some bland, vague words to avoid include "a lot," "a little," "things," "much," and "very." Additionally, phrases like "I think," "I believe," "I feel," "in my opinion," "so as you can see," and "in conclusion," are unnecessary.

- How many linking verbs do you use? The linking verb (usually a form of the verb "to be") has no action, is vastly overused, and produces unimaginative prose. Replace as many of these as possible with action verbs.

- What sentence patterns do you use? Again, you should aim for variety; avoid using the same pattern over and over. Also, try inverting the normal order; for example, try putting a direct object before the subject for emphasis.

- Are all your compound sentences joined in the same way? The usual method is to use a comma and a coordinating conjunction (such as "and," "but," or "yet"). Try experimenting with the semicolon and the dash to add emphasis and variety (but be sure you're using these more sophisticated punctuation devices correctly).

- How many prepositional phrases do you see? Eliminate as many as possible, especially the possessive prepositional phrase. Change "the words of Homer" to "Homer's words."

- Do you use any parallel construction? Develop your ability to produce parallelisms and your writing will appear more polished and memorable. Parallel construction also adds a delightful, sophisticated rhythm to your sentences. You can find examples of parallelism in "Terms for Multiple-Choice and Essay Sections," later in this book, as well as in many of the high-scoring essays in this chapter.

- Do you use any figures of speech? If you practice incorporating the occasional use of alliteration, repetition, imagery, and other figures of speech, your writing will be more vivid and engaging.

- What does your essay sound like? Have a friend read your essay aloud to you and listen to how it sounds.

Finally, a word about vocabulary. Of course, the use of sophisticated language is one of your goals, but do *not* use words you're unfamiliar with. In your practice, *look up* new words in a dictionary before you use them, especially if you find them in a thesaurus. Of course, you are not permitted to use a dictionary or thesaurus during the actual exam. Variety in word choice is as essential as variety in sentences, but don't try to overload an essay with fancy, multisyllabic words. Use succinct words that specifically fit your purpose.

Sample Topics with Student Essays

Now let's examine some sample essays that were written by AP students under timed conditions. They are reproduced here as they were written, including some misused words and spelling and punctuation errors. You'll find a topic, scoring guide, plus sample high- and medium-scoring essays with analysis for each of the two following passages.

Question 1

Suggested time: 40 minutes. This question counts as one-third of the total essay score.

Fanny Burney (Mme d'Arblay) once wrote,

> There is nothing upon the face of the earth so insipid as a medium. Give me love or hate! a friend that will go to jail for me, or an enemy that will run me through the body!

Directions: In a well-thought-out essay, evaluate the validity of Burney's assertion about extremes. Use appropriate evidence to make your argument convincing.

Scoring Guide for Question 1 (Fanny Burney)

9 Essays earning a score of 9 meet the criteria for essays that are scored an 8 and, in addition, are especially full or apt in their analysis or reveal particularly remarkable control of language.

8 Successful

Essays scoring an 8 will **successfully** and substantially evaluate Burney's assertion that there is "nothing so insipid as a medium." They present a well-articulated argument that offers ample and appropriate evidence to support the essay's ideas. The development is thorough, the organization clear and logical. The high-scoring essays present language usage and style that show sophistication, although the writing may contain some minor errors.

7 Essays earning a score of 7 fit the description of essays that are scored a 6 but provide more complete analysis and a more mature prose style.

6 Satisfactory

Essays earning a score of 6 **satisfactorily** evaluate Burney's assertion in a generally interesting fashion. The arguments are usually logically reliable and offer sufficient support. These essays are often developed quite well, but not to as great an extent as the highest-scoring essays. In general, these essays may show a few lapses in control over language usage, but demonstrate such a clear command over diction and syntax that meaning is clear to the reader.

5 The 5-scoring essays understand the task and attempt to evaluate Burney's ideas. The argument is generally clear, but frequently too narrow in scope or superficial in its concept. Development is often too limited and ideas too simplistic. Evidence offered may be only tangentially relevant or may not be adequately or logically examined, leaving the reader to question the validity of examples. Although some lapses in grammar and mechanics may be present, they generally do not interfere with meaning, and the reader can follow the writers' ideas.

4 Inadequate

These lower-scoring essays **inadequately** evaluate the topic. They may misunderstand, misrepresent, or oversimplify Burney's assertion. They may use inappropriate examples or fail to develop them in a convincing manner. Development and organization are frequently flawed. Even though the meaning is usually clear, the writing may demonstrate immature control of English conventions.

3 Essays earning a score of 3 meet the criteria for a score of 4 but demonstrate a less clear understanding of Burney's ideas. The essays may show less control over the elements of writing.

2 Little Success

Essays scoring a 2 achieve **little success** in evaluating Burney's ideas. They may completely misread the passage or substitute a simpler task instead of developing a cohesive argument. Lack of relevant or convincing evidence typically characterizes the lowest-scoring essays, and weak, simplistic logic or nonexistent explanations of any evidence often compound the essays' problems. The prose frequently reveals consistent weaknesses over diction and syntax.

1 These poorly written essays meet the criteria for a score of 2 but are undeveloped, especially simplistic in their analysis, and weak in their control of language.

High-Scoring Essay

Our fascination with extremes is a phenomenon that is unexplainable by any biological method—we have no genuine need for it, and yet Fanny Burney is accurate; this purely human condition is prevalent in nearly all of us. Burney implies a psychological explanation, simple yet multifaceted. In essence, we simply find the extreme to be more interesting. We cannot rely on any scientific techniques to measure such an abstract concept. But perhaps the most effective way to relate Burney's assertion to current public opinion is to look at the press's choices in content. When considering the stories covered by the press, while we are actually looking at events or people which an editorial staff deems newsworthy, in the interest of sales and advertising profits, we can assume that the media caters to the public's interests. Clearly, news about the best or the worst in our world sells. Clearly, the major headlines generating the most interest have all been the result of some sort of extreme. Plane crashes involving hundreds of lives lost, baseball players booming baseballs farther and more frequently, stock market jumps that affect everyone—these are the most readable, most interesting stories. Not the car crash that injured a twenty-five year old man (though it may be just as heart-wrenching); not the consistent .330 batting average of a seasoned baseball veteran (though it may be just as difficult to achieve); and certainly not the steady conglomerate (though it may be just as profitable). Certainly, our hearts and minds gravitate to stories and people that pique our interest.

Hollywood, especially, gears its entertainment to fulfilling this interest. We love to watch the over-the-top, clever and cruel arch-villains who plot to take over the universe and the overly saccharine brave young heroes who valiantly stop their plans (and win the damsel in distress while they're at it). Even ordinary Clark Kent became the strong Superman, perhaps convincing us that we too, would be able to fly, have x-ray vision, and save the world from any evil nemesis. It appears we want movies to represent extremes of good and evil, not just some "insipid" everyman. And certainly, this interest in the extreme is not a recent phenomenon. If we go back to Shakespeare's work, considered by many to be the archetypal settings and characters for so many stories to come, we see that Burney's comment holds no less truth. For instance, in *Hamlet,* we have Horatio, "a friend that will go to jail for me" and Polonius, "an enemy that will run me through the body," occupying different extremes. There can be no medium in effective drama, for our imaginations and emotions feed off characters and conflicts that are more grandiose than our daily lives. It's what the audience wants; it's what the playwright delivers.

Our insistent need for the extreme serves no harmful purpose. Indeed, it has shaped our modern conceptions of drama, comedy, and news, helping us define our psychological boundaries and sparking the imaginations of generations to come.

Analysis of the High-Scoring Essay

The student who wrote this high-scoring essay has a firm grasp on the topic and a clear view of the world. He or she appropriately uses examples from the news media, Hollywood cinema, and Shakespearean drama to prove that Fanny Burney's quotation is an accurate perception of mankind; we do relish extremes over the mediocre. The first paragraph blends the introductory material and its effective thesis into a body paragraph that explores the current state of print journalism. Although the student does not use specific existing headlines or news stories as examples, he or she does not need to—the universal point here is that the news media depicts the extreme in life, and the "generic" examples that are presented here work very well. Plane crashes, outrageous professional baseball salaries, and the excessive ups and downs of the stock market are all examples that the reader can relate to and easily connect to the student's point. The student also slips in a legitimate business rationale for these types of stories: Not only does the public crave them, but the paper also profits by them. This paragraph, nicely on topic, focuses on observations of our modern life and convinces the reader that the media does present extremes in the news, which in turn reflects humanity's desire for such sensationalism.

The next paragraph explores Hollywood movies and Shakespearean drama, again effectively utilizing both to prove that mankind craves extremes in fictional characters. Everyone knows so well the "cruel arch-villain" and the "brave young hero" that Hollywood exaggerates. The student's declaration that we would all like to become a Superman and "save the world from any evil nemesis" both rings true and helps prove Burney's assertion. Middle-of-the-road personalities do not save the world; extreme ones do. The student's use of *Hamlet* gives the essay a sophisticated and cultured flair, not merely because it is a Shakespearean reference but because it also proves the student well read and well rounded. It helps to balance the previous contemporary examples in the essay. Perhaps the *Hamlet* discussion could be developed more, explaining how Horatio and Polonius exemplify these extremes in character, but an essay that is written under timed pressure cannot always elaborate as much as an untimed one. Remember that the AP reader will "reward the writer for what he or she does well," and this writer proves his or her point admirably.

This essay earns its high score through the development of its clear and relevant ideas, as well as its abundant examples, strong organization, and commendable control of written English. The sense of rhythm that is so pleasing to the ear through parallel construction can be observed in such areas as the repetition of the word "clearly" to begin two sentences, the parenthetical "though it may be . . ." phrasing in the first paragraph, and in the sentence, "It's what the audience wants; it's what the playwright delivers" in the second paragraph. Although parallelism is never a specific requirement, any student who effectively uses such sophisticated devices will demonstrate a sense of style that shines through to the reader.

Medium-Scoring Essay

We can't help but be interested by extremes. They represent both the bad and the good of life and are interesting simply because they differ from the typical person. Like scientists who also are interested in differences from the standard, we classify and thus notice these differences. For example, the world records in running have, time and time again, deserved media coverage while the average speed of a typical healthy males may perhaps be an obscure fact. Our societies focus on the individual inevitably results in the few strongest, smartest, quickest being not only isolated but at times revered. The opposite side of the spectrum is similarly true. The publics fascination with, for example, a cereal killer, is only rivaled by its fascination with the fireman who saved twenty lives. Everything in between (with varying degrees), is ordinary and, as Fanny Burney wrote, "insipid."

Perhaps our dedication to seeking out the extremes in life represents our own struggle to find who we are. Extremes provide a watermark to our own situation. Are we that "friend that will go to jail for me" or the "enemy that will run me through the body?" We are most likely in between. But are fascination with this scale is a symbol of our dreams. We certainly cannot achieve such heights (or such lows) but we can often live vicariously through these extreme individuals.

Analysis of the Medium to Low-Scoring Essay

This essay attempts to agree with Burney's assertion; however, it does not make a strong point in doing so, nor does it actually convince the reader. Simply stated, because of its brevity the essay is not fulfilling. The example with which the student begins, that of track-and-field world records, does not work particularly well; it appears that the student has not thought it through. After all, it *does* make sense that a new world's record would "deserve media coverage" while at the same time "average speed of a typical, healthy male" would not. This "average" statistical information can be obtained, but it is not particularly newsworthy on a daily basis, so the example does not make much sense to the reader. The later example of the public's fascination with murderers and heroes is more logically sound, but it is not enough to save the entire paragraph from mediocrity.

The second paragraph appears to be a hastily drawn conclusion; it certainly offers no new examples or ideas to support the student's thesis. Although it may be philosophically interesting to ponder how "seeking out the extremes in life represents our own struggle to find who we are," it does not persuade the reader of the validity of Burney's assertion, and therefore falls flat. This paragraph does not meet the requirement in the directions, namely using "appropriate evidence" to support ideas. It needs stronger organization and development.

The large number of diction and grammatical mistakes also hurt this essay's score. Although the readers want to "reward the writer for what he or she does well," they simply cannot ignore so many errors. Notice the first two sentences. The student claims we are interested "*by*" extremes (an unidiomatic expression to start), then claims "they differ from the typical person," which is not possible. One cannot logically compare "extremes" to "*people*." Notice also the number agreement problem in the phrase "speed of *a* typically healthy *males*." The student also has many diction and/or punctuation mistakes, such as "societies" instead of "society's," "publics" without its apostrophe, and "cereal" instead of "serial." Additionally, the homophone confusion of using "are" instead of "our" strikes the reader as yet another careless error. Although an AP reader can disregard minor mistakes here and there, this essay is riddled with far too many errors to disregard without affecting the score. Therefore, this essay is an example of an extremely low "mid-range" essay. Giving it a score of 4 would be generous.

The essay earns a low score because of its combination of being barely on topic, having weak development, displaying ineffectual organization, and exhibiting numerous mechanical errors.

Question 2

Directions: The following essay comes from Sir Thomas More's *Utopia* (1516). Read the passage carefully, and then write an essay that evaluates the validity of the speaker's ideas in light of contemporary standards. Use appropriate evidence to develop your essay and convince the reader of your ideas.

On Communal Property

By this I am persuaded that unless private property is entirely done away with, there can be no fair distribution of goods, nor can the world be happily governed. As long as private property remains, the largest and far the best part of mankind will be oppressed with an inescapable load of cares and anxieties. This load, I admit, may be lightened somewhat, but cannot be entirely removed. Laws might be made that no one should own more than a certain amount of land nor possess more than a certain sum of money. Or laws might be passed to prevent the prince from growing too powerful and the populace from becoming too strong. It might be made unlawful for public offices to be solicited, or sold, or made burdensome for the officeholder by great expense. Otherwise officeholders are tempted to reimburse themselves by dishonesty and force, and it becomes necessary to find rich men for those offices which ought rather be held by wise men. Such laws, I say, may have as much effect as good nursing has on men who are dangerously sick. Social evils may be allayed and mitigated, but so long as private property remains, there is no hope at all that they may be healed and society restored to good health. While you try to cure one part, you aggravate the disease in other parts. In redressing one evil another is committed, since you cannot give something to one man without taking the same thing from another.

Scoring Guide for Question 2 (Thomas More)

9 Essays earning a score of 9 meet the criteria for essays that are scored an 8 and, in addition, are especially full or apt in their analysis or reveal particularly remarkable control of language.

8 Successful

These well-written essays clearly take a stand concerning More's ideas on communal property and **successfully** support that stand. The thesis is articulate and relevant to the topic. The paper provides strong and relevant evidence intelligently connected to the thesis. Although it need not be without errors, the paper shows a mature command of style and language.

7 Essays earning a score of 7 fit the description of essays that are scored a 6 but provide more complete analysis and a more mature prose style.

6 Satisfactory

These essays contemplate More's ideas on communal property in a **satisfactory** manner but produce a less explicit thesis. Perhaps less relevant or insufficient evidence is offered, and the reader may not be as thoroughly convinced as with a top-scoring paper. Although well written, it may demonstrate some errors while still showing satisfactory control over diction and the essay requirements.

5 The adequate presentation in these essays includes a thesis, but one that is perhaps not as well thought out as in higher-scoring essays. The ideas may be too hastily conceived after a cursory reading of More's concepts. Overall, the argument may not be as strong or convincing. It may appear more opinionated without sufficient evidence to support the opinions. Acceptable organization may be evident, but the style may be much more simplistic than higher-scoring essays.

4 Inadequate

Essays that earn a score of 4 respond to the prompt **inadequately**. These low-scoring essays fail to convince the reader. The weak presentation may include an unsupported or unsubstantiated thesis, weak paragraph development, and/or poor organization. These essays may exhibit confusion in ideas and superficial thinking in the use of evidence. Frequent mechanical errors may persist.

3 Essays earning a score of 3 meet the criteria for a score of 4 but demonstrate a less clear understanding of More's ideas. The essays may show less control over the elements of writing.

2 Little Success

These poorly written essays lack clarity and coherence. They may have an overly obvious thesis or no thesis at all. They may contain little or no evidence, and the connection between the evidence and the thesis may be shallow or nonexistent. These essays may misunderstand the task, may fail to articulate More's attitude, or may substitute a simpler task. These essays may be unusually short and exhibit poor fundamental essay skills. Weak sentence construction may persist, and consistent weaknesses in mechanics may be present.

1 These poorly written essays meet the criteria for a score of 2 but are undeveloped, especially simplistic in their analysis, and weak in their control of language.

High-Scoring Essay

Sir Thomas More's Utopia discusses ideas and conflicts still relevant to society today. He manages to perceptively express the nature of wealth and material goods; and although written over 400 years ago, his essay still reveals essential truths about the attitudes in our contemporary society.

More primarily addresses the issue of ownership of private property and its hindrance upon the fair distribution of wealth. More points out that ownership of private wealth hurts those who have little or none themselves, which makes up the majority of the population. More perceives that "As long as private property remains, the largest and far the best part of mankind will be oppressed with an inescapable load of cares and anxieties." In today's society, More's idea still holds true. The majority of the population does control less than their fair amount of wealth and goods. This is evident not just in America, but also among competing nations of the world. Each day, in countries like Mexico, the poor struggle to keep from getting poorer, while the wealth of many of the rich grows more opulent. Because of this unfair distribution of wealth, the poor have little opportunity to change their worsening situations.

More's concerns also go beyond the poor and encompass another major realm of controversy: politics. More correctly predicts the nature of politics which exists in a society where not everyone is of the same economic class. He suggests that "it might be made unlawful for public offices to be solicited, or sold, or made burdensome for the officeholder by great expense. Otherwise officeholders are tempted to reimburse themselves by dishonesty and force, and it becomes necessary to find rich men for those offices which ought rather be held by wise men." This prediction has certainly come true in contemporary America, where the vast number of politicians tend to come from the upper echelons of society;

conversely, one would be hard-pressed to name a top office-holder who rose from the ranks of the poor underclass. In addition, just as Plato saw the needs for wise, rational men to fill the position of philosopher-king, More also realizes the danger of public offices held by rich men rather than wise men, an event fostered by a society in which unequal distribution of goods exists. Both Plato and More have made a valid point here, and the voting public should be constantly cautioned to question a potential leader's wisdom and rational thinking before they vote.

While More's essays define the evils that burden a private property owning society, More fails to see some of the problems that would follow with completely eradicating the system. More suggests several legal reforms to stop and prevent the amassing of goods by citizens. When this is stopped, however, all incentive to work is taken away. People rarely have the time, the energy, or the interest to work solely for the merit of working. In contemporary society, human nature drives people to work to earn something tangible—be it wealth, or goods, or love. More's reforms are also unfair. While upon a first glance they may sound fair and equal, in reality they are not. This system would be unfair to hard workers who do deserve a reward, and unfair to lazy workers who don't earn what they receive. Instead of promoting equality, this system would promote laziness and remove the incentive to work. In theory this would be a good system. But, in reality, Sir Thomas More's Utopia does not work. The breakdown of the Soviet Union alone disproves More's system.

More's essay perceptively observes some of the major injustices and corruptions within a private property owning society. While these are valid, pertinent issues, More overlooks some of the inherent pitfalls within the system of a society which bans the ownership of private property.

Analysis of the High-Scoring Essay

This thoughtful essay immediately addresses the topic in its first sentence. The writer uses contemporary examples to buttress points and also insightfully comments that More addresses more concepts than money and land distribution. The writer's inclusion of Plato in the third paragraph relevantly extends this idea. In the fourth paragraph, the writer acknowledges that More fails to accurately predict all the consequences of his proposals—the problem that the need for reward is inherent in human nature. Showing both advantages and disadvantages of More's proposal demonstrates the skill of close reading and a high degree of maturity in this writer. To improve this essay, the writer could have worked on a stronger thesis that more accurately addresses the writer's points; notice that the thesis does not allude to any criticism of More's ideas. Some of the vague wording could be made more specific. In general, the essay's ideas are more sophisticated than their presentation.

This essay is well organized and the ideas are supported by examples from contemporary society. Overall, this essay deserves a high score for pointing out the validity of More's ideas for today's society as well as their perhaps mistaken assumptions.

Medium-Scoring Essay

Sir Thomas More's Utopia discusses fair government and equal social status within our society, and identifies the need for people to give up their private property. His ideas (as written about in the essay) are valid in light of contemporary standards.

More's initial position that private property is an unnecessary evil within our society at first appears to be blatantly Communistic. His desires to redistribute wealth and property and to make laws preventing people from earning too much money seem absurd at first glance. However, on further inspection, the reader realizes that some of More's views are valid and relevant to society. More predicts corruption of the government, something that our nation has been experiencing for several decades. This corruption is a result of politicians feeling obligated to remunerate themselves for the great expense they go through as a part of their job. More sums this up very nicely and accurately as he points out that rich men (instead of wise men) take over the offices of government.

Not only do we see the validity of More's views in our current day and age, but personally speaking, I agree with More's beliefs. The greed and self-interest associated with Capitalism are two symptoms of the sickness that comes with private property. It is wrong for a country's government to allow some people to starve on the streets while others are living like kings. More sympathizes for the great majority of people who do not have much private property.

Throughout his essay More proposes solutions to the problem of private property. He advocates altruism and his ideas are shown to be relevant to our society. His essay is very valid in light of today's social standards.

Analysis of the Medium-Scoring Essay

This medium-scoring essay attempts to address the topic. The first paragraph produces a thesis that claims that More's ideas are valid for contemporary society, but little else is presented here. The thesis is not highly thought-provoking, and it contains some redundancy ("as written about in the essay").

The student spends almost half of the second paragraph explaining his or her first impression of More, only to reverse it after a deeper analysis. This student should be commended for looking below the surface, but no evidence is offered to support the student's opinions. This paragraph would be stronger if the student were to include some specific examples of government corruption, rather than merely alluding to them.

The third paragraph becomes a forum for the student's personal beliefs. Once again, the student presents relevant ideas but little evidence for them. The only example included, the idea that the government allows poor people to starve while other live like kings, may indeed be true but is not specific. Stronger development of both ideas and examples would improve this paragraph.

The concluding paragraph merely summarizes the essay's only point, that the writer finds More's ideas valid. There's not much of substance here, and the conclusion doesn't help to convince the reader of the validity of the writer's opinions.

Although this essay does take a stand, it offers only weak support and sometimes simplistic and redundant wording. This essay would be stronger if the student were to include more of More's ideas and test their validity by today's standards. Overall, this essay is adequate, but it is not persuasive enough to merit a higher score.

PART III

DIAGNOSTIC MINI-TEST

The Mini-Test that follows is designed to familiarize you with some of the AP English Language and Composition Exam question types. It will also assist you in assessing some of your strengths and weaknesses. This short assessment includes complete answers and explanations, two essays written by AP students, and analyses of those essays.

The format, levels of difficulty, and question structures are similar to those on the actual AP English Language and Composition Exam. The actual AP Exam is copyrighted and may not be duplicated, and these questions are not taken directly from the actual test.

Answer Sheet for the Mini-Test

Remove this sheet and use it to mark your answers.
Answer sheets for "Section II: Essays" can be found at the end of the book.

Section I
Multiple-Choice Questions

1 Ⓐ Ⓑ Ⓒ Ⓓ Ⓔ
2 Ⓐ Ⓑ Ⓒ Ⓓ Ⓔ
3 Ⓐ Ⓑ Ⓒ Ⓓ Ⓔ
4 Ⓐ Ⓑ Ⓒ Ⓓ Ⓔ
5 Ⓐ Ⓑ Ⓒ Ⓓ Ⓔ
6 Ⓐ Ⓑ Ⓒ Ⓓ Ⓔ
7 Ⓐ Ⓑ Ⓒ Ⓓ Ⓔ
8 Ⓐ Ⓑ Ⓒ Ⓓ Ⓔ
9 Ⓐ Ⓑ Ⓒ Ⓓ Ⓔ
10 Ⓐ Ⓑ Ⓒ Ⓓ Ⓔ

CUT HERE

CUT HERE

Mini-Test

Section I: Multiple-Choice Questions

Time: 12 minutes

10 questions

Directions: This section contains a selection from a prose work and questions on its content, style, and form. Read each section carefully. Choose the best answer of the five choices.

Questions 1–10. Read the passage carefully before you begin to answer the questions.

Mini-Test Passage

On Route 301 south of Tampa, billboards advertising Sun City Center crop up every few miles, with pictures of Cesar Romero and slogans that read FLORIDA'S RETIREMENT COMMUNITY OF THE
(5) YEAR, 87 HOLES OF GOLF, THE TOWN TOO BUSY TO RETIRE. According to a real-estate brochure, the town is "sensibly located . . . comfortably removed from the crowded downtown areas, the highway clutter, the tourists, and the traffic." It is 25 miles
(10) from Sarasota, and 11 miles from the nearest beach on the Gulf Coast. Route 301, an inland route—to be taken in preference to the coast road, with its lines of trucks from the phosphate plants—passes through a lot of swampland, some scraggly
(15) pinewoods, and acre upon acre of strawberry beds covered with sheets of black plastic. There are fields where hairy, tough-looking cattle snatch at the grass between the palmettos. There are aluminum warehouses, cinder-block stores, and trailer
(20) homes in patches of dirt with laundry sailing out behind. There are Pentecostal churches and run-down cafes and bars with rows of pickup trucks parked out front.

Turn right with the billboards onto Route 674,
(25) and there is a green-and-white, suburban-looking resort town. Off the main road, white asphalt boulevards with avenues of palm trees give onto streets that curve pleasingly around golf courses and small lakes. White, ranch-style houses sit back
(30) from the streets on small, impeccably manicured lawns. A glossy, four-color map of the town put out by a real-estate company shows cartoon figures of golfers on the fairways and boats on the lakes, along with drawings of churches, clubhouses, and
(35) curly green trees. The map is a necessity for the visitor, since the streets curve around in a maze

fashion, ending in culs-de-sac or doubling back on themselves. There is no way in or out of Sun City Center except by the main road bisecting the town.
(40) The map, which looks like a child's board game (Snakes and Ladders or Uncle Wiggily), shows a vague area—a kind of no-man's-land—surrounding the town. As the map suggests, there is nothing natural about Sun City Center. The lakes are artifi-
(45) cial, and there is hardly a tree or shrub or blade of grass that has any correspondence in the world just beyond it. At the edges of the development, there are houses under construction, with the seams still showing in the transplanted lawns. From there, you
(50) can look out at a flat, brown plain that used to be a cattle ranch. The developer simply scraped the surface off the land and started over again.

Sun City Center is an unincorporated town of about 8,500 people, almost all of whom are over the
(55) age of 60. It is a self-contained community, with stores, banks, restaurants, and doctors' offices. It has the advertised 87 holes of golf; it also has tennis courts, shuffleboard courts, swimming pools, and lawn-bowling greens. In addition to the regular
(60) housing, it has a "life-care facility"—a six-story apartment building with a nursing home in one wing. "It's a strange town," a clinical psychologist at the University of South Florida, in Tampa, told me before I went. "It's out there in the middle of
(65) nowhere. It has a section of private houses, where people go when they retire. Then it has a section of condos and apartments, where people go when they can't keep up their houses. Then it has a nursing home. Then it has a cemetery." In fact, there is no
(70) cemetery in Sun City Center, but the doctor was otherwise correct.

(75) Sun City Center has become a world unto itself. Over the years, the town attracted a supermarket and all the stores and services necessary to the maintenance of daily life. Now, in addition, it has a golf-cart dealer, two banks, three savings and loan associations, four restaurants, and a brokerage firm. For visitors, there is the Sun City Center Inn. The town has a post office. Five churches have been
(80) built by the residents and a sixth is under construction. A number of doctors have set up offices in the town, and a Bradenton hospital recently opened a satellite hospital with 112 beds. There is no school, of course. The commercial establishments all front
(85) on the state road running through the center of town, but, because most of them are more expensive than those in the neighboring towns, the people from the surrounding area patronize only the super-market, the Laundromat, and one or two others. The
(90) local farmers and the migrant workers they employ, many of whom are Mexican, have little relationship to golf courses or to dinner dances with organ music. Conversely, Sun Citians are not the sort of people who would go to bean suppers in the
(95) Pentecostal churches or hang out at raunchy bars where gravel-voiced women sing "Satin Sheets and Satin Pillows." The result is that Sun Citians see very little of their Florida neighbors. They take trips to Tampa, Bradenton, and Sarasota, but otherwise
(100) they rarely leave the green-and-white developments, with their palm-lined avenues and artificial lakes. In the normal course of a week, they rarely see anyone under sixty.

1. In the first paragraph, the author refers to the "fields where hairy, tough-looking cattle snatch at the grass between the palmettos" in order to

   I. deny the area any pastoral attractiveness
   II. underscore the loss when farmland is subdivided for retirement homes
   III. suggest the savagery of the natural world that can be ordered and made beautiful by human projects

   A. I only
   B. II only
   C. I and III only
   D. II and III only
   E. I, II, and III

2. In the last three sentences of the first paragraph ("There are fields . . . parked out front"), the author uses all of the following EXCEPT

   A. parallel structure
   B. periodic sentences
   C. specific details
   D. direct statements
   E. subject-verb inversions

3. In the quotation at the end of the third paragraph, the use of two sentences with "where" clauses and three sentences beginning with "then" has which of the following effect?

   I. It provides a rhetorical parallelism for an unspoken chronological progression.
   II. It invites the reader to supply the "where" clauses for the last two sentences that begin with "then."
   III. It provides a series of transitions that direct the reader's attention to the speaker.

   A. II only
   B. I and II only
   C. I and III only
   D. II and III only
   E. I, II, and III

4. In the last paragraph, the list of services available in Sun City Center itemized in the sentence in lines 75–77 ("Now, in addition . . . brokerage firm") effectively suggests the residents' concern with

   A. avoiding the idea of death
   B. physical comforts
   C. impressing one another
   D. relaxation
   E. money

5. Which of the following does NOT accurately describe this sentence in the fourth paragraph: "Conversely, Sun Citians are not the sort of people who would go to bean suppers in the Pentecostal churches or hang out at raunchy bars where gravel-voiced women sing 'Satin Sheets and Satin Pillows'" (lines 93–97)?

A. It reinforces the idea of the preceding sentence.

B. It effectively contrasts Sun City Center residents and their neighbors.

C. It recalls details of the description at the end of the first paragraph.

D. It attacks the values of the people who live in the area near Sun City Center.

E. It presents an image that is amusing in its incongruity.

6. The effect of the last paragraph of the passage is to call attention to the

A. age of Sun City Center's residents

B. convenience of life in Sun City Center

C. political indifference of Sun City Center's residents

D. isolation of Sun City Center's residents

E. wealth of Sun City Center's residents

7. Which of the following best describes the diction of the passage?

A. formal and austere

B. informal and documentary

C. abstract

D. artless and colloquial

E. highly metaphorical

8. Which of the following quotations from the passage best sums up its main idea?

A. "As the map suggests, there is nothing natural about Sun City Center." (lines 43–44)

B. "The developer simply scraped the surface off the land and started over again." (lines 51–52)

C. "Sun City Center is an unincorporated town of about 8,500 people, almost all of whom are over the age of 60." (lines 53–55)

D. "In fact, there is no cemetery in Sun City Center, but the doctor was otherwise correct." (lines 69–71)

E. "The result is that Sun Citians see very little of their Florida neighbors." (lines 97–98)

9. A principal rhetorical strategy of the passage as a whole is to

A. depict a small city by presenting information in a chronological narrative

B. portray a place by comparison and contrast

C. raise and then answer questions about the nature of a place

D. progressively narrow the focus from a larger area to a smaller one and its residents

E. develop a discussion of a unique location by using multiple points of view

10. All of the following are characteristics of the style of this passage EXCEPT

A. variety in the length of its sentences

B. infrequent use of the first person

C. infrequent use of adjectives

D. infrequent use of simile

E. frequent use of specific details

Section II: Essay Question

Suggested Time: 40 minutes

Directions: The following passage comes from Michel-Guillaume-Jean de Crèvecoeur's *Letters from an American Farmer* (1782). Read the selection carefully, and then write an essay in which you analyze Crèvecoeur's attitude toward Europeans and Americans, concentrating on how his diction reflects his opinions.

In this great American asylum, the poor of Europe have by some means met together, and in consequence of various causes; to what purpose should they ask one another what countrymen they (5) are? Alas, two thirds of them had no country. Can a wretch who wanders about, who works and starves, whose life is a continual scene of sore affliction or pinching penury; can that man call England or any other kingdom his country? A country that had no (10) bread for him, whose fields procured him no harvest, who met with nothing but the frowns of the rich, the severity of the laws, with jails and punishments; who owned not a single foot of extensive surface of this planet? No! Urged by a variety of motives, here they (15) came. Everything has tended to regenerate them; new laws, a new mode of living, a new social system; here they are become men: in Europe they were as so many useless plants, wanting vegetative mold and refreshing showers; they withered, and were (20) mowed down by want, hunger, and war; but now by the power of transplantation, like all other plants they have taken root and flourished! Formerly they were not numbered in any civil lists of their country, except in those of the poor; here they rank as citizens.

(25) By what invisible power has this surprising metamorphosis been performed? By that of the laws and that of their industry. . . .

What then is the American, this new man? He is either a European, or the descendant of a European, (30) hence that strange mixture of blood, which you will find in no other country. I could point out to you a family whose grandfather was an Englishman, whose wife was Dutch, whose son married a French woman, and whose present four sons have (35) now four wives of different nations. *He* is an American, who leaving behind him all his ancient prejudices and manners, receives new ones from the new mode of life he has embraced, the new government he obeys, and the new rank he holds. (40) He becomes an American by being received in the broad lap of our great *Alma Mater.* Here individuals of all nations are melted into a new race of men, whose labors and posterity will one day cause great changes in the world. Americans are the western (45) pilgrims, who are carrying only with them that great mass of arts, sciences, vigor, and industry which began long since in the east; they will finish the great circle.

Answer Key for the Mini-Test

Section I: Multiple-Choice Questions

1. A
2. B
3. B
4. E
5. D
6. D
7. B
8. A
9. D
10. C

Section II: Essay Question

An essay scoring guide, student essays, and analysis appear beginning on page 51.

Answers and Explanations for the Mini-Test

Section I: Multiple-Choice Questions

From *Cities on a Hill* by Frances Fitzgerald

1. **A.** The passage presents the area around Sun City Center as ugly: "scraggly pinewoods" and a "lot of swampland." Although the land is used for cattle ranching, the prose denies it any charm or beauty. The passage has no concern with making a case for the subdivision as ecologically good (III) or bad (II). In the passage, ecology is not an issue.

2. **B.** These are all loose, not periodic, sentences. Each of the sentences could end after just three or four words. There is parallel structure in the repeated "There are." The sentences are direct statements chiefly made up of specific details. All three sentences place the verbs ("are") before the subjects ("fields," "warehouses," "churches").

3. **B.** The repetition of "it has" and "then it has" is an example of parallel structure, and the chronology progresses from the time when the people first move to Sun City Center to a later time when health begins to fail, to a time of greater weakness, to death (I). The two "where" clauses invite us to add two more "where" clauses into the last two sentences, thus mentally completing the implied parallel construction: "it has a nursing home, where they go when they can't keep up their condos" and "it has a cemetery, where they go when they die" (II). The series does not call attention to the speaker (III).

4. **E.** There are five services listed, and three of the five (banks, savings and loan associations, and a brokerage firm) are specifically related to money. A fourth, the golf-cart dealer, is at least tangentially related to affluence. Choices B, C, and D are plausible, but E, although it may seem obvious, is the best choice.

5. **D.** The sentence reinforces the idea of the sentence before—the alienation of the Sun Citians from their neighbors (choices A and B). The bars and Pentecostal churches were mentioned in the last sentence of the first paragraph (C). The notion of a group of middle-class senior citizens sitting in a run-down café listening to country-western music is amusing in its incongruity (E). The passage is not satiric. Its point is not that Sun Citians or their neighbors are flawed, but that they have nothing in common.

6. **D.** Although the paragraph begins with an account of the stores and services of Sun City Center, even the first sentence insists on this development as "a world unto itself." And the last two-thirds of the paragraph (beginning with "There is no school, of course") gives evidence to support the notion of the residents' isolation from the rest of the world.

7. **B.** Although perhaps not an ideal answer, Choice B is the best of the five choices here. The passage is not formal and austere, not abstract, not artless (although a few phrases could be called colloquial), and not at all metaphorical.

8. **A.** Choices B, C, and D don't really sum up a central idea of the passage. Both A and E are good answers, but A can include the idea of E, while E is more narrow. The whole passage is about the unnaturalness of Sun City Center, its oddness in this geographical area, and the segregation of its residents from their neighbors and from a world where many people are still under 60. "Sun City Center has become a world unto itself" in the last paragraph would also be a good answer.

9. **D.** The best choice here is D. The passage begins with the geography of the central west coast of Florida but narrows to Sun City Center ("Turn right onto Route 674"). The second paragraph maps out the town, while the third and fourth describe its residents. The passage is not a chronological narrative (A), uses contrast only in the last paragraph (B), asks no questions (C), and has only one point of view and one additional quoted comment (D).

10. **C.** The passage varies its sentence length, uses the first person only once (paragraph three), uses very little figurative language, and uses a large number of specific details. It is very dependent on adjectives and, without its adjectives, it would be barren and unrecognizable.

Section II: Essay Question

Scoring Guide for the Essay Question (Michel de Crèvecoeur)

9 Essays earning a score of 9 meet the criteria for essays that are scored an 8 and, in addition, are especially full or apt in their analysis or reveal particularly remarkable control of language.

8 Successful

Essays earning a score of 8 **successfully** and clearly demonstrate understanding of Crèvecoeur's attitude toward Americans and a thorough comprehension of how his diction reflects his attitude. The thesis is articulate and thoughtful. Strong and relevant evidence from Crèvecoeur's essay is included. Thoroughly convincing, these essays show a clear command of essay-writing skills. Although it need not be without errors, these papers show a mature style and use of language.

7 Essays earning a score of 7 fit the description of essays that are scored a 6 but provide more complete analysis, and a more mature prose style.

6 Satisfactory

These essays show a **satisfactory** comprehension of Crèvecoeur's ideas, but the thesis may be less explicit than that of the top-scoring essays. The evidence offered may not be as convincing or thorough, making the essay less persuasive. Still, the essay is fairly convincing and shows clear thinking. The connection between the evidence and Crèvecoeur's attitude may not be as clear as in top-scoring essays. Although well written, it may demonstrate some errors while still showing satisfactory control over diction and the essay requirements.

5 These adequately written essays show some understanding of Crèvecoeur's attitude but may not show clear comprehension of the relationship between his language and his attitude. The thesis may be simplistic and predictable while the evidence offered may be insufficient to prove the writer's points. Evidence presented for Crèvecoeur's attitude may be too brief or understated. Although the presentation of ideas may be acceptable, the paper as a whole is not strongly convincing. Acceptable organization and development may be evident, but the style may not be as sophisticated as that of higher-scoring essays.

4 Inadequate

These low-scoring essays fail to convince the reader because of their **inadequate** response to the prompt. The weak presentation may not demonstrate a clear understanding of Crèvecoeur's ideas. Comprehension of how Crèvecoeur's language communicates his attitude may be minimal. The thesis may be unsubstantiated, paragraph development may be weak, and superficial thinking may be evident. Connection between Crèvecoeur's language and the paper's thesis may be nonexistent or trite. Frequent mechanical errors that distract the reader may be present.

3 Essays earning a score of 3 meet the criteria for a score of 4 but demonstrate a less clear understanding of Crèvecoeur's ideas. The essays may show less control over the elements of writing.

2 Little Success

These poorly written essays lack coherence and clarity. They may present only a brief synopsis of Crèvecoeur's attitude with no mention of how his language reflects that attitude. The thesis may be overly obvious or nonexistent. Little or no evidence may be offered, and the connection between the evidence and the thesis may be shallow or missing. These essays may misunderstand the task, fail to articulate Crèvecoeur's attitude, or may substitute a simpler task. These essays may be unusually short and exhibit poor fundamental essay skills. Weak sentence construction may persist, and frequent weaknesses in mechanics may be present.

1 These poorly written essays meet the criteria for a score of 2 but are undeveloped, especially simplistic in their analysis, and weak in their control of language.

High-Scoring Essay

Many foreigners came to America during the republic's formative years to explore life in the new nation. The writings of de Tocqueville and Charles Dickens commented on the new American character and government in the nineteenth century. Michel-Guillaume-Jean de Crèvecoeur, who wrote *Letters from an American Farmer* in 1782, was not alone in his endeavor, though he was one of the first to visit the new United States. His writing generally reflects a positive image of Americans. While taking note of their humble origins and lack of cultural refinement, he praises the resilience of American citizens. Crèvecoeur's diction, and the positive connotations of the words he uses to describe Americans, clearly present his positive, though occasionally paternal and superior, attitude toward Americans.

Americans are defined by Crèvecoeur largely in terms of the land they left. Their new nation is a haven from a Europe of "severe laws, with jails and punishments." The common folk in England are faced by the "frowns of the rich." The new Americans have left the "refinement" of Europe behind, along with the class system and much else which had restricted them. These images tell as much about Crèvecoeur's attitude toward Europeans as it does toward Americans. The negativity attached to Americans' backgrounds perhaps emphasizes their ultimate determination and drive once they arrived on new soil. Crèvecoeur deliberately uses negative phrases in describing Americans' pasts so that their change in the new country will be even more dramatic.

Crèvecoeur emphasizes the newness of the United States, thus implying a positive impression of the land. While he may look down somewhat on the breeding and manners of the Americans, noting that they come from the lower rungs of European social hierarchy, he certainly believes the new land is good for them. America is a place of "regenerative" powers, with "new laws, a new mode of living, a new social system." Crèvecoeur credits America with encouraging the "flourishing" of the world's poor and unwanted. Might he then be looking down on America, as the "asylum" he describes in the opening sentence, a refuge suitable only for the wretches of sophisticated European life? Perhaps. But he leaves no doubt about the successful attainment of such a goal, lauding it by writing that the "surprising metamorphosis" from wretches to citizens is thanks to American "laws and . . . industry."

Although Crèvecoeur generally presents Americans in laudable terms, a trace of condescension appears in some phrases. America was made up of "wretches" who had previously "wandered about." They had endured lives of "sore affliction or pinching penury." But despite the seeming elitism of Crèvecoeur's description, his word choices elicit sympathy rather than scorn in the attentive reader because he is referring to the Americans' previous lives in Europe. Crèvecoeur makes a careful point of the work ethic of these derelict new countrymen, essentially homeless among the world's nations. Such attention clearly shows that Crèvecoeur is sensitive to the plight of the new Americans.

Crèvecoeur writes as if America has surpassed his expectations as a melting pot of undesirables. He has an optimistic view of the country's role in the future. Compared to crusaders, the Americans he praises are the "western pilgrims" full of the "great mass of arts, sciences, vigor, and industry" that once issued from the east. It is important to note that Crèvecoeur ends his essay on a positive tone, with phrasing that emphasizes greatness. Here, in his conclusion, Crèvecoeur's attitude toward Americans really shines with enthusiasm. They are the nation of the future he believes, and they will deeply influence the future of the world with their newborn splendor.

Analysis of the High-Scoring Essay

This thorough and well-written essay succeeds both in covering the topic and in convincing the reader. The student demonstrates a clear comprehension of the passage and does not merely present a one-sided view of Crèvecoeur. The first paragraph introduces and relates other foreign authors who also addressed the personality of the new Americans. Ultimately, it presents a thoughtful thesis that shows a full understanding of Crèvecoeur's attitude while also mentioning his diction.

In the second paragraph, the student addresses Crèvecoeur's negative statements about the Americans' background in Europe and does a nice job of placing this negativity in context by pointing out that it will be balanced with the "dramatic" changes that take place once the new citizens have become Americans. This paragraph, like those that follow, is thoughtful and articulate, presenting an ample number of specific examples for the student's points and providing connection to the thesis.

The next paragraph addresses the transformation that took place in the Americans after they arrived in the new country. This unified paragraph uses quotations from the passage well and presents interesting ideas from the student. This writer shows the ability to think about and interpret Crèvecoeur's ideas, not simply to present them.

The fourth paragraph describes the "condescension" in some of Crèvecoeur's phrasing; again the student does an admirable job of presenting Crèvecoeur's attitude while remembering that the topic asks for diction analysis. The student clearly sees that, although Crèvecoeur presents many negative ideas about the Americans' background, essentially, he praises Americans.

The essay ends positively, just as Crèvecoeur's does. The student's wording, like Crèvecoeur's, shows optimism and provides a clean ending to a fairly long essay. Influencing the future with "newborn splendor" sums up both Crèvecoeur's attitude and the student's ideas very nicely. Overall, the essay uses sophisticated wording and contains many intelligent ideas. It reads well because it's clear that the student has ideas of his or her own and is not merely listing Crèvecoeur's.

Medium-Scoring Essay

Crèvecoeur was a French writer who wrote about life in the rural parts of America. He has a partly negative attitude about America, and cuts down the Americans many times in his essay. He also gives them some praise for starting over and doing something new. He also praises them for succeeding at something new.

He uses diction to obtain these results. A careful use of diction shows readers that he sometimes doesn't think much of the American people as a whole. He points out that they were the "poor of Europe" who, as "wretches," lived a life of "sore affliction." He also says that "two thirds of them had no country." This hardly sounds like Crèvecoeur admires the Americans background. He stereotypes Americans to all be like this.

Crèvecoeur continues his diatribe against Americans as he calls them "useless plants" in Europe. But finally, he has something more generous to say about Americans as he claims these plants have "taken root and flourished" here in American soil. So, although these Americans were low-life Europeans, once they became Americans they became "new." They became "citizens." Crèvecoeur also notices that Americans work hard and have good laws. I find it interesting that even though he has some good things to say about Americans, he still claims negative things; he believes that once the new Americans arrived, they left behind them all their "ancient prejudices . . . receiving new ones. . . ." We in America today like to believe that we hold no prejudices; at least that's one of the principles that our country was founded on.

Thus it can be seen that Crèvecoeur seemed to have some good thoughts about Americans, but that he was by no means entirely impressed by them. He uses his diction to present his opinions, and very strong diction at that. His wording is surprisingly harsh at times, considering that he seems to want to praise Americans for what they have accomplished, yet he spends so much time degrading their background. His attitude toward Americans is best described as guarded; he certainly does not show Americans in nothing but glowing terms.

Analysis of the Medium-Scoring Essay

This essay, although well organized, clearly shows the student's problems in both reading and writing skills. It begins by attempting to address the topic, but it does so with such a vague thesis that all it essentially sets forth is the simplistic idea that Crèvecoeur is both positive and negative about Americans. How Crèvecoeur's diction establishes that attitude is not yet addressed.

The student then devotes a paragraph to proving how negatively Crèvecoeur viewed the Americans' backgrounds by supplying a fair amount of evidence from Crèvecoeur's text. The student cites several examples of negative wording but also makes mistakes. First, the student borders on a misreading of the passage. In explaining the despair that Americans felt before coming to this country, Crèvecoeur's purpose seems to be to show how much the Americans had to overcome, thus emphasizing their strength. However, this student concentrates on only the negative European experience and transfers that negativity to the Americans *after* they became Americans. The student's second mistake is failing to address the topic clearly, failing to comment on exactly *how* Crèvecoeur's attitude is presented through his diction. This student simply gives the evidence and leaves it to the reader to make the connection.

The next paragraph tries to establish Crèvecoeur's positive attitude toward Americans, but the evidence presented is weak; the student offers little more than that the country is "new" and that people are now "citizens." The student turns again to a negative reading of the text, focusing on Crèvecoeur's claim that Americans have prejudices. Because of this change in direction, the paragraph lacks unity.

The concluding paragraph finally mentions diction again, but again it makes no connection between Crèvecoeur's word choice and the attitude it reflects. Unfortunately, this paragraph is merely summary. Overall, the essay's weaknesses stem from a cursory reading of the passage, weak presentation of evidence, and a lack of attention to the topic of the thesis. Simplistic thinking and simplistic diction combine here to produce a bland essay that fails to convince the reader.

PART IV

PAST AP ENGLISH LANGUAGE ESSAYS

By examining essay topics from previous exams, you can notice trends and become familiar with the question categories to expect. You will find topics from the last 25 years paraphrased in this part. Read them and become comfortable with the question format. Also be aware of the different writing modes the essays require. Top-scoring students can write in a variety of modes.

Past AP English Language and Composition Essay Topics

In the following chart, you will find a paraphrasing of AP English Language and Composition essay topics since 1980. Although an exact topic is never reused, when you read this information you should look for trends and patterns in the essay topics. Examine the different modes the essay category requires. For instance, understand the difference between writing a rhetorical analysis essay and writing an argument essay. Notice that in the argument topics, you may use examples from your observation, experience, or reading to support your ideas. Finally, be aware that the real test will not be printed like this; it will not tell you that the topic is a "rhetorical analysis" one or an "argument" one, for example. However, you should be able to understand what category the topic fits into from your practice.

Year	Question Category	Passage/Topic (Title of Passage and Author)
1980	Argument	Discuss the grounds on which a group could attack or suppress a work (such as a book, movie, and so on), and then defend the work.
	Rhetorical analysis	Two eyewitness accounts of two different funerals are given—one from Henry James, the other from Ralph Ellison. Analyze the differences in their perspectives as seen in their rhetoric.
	Argument	"Querencia" is defined as a "feeling for one's own place"; identify your "own place" and explain its meaning.
1981	Rhetorical analysis	A passage from "The Rattler" by Donald Peattie is given in which he describes coming upon a rattlesnake in the desert. Discuss the passage's effect and how it is created by the author's techniques.
	Rhetorical analysis	A portion of the letter written by George Bernard Shaw after the death of his mother is presented. Describe the author's attitude toward his mother and her cremation; analyze how his language conveys his attitude.
	Argument	A short passage from Thomas Szasz is given that discusses the struggle for definition. Agree or disagree with the author's position and draw upon your experiences, observations, or readings to support your position.
1982	Argument	A passage is given in which the author disagrees with the adage, "Where ignorance is bliss, 'tis folly to be wise." Summarize the passage's reasoning and agree or disagree with the author's opinion.
	Rhetorical analysis	The given passage is a statement of veto from Governor Adlai E. Stevenson to the state congress. Analyze the governor's strategies and devices that make his argument effective.
	Free response	Describe a place so that it conveys a recognizable feeling through specific details without having to state that feeling.
1983	Argument	Analyze both the good and bad effects of a change in society that has occurred or that you would like to see occur.
	Rhetorical analysis	A passage from Thomas Carlyle's *Past and Present* is given. Define the author's attitude toward work, what assumptions he makes about human nature, and how his language persuades the reader of the validity of his position.
	Argument	Agree or disagree with the concept that "when everything is superlative, everything is mediocre" while considering the "ethical and social consequences of language inflation."

(continued)

Year	Question Category	Passage/Topic (Title of Passage and Author)
1984	Argument	Examine the importance of time, how you keep track of time, and what this reveals about you.
	Argument	Two passages are given that have different definitions of freedom. One is by Percy Bysshe Shelley and the other is by John Milton. Discuss the concept expressed in each passage and examine the concepts' differences.
	Rhetorical analysis	A passage from Norman Mailer that describes Paret, a Cuban boxer, is given. Analyze the effect of the passage on the reader and how Mailer's rhetoric produces that effect.
1985	Rhetorical analysis	Two passages describe the Soviet Union's launching of the first satellite in 1957. Analyze the stylistic and rhetorical differences between the passages.
	Rhetorical analysis	Two drafts from the same writer reflect his thoughts about how war changed his attitude about language. Discuss reasons for the writer's additions and deletions and how the revisions affect the passage.
	Argument	The passage implies that television should reflect the real world. Defend one or more of the propositions in the passage.
1986	Rhetorical analysis	Two Native American writers, N. S. Momaday and D. Brown, describe similar landscapes. Analyze how their respective rhetoric reveal their different purposes.
	Rhetorical analysis	Pairs of words similar in meaning but different in connotation are given (for example, "religion" and "cult"). Choose one or more pairs and elaborate on their distinctions.
	Argument	A quote claiming that human nature yearns for patterns, structure, and conformity is given. Agree or disagree with the concept and use your experiences, observations, or readings to back up your opinion.
1987	Argument	Agree or disagree with E. M. Forster's quotation in which he claims the he would rather betray his country than betray a friend.
	Rhetorical analysis	A passage from Zora Neal Hurston's *Dust Tracks on a Road* is given; analyze how her diction and point of view enhance our view of her childhood.
	Free Response	Examine how the language of a specific group you know well, such as an ethnic or social group, reflects that group. Describe the language (sociolect) of that group and discuss its influences.
1988	Argument	A passage from de Tocqueville's *Democracy in America* is given in which he concludes that democracy "throws [man] back forever upon himself alone." Evaluate his ideas.
	Rhetorical analysis	A passage from Frederick Douglass explains how he felt after escaping slavery and arriving in New York in 1838. Analyze how his diverse language presents his various states of mind.
	Free response	Describe a place that might be of interest or significance to others. Include descriptive detail and your attitude regarding this location.
1989	Argument	An announcement from a church bulletin reprinted in a magazine is given; the heading in the magazine implies a criticism of American values. Argue for or against the implied criticism.
	Rhetorical analysis	A passage from Martin Luther King's *Why We Can't Wait* is given; analyze how his rhetoric fits his rhetorical purpose.

Year	Question Category	Passage/Topic (Title of Passage and Author)
	Argument	Describe how one person can be perceived differently at different times or in different situations.
1990	Rhetorical analysis	A passage from Beryl Markham's autobiography is given. Analyze how her rhetoric reflects her personality.
	Rhetorical analysis	Two passages describe the Galapagos Islands. Analyze the stylistic and rhetorical differences between them.
	Argument	Present an argument for or against the Supreme Court ruling that limited the First Amendment rights of student newspapers, claiming that a school newspaper is a "laboratory situation" that can be curbed to remain consistent with the school's "basic educational mission."
1991	Rhetorical analysis	A passage from the composer Igor Stravinsky is given; analyze how his diction and rhetorical devices present his point of view.
	Rhetorical analysis	A passage from Richard Rodriguez's autobiography is given; analyze how his rhetoric and style reflect his attitude toward his family and himself.
	Argument	A biblical quote from Ecclesiastes claims that more knowledge brings more sorrow. Agree or disagree and use your experiences, observations, or readings to support your position.
1992	Rhetorical analysis	A speech from Queen Elizabeth I to her troops during the war with the Spanish Armada is given. Identify her purpose and analyze how she uses language to achieve that purpose.
	Argument	A passage from a Joseph Addison essay in *The Spectator* claims that mankind uses ridicule for bad aims instead of using it to achieve good. Defend, challenge, or qualify the concept, using your experiences, readings, or observations to back up your ideas.
	Rhetorical analysis	A passage from Nancy Mairs about being a "cripple" is given; analyze how she presents herself through language and rhetorical features.
1993	Rhetorical analysis	A passage from Jane Austen and a passage from Charles Dickens are given, each dealing with the subject of marriage. Compare the rhetorical strategies in the passages and the possible effects of each proposal.
	Argument	A passage from H. L. Mencken clarifies his view about the relationship between an artist and society. Defend, qualify, or challenge Mencken's view and support your position with references to particular writers, artists, or composers.
	Rhetorical analysis	A passage from E. M. Forster's essay "My Wood" describes his feeling about owning property that he bought from his book royalties. Analyze how his rhetoric and biblical allusions convey his attitude.
1994	Rhetorical analysis	A passage from Sir George Savile, a member of King Charles II's Privy Council, is given in which he addresses the criticism that the king loves only pleasure. Clarify what attitude Savile wants the reader to adopt and how his rhetorical strategies encourage that attitude.
	Argument	A quotation from Barbara Tuchman's *March of Folly* is given in which she asserts the role that "wooden-headedness" plays in human affairs. Defend, challenge, or qualify her idea, using your readings and/or observations to support your position.

(continued)

Year	Question Category	Passage/Topic (Title of Passage and Author)
	Rhetorical analysis	A passage from Joan Didion's essay "Los Angeles Notebook" is given in which she describes the Santa Ana winds and their effect on people. Analyze how her rhetoric promotes her views.
1995	Argument	A passage is used in which John Ruskin claims that precedence should be given to the soldier over the merchant or manufacturer. Evaluate Ruskin's argument.
	Rhetorical analysis	A column by Ellen Goodman called "The Company Man" is given. Analyze how her language and rhetorical technique convey her attitude.
	Argument	A passage from James Baldwin about the importance of language as the "key to identity" and social acceptance is given. Defend, challenge, or qualify Baldwin's ideas, using your experiences, observations, or readings to develop your opinion.
1996	Rhetorical analysis	A letter from Lady Montagu to her daughter is given, regarding the education of her granddaughter. Analyze the rhetorical strategies and stylistic devices she uses to present her ideas about the role that education played in women's lives in the 18th century.
	Rhetorical analysis	A passage from Gary Soto's autobiography is presented in which he recounts an experience of stealing a pie at age 6. Examine how his rhetoric re-creates both the experience and his ensuing guilt.
	Argument	A passage from Lewis Lapham's *Money and Class in America* is given in which he observes the attitudes of Americans toward wealth. Defend, challenge, or qualify his view, based on your own experience and knowledge.
1997	Rhetorical analysis	A passage from Meena Alexander's autobiography, *Fault Lines,* is given. Analyze how her language represents her "fractured identity."
	Rhetorical analysis	A passage from the autobiography, *Narrative of the Life of Frederick Douglass, an American Slave,* is presented. Analyze how the third paragraph differs stylistically from the rest of the passage and reinforces Douglass's purpose.
	Argument	A passage from Neil Postman, a contemporary social critic, contrasts the view of the future as presented in Orwell's *1984* and Huxley's *Brave New World.* Postman finds Huxley's ideas more relevant. Agree or disagree with Postman's idea, based on your understanding of modern society.
1998	Rhetorical analysis	A letter from Charles Lamb to English Romantic poet William Wordsworth is given. Analyze the techniques Lamb uses to reject an invitation by Wordsworth to visit.
	Argument	A passage from Henry James's novel *The Portrait of a Lady* is given in which two conversationalists present differing views about what constitutes the self. Using your experiences, observations, or readings, develop whichever position you feel has greater validity.
	Rhetorical analysis	Two letters are presented that deal with an advertising company's use of the slogan "It's the Real Thing" to promote a book. One letter is from a Coca-Cola Company executive and the second is a reply from the advertiser. Analyze the rhetorical strategies each writer uses and examine which is more successful in its persuasion.
1999	Rhetorical analysis	Two passages describing Florida's Okefenokee Swamp are presented. Analyze how the rhetoric of each passage reflects each author's purpose.
	Rhetorical analysis	A passage from Jamaica Kinkaid's essay "On Seeing England for the First Time" is given. Analyze how her attitude toward England is presented through her rhetoric.

Year	Question Category	Passage/Topic (Title of Passage and Author)
	Argument	A quotation from Teiresias in Sophocles's play *Antigone* is given in which he observes that "the only crime [in man] is pride." Evaluate the validity of his claim, using your experiences, observations, or readings to support your opinion.
2000	Rhetorical analysis	A passage from Eudora Welty's autobiography, *One Writer's Beginnings,* is given in which she explains the value that reading books has had on her development as a writer. Analyze how her language explores the power of these experiences.
	Rhetorical analysis	A passage from George Orwell is given in which he criticizes Gandhi and makes a point for humans being imperfect instead of saints. Analyze how Orwell disapproves of Gandhi and how effective he is in presenting his own opinion.
	Argument	A quotation is given from the title character in *King Lear,* in which Lear comments on the relationship between wealth and justice. Paraphrase Lear's comment, and then defend, challenge, or qualify that assertion with examples from your readings, experiences, or observations.
2001	Rhetorical analysis	A letter from Marian Evans Lewes (whose pen name was George Eliot) responding to a letter she had received from an American is given. Analyze the rhetorical strategies she uses to establish her ideas about the development of a writer.
	Rhetorical analysis	A passage from Mary Oliver's essay "Owls" is presented. Analyze how her style explains her complex response to the natural world.
	Argument	A passage from Susan Sontag establishes the idea that photography restricts our understanding of the world. Develop the extent to which you agree or disagree, using appropriate evidence.
2002	Rhetorical analysis	The passage presents Abraham Lincoln's second inaugural address, in which he reflects upon the effects of the Civil War and ponders the future of the nation. Using specific references to the text, analyze the rhetorical strategies he uses to create his ideas.
	Rhetorical analysis	In a passage from her memoir, *Moments of Being,* Virginia Woolf muses on her childhood summers in the coastal town of Cornwall, England. Analyze how her language expresses the lifelong importance of these moments from her past.
	Argument	A passage from *Testaments Betrayed* by Milan Kundera, a Czech writer, presents the concept that in order for a man to live free, he must be able to separate his private life from his public one. Using appropriate evidence, explain the extent to which you agree or disagree with his assertion.
2003	Argument	In an excerpt from his 1983 book, *Life the Movie: How Entertainment Conquered Reality,* Neal Gabler explains how entertainment has the capacity to "ruin" society. Using appropriate evidence, explain the extent with which you agree or disagree with his premise.
	Rhetorical analysis	A speech from Alfred M. Green in 1861 asserts that African-Americans should strive for the ability to enlist in the army and prepare to join up. Analyze the methods Green uses to persuade his fellow African Americans to join the Union forces.
	Rhetorical analysis	Two passages that describe large flocks of birds in flight are presented, one from John James Audubon and one from Annie Dillard. Compare and contrast how each author's description of the birds conveys the birds' effect on the writer as an observer of nature.

(continued)

Year	Question Category	Passage/Topic (Title of Passage and Author)
2004	Rhetorical analysis	A letter from Lord Chesterfield to his son, a youth who was traveling far from home, presents a father's advice. Analyze how the rhetorical strategies Lord Chesterfield uses reveal his own values.
	Argument	The concept that "Contemporary life is marked by controversy" is presented. Choose an issue and write an essay, using appropriate evidence, that considers opposing positions and proposes a solution or compromise to the problem.
	Rhetorical analysis	The introduction to *Days of Obligation* by Richard Rodriquez is presented. Analyze how Rodriquez contrasts California and Mexico while he explores and conveys his conflicted feelings about both locations.
2005	Argument	A passage from "Training for Statesmanship" by George F. Kennan, a principal architect of U.S. policy after World War II, is presented. Decide which idea is Kennan's most compelling observation, and argue to what extent that observation still holds true for the United States or any other country, using appropriate evidence.
	Rhetorical analysis	A mock press release from *The Onion*, a satirical and humorous publication, is presented. Analyze the strategies the article uses to satirize how products are marketed to contemporary consumers.
	Argument	A controversial idea from Peter Singer, professor of bioethics, is presented. Noting the need for food and medicine in many parts of the world, he argues that wealthy people should donate all their money that is not needed for basic requirements to overseas aid organizations. Evaluate the pros and cons of his argument, and, using appropriate evidence in this examination, indicate the more persuasive position.

PART V

GLOSSARY OF IMPORTANT TERMS FOR THE AP ENGLISH LANGUAGE AND COMPOSITION EXAM

The following glossary lists technical terms, both literary and grammatical, with which you should be familiar before the AP Exam. It isn't an exhaustive list of every term you might encounter. For example, you won't find parts of speech defined, as it is assumed that AP students are familiar with them. The first section includes terms common in both multiple-choice and essay sections. The second includes terms used exclusively in the essay section.

Terms for the Multiple-Choice and Essay Sections

Some of the following terms may be used in the multiple-choice questions and/or answers, or in essay-section instructions. You might choose to incorporate others into your essay writing, for example, to help explain the effect of a literary device mentioned in the essay prompt.

ad hominem argument   From the Latin meaning "to or against the man," this is an argument that appeals to emotion rather than reason, to feeling rather than intellect.

allegory   The device of using character and/or story elements symbolically to represent an abstraction in addition to the literal meaning. In some allegories, for example, an author may intend the characters to personify an abstraction like hope or freedom. The allegorical meaning usually deals with moral truth or a generalization about human existence.

alliteration   The repetition of sounds, especially initial consonant sounds in two or more neighboring words (as in "she sells sea shells"). Although the term is not used in the multiple-choice section, you can look for alliteration in any essay passage. The repetition can reinforce meaning, unify ideas, and/or supply a musical sound.

allusion   A direct or indirect reference to something that is presumably commonly known, such as an event, book, myth, place, or work of art. Allusions can be historical (like referring to Hitler), literary (like referring to Kurtz in *Heart of Darkness*), religious (like referring to Noah and the flood), or mythical (like referring to Atlas). There are, of course, many more possibilities, and a work may simultaneously use multiple layers of allusion.

ambiguity   The multiple meanings, either intentional or unintentional, of a word, phrase, sentence, or passage.

analogy   A similarity or comparison between two different things or the relationship between them. An analogy can explain something unfamiliar by associating it with, or pointing out its similarity to, something more familiar. Analogies can also make writing more vivid, imaginative, and intellectually engaging.

antecedent   The word, phrase, or clause referred to by a pronoun. The AP English Language and Composition Exam occasionally asks for the antecedent of a given pronoun in a long, complex sentence or in a group of sentences.

antithesis   A figure of speech involving a seeming contradiction of ideas, words, clauses, or sentences within a balanced grammatical structure. The resulting parallelism serves to emphasize opposition of ideas. The familiar phrase "Man proposes, God disposes" is an example of antithesis, as is John Dryden's description in *The Hind and the Panther:* "Too black for heaven, and yet too white for hell."

aphorism   A terse statement of known authorship that expresses a general truth or moral principle. (If the authorship is unknown, the statement is generally considered to be a folk proverb.) An aphorism can be a memorable summation of the author's point.

apostrophe   A figure of speech that directly addresses an absent or imaginary person or personified abstraction, such as liberty or love. The effect may add familiarity or emotional intensity. William Wordsworth addresses John Milton as he writes, "Milton, thou shouldst be living at this hour: England hath need of thee."

atmosphere   The emotional mood created by the entirety of a literary work, established partly by the setting and partly by the author's choice of objects that are described. Even such elements as a description of the weather can contribute to the atmosphere. Frequently, atmosphere foreshadows events. See **mood.**

caricature   A representation, especially pictorial or literary, in which the subject's distinctive features or peculiarities are deliberately exaggerated to produce a comic or grotesque effect. Sometimes caricature can be so exaggerated that it becomes a grotesque imitation or misrepresentation. Synonymous words include *burlesque, parody, travesty, satire, lampoon.*

chiasmus   A figure of speech based on inverted parallelism. It is a rhetorical figure in which two clauses are related to each another through a reversal of terms. The purpose is usually to make a larger point or to provide balance or order. In classical rhetoric, the parallel structures did not repeat words, such as found in Alexander Pope's *Essay on Man:* "His time a moment, and a point his space." However, contemporary standards allow for repeated words; a commonly cited example comes from John F. Kennedy's inaugural address: ". . . ask not what your country can do for you—ask what you can do for your country."

clause   A grammatical unit that contains both a subject and a verb. An independent, or main, clause expresses a complete thought and can stand alone as a sentence. A dependent, or subordinate, clause cannot stand alone as a sentence and must be accompanied by an independent clause. Examine this sample sentence: "Because I practiced hard, my AP scores were high." In this sentence, the independent clause is "my AP scores were high," and the dependent clause is "Because I practiced hard."

colloquialism   Slang or informality in speech or writing. Not generally acceptable for formal writing, colloquialisms give work a conversational, familiar tone. Colloquial expressions in writing include local or regional dialects.

conceit   A fanciful expression, usually in the form of an extended metaphor or surprising analogy between seemingly dissimilar objects. A conceit displays intellectual cleverness due to the unusual comparison being made.

connotation   The nonliteral, associative meaning of a word; the implied, suggested meaning. Connotations may involve ideas, emotions, or attitudes. See **denotation.**

denotation   The strict, literal, dictionary definition of a word, devoid of any emotion, attitude, or color. See **connotation.**

diction   Related to style, diction refers to the writer's word choices, especially with regard to their correctness, clearness, or effectiveness. For the AP Language and Composition Exam, you should be able to describe an author's diction (for example, formal or informal, ornate or plain) and understand the ways in which diction can complement the author's purpose. Diction, combined with syntax, figurative language, literary devices, and so on, creates an author's style. **Note:** This term frequently appears in the essay question's wording. In your thesis, avoid phrases such as, "The author uses diction. . . ." Because diction, by definition, *is word choice,* this phrase really says, "The author chooses words to write . . .", which is as redundant (and silly) as claiming, "A painter uses paints to paint." At least try to put an adjective in front of the word "diction" to help describe it, such as "stark diction" or "flowery and soft diction." See **syntax.**

didactic   From the Greek, "didactic" literally means "instructive." Didactic works have the primary aim of teaching or instructing, especially the teaching of moral or ethical principles.

euphemism   From the Greek for "good speech," euphemisms are a more agreeable or less offensive substitute for generally unpleasant words or concepts. The euphemism may be used to adhere to standards of social or political correctness, or to add humor or ironic understatement. Saying "earthly remains" rather than "corpse" is an example of euphemism.

extended metaphor   A metaphor developed at great length, occurring frequently in or throughout a work. See **metaphor.**

figurative language   Writing or speech that is not intended to carry literal meaning and is usually meant to be imaginative and vivid. See **figure of speech.**

figure of speech   A device used to produce figurative language. Many compare dissimilar things. Figures of speech include, for example, apostrophe, hyperbole, irony, metaphor, metonymy, oxymoron, paradox, personification, simile, synecdoche, and understatement.

generic conventions   This term describes traditions for each genre. These conventions help to define each genre; for example, they differentiate between an essay and journalistic writing or an autobiography and political writing. On the AP Language and Composition Exam, try to distinguish the unique features of a writer's work from those dictated by convention.

genre   The major category into which a literary work fits. The basic divisions of literature are prose, poetry, and drama. However, "genre" is a flexible term; within these broad boundaries exist many subdivisions that are often called genres themselves. For example, prose can be divided into fiction (novels and short stories) or nonfiction (essays, biographies, autobiographies, and so on). Poetry can be divided into such subcategories as lyric, dramatic, narrative, epic, and so on.

Drama can be divided into tragedy, comedy, melodrama, farce, and so on. On the AP Language and Composition Exam, expect the majority of the passages to be from the following genres: autobiography, biography, diaries, criticism, and essays, as well as journalistic, political, scientific, and nature writing.

homily   This term literally means "sermon," but more informally, it can include any serious talk, speech, or lecture involving moral or spiritual advice.

hyperbole   A figure of speech using deliberate exaggeration or overstatement. Hyperboles often have a comic effect; however, a serious effect is also possible. Often, hyperbole produces irony at the same time.

imagery   The sensory details or figurative language used to describe, arouse emotion, or represent abstractions. On a physical level, imagery uses terms related to the five senses; we refer to visual, auditory, tactile, gustatory, or olfactory imagery. On a broader and deeper level, however, one image can represent more than one thing. For example, a rose may present visual imagery while also representing the color in a woman's cheeks. An author, therefore, may use complex imagery while simultaneously employing other figures of speech, especially metaphor and simile. In addition, this term can apply to the total of all the images in a work. On the AP Language and Composition Exam, pay attention to *how* an author creates imagery and the effect of that imagery.

inference/infer   To draw a reasonable conclusion from the information presented. When a multiple-choice question asks for an inference to be drawn from the passage, the most direct, most reasonable inference is the safest answer choice. If an inference is implausible, it's unlikely to be the correct answer. Note that if the answer choice is directly stated, it is *not* inferred and is wrong.

invective   An emotionally violent, verbal denunciation or attack using strong, abusive language.

irony/ironic   The contrast between what is stated explicitly and what is really meant; the difference between what appears to be and what actually is true. Irony is used for many reasons, but frequently, it's used to create poignancy or humor. In general, three major types of irony are used in language:

1. In *verbal* irony, the words literally state the opposite of the writer's (or speaker's) true meaning.
2. In *situational* irony, events turn out the opposite of what was expected. What the characters and readers think ought to happen does not actually happen.
3. In *dramatic* irony, facts or events are unknown to a character in a play or piece of fiction but known to the reader, audience, or other characters in the work.

juxtaposition   Placing dissimilar items, descriptions, or ideas close together or side by side, especially for comparison or contrast.

loose sentence   A type of sentence in which the main idea (independent clause) comes first, followed by dependent grammatical units such as phrases and clauses. If a period were placed at the end of the independent clause, the clause would be a complete sentence. A work containing many loose sentences often seems informal, relaxed, and conversational. See **periodic sentence.**

metaphor   A figure of speech using implied comparison of seemingly unlike things or the substitution of one for the other, suggesting some similarity. Metaphorical language makes writing more vivid, imaginative, thought provoking, and meaningful. See **simile.**

metonymy   A term from the Greek meaning "changed label" or "substitute name," metonymy is a figure of speech in which the name of one object is substituted for that of another closely associated with it. A news release that claims "the White House declared" rather than "the President declared" is using metonymy. This term is unlikely to be used in the multiple-choice section, but you might see examples of metonymy in an essay passage.

mood   This term has two distinct technical meanings in English writing. The first meaning is grammatical and deals with verbal units and a speaker's attitude. The *indicative* mood is used only for factual sentences. For example, "Joe eats too quickly." The *subjunctive* mood is used for a doubtful or conditional attitude. For example, "If I were you, I'd get another job." The *imperative* mood is used for commands. For example, "Shut the door!" The second meaning of mood is literary, meaning the prevailing atmosphere or emotional aura of a work. Setting, tone, and events can affect the mood. In this usage, mood is similar to tone and atmosphere.

narrative   The telling of a story or an account of an event or series of events.

onomatopoeia   A figure of speech in which natural sounds are imitated in the sounds of words. Simple examples include such words as buzz, hiss, hum, crack, whinny, and murmur. This term is not used in the multiple-choice section. If you identify examples of onomatopoeia in an essay passage, note the effect.

oxymoron   From the Greek for "pointedly foolish," an oxymoron is a figure of speech wherein the author groups apparently contradictory terms to suggest a paradox. Simple examples include "jumbo shrimp" and "cruel kindness." This term does not appear in the multiple-choice questions, but there is a slight chance you will see it used by an author in an essay passage or find it useful in your own essay writing.

paradox   A statement that appears to be self-contradictory or opposed to common sense, but upon closer inspection contains some degree of truth or validity. The first scene of *Macbeth,* for example, closes with the witches' cryptic remark "Fair is foul, and foul is fair. . . ."

parallelism   Also referred to as parallel construction or parallel structure, this term comes from Greek roots meaning "beside one another." It refers to the grammatical or rhetorical framing of words, phrases, sentences, or paragraphs to give structural similarity. This can involve, but is not limited to, repetition of a grammatical element such as a preposition or verbal phrase. A famous example of parallelism begins Charles Dickens's novel *A Tale of Two Cities:* "It was the best of times, it was the worst of times, it was the age of wisdom, it was the age of foolishness, it was the epoch of belief, it was the epoch of incredulity. . . ." The effects of parallelism are numerous, but, frequently, they act as an organizing force to attract the reader's attention, add emphasis and organization, or simply provide a pleasing, musical rhythm. Other famous examples include *Julius Caesar*'s "I came, I saw, I conquered," or, as Tennyson's poem "Ulysses" claims, "To strive, to seek, to find, and not to yield."

parody   A work that closely imitates the style or content of another with the specific aim of comic effect and/or ridicule. As comedy, parody distorts or exaggerates distinctive features of the original. As ridicule, it mimics the work by repeating and borrowing words, phrases, or characteristics in order to illuminate weaknesses in the original. Well-written parody offers insight into the original, but poorly written parody offers only ineffectual imitation. Usually an audience must grasp literary allusion and understand the work being parodied in order to fully appreciate the nuances of the newer work. Occasionally, however, parodies take on a life of their own and don't require knowledge of the original.

pedantic   An adjective that describes words, phrases, or general tone that is overly scholarly, academic, or bookish.

periodic sentence   A sentence that presents its central meaning in a main clause at the end. This independent clause is preceded by a phrase or clause that cannot stand alone. For example, "Ecstatic with my AP scores, I let out a loud shout of joy!" The effect of a periodic sentence is to add emphasis and structural variety. See **loose sentence.**

personification   A figure of speech in which the author presents or describes concepts, animals, or inanimate objects by endowing them with human attributes or emotions. Personification is used to make these abstractions, animals, or objects appear more vivid to the reader.

point of view   In literature, the perspective from which a story is told. There are two general divisions of point of view and many subdivisions within those.

1. The *first-person narrator* tells the story with the first-person pronoun, "I," and is a character in the story. This narrator can be the protagonist (the hero or heroine), a participant (a character in a secondary role), or an observer (a character who merely watches the action).

2. The *third-person narrator* relates the events with the third-person pronouns, "he," "she," and "it." Be aware of two main subdivisions: *omniscient* and *limited omniscient.* In the third-person omniscient point of view, the narrator, with godlike knowledge, presents the thoughts and actions of any or all characters. This all-knowing narrator can reveal what each character feels and thinks at any given moment. The third-person limited-omniscient point of view, as its name implies, presents the feelings and thoughts of only one character, and only the actions of all remaining characters. This definition applies in questions in the multiple-choice section. However, on the essay portion of the exam, the term "point of view" carries a different meaning. When you're asked to analyze an author's point of view, address the author's *attitude.*

predicate adjectives   One type of subject complement—an adjective, group of adjectives, or adjective clause that follows a linking verb. It is in the predicate of the sentence, and modifies or describes the subject. For example, in the sentence "My boyfriend is tall, dark, and handsome," the group of predicate adjectives ("tall, dark, and handsome") describes "boyfriend."

predicate nominative   A second type of subject complement—a noun, group of nouns, or noun clause that renames the subject. It, like the predicate adjective, follows a linking verb and is located in the predicate of the sentence. For example, in the sentence "Abe Lincoln was a man of integrity," the predicate nominative is "man of integrity," as it renames Abe Lincoln. Occasionally, this term or the term "predicate adjective" appears in a multiple-choice question.

prose   One of the major divisions of genre, "prose" refers to fiction and nonfiction, including all its forms, because they are written in ordinary language and most closely resemble everyday speech. Technically, anything that isn't poetry or drama is prose. Therefore, all passages in the AP Language and Composition Exam are prose. Of course, prose writers often borrow poetic and dramatic elements.

repetition   The duplication, either exact or approximate, of any element of language, such as a sound, word, phrase, clause, sentence, or grammatical pattern. When repetition is poorly done, it bores, but when it's well done, it links and emphasizes ideas while allowing the reader the comfort of recognizing something familiar. See **parallelism.**

rhetoric   From the Greek for "orator," this term describes the principles governing the art of writing effectively, eloquently, and persuasively.

rhetorical appeal   The persuasive device by which a writer tries to sway the audience's attention and response to any given work. Three rhetorical appeals were defined by Aristotle:

1. *Logos* employs logical reasoning, combining a clear idea (or multiple ideas) with well-thought-out and appropriate examples and details. These supports are logically presented and rationally reach the writer's conclusion.

2. *Ethos* establishes credibility in the speaker. Since by definition "ethos" means the common attitudes, beliefs, and characteristics of a group or time period, this appeal sets up believability in the writer. He or she is perceived as someone who can be trusted and is concerned with the reader's best interests.

3. *Pathos* plays on the reader's emotions and interests. A sympathetic audience is more likely to accept a writer's assertions, so this appeal draws upon that understanding and uses it to the writer's advantage.

rhetorical modes   This flexible term describes the variety, the conventions, and the purposes of the major kinds of writing. Sometimes referred to as modes of discourse, the four most common rhetorical modes and their purposes are as follows:

1. The purpose of *exposition* (or expository writing) is to explain and analyze information by presenting an idea, relevant evidence, and appropriate discussion. The AP Language and Composition Exam essay questions are frequently set up as expository topics.

2. The purpose of *argumentation* is to prove the validity of an idea, or point of view, by presenting sound reasoning, thoughtful discussion, and insightful argument that thoroughly convince the reader. Persuasive writing is a type of argumentation having the additional aim of urging some form of action. Many AP Language and Composition Exam essay questions ask you to form an argument.

3. The purpose of *description* is to re-create, invent, or visually present a person, place, event, or action so that the reader can picture that being described. Sometimes an author engages all five senses in description; good descriptive writing can be sensuous and picturesque. Descriptive writing may be straightforward and objective or highly emotional and subjective.

4. The purpose of *narration* is to tell a story or narrate an event or series of events. This writing mode frequently uses the tools of descriptive writing.

rhetorical question   A question that is asked merely for effect and does not expect a reply. The answer is assumed.

sarcasm   From the Greek meaning "to tear flesh," sarcasm involves bitter, caustic language that is meant to hurt or ridicule someone or something. It may use irony as a device, but not all ironic statements are sarcastic (that is, intending to ridicule). When well done, sarcasm can be witty and insightful; when poorly done, it's simply cruel.

satire   A work that targets human vices and follies, or social institutions and conventions, for reform or ridicule. Regardless of whether or not the work aims to reform humans or their society, satire is best seen as a style of writing rather than a purpose for writing. It can be recognized by the many devices used effectively by the satirist, such as irony, wit, parody, caricature, hyperbole, understatement, and sarcasm. The effects of satire are varied, depending on the writer's goal, but good satire—often humorous—is thought provoking and insightful about the human condition.

simile   An explicit comparison, normally using *"like," "as,"* or *"if."* For example, remember Robbie Burns's famous lines, "O, my love is like a red, red rose / That's newly sprung in June. / O, my love is like a melody, / That's sweetly played in tune." See **metaphor.**

style   The consideration of style has two purposes:

1. An evaluation of the sum of the choices an author makes in blending diction, syntax, figurative language, and other literary devices. Some authors' styles are so idiosyncratic that we can quickly recognize works by the same author (or writer emulating that author's style). Compare, for example, Jonathan Swift to George Orwell, or William Faulkner to Ernest Hemingway. We can analyze and describe an author's personal style and make judgments on how appropriate it is to the author's purpose. Styles can be called flowery, explicit, succinct, rambling, bombastic, commonplace, incisive, or laconic, to name only a few examples.

2. Classification of authors to a group and comparison of an author to similar authors.

By means of such classification and comparison, one can see how an author's style reflects and helps to define a historical period, such as the Renaissance or the Victorian period, or a literary movement, such as the Romantic, Transcendental, or Realist movement.

subject complement   The word (with any accompanying phrases) or clause that follows a linking verb and complements, or completes, the subject of the sentence by either (1) renaming it or (2) describing it. The former is technically called a predicate nominative, the latter a predicate adjective. See **predicate nominative** and **predicate adjective** for examples of sentences. This term is occasionally used in a multiple-choice question.

subordinate clause   Like all clauses, this word group contains both a subject and a verb (plus any accompanying phrases or modifiers), but unlike the independent clause, the subordinate clause cannot stand alone; it does not express a complete thought. Also called a dependent clause, the subordinate clause depends on a main clause, sometimes called an independent clause, to complete its meaning. Easily recognized key words and phrases usually begin these clauses— for example: "although," "because," "unless," "if," "even though," "since," "as soon as," "while," "who," "when," "where," "how," and "that."

syllogism   From the Greek for "reckoning together," a syllogism (or syllogistic reasoning) is a deductive system of formal logic that presents two premises—the first one called "major" and the second "minor"—that inevitably lead to a sound conclusion. A frequently cited example proceeds as follows:

- Major premise: All men are mortal.
- Minor premise: Socrates is a man.
- Conclusion: Therefore, Socrates is mortal.

A syllogism's conclusion is valid only if each of the two premises are valid. Syllogisms may also present the specific idea first ("Socrates") and the general idea second ("All men").

symbol/symbolism   Generally, anything that represents or stands for something else. Usually, a symbol is something concrete—such as an object, action, character, or scene—that represents something more abstract. However, symbols and symbolism can be much more complex. One system classifies symbols in three categories:

1. *Natural* symbols use objects and occurrences from nature to represent ideas commonly associated with them (dawn symbolizing hope or a new beginning, a rose symbolizing love, a tree symbolizing knowledge).

2. *Conventional* symbols are those that have been invested with meaning by a group (religious symbols, such as a cross or Star of David; national symbols, such as a flag or an eagle; or group symbols, such as skull and cross-bones for pirates or the scales of justice for lawyers).

3. *Literary* symbols are sometimes also conventional in the sense that they are found in a variety of works and are generally recognized. However, a work's symbols may be more complicated, such as the whale in *Moby Dick* and the jungle in *Heart of Darkness*. On the AP Language and Composition Exam, try to determine what abstraction an object is a symbol for and to what extent it is successful in representing that abstraction.

syntax   The way an author chooses to join words into phrases, clauses, and sentences. Syntax is similar to diction, but you can differentiate the two by thinking of syntax as referring to *groups* of words, while diction refers to individual words. In the multiple-choice section of the AP Language and Composition Exam, expect to be asked some questions about how an author manipulates syntax. In the essay section, you will need to analyze how syntax produces effects. When you are analyzing syntax, consider such elements as the length or brevity of sentences, unusual sentence constructions, the sentence patterns used, and the kinds of sentences the author uses. The writer may use questions, declarations, exclamations, or rhetorical questions; sentences are also classified as periodic or loose, simple, compound, or complex sentences. Syntax can be tricky for students to analyze. First try to classify *what kind* of sentences the author uses, and then try to determine *how* the author's choices amplify meaning, in other words *why they work* well for the author's purpose.

theme   The central idea or message of a work, the insight it offers into life. Usually, theme is unstated in fictional works, but in nonfiction, the theme may be directly stated, especially in expository or argumentative writing. Frequently a theme can be stated as a "universal truth," that is, a general statement about the human condition, about society, or about man's relation to the natural world.

thesis   In expository writing, the thesis statement is the sentence or group of sentences that directly expresses the author's opinion, purpose, meaning, or proposition. Expository writing is usually judged by analyzing how accurately, effectively, and thoroughly a writer has proven the thesis.

tone   Similar to mood, tone describes the author's attitude toward his or her material, the audience, or both. Tone is easier to determine in spoken language than in written language. Considering how a work would sound if it were read aloud can help in identifying an author's tone. Some words describing tone are "playful," "serious," "businesslike," "sarcastic," "humorous," "formal," "ornate," and "somber." As with attitude, an author's tone in the exam's passages can rarely be described by one word. Expect that it will be more complex. See **attitude** in "Terms for the Essay Section," later in this chapter.

transition   A word or phrase that links different ideas. Used especially, although not exclusively, in expository and argumentative writing, transitions effectively signal a shift from one idea to another. A few commonly used transitional words or phrases are "furthermore," "consequently," "nevertheless," "for example," "in addition," "likewise," "similarly," and "on the contrary."

understatement   The ironic minimizing of fact, understatement presents something as less significant than it is. The effect can frequently be humorous and emphatic. Understatement is the opposite of *hyperbole*. Two specific types of understatement exist:

1. **litotes:** A figure of speech by which an affirmation is made indirectly by denying its opposite. It uses understatement for emphasis, frequently with a negative assertion. Example: "It was no mean feat" means it was quite hard. "He was not averse to a drink" means he drank a lot.

2. **meiosis:** The Greek term for understatement or belittling; a rhetorical figure by which something is referred to in terms less important than it really deserves. It describes something that is very impressive with simplicity. Example: When Mercutio calls his mortal wound a "scratch" in *Romeo and Juliet*.

wit   In modern usage, wit is intellectually amusing language that surprises and delights. A witty statement is humorous, while suggesting the speaker's verbal power in creating ingenious and perceptive remarks. Wit usually uses terse language that makes a pointed statement. Historically, wit originally meant basic understanding. Its meaning evolved to include speed of understanding, and finally (in the early 17th century), it grew to mean quick perception including creative fancy.

Terms for the Essay Section

The following words and phrases have appeared in recent AP Language and Composition Exam essay topics. Although what follows is not a comprehensive list of every word or phrase you might encounter, it will help you understand what you're being asked to do for a topic.

attitude   A writer's intellectual position or emotion regarding the subject of the writing. In the essay section, expect to be asked what the writer's attitude is and how his or her language conveys that attitude. Also be aware that, although the singular term "attitude" is used in this definition and on the exam, the passage will rarely have only one attitude. More often than not, the author's attitude will be more complex, and the student who presents this complexity—no matter how subtle the differences—will appear to be more astute than the student who only uses one adjective to describe attitude. Of course, don't force an attitude that has no evidence in the passage; instead, understand that an accurate statement of an author's attitude is not likely to be a blatantly obvious idea. If it were that simple, the test committee wouldn't ask you to discuss it.

concrete detail   Strictly defined, "concrete" refers to nouns that name physical objects—a bridge, a book, or a coat. Concrete nouns are the opposite of abstract nouns (which refer to concepts like freedom and love). However, as used in the essay portion of the AP Language and Composition Exam, this term has a slightly different connotation. The directions may read something like this: "Provide concrete details that will convince the reader." This means that your essay should include details in the passage; at times, you'll be allowed to provide details from your own life (readings, observations, experiences, and so forth).

descriptive details   When an essay uses this phrase, look for the writer's sensory description. Descriptive detail appealing to the visual sense is usually the most predominant, but don't overlook other sensory details. As usual, after you identify a passage's descriptive details, analyze their effect.

devices   The figures of speech, syntax, diction, and other stylistic elements that collectively produce a particular artistic effect.

language   When you're asked to "analyze the language," concentrate on how the elements of language combine to form a whole—how diction, syntax, figurative language, and sentence structure create a cumulative effect.

narrative devices   This term describes the tools of the storyteller (also used in nonfiction), such as ordering events so that they build to a climactic moment or withholding information until a crucial or appropriate moment when revealing it creates a desired effect. On the essay portion of the exam, this term may also apply to biographical and autobiographical writing.

narrative technique   The style of telling the "story," even if the passage is nonfiction. Concentrate on the order of events and on their detail in evaluating a writer's technique.

persuasive devices   When asked to analyze an author's persuasive devices, look for the words in the passage that have strong connotations—words that intensify the emotional effect. In addition, analyze *how* these words complement the writer's argument as it builds logically. Speeches are often used in this context, because they are generally designed to persuade.

persuasive essay   When asked to write a persuasive essay, you should present a coherent argument in which the evidence builds to a logical and relevant conclusion. Strong persuasive essays often appeal to the audience's emotions or ethical standards.

resources of language   This phrase refers to all the devices of composition available to a writer, such as diction, syntax, sentence structure, and figures of speech. The cumulative effect of a work is produced by the resources of language a writer chooses.

rhetorical features   This phrase refers to how a passage is constructed. If asked to consider rhetorical structure, look at the passage's organization and how the writer combines images, details, or arguments to serve his or her purpose.

sentence structure   When an essay question asks you to analyze sentence structure, look at the type of sentences the author uses. Remember that the basic sentence structures are simple, compound, and complex, and variations created with sentence combining. Also consider variation or lack of it in sentence length, any unusual devices in sentence construction, such as repetition or inverted word order, and any unusual word or phrase placement. As with all devices, be prepared to discuss the effect of the sentence structure. For example, a series of short, simple sentences or phrases can produce a feeling of speed and choppiness, which may suit the author's purpose.

stylistic devices   An essay prompt that mentions stylistic devices is asking you to note and analyze all of the elements in language that contribute to style—such as diction, syntax, tone, attitude, figures of speech, connotations, and repetition.

PART VI

SIX FULL-LENGTH PRACTICE TESTS

This section contains six full-length simulated AP English Language and Composition Exams. The practice tests are followed by complete answers, explanations, and analysis of techniques. In addition, two sample essays written by AP students and analyses of the essays are included for each essay topic.

The format, levels of difficulty, question structures, and number of questions are similar to those found on actual AP English Language and Composition Exams. The actual AP Exam is copyrighted and may not be duplicated; therefore, these questions are not taken from the actual tests.

When taking these exams, try to simulate test conditions by following the time allotments carefully. Remember, the total testing time for each practice test is 3 hours and 15 minutes. Be aware of the time allotted for each section.

Answer Sheet for Practice Test 1

Remove this sheet and use it to mark your answers.
Answer sheets for "Section II: Essays" can be found at the end of the book.

Section I
Multiple-Choice Questions

First Passage

1 Ⓐ Ⓑ Ⓒ Ⓓ Ⓔ
2 Ⓐ Ⓑ Ⓒ Ⓓ Ⓔ
3 Ⓐ Ⓑ Ⓒ Ⓓ Ⓔ
4 Ⓐ Ⓑ Ⓒ Ⓓ Ⓔ
5 Ⓐ Ⓑ Ⓒ Ⓓ Ⓔ
6 Ⓐ Ⓑ Ⓒ Ⓓ Ⓔ
7 Ⓐ Ⓑ Ⓒ Ⓓ Ⓔ
8 Ⓐ Ⓑ Ⓒ Ⓓ Ⓔ
9 Ⓐ Ⓑ Ⓒ Ⓓ Ⓔ
10 Ⓐ Ⓑ Ⓒ Ⓓ Ⓔ
11 Ⓐ Ⓑ Ⓒ Ⓓ Ⓔ
12 Ⓐ Ⓑ Ⓒ Ⓓ Ⓔ
13 Ⓐ Ⓑ Ⓒ Ⓓ Ⓔ
14 Ⓐ Ⓑ Ⓒ Ⓓ Ⓔ

Second Passage

15 Ⓐ Ⓑ Ⓒ Ⓓ Ⓔ
16 Ⓐ Ⓑ Ⓒ Ⓓ Ⓔ
17 Ⓐ Ⓑ Ⓒ Ⓓ Ⓔ
18 Ⓐ Ⓑ Ⓒ Ⓓ Ⓔ
19 Ⓐ Ⓑ Ⓒ Ⓓ Ⓔ
20 Ⓐ Ⓑ Ⓒ Ⓓ Ⓔ
21 Ⓐ Ⓑ Ⓒ Ⓓ Ⓔ
22 Ⓐ Ⓑ Ⓒ Ⓓ Ⓔ
23 Ⓐ Ⓑ Ⓒ Ⓓ Ⓔ
24 Ⓐ Ⓑ Ⓒ Ⓓ Ⓔ
25 Ⓐ Ⓑ Ⓒ Ⓓ Ⓔ
26 Ⓐ Ⓑ Ⓒ Ⓓ Ⓔ
27 Ⓐ Ⓑ Ⓒ Ⓓ Ⓔ
28 Ⓐ Ⓑ Ⓒ Ⓓ Ⓔ

Third Passage

29 Ⓐ Ⓑ Ⓒ Ⓓ Ⓔ
30 Ⓐ Ⓑ Ⓒ Ⓓ Ⓔ
31 Ⓐ Ⓑ Ⓒ Ⓓ Ⓔ
32 Ⓐ Ⓑ Ⓒ Ⓓ Ⓔ
33 Ⓐ Ⓑ Ⓒ Ⓓ Ⓔ
34 Ⓐ Ⓑ Ⓒ Ⓓ Ⓔ
35 Ⓐ Ⓑ Ⓒ Ⓓ Ⓔ
36 Ⓐ Ⓑ Ⓒ Ⓓ Ⓔ
37 Ⓐ Ⓑ Ⓒ Ⓓ Ⓔ
38 Ⓐ Ⓑ Ⓒ Ⓓ Ⓔ
39 Ⓐ Ⓑ Ⓒ Ⓓ Ⓔ
40 Ⓐ Ⓑ Ⓒ Ⓓ Ⓔ
41 Ⓐ Ⓑ Ⓒ Ⓓ Ⓔ
42 Ⓐ Ⓑ Ⓒ Ⓓ Ⓔ
43 Ⓐ Ⓑ Ⓒ Ⓓ Ⓔ

Fourth Passage

44 Ⓐ Ⓑ Ⓒ Ⓓ Ⓔ
45 Ⓐ Ⓑ Ⓒ Ⓓ Ⓔ
46 Ⓐ Ⓑ Ⓒ Ⓓ Ⓔ
47 Ⓐ Ⓑ Ⓒ Ⓓ Ⓔ
48 Ⓐ Ⓑ Ⓒ Ⓓ Ⓔ
49 Ⓐ Ⓑ Ⓒ Ⓓ Ⓔ
50 Ⓐ Ⓑ Ⓒ Ⓓ Ⓔ
51 Ⓐ Ⓑ Ⓒ Ⓓ Ⓔ
52 Ⓐ Ⓑ Ⓒ Ⓓ Ⓔ
53 Ⓐ Ⓑ Ⓒ Ⓓ Ⓔ
54 Ⓐ Ⓑ Ⓒ Ⓓ Ⓔ
55 Ⓐ Ⓑ Ⓒ Ⓓ Ⓔ

CUT HERE

CUT HERE

Practice Test 1

Section I: Multiple-Choice Questions

Time: 60 minutes

55 questions

Directions: This section consists of selections from prose works and questions on their content, style, and form. Read each selection carefully. Choose the best answer of the five choices.

Questions 1–14. Read the following passage carefully before you begin to answer the questions.

First Passage

The written word is weak. Many people prefer life to it. Life gets your blood going, and it smells good. Writing is mere writing, literature is mere. It appeals only to the subtlest senses—the imagina-
(5) tion's vision, and the imagination's hearing and the moral sense, and the intellect. This writing that you do, that so thrills you, that so racks and exhilarates you, as if you were dancing next to the band, is barely audible to anyone else. The reader's ear
(10) must adjust down from loud life to the subtle, imaginary sounds of the written word. An ordinary reader picking up a book can't yet hear a thing; it will take half an hour to pick up the writing's modulations, its ups and downs and louds and softs.
(15) An intriguing entomological experiment shows that a male butterfly will ignore a living female butterfly of his own species in favor of a painted cardboard one, if the cardboard one is big. If the cardboard one is bigger than he is, bigger than any
(20) female butterfly ever could be. He jumps the piece of cardboard. Over and over again, he jumps the piece of cardboard. Nearby, the real, living butterfly opens and closes her wings in vain.
Films and television stimulate the body's senses
(25) too, in big ways. A nine-foot handsome face, and its three-foot-wide smile, are irresistible. Look at the long legs on that man, as high as a wall, and coming straight toward you. The music builds. The moving, lighted screen fills your brain. You do not
(30) like filmed car chases? See if you can turn away. Try not to watch. Even knowing you are manipulated, you are still as helpless as the male butterfly drawn to painted cardboard.

That is the movies. That is their ground. The
(35) printed word cannot compete with the movies on their ground, and should not. You can describe beautiful faces, car chases, or valleys full of Indians on horseback until you run out of words, and you will not approach the movies' spectacle. Novels
(40) written with film contracts in mind have a faint but unmistakable, and ruinous, odor. I cannot name what, in the text, alerts the reader to suspect the writer of mixed motives; I cannot specify which sentences, in several books, have caused me to read
(45) on with increasing dismay, and finally close the books because I smelled a rat. Such books seem uneasy being books; they seem eager to fling off their disguises and jump onto screens.
Why would anyone read a book instead of
(50) watching big people move on a screen? Because a book can be literature. It is a subtle thing—poor thing, but our own. In my view, the more literary the book—the more purely verbal, crafted sentence by sentence, the more imaginative, reasoned, and
(55) deep—the more likely people are to read it. The people who read are the people who like literature, after all, whatever that might be. They like, or require what books alone have. If they want to see films that evening, they will find films. If they do
(60) not like to read, they will not. People who read are not too lazy to flip on the television; they prefer books. I cannot imagine a sorrier pursuit than struggling for years to write a book that attempts to appeal to people who do not read in the first place.

GO ON TO THE NEXT PAGE

1. Which of the following terms can be used to describe the imagery of the last sentence in the first paragraph ("An ordinary . . . and softs")?

   I. Simile
   II. Metaphor
   III. Synthesthetic

   A. I only
   B. II only
   C. I and III only
   D. II and III only
   E. I, II, and III

2. In the second paragraph of the passage, the speaker employs a(n)

   A. concession to an opposing point of view
   B. cause and effect relationship
   C. simile
   D. metaphor
   E. extended definition

3. Which of the following best describes how the second and third paragraphs are related?

   A. The second paragraph makes an assertion that is qualified by the third paragraph.
   B. The second paragraph asks a question that is answered by the third paragraph.
   C. The second paragraph describes a situation that is paralleled in the third paragraph.
   D. The second paragraph presents as factual what the third paragraph presents as only a possibility.
   E. There is no clear relationship between the two paragraphs.

4. The "nine-foot handsome face" (line 25) refers to

   A. the female butterfly
   B. literary creativity
   C. a television image
   D. an image in the movies
   E. how the imagination of a reader may see a face

5. In the fourth paragraph, the speaker argues that

   I. action scenes are better in films than in books
   II. novels written with an eye on future film adaptation stink
   III. novels specifically written to be adapted into films do not make superior films

   A. II only
   B. I and II only
   C. I and III only
   D. II and III only
   E. I, II, and III

6. The last sentence of the fourth paragraph ("Such books . . . onto screens") contains an example of

   A. personification
   B. understatement
   C. irony
   D. simile
   E. syllogism

7. According to the passage, literature is likely to be characterized by all of the following EXCEPT

   A. colloquial language
   B. imagination
   C. verbal skill
   D. moral sense
   E. intelligence

8. In the last sentence of the last paragraph, the phrase "sorrier pursuit" can be best understood to mean

   A. more regretful chase
   B. poorer occupation
   C. more sympathetic profession
   D. sadder expectation
   E. more pitiful striving

9. In the last paragraph, the phrase "a poor thing, but our own" is adapted from Shakespeare's "a poor . . . thing, sir, but mine own." The change from the singular to the plural pronoun is made in order to

   A. avoid the use of the first person
   B. include all readers of this passage who prefer literature
   C. avoid direct quotation of Shakespeare and the appearance of comparing this work to his
   D. suggest that the number of readers is as great as the number of moviegoers
   E. avoid overpraising literature compared to films, which are more popular

10. The sentences "The written word is weak" (line 1), "An ordinary reader . . . a thing" (lines 11–12), and "The printed word . . . should not" (lines 34–36) have in common that they

A. concede a limitation of the written word
B. assert the superiority of film to writing
C. do not represent the genuine feelings of the author
D. deliberately overstate the author's ideas
E. are all ironic

11. With which of the following statements would the speaker of this passage be most likely to disagree?

A. Life is more exciting than writing.
B. People who dislike reading should not be forced to read.
C. Good books will appeal to those who do not like to read as well as to those who do.
D. The power of film is irresistible.
E. Novels written for people who hate reading are folly.

12. The passage in its entirety is best described as about the

A. superiority of the art of writing to the art of film
B. difficulties of being a writer
C. differences between writing and film
D. public's preference of film to literature
E. similarities and differences of the novel and the film

13. Which of the following best describes the organization of the passage?

A. A five-paragraph essay in which the first and last paragraphs are general and the second, third, and fourth paragraphs are specific.
B. A five-paragraph essay in which the first two paragraphs describe writing, the third and fourth paragraphs describe film, and the last paragraph describes both writing and film.
C. Five paragraphs with the first about literature; the second about butterflies; and the third, fourth, and fifth about the superiority of film.
D. Five paragraphs with the first and last about writing, the third about film, and the fourth about both film and writing.
E. Five paragraphs of comparison and contrast, with the comparison in the first and last paragraphs and the contrast in the second, third, and fourth.

14. All of the following rhetorical devices are featured in the passage EXCEPT

A. personal anecdote
B. extended analogy
C. short sentence
D. colloquialism
E. irony

GO ON TO THE NEXT PAGE

Question 15–28. Read the following passage carefully before you begin to answer the questions.

Second Passage

These are the times that try men's souls. The summer soldier and the sunshine patriot will, in this crisis, shrink from the service of their country; but he that stands it now deserves the love and (5) thanks of man and woman. Tyranny, like hell, is not easily conquered; yet we have this consolation with us, that the harder the conflict, the more glorious the triumph. What we obtain too cheap, we esteem too lightly: it is dearness only that gives everything (10) its value. Heaven knows how to put a proper price upon its goods; and it would be strange indeed if so celestial an article as freedom should not be highly rated. Britain, with an army to enforce her tyranny, has declared that she has a right not only to tax, but (15) "to bind us in all cases whatsoever," and if being bound in that manner is not slavery, then is there not such a thing as slavery upon earth. Even the expression is impious; for so unlimited a power can belong only to God. . . .

(20) I have as little superstition in me as any man living, but my secret opinion has ever been, and still is, that God Almighty will not give up a people to military destruction, or leave them unsupportedly to perish, who have so earnestly and so repeatedly (25) sought to avoid the calamities of war, by every decent method which wisdom could invent. Neither have I so much of the infidel in me as to suppose that He has relinquished the government of the world, and given us up to the care of devils; and as (30) I do not, I cannot see on what grounds the King of Britain can look up to heaven for help against us: a common murderer, a highwayman, or a housebreaker has as good a pretense as he. . . .

I once felt all that kind of anger, which a man (35) ought to feel, against the mean principles that are held by the Tories: a noted one, who kept a tavern at Amboy, was standing at his door, with as pretty a child in his hand, about eight or nine years old, as I ever saw, and after speaking his mind as freely as he (40) thought was prudent, finished with this unfatherly expression, "Well! Give me peace in my day." Not a man lives on the continent but fully believes that a separation must some time or other finally take place, and a generous parent should have said, "If (45) there must be trouble, let it be in my day, that my children may have peace"; and this single reflection, well applied, is sufficient to awaken every man to duty. Not a place upon earth might be so happy as America. Her situation is remote from all the wran- (50) gling world, and she has nothing to do but to trade with them. A man can distinguish himself between temper and principle, and I am as confident, as I am that God governs the world, that America will never be happy till she gets clear of foreign dominion. (55) Wars, without ceasing, will break out till that period arrives, and the continent must in the end be conqueror; for though the flame of liberty may sometimes cease to shine, the coal can never expire. . . .

The heart that feels not now is dead: the blood of (60) his children will curse his cowardice who shrinks back at a time when a little might have saved the whole, and made them happy. I love the man that can smile in trouble, that can gather strength from distress, and grow brave by reflection. 'Tis the (65) business of little minds to shrink; but he whose heart is firm, and whose conscience approves his conduct, will pursue his principles unto death. My own line of reasoning is to myself as straight and clear as a ray of light. Not all the treasures of the (70) world so far as I believe, could have induced me to support an offensive war, for I think it murder; but if a thief breaks into my house, burns and destroys my property, and kills or threatens to kill me, or those that are in it, and to "bind me in all cases (75) whatsoever" to his absolute will, am I to suffer it? What signifies it to me, whether he who does it is a king or a common man; my countryman or not my countryman; whether it be done by an individual villain, or an army of them? If we reason to the root (80) of things we shall find no difference; neither can any just cause be assigned why we should punish in the one case and pardon in the other.

15. The essay appears to be addressed to

A. the British government
B. British citizens
C. Americans
D. the American government
E. all oppressed people

16. When the speaker addresses the "summer soldier and the sunshine patriot," he is most likely referring to

A. the American army's reserve soldiers
B. those citizens who are infidels
C. the British soldiers stationed in America
D. those who support the revolution only when convenient
E. the government's specialized forces

17. The speaker's style relies on heavy use of

A. allegory and didactic rhetoric
B. aphorism and emotional appeal
C. symbolism and biblical allusion
D. paradox and invective
E. historical background and illustration

18. Which of the following does the speaker NOT group with the others?

A. common murderer
B. highwayman
C. housebreaker
D. king
E. coward

19. The "God" that the speaker refers to can be characterized as

A. principled
B. vexed
C. indifferent
D. contemplative
E. pernicious

20. Which of the following rhetorical devices is NOT one of the speaker's tools?

A. anecdote
B. simile
C. aphorism
D. understatement
E. symbolism

21. According to the speaker, freedom should be considered

A. that which will vanquish cowards
B. one of the most valuable commodities in heaven
C. that which can be achieved quickly
D. desirable but never attainable
E. an issue only governments should negotiate

22. The speaker's purpose in using the phrase "with as pretty a child . . . as I ever saw" (lines 37–39) is most likely to

A. prove that the tavern owner has a family
B. display his anger
C. add emotional appeal to his argument
D. symbolically increase the tavern owner's evil
E. dismiss traditional values

23. Which of the following would NOT be considered an aphorism?

A. "Tyranny, like hell, is not easily conquered. . . ." (lines 5–6)
B. ". . . the harder the conflict, the more glorious the triumph." (lines 7–8)
C. "What we obtain too cheap, we esteem too lightly. . . ." (lines 8–9)
D. "Not a place upon earth might be so happy as America." (lines 48–49)
E. ". . . though the flame of liberty may sometimes cease to shine, the coal can never expire. . . ." (lines 57–58)

24. As seen in lines 48–58, the speaker feels that, in an ideal world, America's role in relation to the rest of the world would be

A. only one of commerce
B. one of aggressive self-assertion
C. more exalted than Britain's
D. sanctified by God
E. one of complete isolationism

25. The rhetorical mode that the speaker uses can best be classified as

A. explanation
B. description
C. narration
D. illustration
E. persuasion

GO ON TO THE NEXT PAGE

26. Which of the following best describes the rhetorical purpose in the sentence "The heart that feels not now is dead . . ." (lines 59–62)?

    A. to suggest that children should also join the revolution

    B. to plant fear in people's hearts

    C. to plead to the king once again for liberty

    D. to encourage retreat in the face of superior force

    E. to encourage support by an emotional appeal to all American Patriots

27. All of the following rhetorical devices are particularly effective in the last paragraph of the essay EXCEPT

    A. aphorism

    B. simile

    C. deliberate ambivalence

    D. parallel construction

    E. analogy

28. The main rhetorical purpose in the essay can best be described as

    A. a summons for peace and rational thinking

    B. overemotional preaching for equality

    C. a series of unwarranted conclusions

    D. a patriotic call to duty and action

    E. a demand for immediate liberty

Questions 29–43. Read the following passage carefully before you begin to answer the questions.

Third Passage

When Charles Lamb was seven years old, his father's employer, Samuel Salt, obtained for him admission to the famous school in London for poor boys, called Christ's Hospital. In the same year, young Samuel Taylor Coleridge also came to the school, and between the future author of The Rime of the Ancient Mariner *and the gentle, nervous, stammering Charles Lamb there sprang up a friendship that lasted more than 50 years and was one of the happiest influences in their lives. Lamb wrote of the old schooldays in* Christ's Hospital Five-and-Thirty Years Ago[1]. *For the sake of innocent mystification, he chose to write as if he were Coleridge.*

In Mr. Lamb's "Works,"[2] published a year or two since, I find a magnificent eulogy on my old school, such as it was, or now appears to him to have been, between the year 1782 and 1789. It hap-
(5) pens, very oddly, that my own standing at Christ's was nearly corresponding with his; and, with all gratitude to him for his enthusiasm for the cloisters, I think he has contrived to bring together whatever can be said in praise of them, dropping all the other
(10) side of the argument most ingeniously.

I remember L. at school; and can well recollect that he had some particular advantages, which I and others of his schoolfellows had not. His friends lived in town, and were near at hand; and he had
(15) the privilege of going to see them, almost as often as he wished, through some invidious distinction, which was denied to us. The present worthy sub-treasurer to the Inner Temple[3] can explain how that happened. He had his tea and hot rolls in a morn-
(20) ing, while we were battening upon our quarter of a penny loaf—our *crug*—moistened with attenuated small beer, in wooden piggins, smacking of the pitched leathern jack it was poured from. Our Monday's milk porritch, blue and tasteless, and the
(25) pease soup of Saturday, coarse and choking, were enriched for him with a slice of "extraordinary bread and butter," from the hot-loaf of the Temple. The Wednesday's mess of millet, somewhat less than repugnant—(we had three banyan[4] to four
(30) meat days in the week)—was endeared to his palate with a lump of double-refined, and a smack of ginger (to make it go down the more glibly) or the fragrant cinnamon. In lieu of our *half-pickled* Sundays, or *quite fresh* boiled beef on Thursdays
(35) (strong as *caro equina*[5]), with detestable marigolds floating in the pail to poison the broth—our scanty

mutton scrags on Fridays—and rather more savoury, but grudging, portions of the same flesh, rotten-roasted or rare, on the Tuesdays (the only dish
(40) which excited our appetites, and disappointed our stomachs, in almost equal proportion)—he had his hot plate of roast veal, or the same tempting griskin (exotics unknown to our palates), cooked in the paternal kitchen (a great thing), and brought him
(45) daily by his maid or aunt! I remember the good old relative[6] (in whom love forbade pride) squatting down upon some odd stone in a by-nook of the cloisters, disclosing the viands (of higher regale[7] than those cates[8] which the ravens ministered to the
(50) Tishbite[9]); and the contending passion of L. at the unfolding. There was love for the bringer; shame for the thing brought, and the manner of its bringing; sympathy for those who were too many to share in it; and, at top of all, hunger (eldest,
(55) strongest of the passions!) predominant, breaking down the stony fences of shame, and awkwardness, and a troubling over-consciousness.

[1] London Magazine, *November 1820.*

[2] *The first collection of Lamb's writings representing this period of his literary work was published in 1818. Among this material was an essay entitled "Recollections of Christ's Hospital," in which Lamb paid a fine tribute of praise to this charitable institution for the education and support of the young. In the present essay, however, he presents another side of the picture, showing the grievances, real and imaginary, of the scholars, together with some of the humorous aspects of the regulations and traditions of the school. Coleridge in* Biographia Literaria *has drawn a companion picture of the better side of Christ's Hospital discipline, and Leigh Hunt, who was a scholar two or three years later than Lamb, has also described in his* Autobiography *the life and ideals of the famous school.*

[3] *Randall Norris, a family friend.*

[4] *Vegetable days.*

[5] *Horseflesh.*

[6] *In a letter to Coleridge, January 1797, Lamb writes: "My poor old aunt, whom you have seen, the kindest, goodest creature to me when I was at school; who used to toddle there to bring me good things, when I, school-boy like, only despised her for it, and used to be ashamed to see her come and sit herself down on the old coal-hole steps as you went into the grammar school, and open her apron, and bring out her bason, with some nice thing she had caused to be saved for me."*

[7] *Banquet.*

[8] *Dainties.*

[9] *The prophet Elijah; see I Kings xvii.*

GO ON TO THE NEXT PAGE

29. In paragraph one, the speaker suggests that

    A. Lamb's recollections are an accurate depiction of the school

    B. Lamb has chosen to ignore negative memories from his school years

    C. Coleridge remembers the school years exactly as Lamb did

    D. Coleridge would write a very different reminiscence of his school days

    E. Coleridge concurs with the accuracy of Lamb's account of the school

30. Within context, the speaker uses the word "invidious" (line 16) to mean

    A. gratuitous

    B. fortuitous

    C. undeniable

    D. justifiable

    E. discriminatory

31. The speaker implies that the specific reason Lamb enjoyed the privilege of visiting his friends in town was because

    A. his aunt secured him special favors

    B. he was a favorite of the schoolmaster

    C. someone was bribed at the Inner Temple

    D. he crept off the school grounds against rules

    E. they gave special treatment to the sub-treasurer

32. The speaker's description of Lamb's food serves to

    A. juxtapose Lamb's relative wealth with the other boys' poverty

    B. enhance fond memories in all of the boys

    C. explain why his aunt had to deliver extra victuals

    D. exemplify how superior he felt toward the other boys

    E. dispel common myths of British boarding schools

33. The passage contains all of the following EXCEPT

    A. alliteration

    B. complex sentences with clarifying clauses

    C. revolting gustatory imagery

    D. metaphor

    E. historical allusion

34. The italics in *"quite fresh"* (line 34) serve the rhetorical purpose of

    A. establishing how carefully the boys' meals were prepared

    B. reinforcing the speaker's genuine feelings

    C. carefully balancing the positive and negative aspects of their meals

    D. emphasizing how stale the beef was

    E. highlighting the need for Lamb's aunt to bring food

35. The image of the "marigolds floating" (lines 35–36) emphasizes

    A. the beauty and comfort that nature can offer in uncomfortable situations

    B. a feeble attempt to hide the horror of the meal

    C. a pleasant table complement to the meal

    D. the cook's creativity in presenting meals

    E. the need to cover ugliness in the world with natural images

36. The speaker's rhetorical purpose in describing the food of every day of the week is to

    A. emphasize the consistency of the inedible food

    B. ensure a thorough and complete picture of daily life

    C. contradict the idea that the boys were poorly fed

    D. establish how Lamb's food was far superior

    E. intimate the inequities of the school system

37. The underlying purpose of Lamb's pretending to be Coleridge can best be described as

    A. a desire to emulate Coleridge's artistic genius

    B. a yearning to hide his stammering

    C. an inoffensive attempt to hide his nervousness

    D. an effort to protect his family's identity

    E. an easy way to mask his true feelings

38. The "contending passion of L." (line 50) suggests that Lamb

  A. showed unbounded enthusiasm for his aunt's gifts

  B. willingly shared the food with those less fortunate

  C. demonstrated indisputable affection for his aunt

  D. suffered a conflict between embarrassment and affection that his aunt's actions caused

  E. knew all the students were aware of his conflicted feelings

39. The description of Lamb's aunt implies that

  A. her love for her nephew outweighed her embarrassment at crouching and waiting for him, with food in her apron

  B. she brought her nephew food solely because the school was too stingy to feed him well

  C. she provided him with the food his own family could not afford

  D. she wished she could have brought food for all the boys

  E. she had made previous arrangements with the school officials to deliver Lamb's food

40. Which of the following emotions does Lamb NOT experience when his aunt brings him gifts?

  A. ignominy

  B. affection

  C. compassion

  D. discomfiture

  E. antipathy

41. Lamb's letter to Coleridge (note #6) infers that

  A. he remains steadfast in his reaction to her deeds

  B. he and his aunt were only close while he was at school

  C. Lamb and Coleridge both enjoyed the victuals that his aunt delivered

  D. he now better understands his conflicted reactions to her kindness

  E. Coleridge had inquired about Lamb's behavior toward his aunt

42. Note #2 presents the perception that

  A. the three authors collaborated on their memoirs

  B. Leigh Hunt disagrees with Lamb's and Coleridge's recollections

  C. the three authors mainly recall the benefits of attending Christ's Hospital

  D. the three authors were equally mistreated while at school

  E. Coleridge and Hunt had more advantages while at school

43. Which of the following phrases most clearly contradicts the rhetorical purpose of the passage as a whole?

  A. ". . . my old school, such as it was, or now appears to him to have been . . ." (lines 2–4)

  B. ". . . he has contrived to bring together whatever can be said in praise of them . . ." (lines 8–9)

  C. ". . . can well recollect that he had some particular advantages . . ." (lines 11–12)

  D. ". . . the only dish which excited out appetites, and disappointed our stomachs, in almost equal proportion . . ." (lines 39–41)

  E. ". . . the good old relative (in whom love forbade pride) . . ." (lines 45–46)

GO ON TO THE NEXT PAGE

Questions 44–55. Read the following passage carefully before you begin to answer the questions.

Fourth Passage

Studies serve for delight, for ornament, and for ability. Their chief use for delight is in privateness and retiring; for ornament, is in discourse; and for ability, is in the judgment and disposition of busi-
(5) ness; for expert men can execute, and perhaps judge of particulars, one by one; but the general counsels, and the plots and marshaling of affairs come best from those that are learned. To spend too much time in studies is sloth; to use them too much
(10) for ornament is affectation; to make judgment wholly by their rules is the humor of a scholar. They perfect nature, and are perfected by experience; for natural abilities are like natural plants, that need pruning by study; and studies themselves do give
(15) forth directions too much at large, except they be bounded in by experience. Crafty men condemn studies, simple men admire them, and wise men use them; for they teach not their own use; but that is a wisdom without them and above them, won by
(20) observation. Read not to contradict and confute, nor to believe and take for granted, nor to find talk and discourse, but to weigh and consider. Some books are to be tasted, others to be swallowed, and some few to be chewed and digested; that is, some
(25) books are to be read only in parts; others to be read but not curiously; and some few to be read wholly, and with diligence and attention. Some books also may be read by deputy, and extracts made of them by others; but that would be only in the less

(30) important arguments and the meaner sort of books; else distilled books are, like common distilled water, flashy things. Reading maketh a full man; conference a ready man; and writing an exact man. And therefore, if a man write little, he had need
(35) have a great memory; if he confer little, he had need have a present wit; and if he read little, he had need have much cunning, to seem to know that he doth not. Histories make men wise; poets, witty; the mathematics, subtle; natural philosophy, deep;
(40) moral, grave; logic and rhetoric, able to contend: *Abeunt studia in mores*![1] Nay, there is no stand or impediment in the wit but may be wrought out by fit studies; like as diseases of the body may have appropriate exercises. Bowling is good for the stone
(45) and reins, shooting for the lungs and breast, gently walking for the stomach, riding for the head, and the like. So if a man's wit be wandering, let him study the mathematics; for in demonstrations, if his wit be called away never so little, he must begin
(50) again. If his wit be not apt to distinguish or find differences, let him study the schoolmen; for they are *cymini sectores*![2] If he be not apt to beat over matters, and to call up one thing to prove and illustrate another, let him study the lawyers' cases. So every
(55) aspect of the mind may have a special receipt.

[1] *"Studies from character," Ovid.*

[2] *Literally, "cutters of cumin seed," or hair splitters.*

44. The audience that might benefit the most from the speaker's ideas is likely to be those who

    A. have returned to university study
    B. think studies are unnecessary
    C. are poor readers
    D. already have university degrees
    E. are successful in business

45. The word "humor" (line 11) can be best defined as

    A. mirth
    B. benefit
    C. excuse
    D. aspiration
    E. temperament

46. According to the passage, reading is beneficial when supplemented by

    A. academic necessity
    B. literary criticism
    C. personal experience
    D. brief discussion
    E. historical background

47. A prominent stylistic characteristic of the sentence "Read not to . . . weigh and consider" (lines 20–22) is

    A. understatement
    B. metaphor
    C. hyperbole
    D. parallel construction
    E. analogy

48. The sentence "They perfect nature . . . by experience" (lines 11–16) most probably means that

    A. a professor should emphasize reading over personal experience

    B. the message in some books is too complex to be understood by the common person

    C. the ideas in books are readily accessible to one who reads widely

    D. people misspend valuable time in the pursuit of evasive knowledge

    E. everything one learns in books cannot necessarily be applied directly to real-life situations

49. In context, the word "observation" (line 20) is analogous to

    A. "experience" (line 12)

    B. "directions" (line 15)

    C. "studies" (line 17)

    D. "wisdom" (line 19)

    E. "believe" (line 21)

50. According to the passage, which of the following are reasonable uses for one's studies?

    I. private enjoyment

    II. intelligent conversation

    III. sound judgment

    A. I only

    B. II only

    C. III only

    D. II and III only

    E. I, II, and III

51. What paradox about studies does the speaker present?

    A. Crafty men may be tempted to ignore studies.

    B. Those who are too consumed by studies become indolent.

    C. Some books can never be completely understood.

    D. Not all books are approached the same way.

    E. Some "defects of the mind" can never be remedied.

52. Which of the following does the speaker imply is the greatest error a reader can commit?

    A. reading voluminously

    B. reading only excerpts

    C. reading only what professors recommend

    D. reading without thinking

    E. reading only for pleasure

53. Which of the following phrases may be seen as rhetorically similar to "Some books are to be tasted . . . chewed and digested" (lines 22–24)?

    I. "natural abilities . . . need pruning by study" (lines 13–14)

    II. "Some books also may be read . . . by others" (lines 27–29)

    III. "like as diseases . . . have appropriate exercises" (lines 43–44)

    A. I only

    B. II only

    C. II and III only

    D. I and III only

    E. I, II, and III

54. In context, the phrase "not curiously" (line 26) means

    A. with questions in mind

    B. with great interest

    C. without much scrutiny

    D. without strong background

    E. with personal interpretation

55. Stylistically, the sentence "Reading maketh a full man . . . writing an exact man" (lines 32–33) is closest in structure to

    A. "To spend too much time . . . the humor of a scholar." (lines 8–11)

    B. "They perfect nature, and are perfected by experience . . . bounded in by experience." (lines 11–16)

    C. "Some books also may be read by deputy . . . flashy things." (lines 27–32)

    D. "Nay, there is no stand or impediment . . . exercises." (lines 41–44)

    E. "So if a man's wit be wandering . . . begin again." (lines 47–50)

IF YOU FINISH BEFORE TIME IS CALLED, CHECK YOUR WORK ON THIS SECTION ONLY. DO NOT WORK ON ANY OTHER SECTION IN THE TEST.

Section II: Essay Questions

Time: 2 hours, 15 minutes

3 questions

Question 1

(Reading time—15 minutes. Suggested writing time—40 minutes. This question counts one-third of the total essay section score.)

Directions: The prompt that follows is based on six accompanying sources. This essay requires you to integrate a variety of sources into a coherent, well-written essay. Refer to the sources, both directly and indirectly, to support your position. Avoid mere paraphrasing or summarizing. Your argument should be the central focus; the use of the sources should support your argument.

Introduction

The media has been influential in the world's reaction to natural disasters, terrorist attacks, and school shootings since the advent of radio and television. What exactly has this influence been and how has it affected the amount of people who help or care for the victims of these disasters? Has it encouraged people to help or has it merely shown them that they are the lucky ones who were not involved in each particular disaster?

Assignment

Read the following sources carefully. **Then, in an essay that synthesizes at least three of the sources for support, take a position that defends, challenges, or qualifies the notion that the media has had a positive influence on the effects of disasters.**

Refer to the sources as Source A, Source B, and so on; authors' names and titles are included for your convenience.

Source A (ISDR)

Source B (Lisset)

Source C (Floroiu)

Source D (Bluestein)

Source E (political cartoon)

Source F (Global Issues)

Source A

"ISDR Joins Asia-Pacific Broadcasting Union to boost information, education on disasters." 10 June 2005. UNESCAP News Services. 25 Sept. 2005. N. page. Available at www.unescap.org/unis/press/2005/jun/n26.asp.

The following passage is an excerpted online article that tells us about new radio and television programs that will educate and prepare people for natural disasters in the Asia-Pacific countries.

ISDR (International Strategy for Disaster Reduction) considers media an essential partner to enhance public safety and adverse impacts of natural disasters. Media are not only part of the early warning chain; they are the best channel to prepare communities for disasters. They can help educate people on the need to reduce risk by regularly informing on the hazards and social vulnerabilities that may lead to disasters. Media also play an important role in convincing Governments and citizens to invest in disaster reduction", says Salvano Briceño, Director of the ISDR secretariat.

"It is just the beginning of a new collaboration. We are planning to promote educational programmes like the ones we are already developing in Africa, in Latin America and the Caribbean, and incite broadcasters to invest more in disaster reduction. Education and preparedness are the key to reduce the number of affected people by natural hazards every year. If people know what to do, they can save their own life. Education on disasters should be part of the school's curriculum like it is in Japan and Cuba, for instance. The more people are aware of the risks they face, the better chance they have to save their lives when hazards strikes," says Mr. Briceño.

"Broadcasters have a responsibility to educate people and raise their awareness of the dangers of natural disasters. They can do this by airing public service announcements, producing special programmes to mark the anniversaries of previous disasters and creating other content, says David Astley, Secretary-General of the ABU. The ABU is well positioned to both coordinate the improvement of emergency warning systems through television and radio among broadcasters across the Pacific region and to assist in the development of content designed to educate audiences in advance on how to respond in the event of emergencies and natural disasters."

GO ON TO THE NEXT PAGE

Source B

Lissit, Robert. "The Privacy Piercers." *The World and I*, July 1999: vol. 14.

The following is an excerpted magazine article discussing the effects media has on the lives of the victims of disasters.

For example, when Pan Am 103 was blown out of the sky by a terrorist bomb on December 21, 1988, raining blazing debris on the Scottish village of Lockerbie, thousands of media people descended on the hamlet. They stalked and hounded residents for weeks in a relentless hunt for "reaction" to the horrible deaths of 259 people aboard the plane and 11 more on the ground.

And for years afterward on the anniversary of the disaster, the media spectacle was repeated, contributing to anguish and lack of closure among the families of Pan Am 103 victims and Lockerbie residents.

But a few developments are providing hope for protecting people's privacy when media feeding frenzies occur. For instance, in the months leading up to last year's tenth anniversary of the Pan Am 103 tragedy, Lockerbie residents formed a committee that set up all interviews and directed coverage of memorial events.

In addition, when 229 people perished in the ocean in the crash of Swissair Flight 111 off Nova Scotia on September 2, 1998, the airline company did not hesitate to take charge of the media melee. Company officials made sure that relatives of those aboard the flight were protected from intrusive reporting while journalists still got as much information as possible.

Nevertheless, victims of terrorism, their friends, and their relatives are remembered by the stories and pictures sent out by the media.

Source C

Floroiu, Ruxandra. *Altering America: Effective Risk Communication.* Washington, D.C.: The National Academic Press, 2002.

The following excerpt is from a book discussing risk communications to the public about various kinds of hazards and disasters.

The sixth Natural Disasters Roundtable (NDR) forum, "Alerting America: Effective Risk Communication," was held on October 31, 2002 at the National Academies in Washington, D.C. Approximately 140 participants from government, academia, business, industry and civil society attended the one-day forum. The objective of the forum was to provide the opportunity for researchers, decision-makers, practitioners and other stakeholders to exchange views and perspectives on communicating risk information to the public about various kinds of hazards and disasters.

Effective and consistent risk communication is vital to disaster reduction and response. Formal and informal groups and the media are important channels for risk communication. And technology is playing an increasingly crucial role, making it possible to track potential disaster agents, alert authorities, and educate and warn the public in a more timely manner. However, underlying the public response to risk communication are other factors such as social structure, norms, resources and risk perception, which is embedded in past experience and group interaction.

GO ON TO THE NEXT PAGE

Source D

Bluestein, Jane. *Creating Emotionally Safe Schools: A Guide for Educators and Parents.* Albuquerque, New Mexico: Health Communications, Inc., 1996–2004.

The following is an excerpt from a book discussing the Columbine school shootings and its psychological effects on society.

So it goes with safety in schools. Invariably, whenever somebody brings up the topic. The conversation seems to focus on one little piece of this reality—usually a headline-grabbing instance of violence or vandalism. However, if we apply the "big-picture" perspective to this issue, we realize that the more extreme breaches of school safety are only a very small part of a much larger issue. Unfortunately, despite our efforts to place these events in a larger context, we can easily become fixated on the intensity of a terrible moment, and lose our sense of multidimensional reality in which the events occurred. When our focus narrows to one little corner of the picture, we can neglect the millions of other details that are also a part of the scenery, much less how all these threads are woven together or how they impact one another. When our vision fails to go beyond the immediacy of the moment, our lack of perspective can have serious consequences, particularly with regard to how we respond to the event and the solutions we propose.

Source E

Adapted from *Green Left Weekly.* Issue #592. 4 Aug. 2004. N. page. Available at greenleft.org.au.

The following political cartoon is about September 11, a spoof on the media and how movies and the news affect people's views on national disasters.

Source F

"Hurricane Katrina—Rejuvenating the Mainstream Media?" Available at www.globalissues.org/HumanRights/ Media/USA.asp#HurricaneKatrinaRejuvenatingtheMainstreamMedia.

The following is an online article about the effects of Hurricane Katrina on the media.

It has not gone unnoticed by many that the American mainstream media has become more critical of power in the wake of Hurricane Katrina and the poor response of authorities and George Bush in its aftermath. Many have wondered if this finally means the mainstream media will do what it is supposed to: provide a quality service, critiquing claims rather than simply reporting them, and fundamentally, allowing people to make informed decisions.

Media watchdog *FAIR* is guarded in its optimism noting that not all reporting has been that good. In addition:

In the aftermath of Hurricane Katrina, a more aggressive press corps seems to have caught the White House public relations team off-balance—a situation the White House has not had to face very often in the last five years. Many might wonder why it took reporters so long; as Eric Boehlert wrote in Salon.com (9/7/05):

"It's hard to decide which is more troubling: that it took the national press corps five years to summon up enough courage to report, without apology, that what the Bush administration says and does are often two different things, or that it took the sight of bodies floating facedown in the streets of New Orleans to trigger a change in the press's behavior."

Question 2

(Suggested time—40 minutes. This question counts one-third of the total essay section score.)

In the following two passages, Virginia Woolf describes two different meals that she was served during a university visit; the first meal was served at the men's college, while the second meal was served at the women's college.

Directions: Read the two passages carefully; then write an essay in which you analyze Woolf's underlying attitude toward women's place in society as she describes the two meals. Discuss how such elements as narrative structure, manipulation of language, selection of detail, and tone contribute to the rhetorical effect of the passage.

Passage I

It is a curious fact that novelists have a way of making us believe that luncheon parties are invariably memorable for something very witty that was said, or for something very wise that was done. But they seldom spare a word for what was eaten. It is part of the novelist's convention not to mention soup and salmon and ducklings, as if soup and a salmon and ducklings were of no importance whatsoever, as if nobody ever smoked a cigar or drank a glass of wine. Here, however, I shall take the liberty to defy that convention and to tell you that the lunch on this occasion began with soles, sunk in a deep dish, over which the college cook had spread a counterpane of the whitest cream, save that it was branded here and there with brown spots like the spots on the flanks of a doe. After that, came the partridges, but if this suggests a couple of bald, brown birds on a plate you are mistaken. The partridges, many and various, came with all their retinue of sauces and salads, the sharp and the sweet, each in its order; their potatoes, thin as coins but not so hard; their sprouts, foliated as rosebuds but more succulent. And no sooner had the roast and its retinue been done with than the silent serving-man, the Beadle himself perhaps in a milder manifestation, set before us, wreathed in napkins, a confection which rose all sugar from the waves. To call it pudding and so relate it to rice and tapioca would be an insult. Meanwhile the wineglasses had flushed yellow and flushed crimson; had been emptied; had been filled. And thus by degrees was lit, halfway down the spine, which is the seat of the soul, not that hard little electric light which we call brilliance, as it pops in and out upon our lips, but the more profound, subtle and subterranean glow, which is the rich yellow flame of rational intercourse. No need to hurry. No need to sparkle. No need to be anybody but oneself. We are all going to heaven . . . in other words, how good life seemed, how sweet its rewards, how trivial this grudge or that grievance, how admirable friendship and the society of one's kind, as, lighting a good cigarette, one sunk among the cushions in the window-seat.

Passage II

Here was my soup. Dinner was being served in the great dining-hall. Far from being spring it was in fact an evening in October. Everybody was assembled in the big dining-room. Dinner was ready. Here was the soup. It was a plain gravy soup. There was nothing to stir the fancy in that. One could have seen through the transparent liquid any pattern that there might have been on the plate itself. But there was no pattern. The plate was plain. Next came beef with its attendant greens and potatoes—a homely trinity, suggesting the rumps of cattle in a muddy market, and sprouts curled and yellowed at the edge, and bargaining and cheapening, and women with string bags on Monday morning. There was no reason to complain of human nature's daily food, seeing that the supply was sufficient and coal-miners doubtless were sitting down to less. Prunes and custard followed. And if any one complains that prunes, even when mitigated by custard, are an uncharitable vegetable (fruit they are not), stringy as a miser's heart and exuding a fluid such as might run in miser's veins who have denied themselves wine and warmth for eighty years and yet not given to the poor, he should reflect that there are people whose charity embraces even the prune. Biscuits and cheese came next, and here the water-jug was liberally passed round, for it is the nature of biscuits to be dry, and these were biscuits to the core. That was all. The meal was over. Everybody scraped their chairs back; the swing-doors swung violently to and fro; soon the hall was emptied of every sign of food and made ready no doubt for breakfast next morning.

GO ON TO THE NEXT PAGE

Question 3

(Suggested time—40 minutes. This question counts one-third of the total essay section score.)

Directions: Read the following excerpt from Ralph Waldo Emerson's speech, "The American Scholar," which was delivered at Cambridge on August 31, 1837. Then write a well-reasoned essay that defends, challenges, or qualifies Emerson's ideas about books and their usefulness. Use appropriate evidence to develop your essay.

The theory of books is noble. The scholar of the first age received into him the world around; brooded thereon; gave it the new arrangement of his own mind, and uttered it again. It came into him—life; it went out from him—truth. It came to him—short-lived actions; it went out from him—immortal thoughts. It came to him—business; it went from him—poetry. It was—dead fact; now, it is quick thought. It can stand, and it can go. It now endures, it now flies, it now inspires. Precisely in proportion to the depth of mind from which it issued, so high does it soar, so long does it sing.

Or, I might say, it depends on how far the process had gone, of transmuting life into truth. In proportion to the completeness of the distillation, so will the purity and imperishableness of the product be. But none is quite perfect. . . . Each age, it is found, must write its own books; or rather, each generation for the next succeeding. The books of an older period will not fit this.

Yet hence arises a grave mischief. The sacredness which attaches to the act of creation—the act of thought— is instantly transferred to the record. The poet chanting, was felt to be a divine man. Henceforth the chant is divine also. The writer was a just and wise spirit. Henceforth it is settled, the book is perfect; as love of the hero corrupts into worship of his statue. Instantly, the book becomes noxious. The guide is a tyrant. . . . The sluggish and perverted mind of the multitude, always slow to open to the incursions of Reason, having once so opened, having once received this book, stands upon it, and makes an outcry, if it is disparaged. Colleges are built on it. Books are written on it by thinkers, not by Man Thinking; by men of talent, that is, who start wrong, who set out from accepted dogmas, not from their own sight of principles. Meek young men grow up in libraries, believing it their duty to accept the views which Cicero, which Locke, which Bacon, have given, forgetful that Cicero, Locke, and Bacon were only young men in libraries when they wrote these books.

Hence, instead of Man Thinking, we have the book-worm. . . .

Books are the best of things, well used; abused, among the worst.

Answer Key for Practice Test 1

Section I: Multiple-Choice Questions

First Passage

1. D
2. B
3. C
4. D
5. B
6. A
7. A
8. B
9. B
10. A
11. C
12. C
13. D
14. E

Second Passage

15. C
16. D
17. B
18. E
19. A
20. D
21. B
22. C
23. D
24. A
25. E
26. E
27. C
28. D

Third Passage

29. B

30. E

31. C

32. A

33. E

34. D

35. B

36. A

37. C

38. D

39. A

40. E

41. D

42. C

43. B

Fourth Passage

44. B

45. E

46. C

47. D

48. E

49. A

50. E

51. B

52. D

53. D

54. C

55. A

Section II: Essay Questions

Essay scoring guides, student essays, and analyses appear beginning on page 108.

Practice Test 1 Scoring Worksheet

Use the following worksheet to arrive at a probable final AP grade on Practice Test 1. Because being objective enough to estimate your own essay is sometimes difficult, you can use the sample essay answers that follow to approximate an essay score for yourself. You might also give your essays (along with the sample essays) to a teacher, friend, or relative to score if you feel confident that the individual has the knowledge necessary to make such a judgment and that he or she will feel comfortable in doing so.

Section I: Multiple-Choice Questions

_____ − (¼ or .25 × _____) = _____
right   wrong   multiple-choice
answers   answers   raw score

_____ × 1.2272 = _____ (of possible 67.5)
multiple-choice   multiple-choice
raw score   converted score

Section II: Essay Questions

_____ + _____ + _____ = _____
question 1   question 2   question 3   essay
raw score   raw score   raw score   raw score

_____ × 3.0556 = _____ (of possible 82.5)
essay   essay
raw score   converted score

Final Score

_____ + _____ = _____ (of possible 150)
multiple-choice   essay   final
converted score   converted score   converted score

Probable Final AP Score

Final Converted Score	Probable AP Score
150–104	5
103–92	4
91–76	3
75–50	2
49–0	1

Answers and Explanations for Practice Test 1

Section I: Multiple-Choice Questions

First Passage

From *The Writing Life* by Annie Dillard

1. **D.** The figure is a metaphor, not a simile. Synesthetic imagery moves from the stimulation of one sense to a response by another sense, as a certain odor induces the visualization of a certain color. Here, the act of reading, a visual stimulus, produces sounds.

2. **B.** The paragraph describes a cause (the large cardboard butterfly) and its effect ("He jumps the piece of cardboard"). The paragraph does not contain any metaphors, similes, extended definitions, or concessions to an opposing view. The paragraph is used to compare the butterfly's and the human's response to size, but the comparison is not made in this paragraph.

3. **C.** The first sentence of the third paragraph makes clear the relevance of the second. As the butterfly automatically responds to size, so humans respond to the larger-than-life stimuli of films. The last sentence makes the comparison explicit with its simile. The third paragraph doesn't qualify the second (A and D). The second paragraph doesn't ask why butterflies behave as they do (B).

4. **D.** The nine-foot handsome face with its three-foot-wide smile is an image on the movie screen to which we cannot help responding. Since the point of the paragraph is the irresistible appeal of size, the reference is to the larger-than-life film rather than to the television set.

5. **B.** Although the author claims she can recognize and will dislike a book when written with an eye on film adaptation, she makes no comment on the quality of the films these books may become. The first four sentences of the paragraph assert the superiority of films in depicting spectacle and scenes of action. Her dissatisfaction with novels written for film adaptation is expressed twice in terms of smell: "a faint but unmistakable, and ruinous odor" and "I smelled a rat."

6. **A.** The figure here is personification. The metaphor compares books to people (who can be "uneasy," "eager," and wear "disguises"). The figure is neither understood nor ironic. It is a metaphor, not a simile or a syllogism.

7. **A.** The question uses the phrase "according to the passage," and although the writer uses colloquial language ("smell a rat"), she doesn't call it a characteristic of literature. These qualities are cited in the first paragraph ("the imagination's vision . . . the moral sense . . . the intellect") and the last ("the more purely verbal, crafted sentence by sentence, the more imaginative").

8. **B.** The phrase means something like "a greater waste of time." The best of the five choices here is "poorer occupation." "Sorry" here means "sad" or "pathetic" (a sorry excuse), and "pursuit" means "occupation," not "chase."

9. **B.** Choice A can't be right, since "our" is the first-person plural possessive pronoun. The phrase, like most of the passage, makes only modest claims for literature, based upon the greater subtlety of the verbal appeal. The move from the first-person singular ("I") of the fourth paragraph to the plural here seems intended to assert a solidarity with the people "who like literature." Choice E explains the phrase "a poor thing," but the question asks about the plural "our." Choice D is untrue and C most unlikely. Many readers won't notice the allusion at all, and if they do, they won't see that it is an oblique form of self-promotion.

10. **A.** Throughout the passage, the author frankly admits the limitations of the written word and concedes advantages to film in certain areas. All three of these sentences admit that writing is not powerful, or not immediately so, or not as effective in some areas as other forms of expression. The first two don't deal with film (B). Choices C, D, and E are all untrue. The passage is genuine and doesn't employ overstatement of irony.

11. **C.** The first paragraph supports the idea that life is more exciting than writing. The whole passage suggests that reading is a special taste that some people have acquired, but it makes no case for forcing literature upon those who prefer film or television. In fact, the last sentence contends that the attempt to win over nonreaders is foolish (E). The third paragraph calls film "irresistible." The passage makes no claim of universal appeal for even the best books (C). Literature, it calmly argues, will appeal to those who like literature.

12. **C.** The focus of the passage is on the nature of writing and film and their differences. The only mention of the novel is of the book written to be made into film (E). The passage ignores the difficulties of being a writer (B). Although the author may agree with the ideas of A and C, neither is the central concern of this passage.

13. **D.** The first and last paragraphs are primarily about writing. The second paragraph, about the butterfly, is an analogy for the appeal of the big—the film as opposed to literature—and the third and fourth paragraphs are about films and novels written to become films. Choice E misrepresents the first, second, and final paragraphs. Choice A misrepresents the entire passage.

14. **E.** The passage doesn't employ irony. There is a personal anecdote in the description of the author's reading novels written for film (paragraph four), an extended analogy in paragraphs two (the butterfly) and three (the film), short sentences throughout the passage, and colloquialism in a phrase like "I smelled a rat."

Second Passage

From *The American Crisis* by Thomas Paine

15. **C.** It is the author's intent that American citizens will read this essay and thus become inspired to support the revolution. There is no indication that he is speaking to the government of either Great Britain or America, choices A and D. British citizens, Choice B, is an unreasonable answer, unsupported by the essay. Choice E is far too general; the author is speaking only to the oppressed people of America, not of the entire world.

16. **D.** The "summer soldier" and the "sunshine patriot" serve their country only when conditions are favorable to themselves, a behavior akin to that of the proverbial "fair-weather friend." These conditionally patriotic citizens, who want to get involved only on their own terms, are the target of the author's criticism in this sentence. Choices A and E are unreasonable; neither army reserves nor Special Forces existed at this time. Choice B also makes no sense; while the word "infidel" is used in the second paragraph, it has nothing to do with the quotation given. Choice C is contradictory to the meaning of the quotation given; if the professional British soldiers were instead "summer soldiers," the revolution would be easier to accomplish.

17. **B.** The essay is filled with aphorisms—brief, witty sayings—and emotional appeals. Examples of aphorisms here are "the harder the conflict, the more glorious the triumph" (lines 7–8) and "What we obtain too cheap, we esteem too lightly" (lines 8–9). The author appeals to emotions in his claim that a man's children will curse his cowardice if he fails to act now. Answer A is inaccurate because, although it can be argued that parts of the essay are allegorical, it does not use didactic rhetoric. The author's purpose is clearly to persuade, not to teach, and the rhetoric is too highly charged with emotion to be described as didactic. Choice C is only partially correct. An argument can be made that the essay uses symbolism; for example, the man who runs the tavern at Amboy may be a symbol for all that the author considers to be wrong with American citizens. But this lone example does not constitute "heavy use." Although "God" is mentioned in three of the four paragraphs, those references are not technically biblical allusion. The author does not use paradox and invective (D) or historical background and illustration (E).

18. **E.** The author groups the King of Britain with murderers, highwaymen, and housebreakers (lines 30–33) but not with cowards. The line "the blood of his children will curse his cowardice" (lines 59–60) refers to Americans who fail to support the revolution, not to the king.

19. **A.** God, as characterized here, is a just and principled deity who will not let a people perish through military destruction because they have "earnestly and so repeatedly sought to avoid the calamities of war" (lines 24–25). Nor, the author suggests, will this God abandon humans, giving them up "to the care of devils" (line 29). None of the references to God are negative, so "vexed" (angry), "indifferent," and "pernicious" (extremely destructive) are inappropriate answers. Choice D ("contemplative") implies merely that God meditates, but the author suggests a more active God.

20. D. The author's forceful language is nearly the opposite of understatement. He uses anecdote (the story of the tavern owner), simile (for example, "clear as a ray of light," line 69), aphorisms (for example, "What we obtain too cheap, we esteem too lightly," lines 8–9), and symbolism (for example, the story of the tavern owner).

21. B. In lines 10–13, the author claims that "Heaven knows how to put a proper price upon its goods; and it would be strange indeed if so celestial an article as freedom should not be highly rated." Choice A is inaccurate because the author never addresses the relationship between freedom and cowardice. C contradicts the essay. The author states strongly that freedom does not come easily. D also contradicts the essay; the author hopes that one day Americans will know true freedom. E is not addressed in the essay.

22. C. The image of the tavern owner holding the hand of his child is likely designed to increase the emotional appeal of this essay, appealing to every man's desire to protect his family, even if he has to fight in order to save it. As the author says, it is "sufficient to awaken every man to duty." Choice A is too simplistic. True, the mention of the child shows that this man has a family, but introducing that fact is not the purpose of the reference. Answer B is incorrect because it isn't the image of the child that provokes the author's anger, but the image of the child's complacent father. The author may feel that the tavern owner is "evil," but the child's image doesn't symbolically increase the evil (D). Choice E contradicts the passage. The author appeals to the traditional values of family and freedom.

23. D. Since aphorisms are short, proverbial sayings of general truth, Choice D doesn't fit the definition but rather may be more accurately considered a cliché.

24. A. The author states that America's "situation is remote from the entire wrangling world, and she has nothing to do but to trade with them" (lines 49–51). The author does picture America as the "conqueror" but only with regard to winning its freedom from Britain, which makes Choice B too strong a statement to be correct. The author never implies that America should be greater than Britain (C) or sanctified by God (D). Choice E contradicts the passage; if a country conducts trade, its stance is not one of "complete isolationism."

25. E. The author hopes to encourage his readers to take action, and he writes persuasively to achieve that aim.

26. E. There is a strong emotional appeal as the author warns American men that their children will think them cowards and, as he claims, that the heart of a reader who does not feel as he does is "dead." Choice A has no support in the essay. Choice B isn't his purpose, the outcome he desires. He wants men to join the revolution, to take action, not simply to be afraid. C is inaccurate because the sentence quoted in this question is not directed to the king, but to American citizens. There is no mention of the superiority of either American or British forces and no mention of the advisability of retreat (D).

27. C. The author demonstrates no ambivalence in this paragraph. He takes a strong stand without vacillation. The paragraph does include the other devices listed. For example, aphorism ("'Tis the business of little minds to shrink," lines 64–65), simile ("My own line of reasoning is . . . as straight and clear as a ray of light," lines 67–69), parallel construction ("What signifies it to me . . . an army of them?", lines 76–79), and analogy (the comparison of the king to common thieves, line 72 to end).

28. D. Clearly, this author hopes his readers will feel that it is their patriotic duty toward America to join in supporting the revolution. While the author might value "peace and rational thinking," he also clearly suggests that revolution now is necessary to produce later peace. The negative "overemotional" and "unwarranted" in choices B and C should alert you to the fact that these are not likely answers. The essay contradicts Choice E. The author suggests that "Tyranny, like hell, is not easily conquered," that is, freedom will not come immediately. In addition, the essay's primary purpose is to persuade Americans to join in the struggle to win their liberty, not simply to demand that the British government grant it to them.

Third Passage

From *The Complete Letters of Charles Lamb*

29. B. The final sentence of the first paragraph verifies that Lamb "contrived to bring together whatever can be said in praise of them, dropping all the other side of the argument. . . ." This paragraph offers no evidence of Coleridge's opinion of Lamb's recollections, or any hint of what Coleridge would have written differently.

30. **E.** Given that the other boys at the school did not have the special privileges that Lamb had, the best synonymous term for "invidious" is "discriminatory." The other answer choices are all too positive or neutral.

31. **C.** The passage states that the "present worthy sub-treasurer to the Inner Temple can explain how that happened." Thus, one can infer that someone had likely bribed a member of the Inner Temple to obtain Lamb's special privileges. The passage offers no evidence that Lamb's aunt was the one who secured the favors (Choice **A**). Choice E is incorrect for two reasons: No evidence is offered that his friends were the ones who gave any special treatment, and the passage does not explicitly clarify that the sub-treasurer was the one who was bribed.

32. **A.** The speaker extensively describes Lamb's daily food to provide a sharp contrast to the other boys' meals, thereby emphasizing their class differences. The idea that Lamb felt superior to the other boys (Choice D), contradicts the speaker's claim that Lamb felt sympathy for the other boys. Choice E is incorrect because the passage reinforces common ideas about British boarding schools instead of dispelling them.

33. **E.** The passage contains no references to any historical events, but all other answer choices can be found. Alliteration (Choice A) appears in phrases like "rotten-roasted or rare." Examples of complex sentences (Choice B) are present throughout the second paragraph, as are the negative descriptions of the boys' food (Choice C). Finally, the speaker turns the food descriptions into a metaphor (Choice D) that illustrates the harsh conditions of the school.

34. **D.** The decision to italicize the phrase *"quite fresh"* emphasizes that the phrase is a tongue-in-cheek inaccurate description of the beef. In addition, comparing the beef to horseflesh *("caro equina")* in the same sentence reinforces the sarcastic tone and ironic negativity.

35. **B.** This answer choice is the only one that conveys the speaker's negative reaction to the marigolds, emphasizing how feeble this use of flowers is with wording like "detestable" and "poison the pail." The passage provides no evidence that the marigolds, an image of nature, offer comfort or cover for the ugliness of the world.

36. **A.** The descriptive phrases that accompany each meal's presentation overstate how the food so horrified the boys' palates. Phrases such as "blue and tasteless" and "floating in the pail to poison the broth" are surely exaggerated, making the overall experience more intense. Choice B overstates the case; only the boys' meals are described, not all that encompasses "daily life."

37. **C.** The introductory material states that Lamb wrote in the guise of Coleridge "for the sake of innocent mystification" and that he was "gentle, nervous." Therefore, it is reasonable to infer that Lamb hoped to hide his nervousness as inoffensively as possible. Although Choice B may perhaps seem plausible, the word "yearning" in this answer choice does not really address an effect; instead, it more likely represents Lamb's *purpose,* and hiding his stammering is an unreasonable idea. The remaining answer choices have no evidence in the passage.

38. **D.** The "contending passion" is the ambivalence that Lamb felt over his aunt's actions; this is clarified in the last sentence of the passage, with the use of sharply contrasting words such as "love" and "shame."

39. **A.** The passage describes Lamb's aunt as one "in whom love forbade shame," thus her familial love overcame any potential indignity she may have felt. Answer B is inaccurate because the phrase "school was too stingy" is too strong; the passage has no evidence to point out that this is the reason *why* his aunt brought food. Answer choices C, D, and E also have no evidence in the passage.

40. **E.** Lamb does not feel antipathy, an extreme hatred, toward his aunt. All the other choices, such as Choice A, ignominy, which is a synonym for embarrassment, describe emotions that Lamb *does* feel.

41. **D.** Note #6 clarifies that, in retrospect, Lamb views his aunt's actions far differently from the way he did at the time; with hindsight, he understands that he was acting in a "school-boy like" manner, and he now better comprehends his mixed feelings about gaining extra food while watching his aunt lose her dignity. Choices B and E have no evidence in the passage; choices A and C are contradicted in the passage.

42. **C.** Note #2 states that "Lamb paid a fine tribute of praise," Coleridge "has drawn a companion picture of the better side," and Hunt "also described . . . the life and ideals of the school." All incorrect answer choices have no evidence in the note.

43. **B.** The phrase "contrived to bring together whatever can be said in praise of them" is contradicted clearly in the passage as the speaker repeatedly describes the horribly unappetizing and inedible food. This answer opposes the rhetorical purpose of the passage as a whole.

Fourth Passage

From "Of Studies" by Francis Bacon

44. B. Most of these comments explain the benefits of studies (for pleasure, discussion, business, and so forth). Thus, the audience that would most benefit from this essay's message is likely to be those who think they don't need studies. Choices A, D, and E name audiences who are probably already aware of the benefits of studies. Poor readers (Choice C) don't necessarily need to be convinced of the benefits of studies but rather may need to improve their reading skills.

45. E. The author explains how students may focus on their studies incorrectly. One may spend too much time in studies and thus be guilty of sloth, or one may use them only to impress others (displaying affectation). Also, one may make judgments based solely upon studies, failing to consider real-life experience. The author uses the term "humor," while modern writers might label the scholars' tendency as temperament, or disposition.

46. C. The author claims, in line 12, that studies "are perfected by <u>experience</u>" and in line 16, that they are "bounded in by <u>experience.</u>"

47. D. Parallel construction is evident—"to contradict and confute," "to believe and take," "to find talk and discourse," "to weigh and consider."

48. E. The author, in this sentence, discusses how people need to "prune" their natural abilities by study. At the same time, however, studies need to be "bounded in by experience." The message is one of moderation and inclusion—neither studies nor experiences should be relied on exclusively or predominantly.

49. A. The wisdom "won by observation" (lines 19–20) is analogous to that "perfected by experience" (line 12). In both instances, the author recommends reading to gain knowledge but also incorporating life's observations and experiences to obtain wisdom.

50. E. The author suggests all three of these uses in the second sentence. Personal reading brings "delight" (enjoyment), contributes to "discourse" (intelligent conversation), and aids in the "disposition of business" (sound judgment).

51. B. "To spend too much time in studies is sloth" (lines 8–9) paradoxically suggests that too much work on studies can lead to laziness and lack of work. In other words, overemphasis on studies avoids work in the outside world. Choices A, D, and E are not paradoxes. Although Choice C might have paradoxical elements, it is not mentioned in the essay.

52. D. In lines 20–22, the author claims that one should read "not to contradict and confute, nor to believe and take for granted, nor to find talk and discourse, but to <u>weigh and consider</u>." A reader should *think*. Reading voluminously or only for pleasure, choices A and E, are not necessarily "errors." Choices B and C are perhaps reading mistakes, but the non-thinking reader is presented as the greater problem.

53. D. The sentence in this question uses analogy, comparing reading to eating. In I, reading is compared to pruning a plant. In III, a third analogy compares "impediments" in understanding to physical diseases of the body. There is no analogy in II.

54. C. This sentence discusses how readers might adapt their reading style to the subject matter and their purpose. By reading "not curiously," the author means reading without great care or scrutiny, reading cursorily. Choices A, B, and E directly contradict the idea of reading without considerable scrutiny.

55. A. The sentence in the question contains parallel construction in which three ideas make up the sentence. Choice A uses the same structure, presenting three similarly phrased ideas that make up the sentence.

Section II: Essay Questions

Question 1

Scoring Guide for Question 1 (Media Influence on Natural Disasters)

9 Essays that earn a score of 9 meet the criteria for essays that receive a score of 8. In addition, they are especially sophisticated in the use of language, explanation, and argument.

8 Successful

These essays respond to the prompt **successfully,** employing ideas from at least three of the sources from the prompt. They take a position that defends, challenges, or qualifies the claim that the media has had a positive influence on the effects of natural disasters. They effectively argue the position and support the argument with appropriate evidence. The control of language is extensive and the writing errors are minimal.

7 These essays meet the criteria for essays that receive a score of 6 but provide more depth and strength to the argument and evidence. The prose style is mature and shows a wide control over language.

6 Satisfactory

These essays respond to the prompt **satisfactorily.** Using at least three of the sources from the prompt, these essays take a position that defends, challenges, or qualifies the claim that the media has had a positive influence on the effects of natural disasters. The position is adequately argued with support from appropriate evidence, although without the precision and depth of top-scoring essays. The writing may contain minor errors in diction or in syntax, but the prose is generally clear.

5 These essays take a position that defends, challenges, or qualifies the claim that the media has had a positive influence on the effects of natural disasters. It supports the position with generally appropriate evidence, but may not adequately quote, either directly or indirectly, from three sources in the prompt. These essays may be inconsistent, uneven, or limited in the development of their argument. Although the writing usually conveys the writer's ideas and perspectives, it may demonstrate lapses in diction or syntax or an overly simplistic style.

4 Inadequate

These essays respond to the prompt **inadequately.** They have difficulty taking a clear position that defends, challenges, or qualifies the claim that the media has had a positive influence on the effects of natural disasters. The evidence may be insufficient or may not utilize enough sources from the prompt. The prose conveys the writer's ideas but suggests immature control over the elements of effective writing.

3 These essays meet the criteria for a score of 4 but reveal less success in taking a position that defends, challenges, or qualifies the claim that the media has had a positive influence on the effects of natural disasters. The presentation of evidence and arguments is unconvincing. These writers show little or no control over the elements of effective writing.

2 Little Success

These essays demonstrate **little success** at taking a position that defends, challenges, or qualifies the claim that the media has had a positive influence on the effects of natural disasters and show little success in presenting it clearly and with appropriate evidence from the sources in the prompt. These essays may misunderstand the prompt, may fail to establish a position with supporting evidence, or may substitute a simpler task by replying tangentially with unrelated, erroneous, or unsuitable explanation, argument, and/or evidence. The prose frequently demonstrates consistent weaknesses in the conventions of effective writing.

1 These essays meet the criteria for a score of 2 but are undeveloped, especially simplistic in their explanation, argument and/or evidence, or weak in their control of writing.

High-Scoring Essay

The media has assumed a reputation of candor coupled with benevolence, for the media links desperate people in desperate situations to magnanimous audiences, who, theoretically, are only too eager to help. In a media-perpetuated myth, newspapers, radio, internet, and television supposedly serve the distinct purpose of objectively presenting adversity while respecting victims. Thus, the media has tailored for itself an image of an entity that respects victims of disastrous situations, yet simultaneously provides the public with objective reporting. This is not so. The media simply is not able to live up to its self-created reputation. Rather than providing a service to the public and victims following a disaster, the media compromises the integrity of its broadcasts, disregards victims, and alienates audiences, ultimately doing a disservice to the public.

The Columbine High School shooting was a tragedy that shocked a community and frightened a nation. Naturally, the media focused on the shootings, but according to Jane Bluestein, the media did not emphasize the "big-picture" (Source D). The media depicted the shootings with graphic imagery and emotional social commentary, an illogical format that caused their audiences to "lose their sense of multidimensional reality in which the events occurred" (Source D). Thus, the Columbine example depicts how media focuses on one "little corner of the picture" and fails to acknowledge "millions of other details that are part of the scenery" (Source D). Such incomplete coverage, exemplified by Bluestein's argument, illustrates how the media inadequately reports a disaster or a tragedy. Furthermore, Source F details what the media *should* be doing, namely "provid[ing] a quality service, critiquing claims rather than simply reporting them, and fundamentally, allowing people to make informed decisions." Instead of inadequate and sensationalist coverage such as the Columbine School shooting, the media should be striving for the objective and complete coverage it pretends to present.

It is difficult to regard media in a favorable light when one considers the information from Robert Lissit's article, "The Privacy Piercers" (Source B). The media does not help disaster victims; it is in media's best interest to report the news and in its quest to get information, in its quest to get the scoop before rivals, the media can easily turn into a ruthless and unwelcome guest, knowing the audience will not turn away from horrific images. Take, for example the residents of Lockerbie, Scotland and the relatives of the infamous Pan Am 103 flight who had already suffered enough after 270 people died on December 21, 1988, as the plane was blown out of the sky by terrorists (Source B). Apparently the victims' relatives and friends couldn't mourn in peace as "[reporters] stalked and hounded residents for weeks in a relentless hunt for a reaction to the horrible deaths" (Source B). This was not an isolated incident of the press harassing victims. According to Source B, in 1998 Swissair officials were forced to shield relatives and friends from the "media melee" and "intrusive reporting" after one of its airliners crashed off Nova Scotia. Recall also the unrelenting images of victims that were broadcast after the 2004–2005 tsunami, or the nonstop footage of Hurricanes Katrina and Rita, or the Pakistan earthquake; all of these disasters were replayed over and over ad nauseam until the public became immune to the victims' plight. There is ample evidence that describes the media as culprits— they feed the public incomplete information and hurt the victims with ruthless reporting.

In October of 2002, some of America's brightest minds convened for a seminar on effective risk communication (Source C). Effective risk communicators include different aspects of the media, for instance, television and radio. The media is an "important channel for risk communication," an asset to authorities, and a source of public information, yet Source C explicitly states that society's "social structure, norms, and risk perception" undermine media's post-disaster effectiveness.

Thus, in spite of media's disaster education in Latin America (Source A) and roundtable discussions (Source C), media coverage of disasters does a disservice. Reporting on disasters in an incomplete manner, while intrusively disregarding victims' welfare, and failing to effectively reach the public, the media displays the hallmarks of a public service gone awry.

Analysis of High-Scoring Essay

This very thorough essay demonstrates just how much argumentation a thoughtful writer can include. Freely synthesizing the sources and contemporary events, this writer presents an intelligent discussion of the shortcomings of the media regarding their reporting of disasters. Taking a negative stand, the essay systematically criticizes the media's intrusive nature and poor reporting. The writer demonstrates a strong command of diction and syntax, presenting sophisticated phrasing like "candor coupled with benevolence" and "links desperate people in desperate situations with magnanimous audiences." Additionally, the simple sentence, "This is not so," packs a punch because of its brevity and its being surrounded by longer, more complex sentences.

The first body paragraph presents evidence from Source D regarding the Columbine High School shooting incident. Making the point that combining "graphic imagery" with "emotional social commentary" creates an "illogical format," the writer astutely explains how the media manipulates their audience while presenting incomplete information. The statement from Source F regarding the role the media should ideally play in a society adds depth, both by synthesizing multiple sources in the same paragraph and by bringing this particular one to a logical conclusion.

The next paragraph examines yet another negative aspect of the media: its members relentlessly hounding the victims of disasters, knowing that such coverage sells. This touches on a universal truth; humanity is compelled to watch images of horror while simultaneously being repelled by them. The writer implicitly understands this concept and uses it to further the essay's argument. By citing multiple examples from Source C and from contemporary incidents, the writer makes as thorough a case as one can expect in any 40-minute essay. All of the examples are relevant and demonstrate that the writer is not merely repeating the information from the sources, but instead is digesting the ideas, mulling them over, and then producing an intelligent, albeit one-sided, argument against the media.

The following paragraph feels as if the writer is running out of steam (or time!), as its development pales in comparison with the previous paragraphs; however, this is the only weak point in an otherwise well-developed and thoughtful essay. The writer does manage to point out that the media try to effect "risk communication," but follows it up with Source C's criticism that society is not inclined to heed such ideas. This paragraph is not a terribly strong one, as it mainly just reports what Source C has to say; however, it does expand the essay's critique of the media.

The conclusion too is brief, basically just a summary, but it does bring in another source from the prompt, which highlights the writer's overall attention to detail. The essay ends with a very poignant phrase; by stating that the media is a "public service gone awry," the writer reasserts the essay's thesis with finality and conviction. Indeed, this essay truly earns its high score.

Medium-Scoring Essay

Media has a powerful influence upon our lives. Not only does it provide us with news; it subtly shapes our opinions. Media, be it television, magazines, radio, has demonstrated the ability to affect a broad audience. Recent natural disasters and terrorist attacks have been thoroughly reported by the media. When the media portrays a natural disaster it serves one distinct purpose. Over and over, the media has shown that it chooses to consistently display world tragedy in such a way as to convey feelings of closeness and empathy to its audience. Thus, the effects of the media are great, and media attention is beneficial for victims of disasters because it shares their plight with a sympathetic world audience.

The 21st century is an age of technology. Television, radio, and the internet are mediums of media that can convey news quickly and effectively. Source C, an excerpt from a seminar on risk communication, clearly viewed media as an important method to limit the effects of a natural disaster. Media can help limit a disaster's immediate effects, "[media can] track potential disaster agents, alert authorities, and educate and warn the public in a timely manner" (Source C). Media effectively helps victims of a disaster while helping educate the public in order to limit damage and death in future incidents. The seminar's participants from businesses, industry, and civil services (Source C) exemplified the interest in effectively utilizing media to help in disaster situations.

While Source A acknowledges the importance of media immediately following a disaster, the article emphasizes the importance of educational media that limits the effects of future. The article states, "If people know what to do, they can save their own life." Mr. Briceno, the chairman of the committee that held the forum on disasters asserted, "The people are aware of the risks they face, the better chance they have to save their lives when hazards strike" (Source A).

Source F acknowledges that Hurricane Katrina, while a horrible event, at least caused the media to question the administration's ability to help those in need, and in the process of showing the world the devastation from the hurricane, brought tremendous sympathy for those victims of the storm. If we had not seen the images of the people who suffered, we would not have felt for them so much. Therefore, the media helped the victims.

Media has proved itself to be an integral component in disaster relief. Helping people immediately after a disaster and in the ensuing months, media has aided authorities, raised money, and educated potential future victims. Thus, media is a valuable tool in disaster relief.

Analysis of Medium-Scoring Essay

This essay tries to present a coherent argument about the benefits that the media provides after disasters, but it is not terribly convincing because of its simplistic approach. For instance, one sentence in the introduction claims that the media has "one distinct purpose" in reporting disasters: drawing out the audience's sympathy. Surely this naïve thinking exposes an unwarranted assumption; surely the media has many purposes in reporting "world tragedies." A writer who displays such one-dimensional thinking early on frequently produces an essay that oversimplifies. Although it is true that media exposure may indeed evoke a sympathetic reaction in the viewers, that alone does not necessarily produce any tangible benefit for the victims. Viewer sympathy alone will not house or feed victims.

The first body paragraph addresses the potential good works that the media can do, such as helping to limit the damage from natural disasters by providing warnings to the public and officials of imminent danger. However, the writer seems to have forgotten the thesis of the essay; this paragraph includes no evidence for the concept that the media elicits sympathy in a viewing audience. Although this body paragraph does address some good that the media can do, it does not really relate to the introductory paragraph. Unfortunately, this poor organization does not bode well for the essay.

The second body paragraph suffers from similar organizational problems; it does not support the thesis about eliciting sympathy. Just like the previous paragraph, this one focuses on ways in which the media can help circumvent negative effects of disasters with pre-planning; perhaps the writer would have been better served had he or she changed the thesis to fit what the body paragraphs actually discuss. Furthermore, the weak development of this paragraph is apparent because it contains only three sentences, two of which are merely quotations from the source. In other words, the writer barely hints at any interesting ideas and barely develops them.

The last body paragraph attempts to get back on track and address how the media elicited sympathy for Hurricane Katrina victims. However, the writer uses Source F, which does not really present that idea; this source centers on the concept of how, after the hurricane, the media moved to a more aggressive stand in presenting discrepancies between the administration's statements and actions. Therefore, the writer's leap of logic, jumping from an article that criticizes the administration to the idea that photos of hurricane victims cause sympathy in the viewers, is a flaw no reader can ignore. It appears that the writer is grasping at straws, searching for any phrase in the sources that might somehow support the thesis, but he or she falls far short of composing a convincing argument.

The essay concludes too quickly with the concept that "helping people immediately after a disaster and in the ensuing months, media has aided authorities, raised money, and educated potential future victims." Unfortunately, these ideas are simply not proven in this essay. Overall, the essay demonstrates the logical flaws that occur when a writer jumps in and begins writing too quickly, without thinking through his or her positions and *how* the sources can help establish them. The essay's organization would also benefit from greater sophistication. Instead of using the facile "one-source-per-paragraph" method, the essay could successfully demonstrate more complexity if the writer integrated more sources into each paragraph. Always keep in mind that this is the *synthesis* essay; keep your focus on the concept of synthesis and use it to your advantage as you think deeply about the topic and navigate your way, exploring a variety of ideas.

Question 2

Scoring Guide for Question 2 (Virginia Woolf)

9 These essays meet the criteria for essays that receive a score of an 8, and in addition, they are deeper in their analysis and frequently reveal an exquisite use of language.

8 Successful

These well-written essays clearly and **successfully** demonstrate an understanding of Woolf's attitude about women in society, while also analyzing how the author's structure, diction, tone, and detail convey that attitude. These essays present a clear, relevant thesis supported by strong evidence from the passage. Analysis of the evidence and how it reflects the author's attitude about women in society is insightful. Not necessarily without flaws, these essays still show maturity in their use of language and sentence structure.

7 These essays meet the requirements for essays that score a 6 and, in addition, provide a more complete and deeper analysis of Woolf's attitude and a more mature prose style.

6 Satisfactory

Well presented, these essays **satisfactorily** describe Woolf's attitude about women in society, but perhaps less explicitly than do the high-scoring essays. Discussion of the author's techniques may be less thorough, or evidence presented may be less specific. Connection between the evidence and the thesis may be less insightful. Although some errors may be present, the essay, overall, shows satisfactory control of format and language.

5 These average essays may recognize the author's attitude about women in society but may be less precise in discussing that attitude. Attempts to analyze the author's language may be simplistic, or evidence offered may be insufficient to prove the thesis adequately. Organization may be clear but not as effective as that of the better-written papers. Inconsistencies in the command of language may be present.

4 Inadequate

These essays attempt to address the essay question but **inadequately** address the author's attitude. They may not complete all of the tasks of the question. Not having enough evidence for the writer's ideas may be a problem. Insights may be inaccurate or superficial. These essays may convey ideas, but their weak control over language may distract the reader's attention. Frequent errors in mechanics may be present.

3 Essays earning a score of 3 meet the criteria for a score of 4 but demonstrate less understanding of Woolf's attitude and show a lack of depth in analysis. These essays may show little control over the elements of writing.

2 Little Success

These essays fail to respond sufficiently to the question or the passage and therefore demonstrate **little success** in responding to the prompt. They may fail to recognize the author's attitude or may misread the passage so as to distort it. With little or no evidence offered, these essays have little success in persuading the reader, and the connection between the evidence and the thesis may be shallow or nonexistent. Persistent weaknesses may be evident in the basic elements of composition or writing skills.

1 These poorly written essays meet the criteria for a score of 2 but are undeveloped, especially simplistic in their analysis, and weak in their control of language.

High-Scoring Essay

The differences between men's and women's colleges were considerable in Virginia Woolf's day. Rather than assert this in a pedestrian, expository way, Woolf uses the respective meals served at each college to illustrate the discrepancies between the schools. The meals are a metaphorical device, akin to a poetic conceit; Woolf makes a far more forceful, profound distinction between the male and female schools through such juxtaposition than if she had merely enumerated their inconsistencies. Woolf details the relative poverty of the women's school,

and therefore women's position in society, through varied sentence structure, diction and imagery between the descriptions of the meals.

Fundamentally different premises underlie each meal. The men's meal is a luxury to be enjoyed, the women's a metabolic necessity to be endured. Woolf, in describing the men's meal, dismisses the notion that ". . . soup and salmon and ducklings were of no importance whatsoever, as if nobody ever smoked a cigar or drank a glass of wine." She offers a breathless explanation of the sensual joy the meal affords. Diction and sensory detail showcase the piquant pleasure to be taken in foods "spread . . . of the whitest cream," "Sharp and sweet . . . succulent." The men's meal is a catalyst for the "profound, subtle and subterranean glow . . . of rational intercourse." Of course, no similar premium is put on rational intercourse among women, judging by the amenities of the women's meal. They drink not wine "flushed crimson," but rather eat "transparent . . . plain gravy soup." Dry biscuits and water replace partridges, and such victuals provide no stimulus for enlightened conversation; when the eating is done, the women rise and that is all.

Woolf describes the women's meal in plain language, in blunt, staccato, repetitive bursts: "Here was my soup . . . Dinner was ready. Here was the soup. It was plain gravy soup . . . The plate was plain." All the eloquent wordiness has vanished. The images are those of poverty and ugliness, and the meal is only justified as being superior to

that of a coal miner. The prunes are ". . . stringy as a miser's heart and exuding a fluid such as might run in misers' veins . . ." In contrast, the other meal's imagery is that of opulence. The potatoes are like coins, the sprouts "foliated as rosebuds." This is a meal fit for kings, and the diction is suggestive of royalty: "The partridges . . . came with all their retinue . . ." The men are reassured by the meal that they are all going to heaven; the women's meal is a hurried "homely trinity."

As a metaphor for the chasm separating male and female education, and society as a whole, Woolf's piece is mordantly effective. Her point is made with more economy and vivacity through anecdote than it would be through explanation or a propounding of evidence about the inferiority of female schools. By painting the male university as lavish and its female counterpart as lowly, Woolf succeeds in crystallizing her attitude for readers.

Analysis of the High-Scoring Essay

This writer addresses the question; he or she also demonstrates a deep understanding of the subtle differences between the two passages. This writer's thesis is relevant and on-topic. The body paragraphs provide ample evidence for ideas, and the quotations are used effectively to prove this writer's points. This paper does not merely dwell on the obvious aspects of the passage but probes more deeply into the ramifications of the two meals. Especially effective is the section in which the writer demonstrates how Woolf's diction suggests the meaning of each meal. For example, reread the end of the fourth paragraph as this writer connects the word "retinue" with royalty and goes on to suggest what that royal meal does for the men (it reassures them that they are going to heaven). This type of thinking demonstrates the level of analysis necessary for a high score; the writer understands *how* the language of the essay helps to create an effect.

The vocabulary and sentence structure are also very sophisticated, as they should be in top-scoring essays. The phrasing is creative and pleasing. Wording such as "akin to a poetic conceit," "a metabolic necessity," "piquant pleasure," and "mordantly effective" are just a few of the phrases that sing to the reader's ear. In addition, this writer demonstrates a keen sense of sentence structure and thus adds sufficient variety in both sentence pattern and length.

Although very well written, this essay could be improved by providing a stronger connection between ideas, evidence, and thesis. Also, a more profound point could be made about the deeper issues involved in the "chasm separating male and female education." In addition, the writer could concentrate more on Woolf's attitude *as* he or she presents the evidence. However, these criticisms are not significant enough to lower the essay's score. Essays that are this thorough, organized, and well presented, indeed, earn a high score.

Medium-Scoring Essay

Meals are important, but they are often ignored or not thought of much. People often eat in a hurry, and often they don't pay much attention to the details of what they are actually eating.

Virginia Woolf calls readers' attention to this in the selection about two meals which she had when she was at the university. She had one of these at the men's college and the other at the women's college. They were very different in the food but also in the whole atmosphere of the place where she ate.

Woolf says that though people don't often notice it, the food we eat tells us important things about where we are. She compares the two parts of the university with the different meals. She uses narrative structure, details and tone to present her attitude about the two meals and inform readers of which one she likes better, and why.

The first meal she describes, which is at the men's college, is the one which Woolf likes better. The reasons become obvious for this, because the food is far more appetizing and the atmosphere is just nicer generally. Woolf uses lots of details and metaphors to describe this meal, and often her descriptions are full of imagery. It is all very fancy, with a uniformed waiter serving roast, and Woolf drinks a lot of wine, which sends a glow down her spine. She comments that all the other eaters were very friendly and everything seemed nice and happy after the meal. "We are all going to heaven" she says after the meal. It is almost a religious experience for them.

The second meal is at the women's college, and Woolf's attitude toward it is not as positive. That is understandable, but the food is not even close to as good. Woolf uses lots of metaphors to make the food seem gross and very repulsive. The beef is like "the rumps of cattle in a muddy market, and sprouts curled and yellowed at the edge" she says. The prunes are stringy and miserly, and instead of the good pudding that she ate at the men's college, she has to eat custard that is not nearly so good. The biscuits are dry and unappetizing, which makes for a meal that is not very appealing. She doesn't talk about friends or smoking at this meal, which makes it far less homely than the men's meal.

Thus, through her metaphors and affective descriptions of the food at the two meals, Woolf compares them and strongly shows her attitude to the readers. She makes one realize that even though we don't often think about meals, they are important. The differences are something to realize, and Woolf's excellent description helps you do just that.

Analysis of the Medium-Scoring Essay

This essay earns a medium score because it recognizes some of the differences between the two meals. However, it doesn't merit a higher score because it fails to address Woolf's attitudes as displayed through her description of the meals. The introductory remarks go on far too long (for three paragraphs). When the thesis is finally stated, it's bland and obvious, as is the entire essay. This writer mentions that Woolf presents her attitudes but never clarifies what he or she thinks these attitudes are; basically, the thesis merely restates portions of the question.

This writer has chosen to discuss the two meals separately, in two paragraphs, a technique which doesn't allow for strong comparison. This writer does accurately present some evidence, but in many cases, it is not sufficient. For example, where are the metaphors to which the writer refers? Since they aren't included in the essay, the reader is left guessing. The writer does see some interesting description in the passages but fails to make an intelligent point about it, and the analysis offered is shallow and obvious. Also, no connection is made between the evidence presented and the major topic of Woolf's attitude.

In addition, this essay demonstrates some stylistic and grammatical problems and is not helped by the use of unsophisticated words and phrases such as "things," "a lot," and "not as good." Some awkward sentences tend to distract the reader's attention from this writer's ideas. Incorrect word choices, such as "affective" instead of "effective," show that this writer doesn't have a strong command of the language. This difficulty is further demonstrated by pronoun problems such as the use of "you" in the last sentence and "them" at the end of the fourth paragraph.

The positive aspects of this essay are few; it does try to make a point, and it follows many of the conventions of proper writing style. However, its numerous errors and uninteresting, obvious ideas keep the essay from achieving a higher score.

Question 3

Scoring Guide for Question 3 (Ralph Waldo Emerson)

9 These essays meet the criteria for essays that receive a score of an 8, and in addition, they are deeper in the understanding of Emerson's ideas and frequently reveal an exquisite use of language.

8 Successful

These well-written essays **successfully** take a stand concerning Emerson's ideas about the usefulness of books and substantially support it. The thesis is well thought out and relevant to the topic. The paper provides ample evidence to prove the ideas and clearly connects the evidence to the thesis. Thoroughly convincing, these papers demonstrate a significant understanding of the needs of the essay. Although they need not be without errors, these essays show a mature command of style and language.

7 These essays meet the requirements for essays that score a 6 and, in addition, demonstrate a thorough understanding of the author's ideas, while providing stronger and more relevant evidence. The prose style is generally more mature.

6 Satisfactory

These essays demonstrate a **satisfactory** understanding of Emerson's ideas but produce a less explicit thesis than that of higher-scoring essays. Perhaps less relevant evidence is offered, making these essays less persuasive. Still, they are fairly convincing and show clear thinking. The connection between the evidence and the thesis may not be as articulate as in top-scoring essays. Although well written, these essays may demonstrate some errors while still showing satisfactory control over diction and the essay requirements.

5 These adequately written essays show some understanding of Emerson's ideas but produce a thesis that may be weak or predictable. The opinions may be too hastily conceived after a cursory reading of Emerson's concepts. Overall, the argument, although acceptable, may not be persuasive or thought-provoking. It may appear opinionated without sufficient evidence to support the opinions. Acceptable organization may be evident, but the style may not be as sophisticated as that of higher-scoring essays.

4 Inadequate

These low-scoring, **inadequate** essays fail to convince the reader. The weak presentation may show an unsubstantiated thesis or no thesis at all, weak paragraph development and/or weak organization, insufficient evidence for points made, or superficial thinking. Confusion about Emerson's ideas may be evident, and frequent mechanical errors may be present.

3 These essays earning a score of 3 meet the criteria for a score of 4 but demonstrate little understanding of the ideas. Frequently these essays suffer from a lack of evidence to support the arguments made. These essays may show little control over the elements of writing.

2 Little Success

These poorly written essays lack coherence and clarity and therefore show **little success** in addressing the prompt. The thesis may be overly obvious or absent. Little or no evidence may be offered for the thesis, and connection between the evidence and the thesis may be shallow or nonexistent. These essays may be unusually short and exhibit poor fundamental essay skills. Weak sentence construction may persist, and persistent weaknesses in command of the language may be present.

1 These poorly written essays meet the criteria for a score of 2 but are undeveloped, especially simplistic in their analysis, and weak in the control of language.

High-Scoring Essay

Ralph Waldo Emerson is perhaps overly strident in his speech, "The American Scholar." But such zeal serves to make a trenchant point about the tendency toward rigid reverence of "Great Works," as if each were the Holy Grail itself. He asserts: "Books are the best of things, well used; abused, among the worst." Emerson delivers a stinging indictment of "bookworms." He argues that even the greatest thinkers were once humble students. The danger, Emerson claims, is that of transferring our respect from the venerable acts of creation, of thought, to that endeavor's imperfect product. He believes scholars must not so prostrate themselves before the majesty of profound <u>works</u> that they forget their <u>creators</u>, whom they should emulate in creative thought. They should not idolize the books themselves in a sort of cult of inferiority, Emerson says, but rather write their own books, their own truths, undertake their own sacred acts of creation.

In a strict sense, these points are valid. But Emerson goes beyond these points; he overstates his case. He is treading the ground between the good scholar and the singular genius. Perhaps, given his own stature, it is only fitting that he should hold us to such lofty standards. Nevertheless, his warnings against showing too much respect for books are not altogether true. Such arguments, about the paramount importance of individual thought, can readily be misused to justify a dismissal of the past. Often such self-indulgent, arrogant, arguments are used by those less gifted than Emerson as an excuse to disregard the wisdom that has come before them.

A social critic recently said, "It's fine to learn how to think, but what's the point if you have nothing to think about?" The modern education system has sought to shoulder the burden of "teaching students how to think," often elevating such a subjective goal to status superior to teaching facts and sharing insights about past generations. In short, they focus more on method and process than what students actually learn.

Some students graduate from American high schools ignorant of when the Civil War occurred or the difference between the Preamble and the Constitution and Das Kapital. Reading and digesting the thoughts of the past is as essential as learning the rules of grammar so as to intelligently violate them. In light of today's high illiteracy rate, society's problems hardly include too many people being "bookworms" or attempting to follow the doctrines of Plato or John Locke or Mahatma Gandhi.

We as Americans share a heritage of ideas. Common assumptions must be examined so that we understand where such "conventional wisdom" came from, for it is only then that we may change the portions of it which may be unjust or clouded by bias. Certainly great books should not be locked away, immune from criticism. Neither, however, should they be lambasted out of visceral ignorance, in the name of "individuality."

Studying and learning from the works of the past, and creating new original writing and thought in the present are not mutually exclusive propositions. Most scholars lack Emerson's genius, but they will be hard-pressed to find a spark of creativity by meditating in the dark.

Emerson implies that ideas are not great in and of themselves. But ideas can be great. Proof resides in the overwhelming numbers of anonymous poems that fill anthology books. How many aphorisms are repeated daily by speakers who know not whether they generated from the tongue of Winston Churchill or Will Rogers? This is not to suggest that great ideas cannot be proved wrong. That Emerson denies perfection to any ideas is hardly a danger. Since no writer, however brilliant, is perfect, it is perfectly safe to acknowledge certain ideas as great, without granting them perfection and immunity.

When people do not know the past, they face the peril of perpetually re-inventing the wheel—blissfully ignorant of their tendency toward trite alliteration or insipid clichés.

Analysis of the High-Scoring Essay

This thorough, thoughtful, and well-written essay deserves a high score. It begins with the topic and promptly takes a relevant position on the issue of studying from books and ideas of the past. The writer shows a clear understanding of Emerson's ideas by examining and elaborating on the major points.

The writer then points out a major dilemma inherent in a facile acceptance of Emerson's ideas—that of dismissing the past and the wisdom that has come before.

The essay proceeds with a two-paragraph discussion of the state of education today, pointing out the dual needs of teaching both facts and the thinking process. These paragraphs are particularly relevant to the topic, and the examples are presented with insight. The writer also acknowledges our American heritage and the necessity of using books to understand that heritage so that the country's great ideas are not hidden away. These paragraphs demonstrate a deep-thinking writer, one who is aware of the world and presents complex ideas with clarity and sophistication.

The next paragraph counters Emerson's position with optimism—the writer claims that we can have it all; we can learn from the past and still become clear, independent thinkers who create new ideas. The essay points out that great new ideas do exist and cites contemporary, anonymous poems as examples of these new ideas. The writer also acknowledges that ideas can be great while being imperfect and that such imperfection is no reason to dismiss them entirely.

The essay's brief conclusion reminds the reader that humans may be doomed to repeat their mistakes and to reinvent the wheel unless they learn from the great ideas of the past. Overall, this essay's points are valid. Without dismissing Emerson lightly, the student intelligently discusses his concepts.

Medium-Scoring Essay

The process of finding meaningful things in life is not always clear. It is not simple to discover what is true and what is just fancy rhetoric or skirting of the issues. Ralph Waldo Emerson, considered one of our best writers and speakers, gave a speech in Cambridge in 1837, where he talked about books and how they can help us to find the truth which we are seeking in our life.

Emerson said in his speech that books are noble and age-old scholars gave arrangement to the life they saw and organized it. Then they put it into the books that they wrote, and produced a new truth for people to refer to. But he also says that each new generation of Americans has to write their own books. They have to discover their own versions of the truth, and what that truth actually means to them.

He was right. He was also right when he said that we can't just go by what was said then, because the ones who wrote the books that fill our libraries were just young and naïve when they authored those books. How can we be sure they are right, just because they are old? Why are they elevated to the status of classics as if they are perfect?

He says you shouldn't spend all your time in the library, however, I know some people who do just this. The result is that instead of having their own ideas, they just listen to all the old ones, and their creativity is stifled.

I agree that it is more important to be a thinking man than one who just accepts everything. You need to have the freedom to have your own ideas, to let them flow without being influenced by principles and underlying ideas already presented in books. These ideas might be right, but if everyone only reads them without thinking for themselves, the country will be full of brainwashed people. They might be well educated, but what will be the price of that education?

He said that books can be best if they are used well, but among the worst of things if they are abused. What this actually encourages is for one to be intelligent about reading and not to believe everything that you read. Also, he says that we should not be bookworms, so caught up in the details of what people said in the past that we don't bother to think our own thoughts about the present or concerning issues of the future that are important to our society. This is the centerpiece of his speech. He means that books have a noble "theory." He also means that in practice we must live up to that theory. We must live up to that theory by not being blind or gullible. Instead, we must be Thinking Men and not thinkers only. He talked about how what we observe has to be filtered in to the truth by our own original ideas. We have to use books wisely, Emerson believed, and I agree wholeheartedly.

Analysis of the Medium-Scoring Essay

This essay would score at the low end of the medium range. It begins with a vague introduction that essentially restates a few points from Emerson's speech. The writer does not yet state a thesis or take a position.

The second paragraph continues this trend, merely paraphrasing Emerson's speech without thinking critically about those ideas. An essay that *only* paraphrases the passage will never score in the upper range.

Finally, the third paragraph presents an opinion and takes a position, although it is repetitively worded. The writer seems to have finally started thinking as he or she questions the validity of older books and the pedestal upon which the classics have been placed.

The fourth paragraph is probably the best in this essay and saves the score from sinking even lower. The writer uses personal experience as an example, citing other friends who have become "stifled" in their creativity by spending too much time in the library, consuming old books and old ideas without thinking while they read. The writer apparently understands the need for everyone to become an individual thinker, an analyzer of ideas.

However, the next paragraph reverts to simple paraphrasing. It offers no additional commentary and, therefore, falls flat.

The essay reaches an adequate conclusion, explaining the need to read wisely and not be gullible. Ultimately, the writer manages to insert enough of his or her own commentary about Emerson's concepts to salvage the score. However, this essay could be greatly improved by reducing the paraphrasing and including much more analysis and evidence. Remember that this topic specifically directs students to "use appropriate evidence" to develop the essay. This writer has barely accomplished that goal and, thus, the score suffers.

Answer Sheet for Practice Test 2

Remove this sheet and use it to mark your answers.
Answer sheets for "Section II: Essays" can be found at the end of the book.

Section I
Multiple-Choice Questions

First Passage

1 Ⓐ Ⓑ Ⓒ Ⓓ Ⓔ
2 Ⓐ Ⓑ Ⓒ Ⓓ Ⓔ
3 Ⓐ Ⓑ Ⓒ Ⓓ Ⓔ
4 Ⓐ Ⓑ Ⓒ Ⓓ Ⓔ
5 Ⓐ Ⓑ Ⓒ Ⓓ Ⓔ
6 Ⓐ Ⓑ Ⓒ Ⓓ Ⓔ
7 Ⓐ Ⓑ Ⓒ Ⓓ Ⓔ
8 Ⓐ Ⓑ Ⓒ Ⓓ Ⓔ
9 Ⓐ Ⓑ Ⓒ Ⓓ Ⓔ
10 Ⓐ Ⓑ Ⓒ Ⓓ Ⓔ
11 Ⓐ Ⓑ Ⓒ Ⓓ Ⓔ
12 Ⓐ Ⓑ Ⓒ Ⓓ Ⓔ
13 Ⓐ Ⓑ Ⓒ Ⓓ Ⓔ
14 Ⓐ Ⓑ Ⓒ Ⓓ Ⓔ

Second Passage

15 Ⓐ Ⓑ Ⓒ Ⓓ Ⓔ
16 Ⓐ Ⓑ Ⓒ Ⓓ Ⓔ
17 Ⓐ Ⓑ Ⓒ Ⓓ Ⓔ
18 Ⓐ Ⓑ Ⓒ Ⓓ Ⓔ
19 Ⓐ Ⓑ Ⓒ Ⓓ Ⓔ
20 Ⓐ Ⓑ Ⓒ Ⓓ Ⓔ
21 Ⓐ Ⓑ Ⓒ Ⓓ Ⓔ
22 Ⓐ Ⓑ Ⓒ Ⓓ Ⓔ
23 Ⓐ Ⓑ Ⓒ Ⓓ Ⓔ
24 Ⓐ Ⓑ Ⓒ Ⓓ Ⓔ
25 Ⓐ Ⓑ Ⓒ Ⓓ Ⓔ
26 Ⓐ Ⓑ Ⓒ Ⓓ Ⓔ

Third Passage

27 Ⓐ Ⓑ Ⓒ Ⓓ Ⓔ
28 Ⓐ Ⓑ Ⓒ Ⓓ Ⓔ
29 Ⓐ Ⓑ Ⓒ Ⓓ Ⓔ
30 Ⓐ Ⓑ Ⓒ Ⓓ Ⓔ
31 Ⓐ Ⓑ Ⓒ Ⓓ Ⓔ
32 Ⓐ Ⓑ Ⓒ Ⓓ Ⓔ
33 Ⓐ Ⓑ Ⓒ Ⓓ Ⓔ
34 Ⓐ Ⓑ Ⓒ Ⓓ Ⓔ
35 Ⓐ Ⓑ Ⓒ Ⓓ Ⓔ
36 Ⓐ Ⓑ Ⓒ Ⓓ Ⓔ
37 Ⓐ Ⓑ Ⓒ Ⓓ Ⓔ
38 Ⓐ Ⓑ Ⓒ Ⓓ Ⓔ
39 Ⓐ Ⓑ Ⓒ Ⓓ Ⓔ
40 Ⓐ Ⓑ Ⓒ Ⓓ Ⓔ
41 Ⓐ Ⓑ Ⓒ Ⓓ Ⓔ

Fourth Passage

42 Ⓐ Ⓑ Ⓒ Ⓓ Ⓔ
43 Ⓐ Ⓑ Ⓒ Ⓓ Ⓔ
44 Ⓐ Ⓑ Ⓒ Ⓓ Ⓔ
45 Ⓐ Ⓑ Ⓒ Ⓓ Ⓔ
46 Ⓐ Ⓑ Ⓒ Ⓓ Ⓔ
47 Ⓐ Ⓑ Ⓒ Ⓓ Ⓔ
48 Ⓐ Ⓑ Ⓒ Ⓓ Ⓔ
49 Ⓐ Ⓑ Ⓒ Ⓓ Ⓔ
50 Ⓐ Ⓑ Ⓒ Ⓓ Ⓔ
51 Ⓐ Ⓑ Ⓒ Ⓓ Ⓔ
52 Ⓐ Ⓑ Ⓒ Ⓓ Ⓔ
53 Ⓐ Ⓑ Ⓒ Ⓓ Ⓔ
54 Ⓐ Ⓑ Ⓒ Ⓓ Ⓔ
55 Ⓐ Ⓑ Ⓒ Ⓓ Ⓔ

CUT HERE

CUT HERE

Practice Test 2

Section I: Multiple-Choice Questions

Time: 60 minutes

55 questions

Directions: This section consists of selections from prose works and questions on their content, form, and style. Read each selection carefully. Choose the best answer of the five choices.

Questions 1–14. Read the following passage carefully before you begin to answer the questions.

First Passage

Here then was I (call me Mary Beton, Mary Seton, or Mary Carmichael or by any name you please—it is not a matter of any importance) sitting on the banks of a river a week or two ago in fine
(5) October weather, lost in thought. That collar I have spoken of, women and fiction, the need of coming to some conclusion on a subject that raises all sorts of prejudices and passions, bowed my head to the ground. To the right and left bushes of some sort,
(10) golden and crimson, glowed with the colour, even it seemed burnt with the heat, of fire. On the further bank the willows wept in perpetual lamentation, their hair about their shoulders. The river reflected whatever it chose of sky and bridge and burning
(15) tree, and when the undergraduate had oared his boat through the reflections they closed again, completely, as if he had never been. There one might have sat the clock round lost in thought. Thought—to call it by a prouder name than it
(20) deserved—had let its line down into the stream. It swayed, minute after minute, hither and thither among the reflections and weeds, letting the water lift it and sink it, until—you know the little tug— the sudden conglomeration of an idea at the end of
(25) one's line: and then the cautious hauling of it in, and the careful laying of it out? Alas, laid on the grass how small, how insignificant this thought of mine looked; the sort of fish that a good fisherman puts back into the water so that it may grow fatter
(30) and be one day worth cooking and eating. I will not trouble you with that thought now, though if you look carefully you may find it for yourselves. . . .

But however small it was, it had, nevertheless, the mysterious property of its kind—put back
(35) into the mind, it became at once very exciting and

important; and as it darted and sank, and flashed hither and thither, set up such a wash and tumult of ideas that it was impossible to sit still. It was thus that I found myself walking with extreme rapidity
(40) across a grass plot. Instantly a man's figure rose to intercept me. Nor did I at first understand that the gesticulations of a curious-looking object, in a cut-away coat and evening shirt, were aimed at me. His face expressed horror and indignation. Instinct
(45) rather than reason came to my help; he was a Beadle; I was a woman. This was the turf; there was the path. Only the Fellows and Scholars are allowed here; the gravel is the place for me. Such thoughts were the work of a moment. As I regained
(50) the path the arms of the Beadle sank, his face assumed its usual repose, and though turf is better walking than gravel, no very great harm was done. The only charge I could bring against the Fellows and Scholars of whatever the college might happen
(55) to be was that in protection of their turf, which has been rolled for 300 years in succession, they had sent my little fish into hiding.

What an idea it had been that had sent me so audaciously trespassing I could not now remember.
(60) The spirit of peace descended like a cloud from heaven, for if the spirit of peace dwells anywhere, it is in the courts and quadrangles of Oxbridge on a fine October morning. Strolling through those colleges past those ancient halls the roughness of the
(65) present seemed smoothed away; the body seemed contained in a miraculous glass cabinet through which no sound could penetrate, and the mind, freed from any contact with facts (unless one trespassed on the turf again), was at liberty to settle
(70) down upon whatever meditation was in harmony

GO ON TO THE NEXT PAGE

with the moment. As chance would have it, some stray memory of some old essay about revisiting Oxbridge in the long vacation brought Charles Lamb to mind. . . . Indeed, among all the dead . . . Lamb is (75) one of the most congenial. . . . For his essays are superior . . . because of that wild flash of imagination that lightning crack of genius in the middle of them which leaves them flawed and imperfect, but starred with poetry. . . . It then occurred to me that (80) the very manuscript itself which Lamb had looked at was only a few hundred yards away, so that one could follow Lamb's footsteps across the quadrangle to that famous library where the treasure is kept. Moreover, I recollected, as I put this plan into execu- (85) tion, it is in this famous library that the manuscript of Thackeray's *Esmond* is also preserved . . . but

here I was actually at the door which leads to the library itself. I must have opened it, for instantly there issued, like a guardian angel barring the way (90) with a flutter of black gown instead of white wings, a deprecating, silvery, kindly gentleman, who regretted in a low voice as he waved me back that ladies are only admitted to the library if accompanied by a Fellow of the College or furnished with a (95) letter of introduction.

That a famous library has been cursed by a woman is a matter of complete indifference to a famous library. Venerable and calm, with all its treasures safe locked within its breast, it sleeps forever. (100) Never will I wake those echoes, never will I ask for that hospitality again.

1. According to the passage, the narrator uses several names (lines 1–2) in order to

   A. make a universal statement about all humankind
   B. deemphasize her personal identity
   C. introduce her many pseudonyms as an author
   D. attempt to impress the reader with her literacy
   E. mask her true identity from the reader

2. The literary device used to describe the speaker's thought "Thought . . . eating" (lines 19–30) is

   A. a simile
   B. a metaphor
   C. personification
   D. an apostrophe
   E. hyperbole

3. In the phrase "you know the little tug" (line 23), the speaker abstractly refers to

   A. a fish's pull on a fishing line
   B. the Beadle's insisting she move off the lawn
   C. the annoying loss of a thought
   D. the sudden awareness of an idea
   E. the pull of her guilty conscience

4. The effect that the Beadle has on the narrator is to

   A. encourage her pursuit of knowledge
   B. cause her thoughts to retreat
   C. assure her of correct directions
   D. condemn the women's movement
   E. inquire if she needs additional assistance

5. It can be inferred that the narrator realizes that she cannot remember her thought because

   A. it passes so quickly
   B. the student rowing by interrupts it
   C. it is not important enough
   D. it does not compare to a great author's ideas
   E. it is so carefully and slowly thought out

6. The lawn and library serve the purpose of

   A. symbolizing the obstacles that women face
   B. reminding readers of the rigors of university study
   C. contrasting relaxation with research
   D. introducing the existence of equality for women
   E. minimizing the author's point about women's roles

7. The passage contains all of the following rhetorical devices EXCEPT

   A. personification
   B. metaphor
   C. simile
   D. literary allusion
   E. allegory

8. The speaker's purpose in the passage is to

   A. explain her anger at the Beadle
   B. personify nature's splendor
   C. illustrate how men can inhibit women's intellectual pursuits
   D. recall the enticing glory of university study
   E. preach her beliefs about women's roles in society

9. The organization of the passage could be best characterized as

   A. stream of consciousness mixed with narration of specific events
   B. comparison and contrast of two incidents
   C. exposition of the women's movement and the author's opinions
   D. description of both external reality and the author's thoughts
   E. flowing smoothly from general ideas to specific statements

10. The pacing of the sentence "But however small it was . . . it was impossible to sit still" (lines 33–38)

    A. reflects the acceleration of her thoughts
    B. represents a continuation of the pace of the description of the river
    C. contrasts with the fish metaphor
    D. suggests a sluggishness before the Beadle's interruption
    E. parallels that of the description of the library doorman

11. The speaker's description of the Beadle and the library doorman serves to

    A. confirm the horror of what she has done
    B. frighten women away from universities
    C. encourage women to rebel against men
    D. contrast the men's manners
    E. satirize the petty men who enforce the rules

12. The phrase "for instantly there issued . . . waved me back" (lines 88–92) can best be characterized as containing

    A. obvious confusion from the doorman
    B. metaphorical reference to a jailer
    C. awed wonder at the man's position
    D. humorous yet realistic description
    E. matter-of-fact narration

13. At the time of the occurrences she describes, the speaker probably felt all of the following EXCEPT

    A. indignation
    B. bewilderment
    C. delight
    D. exasperation
    E. repression

14. The pattern of the passage can best be described as

    A. alternating between a description of external reality and internal commentary
    B. the presentation of a social problem followed by its resolution
    C. general statements followed by illustrative detail
    D. presentation of theory followed by exceptions to that theory
    E. comparison and contrast of great authors' ideas

GO ON TO THE NEXT PAGE

Practice Test 2

Questions 15–26. Read the following passage carefully before you begin to answer the questions.

Second Passage

[Alexander Pope] professed to have learned his poetry from Dryden, whom, whenever an opportunity was presented, he praised through his whole life with unvaried liberality; and perhaps his character

(5) may receive some illustration if he be compared with his master.

Integrity of understanding and nicety of discernment were not allotted in a less proportion to Dryden than to Pope. The rectitude of Dryden's

(10) mind was sufficiently shown by the dismission of his poetical prejudices, and then rejection of unnatural thoughts and rugged numbers. But Dryden never desired to apply all the judgment that he had. He wrote, and professed to write, merely for the

(15) people, and when he pleased others, he contented himself. He spent no time in struggles to rouse latent powers; he never attempted to make that better which was already good, nor often to mend what he must have known to be faulty. He wrote, as he tells

(20) us, with very little consideration; when occasion or necessity called upon him, he poured out what the present moment happened to supply, and, when once it had passed the press, ejected it from his mind: for when he had no pecuniary interest, he had no further

(25) solicitude.

Pope was not content to satisfy; he desired to excel, and therefore always endeavored to do his best: he did not court the candor, but dared the judgment of his reader, and, expecting no indulgence from

(30) others, he showed none to himself. He examined lines and words with minute and punctilious observation, and retouched every part with indefatigable diligence, till he had left nothing to be forgiven. . . .

His declaration that his care for his works

(35) ceased at their publication was not strictly true. His parental attention never abandoned them; what he found amiss in the first edition, he silently corrected in those that followed. He appears to have revised the *Iliad,* and freed it from some of its im-

(40) perfections, and the *Essay on Criticism* received many improvements after its first appearance. It will seldom be found that he altered without adding clearness, elegance, or vigor. Pope had perhaps the judgment of Dryden; but Dryden certainly wanted

(45) the diligence of Pope.

In acquired knowledge, the superiority must be allowed to Dryden, whose education was more scholastic, and who before he became an author had been allowed more time for study, with better

(50) means of information. His mind has a larger range, and he collects his images and illustrations from a more extensive circumference of science. Dryden knew more of man in his general nature, and Pope in his local manners. The notions of Dryden were

(55) formed by comprehensive speculation, and those of Pope by minute attention. There is more dignity in the knowledge of Dryden, and more certainty in that of Pope.

Poetry was not the sole praise of either; for both

(60) excelled likewise in prose; but Pope did not borrow his prose from his predecessor. The style of Dryden is capricious and varied; that of Pope is cautious and uniform. Dryden obeys the motions of his own mind; Pope constrains his mind to his own rules of

(65) composition. Dryden is sometimes vehement and rapid; Pope is always smooth, uniform, and gentle. Dryden's page is a natural field, rising into inequalities, and diversified by the varied exuberance of abundant vegetation; Pope's is a velvet lawn, shaven

(70) by the scythe, and leveled by the roller.

Of genius, that power which constitutes a poet; that quality without which judgment is cold, and knowledge is inert, that energy which collects, combines, amplifies, and animates; the superiority

(75) must, with some hesitation, be allowed to Dryden. It is not to be inferred that of this poetical vigor Pope had only a little, because Dryden had more; for every other writer since Milton must give place to Pope; and even of Dryden it must be said, that, if

(80) he has brighter paragraphs, he has not better poems. Dryden's performances were always hasty, either excited by some external occasion, or extorted by domestic necessity; he composed without consideration, and published without correction. What his

(85) mind could supply at call, or gather in one excursion, was all that he sought, and all that he gave. The dilatory caution of Pope enabled him to condense his sentiments, to multiply his images, and to accumulate all that study might produce or chance

(90) might supply. If the flights of Dryden therefore are higher, Pope continues longer on the wing. If of Dryden's fire the blaze is brighter, of Pope's the heat is more regular and constant. Dryden often surpasses expectation, and Pope never falls below

(95) it. Dryden is read with frequent astonishment, and Pope with perpetual delight.

15. The essay's organization could best be described as

    A.   exposition of a thesis followed by illustrations

    B.   chronological presentation of each author's works

    C.   presenting ideas based on their order of importance

    D.   basing each paragraph on a different argument

    E.   comparison of and contrast between the two writers

16. In context, "candor" (line 28) can be interpreted to mean

    A.   kindness

    B.   criticism

    C.   excellence

    D.   sincerity

    E.   indifference

17. In each of the following pairs of words, the first refers to Dryden, the second to Pope. Which pair best describes their prose style?

    A.   dignified vs. simplistic

    B.   passionate vs. lyrical

    C.   unsystematic vs. harmonious

    D.   punctilious vs. careless

    E.   pedantic vs. impetuous

18. Which of the following best describes Pope's attitude toward his own writing?

    A.   "[he] dared the judgment of his reader" (lines 28–29)

    B.   "His parental attention never abandoned them" (lines 35–36)

    C.   "It will seldom be found that he altered without adding clearness" (lines 41–43)

    D.   "Pope is cautious and uniform" (lines 62–63)

    E.   "Pope continues longer on the wing" (line 91)

19. The passage's points could be more convincing if the writer were to offer

    A.   less emphasis on Pope's writing and editing diligence

    B.   more direct language to present his ideas about the authors

    C.   more discussion of Dryden's editing theories

    D.   more point-by-point comparisons of each author's prose

    E.   specific examples from each poet's work to support his opinions

20. Which of the following is NOT found in the essay?

    A.   For Pope, good writing meant rewriting.

    B.   Both authors were productive.

    C.   Dryden is the superior prose writer.

    D.   Dryden follows his own mind more than Pope does.

    E.   Pope's writing is like a manicured lawn.

21. Which of the following best characterizes Dryden's method of writing?

    A.   "he never attempted to make that better that which was already good" (lines 17–18)

    B.   "he poured out what the present moment happened to supply" (lines 21–22)

    C.   "when he had no pecuniary interest, he had no further solicitude" (lines 24–25)

    D.   "His mind has a larger range" (line 50)

    E.   "the superiority must, with some hesitation, be allowed to Dryden" (lines 74–75)

22. Although Pope did not have as strong a scholastic background as did Dryden, the writer implies that Pope

    A.   chose subjects unrelated to Dryden's

    B.   had great familiarity with his subject matter

    C.   feigned completing university study

    D.   compensated by emulating Dryden

    E.   undermined any effort on his behalf

Practice Test 2

GO ON TO THE NEXT PAGE

23. According to the passage, genius can invigorate which of the following in an author?

    I.   judgment
    II. knowledge
    III. power

    A. I only
    B. III only
    C. I and II only
    D. II and III only
    E. I, II, and III

24. What does the speaker suggest as the main reason that Dryden's writing style labels him as genius?

    A. the apparent effortlessness of his writing
    B. the fact that he "continues longer on the wing" (line 91)
    C. the fact that his prose is a "natural field" (line 67)
    D. the fact that his academic studies prepare him so well
    E. the fact that the age he lived in was noted for intelligence

25. In lines 67–70 ("Dryden's page . . . roller"), which of the following literary devices is used to summarize the differences between Dryden's and Pope's prose?

    A. syllogism
    B. personification
    C. understatement
    D. metaphor
    E. simile

26. Of the following, which is NOT a major distinction the speaker draws between Dryden and Pope?

    A. their educational foundation
    B. their prose style
    C. their skill in writing
    D. their vigor in writing
    E. their editing practice

Questions 27–41. Read the following passage carefully before you begin to answer the questions.

Third Passage

It is remarkable that there is little or nothing to be remembered written on the subject of getting a living; how to make getting a living not merely honest and honorable, but altogether inviting and (5) glorious; for if *getting* a living is not so, then living is not. One would think, from looking at literature, that this question had never disturbed a solitary individual's musings. Is it that men are too much disgusted with their experience to speak of it? The (10) lesson of value which money teaches, which the Author of the Universe has taken so much pains to teach us, we are inclined to skip altogether. As for the means of living, it is wonderful how indifferent men of all classes are about it, even reformers, so (15) called,—whether they inherit, or earn, or steal it. I think that Society has done nothing for us in this respect, or at least has undone what she has done. Cold and hunger seem more friendly to my nature than those methods which men have adopted and (20) advise to ward them off.

The title *wise* is, for the most part, falsely applied. How can one be a wise man, if he does not know any better how to live than other men?—if he is only more cunning and intellectually subtle? (25) Does Wisdom work in a tread-mill? or does she teach how to succeed *by her example*? Is there any such thing as wisdom not applied to life? Is she merely the miller who grinds the finest logic? Is it pertinent to ask if Plato got his *living* in a better way (30) or more successfully than his contemporaries,—or did he succumb to the difficulties of life like other men? Did he seem to prevail over some of them merely by indifference, or by assuming grand airs? Or find it easier to live, because his aunt remem- (35) bers him in her will? The ways in which most men get their living, that is, live, are mere makeshifts, and a shirking of the real business of life,—chiefly because they do not know, but partly because they do not mean, any better.

(40) The rush to California, for instance, and the attitude, not merely of merchants, but of philosophers and prophets, so called, in relation to it, reflect the greatest disgrace on mankind. That so many are ready to live by luck, and so get the means of com- (45) manding the labor of others less lucky, without contributing any value to society! And that is called enterprise! I know of no more startling development of the immorality of trade, and all the common modes of getting a living. The philosophy and poetry (50) and religion of such a mankind are not worth the dust of a puffball. The hog that gets his living by rooting, stirring up the soil so, would be ashamed of such company. If I could command the wealth of all the world by lifting my finger, I would not pay *such* (55) a price for it. Even Mahomet knew that God did not make this world in jest. It makes God to be a moneyed gentleman who scatters a handful of pennies in order to see mankind scramble for them. The world's raffle! A subsistence in the domains of (60) Nature a thing to be raffled for! What a comment, what a satire, on our institutions! The conclusion will be, that mankind will hang itself upon a tree. And have all the precepts in all the Bibles taught men only this? And is the last and most admirable (65) invention of the human race only an improved muck-rake? Is this the ground on which Orientals and Occidentals meet? Did God direct us so to get our living, digging where we never planted,—and He would, perchance, reward us with lumps of gold?

(70) God gave the righteous man a certificate entitling him to food and raiment, but the unrighteous man found a *facsimile* of the same in God's coffers, and appropriated it, and obtained food and raiment like the former. It is one of the most extensive systems of (75) counterfeiting that the world has ever seen. I did not know that mankind was suffering for want of gold. I have seen a little of it. I know that it is very malleable, but not so malleable as wit. A grain of gold will gild a great surface, but not so much as a grain (80) of wisdom.

The gold-digger in the ravines of the mountains is as much a gambler as his fellow in the saloons of San Francisco. What difference does it make whether you shake dirt or shake dice? If you win, (85) society is the loser. The gold-digger is the enemy of the honest laborer, whatever checks and compensations there may be. It is not enough to tell me that you worked hard to get your gold. So does the Devil work hard. The way of transgressors may be (90) hard in many respects. The humblest observer who goes to the mines sees and says that gold-digging is of the character of a lottery; the gold thus obtained is not the same thing with the wages of honest toil. But, practically, he forgets what he has seen, for he (95) sees only the fact, not the principle, and goes into trade there, that is, buys a ticket in what commonly proves another lottery, where the fact is not so obvious.

GO ON TO THE NEXT PAGE

27. The speaker believes that "getting a living" must be both

    A. moral and pious
    B. ethical and admirable
    C. accessible and sensible
    D. desirable and attainable
    E. humble and profitable

28. According to the speaker, although man must earn money, he is indifferent to

    A. religion
    B. society
    C. cold and hunger
    D. lessons of value
    E. laborers

29. The speaker asserts that

    A. we have forgotten the proper value of money
    B. good, hard work will save mankind
    C. the world operates solely on luck
    D. religion fails to address the merit of labor
    E. gold-digging is acceptable under certain conditions

30. The "Author of the Universe" (line 11) can be interpreted as a

    A. symbol for cosmic consciousness
    B. metaphor for a contemporary writer
    C. symbol for judgment
    D. metaphor for all artists
    E. metaphor for God

31. The speaker's rhetorical purpose in referring to Plato is to

    A. make the point about gold-digging more universal and timeless
    B. qualify the assertions about gold-diggers and their luck
    C. question whether ancient philosophers faced the same dilemmas that others do
    D. consider the ancient philosopher's premises about morality in society
    E. create an authoritative tone to lend credence to the argument

32. What is the antecedent for "it" (line 55)?

    A. "immorality" (line 48)
    B. "philosophy" (line 49)
    C. "hog" (line 51)
    D. "wealth" (line 53)
    E. "world" (line 54)

33. Which of the following is the best example of aphorism?

    A. "The ways in which most men . . . any better." (lines 35–39)
    B. "Nature a thing to be raffled for!" (line 60)
    C. "A grain of gold . . . a grain of wisdom." (lines 78–80)
    D. "What difference does it make . . . shake dice?" (lines 83–84)
    E. "So does the Devil work hard." (lines 88–89)

34. An unstated assumption of the speaker is that

    A. philosophers should work harder to apply their teachings
    B. a pig would be mortified by some men
    C. society is gradually improving
    D. true wisdom comes only though hard work
    E. what appears honest to one can be harmful to society

35. The author's comments about the California gold rush serve the purpose of

    A. comparing gold-diggers to the ancient Greeks
    B. illustrating how immorally men are earning a living
    C. explaining the relationship of Orientals to Occidentals
    D. sensationalizing a topical and popular occupation
    E. criticizing those who think gold-digging is romantic

36. Which of the following negative phrases is, in context, a qualified negative?

    A. "men are . . . disgusted with their experience" (lines 8–9)

    B. "Cold and hunger" (line 18)

    C. "the greatest disgrace on mankind" (lines 42–43)

    D. "the unrighteous man" (line 71)

    E. "society is the loser" (line 85)

37. The essay contains all of the following rhetorical devices EXCEPT

    A. simile

    B. historical allusion

    C. rhetorical question

    D. syllogistic reasoning

    E. religious reference

38. The sentence "A grain of gold . . . a grain of wisdom" (lines 78–80) can best be restated as

    A. knowledge is more valuable than gold

    B. gold-diggers must work harder than philosophers

    C. gold will last longer than knowledge

    D. erudition takes longer to achieve than money

    E. money has no practical purpose

39. The tone of the essay can best be described as

    A. condescending

    B. skeptical

    C. worrisome

    D. indignant

    E. pedestrian

40. Which of the following is NOT part of the speaker's argument against gold-digging?

    A. "The hog . . . would be ashamed of such company." (lines 51–53)

    B. "digging where we never planted" (line 68)

    C. "I know that it is very malleable" (lines 77–78)

    D. "the enemy of the honest laborer" (lines 85–86)

    E. "of the character of a lottery" (line 92)

41. Which of the following is NOT discussed in the passage?

    A. Man can learn to improve his lot in life.

    B. Authors have not addressed "getting a living."

    C. Gamblers have damaged society.

    D. The title "wise" may be misapplied.

    E. Men are too easily lured by monetary rewards.

GO ON TO THE NEXT PAGE

Questions 42–55. Read the following passage carefully before you begin to answer the questions.

Fourth Passage

This excerpt describes a daring and dangerous long-distance flight by Igor Sikorsky in his new flying machine, the Il'ya Muromets. *This gigantic 4-engine biplane was emblematic of the opulence and contradictions of Imperial Russia at the zenith of its power and glory. The* Muromets' *appointments bespoke luxury, yet her aerodynamics were of the most primitive order. She boasted unprecedented size and payload, yet she was severely under-powered. After only a few test flights, Sikorsky's confidence and patriotic courage overcame his doubts and the risky flight took off at 1:00 a.m. on June 30, 1914.*

Sikorsky determined to fly from St. Petersburg to Kiev, the city of his birth, a distance of 1,200 kilometers. . . . The heavily loaded plane staggered along at about 400 feet of altitude. Then, disaster

(5) struck. The right inboard engine fractured a fuel line, and the exhaust immediately ignited it, triggering a blowtorch of flame jetting back 12 feet behind the engine, playing on the wing surface and wing struts.[1] Without hesitation pilot-navigator

(10) Lieutenant Lavrov and mechanic Vladimir Panasiuk went out on the wing; the quick-thinking Lavrov leaned over the roaring jet of flame, reached down, and closed a fuel valve, shutting off the flow. Then the two men, using their greatcoats,

(15) smothered the flame.

After conferring with the crew, Sikorsky decided to climb. . . . Just above 5,000 feet they broke out into the clear, into a brilliant blue sky above the puffy, white, sunlit clouds. It was a Jules Verne mo-

(20) ment, one that Sikorsky must have recognized and desired ever since as a child he had avidly read *Robur-le-conquérant* with its imaginary open-air promenade above the clouds. Sikorsky turned the plane over to Prussis, had a cup of coffee, put on

(25) his greatcoat, and then stepped out on the upper bridge, keeping his position by holding the rails. "Only a few times in my life have I seen such a majestic and beautiful spectacle as I did then," he recalled later. "Our ship was gliding along a few

(30) hundred feet above a sparkling white surface. The air was calm and the plane seemed motionless with its huge yellow wings. . . . All around me there was a fairyland, formed by clouds."[2]

Cold finally forced Sikorsky indoors, where he

(35) rested in his cabin. Two hours later, when it was time to descend into Kiev, Sikorsky took over, and the plane plunged into a gloomy, dark, and turbulent world of clouds . . . it began to thin and finally,

at about 900 feet, they broke out, and there, dead

(40) ahead, miraculously, were the domes of Kiev's famed cathedral. Sikorsky throttled the four faithful Argus engines back and set up a straight-in gliding approach, landing on the muddy field without further ado, tired and worn, but understandably

(45) jubilant at having proven the practicality of the long-range airplane. . . . Only one dignitary, the secretary of the Kiev Aeronautical Society, was there to greet them. He did not offer the reception they might have expected; after only the briefest of

(50) perfunctory congratulations, he told them the latest news: the archduke Franz Ferdinand and his wife had been assassinated by Serbian terrorists in the little Balkan city of Sarajevo.[3] An extraordinary lack of security that lead to a near-fatal bombing

(55) earlier in the day; the inexplicable (and suspicious) misdirection of the motorcade off Appel Quay, requiring it to reverse course so that the archduke's car halted directly in front of Gavrilo Princip; the assassin himself—a trained, fanatical 19-year-old

(60) Bosnian Serb gunman, "tiresome, ego, mare eyed, consumptive looking"[4]—all this culminated in two well-aimed shots from Princip's Browning pistol that irretrievably shattered and reshaped not only European life but the entire course of subsequent

(65) world history.[5]

The airplane—the "annihilator of time and space," the embodiment of speed, even more than the locomotive—promised to create a world of convenient travel. Thus Sikorsky's flight from

(70) St. Petersburg to Kiev had an innocence about it that captured at once the romance, the hope, and—yes—the naiveté of early flying. A young man reveling in his creation, he stood outside as his machine droned along above the clouds, drinking

(75) in the bright sky and sun, living in the fictional adventures of his childhood, seeing the beauty of the cavernous vista around him, and like the world he was in, not thinking of the dark, turbulent storm hidden within all that beauty. Fellow aviators gen-

(80) erally behaved the same. They flew in competitions, crossed frontiers, admired the vistas, flung their aircraft about with increasing abandon, seemingly oblivious that soon they would participate in a far more deadly international competition, cross-

(85) ing into each other's frontiers, observing troop movements below, and flinging their aircraft about in desperate attempts to evade or destroy.

[1] Sikorsky, Winged-S, 108. Finne, Sikorsky: The Russian Years, 49, asserts that it was the left inboard engine that fractured its fuel line and caught fire, but I have relied on Sikorsky's own account, which states that it was the right inboard engine.

[2] Ibid., 113

[3] Ibid., 115.

[4] British minister of trade Alan Clark's evocative reflection upon seeing a photograph of the young assassin in the Princip museum, Sarajevo, in October 1986. He added, "Something between Seventies CND and Baader-Meinhof." CND refers to leftist anti-nuclear Campaign for Nuclear Disarmament, and Baader-Meinhof is a reference to one of the more murderous leftist terrorist organizations of the late Cold War. Alan Clark, Diaries (London: Phoenix, 1993), 146.

[5] There is an excellent summary of the events leading to assassination in Edward Crankshaw's The Fall of the House of Hapsburg (New York: Popular Library, 1963 ed.), 402–406. Earlier in the day, Franz Ferdinand himself had to deflect a potentially fatal hand grenade hurled at his car; enormously (if foolishly) brave, he pressed on with the visit, and was in the second car of the motorcade, which was forced to halt and back up when the mayor's car made a wrong right-hand turn. "Security precautions," Crankshaw has rightly concluded, "were practically nil" (403).

42. Considering the passage as a whole, one can conclude that early aviation

A. was a moderately successful means of mass transportation
B. was rarely successful until the impetus of World War I
C. was very dangerous but worth the effort
D. was never pleasurable for the pioneers of early flight
E. usually ended in disaster that was unavoidable

43. The effect of the short, three-word sentence in lines 4–5 is to

A. modify details in the preceding sentences
B. sound like a direct quote from Sikorsky
C. paraphrase a famous quotation from an earlier work
D. diminish the speaker's surprise
E. add emphasis to the stark reality of the near-catastrophe

44. The description of the actions of the Lavrov and Panasiuk in lines 9–15 implies that the speaker believes that Lavrov and Panasiuk

A. were the only members of the crew who were brave enough to act decisively
B. took an unnecessary chance
C. should not have acted without orders
D. did not follow proper procedures
E. prove, through their own actions, the value of quick and effective action, even at the risk of one's own life

45. The speaker's reference to Jules Verne serves the rhetorical purpose of

A. establishing that, only a few years before this extraordinary flight, the very idea that man could fly was science-fiction
B. establishing that Sikorsky was a Jules Verne fan who lived in a fantasy world
C. suggesting that the speaker shares Sikorsky's fascination with Jules Verne
D. paying homage to the legions of Jules Verne fans
E. showing that aviation had not really advanced since Sikorsky was a child

46. The intended rhetorical effect of the quotation from Sikorsky in lines 27–33 is

A. to describe the view with strong imagery
B. to allow the reader to appreciate the excellent weather
C. to explain exactly how high over the clouds the aircraft is flying
D. to emphasize that this fantastic spectacle is unprecedented in human history
E. to show how the speaker feels the need to use direct quotes in his writing

47. An unstated rhetorical purpose for the speaker's use of the word "faithful" in referring to the aircraft's four engines in lines 41–42 is most likely

A. to refer to Sikorsky's religious faith
B. to allude to the great cathedral in Kiev
C. to chronicle the "four faithful" Russian Orthodox Saints
D. to create the image of the engines as living beings and as obedient servants
E. to acknowledge the name of the engine manufacturer

GO ON TO THE NEXT PAGE

131

48. Following Alan Clark's quote (lines 60–61), the speaker's rhetorical purpose in adding note #4 is to

    A. reinforce the physical description of Princip through comparisons to later terrorists

    B. provide a first-hand description of the Princip Museum in Kiev

    C. provide concrete documentation of Sikorsky's log of the flight

    D. provide a contrasting perspective of the motives of Gavrilo Princip and other terrorists

    E. reference an excellent summary of the events leading to the assassination

49. The image of Sikorsky standing outside his aircraft "drinking in the bright sun and sky . . . living in fiction . . . seeing the beauty . . . [but] not thinking of the dark turbulent storm hidden within all that beauty" (lines 74–79) is a metaphor for

    A. the bad weather below, where they must eventually return to Earth

    B. the coming Great War, in which the opening shots had already been fired

    C. Sikorsky's as-yet-unacknowledged loss of faith in his own creation

    D. the symbolic return to the homeland that all adventurers must make

    E. Sikorsky turning his back on the "old world"

50. The phrase that most clearly identifies the speaker's intended metaphorical impression of Sikorsky's successful flight is

    A. "The airplane—the 'annihilator of time and space'" (lines 66–67)

    B. "Sikorsky's flight . . . had an innocence about it that captured . . . the naiveté of early flying" (lines 69–72)

    C. "A young man reveling in his creation" (lines 72–73)

    D. ". . . living in the fictional adventures of his childhood" (lines 75–76)

    E. ". . . the dark turbulent storm hidden within all that beauty" (lines 78–79)

51. The passage contains all of the following literary devices EXCEPT

    A. character development

    B. literary allusions

    C. vivid descriptions of action

    D. primary-source quotations

    E. metaphorical allusions

52. The following phrases all refer to the inadequate security precautions for Franz Ferdinand EXCEPT

    A. "An extraordinary lack of security" (lines 53–54)

    B. "the inexplicable (and suspicious) misdirection of the motorcade" (lines 55–56).

    C. "the archduke's car halted directly in front of Gavrilo Princip" (lines 57–58)

    D. "Tiresome, ego, mare eyed, consumptive looking" (lines 60–61)

    E. "'Security precautions,' Crankshaw has rightfully concluded, 'were practically nil.'" (note #5)

53. Considering the information in note #1, one can infer that the speaker

    A. concludes that it was really the *left inboard* engine that caught on fire

    B. concludes that it was really the *right outboard* engine that caught fire

    C. has meticulously researched his subject; he relies on Sikorsky's own account, which contradicts Finne's conclusion

    D. relies on the information in a book by Finne, *Sikorsky: The Russian Years*

    E. has trouble deciding the facts, because he is confronted with differing historical narratives

54. One can gather all of the following facts or inferences from note #5 EXCEPT

    A. Another assassination attempt occurred earlier that same day.

    B. Franz Ferdinand himself repelled a hand grenade, but he pressed on with the visit.

    C. A wrong turn by the mayor's car may have contributed to the assassination.

    D. Franz Ferdinand's bravado in the face of danger may have contributed to his own assassination.

    E. Security precautions in Sarajevo were particularly stringent that day.

55. Considering the passage as a whole, the speaker's primary rhetorical purpose is to

    A. establish a strong argument against manned flight

    B. juxtapose the danger and excitement of a history-making flight with a simultaneous history-changing event in Sarajevo

    C. establish the speaker's condescending attitude toward the early aviation pioneers

    D. criticize the negligent security surrounding Archduke Ferdinand

    E. explain the intricacies of aircraft maneuverability

IF YOU FINISH BEFORE TIME IS CALLED, CHECK YOUR WORK ON THIS SECTION ONLY. DO NOT WORK ON ANY OTHER SECTION IN THE TEST.

Section II: Essay Questions

Time: 2 hours, 15 minutes

3 questions

Question 1

(Reading time—15 minutes. Suggested writing time—40 minutes. This question counts one-third of the total essay section score.)

Directions: The prompt that follows is based on six accompanying sources. This essay requires you to integrate a variety of sources into a coherent, well-written essay. Refer to the sources, both directly and indirectly, to support your position. Avoid mere paraphrasing or summarizing. Your argument should be the central focus; the use of the sources should support your argument.

Introduction

The National Endowment for the Arts is an independent federal agency that has been awarding grants to contemporary visual and performing artists since 1965. This grant money comes from American taxpayers. Much of the visual art that is funded by federal grants has been labeled controversial. Should such controversy continue being funded by unsure taxpayers? How does society today look at art as a contribution to American culture and how does it affect the public's view of the spending habits of the United States government?

Assignment

Read the following sources (including any introductory information) carefully. **Then, in an essay that synthesizes at least three of the sources for support, take a position that defends, challenges, or qualifies the claim that the United States government should continue to award grants to artists through the National Endowment for the Arts.**

Refer the sources as Source A, Source B, etc.; authors' names are included for your convenience.

Source A (Brooks)

Source B (Cole)

Source C (Parachini)

Source D (Parachini)

Source E (*Los Angeles Times*)

Source F (National Endowment for the Arts)

Source A

Brooks, Arthur C. "Do Public Subsidies Leverage Private Philanthropy for the Arts?" Nonprofit and Voluntary Sector Quarterly, 1999 28: 32–45.

The following passage is excerpted from an article about the relationship between government funding and private donations to the arts.

The idea that private philanthropy depends positively on public subsidies has commonly been heard of late in the debate over the need for government participation in the provision of the arts in the United States. According to the American Arts Alliance (1995), "Last year [1994], $123 million in [National Endowment for the Arts (NEA)] grants leveraged more than $1.3 billion." This statement imputes causality to the NEA grants: They were in some way responsible for the generation of more than 10 times as much in non-NEA donations.

This argument relies principally on the assumption that donors respond to the added incentives that matching funds from government grants provide: Because NEA dollars require at least equal matching from other sources, these dollars must have elicited at least that amount in donations from the private sector. Other explanations are also commonly heard as to why there should be a positive relationship between public funding and private philanthropy. For example, it has been argued that grants from the government to an organization can bring that organization to the attention of private donors as the object of support. Similarly, being a recipient of government funding requires a certain level of financial accountability and responsibility, which private donors find attractive.

Is it reasonable to claim that government funding to the arts will have this leveraging effect? Some might say not and make the argument that just the opposite effect should obtain: Public funds should tend to "crowd out" private donations, so private donations are likely made in spite of the NEA subsidies rather than because of them. There are three general reasons why this crowding out might occur.

First, the sense of responsibility and public enthusiasm to support a social cause might be diminished if the government takes responsibility for its funding.

Second, subsidies to arts firms may indeed be a signal of quality but not good quality: They might appear to be a bailout of arts firms in dire straits. Although this may attract some donors, others may be driven away by the prospect of a failed project.

Finally, to the extent that higher government subsidies are paid for with higher taxes, individuals have less disposable income and hence do not donate as much as they otherwise might. This is probably insignificant in the United States, where tax revenues (at all levels of government) allocated to the arts in 1987 amounted to just $3.30 per person.

GO ON TO THE NEXT PAGE

Source B

Cole, David. "The Culture War; When the Government Is a Critic." *Los Angeles Times,* 3 Oct. 1999, home ed.: pg. 1.

The following article discusses the government's role in funding controversial art.

New York City Mayor Rudolph W. Giuliani, who threatened in true New York fashion to bring the Brooklyn Museum to its knees if it went ahead with an art exhibition that he finds "sick," is only the latest in a none-too-distinguished line of government officials who decide to become art critics. The mayor's most prominent precursor is Sen. Jesse Helms (R-N.C.), who, in 1989, objected vociferously to federal funding of a Robert Mapplethorpe exhibition on the ground that it was homoerotic, thereby launching a decade-long cultural battle over the National Endowment for the Arts. Five years earlier, Rep. Mario Biaggi of New York objected to NEA funding of a Metropolitan Opera production of Verdi's "Rigoletto," which he considered denigrating to Italians. Long before that, there was the Inquisition, which tried the painter Paolo Veronese in 1573 for his allegedly sacrilegious depiction of the Last Supper.

This cast of characters should be enough to illustrate why we need to limit government officials' ability to mandate "politically correct" art. Giuliani's heavy-handed tactics underscore the point. His objection apparently focuses on a single painting in a Brooklyn Museum exhibit that opened yesterday, Chris Ofili's "Holy Virgin Mary," a representation of the Virgin Mary with elephant dung on her breast. The mayor objects that the painting is anti-Catholic, which it may or may not be. (Ofili is himself a Catholic who attends church.) When ordinary people decide they don't like such a painting, they generally stay away or turn away. But that's not enough for the mayor. He dislikes this painting so much he doesn't want anyone else to see it.

In light of the prevalence of government subsidies, if the state were free to deny funds to those whose speech it finds disagreeable, freedom of expression would be rendered meaningless. The postmaster could deny subsidies to newspapers that criticized the president. Broadcast stations could be put off the air, nonprofit groups denied their tax exemptions and university faculty fired for expressing controversial views.

This is not a hypothetical concern. Such arguments were widely advanced in the 1950s and 1960s to justify legislative efforts to exclude suspected communists from public universities. The Supreme Court, however, ruled that such claims could not be squared with the principle of academic freedom protected by the 1st Amendment. As a result, even though no professor has a right to be on the government payroll, the court struck down as unconstitutional efforts to deny jobs to those who declined to take an oath against communism.

Two years ago, the Supreme Court had an opportunity to make clear that the same principle applied to public funding of the arts, in National Endowment for the Arts vs. Finley, which challenged a law that required the NEA to "take into consideration general standards of decency" in allocating arts grants. The lower courts held the law unconstitutional. But the Supreme Court ducked the issue, interpreting the statute not to bar funding of indecent or offensive art to be merely advisory. In doing so, however, the majority rejected the view, adopted by Justices Antonin Scalia and Clarence Thomas, that the government has a free hand when subsidizing speech.

Source C

Parachini, Allan. "NEA Issues New Obscenity Guidelines Arts . . ." *Los Angeles Times,* 11 Jul. 1990, home ed.: pg. 1.

The following article addresses the wording of NEA guidelines.

The National Endowment for the Arts issued formal obscenity-control guidelines on Tuesday that indicated the arts agency intends to ignore the most controversial phrase in a law passed last year that has provoked a furor in the arts community.

The NEA action may have been intended to both placate a disgruntled arts community, and to create the appearance for endowment political critics that the NEA acted decisively to define what constitutes obscene art it will refuse to fund.

The phrase in question—which appears in the NEA's 1990 appropriations bill—says NEA funds may not be used to produce works that may be considered obscene, "including, but not limited to, depictions of sadomasochism, homoeroticism, the sexual exploitation of children or individuals engaged in sex acts."

The phrase quoted above does not appear in the new endowment policy statement clarifying "The Definition of 'Obscene'." The new policy is now identical to the legal definition of obscenity established by the U.S. Supreme Court.

The endowment has said it would retain a requirement that grantees sign a written certification that anything created under NEA grants will not be obscene.

GO ON TO THE NEXT PAGE

Source D

Parachini, Allan. "NEA and the Arts: The Turmoil Continues Endowment . . ." *Los Angeles Times,* 16 Nov. 1989, home ed.: pg. 1.

The following article discusses an art exhibit that lost NEA funding.

Frohnmayer insisted the decision to cancel the "Witnesses" grant did not indicate a lessening of NEA concern with the AIDS epidemic. The show is part of a national arts observance planned for Dec.1 called Visual AIDS, in which more than 500 arts organizations will schedule special shows, symbolic closures or other events.

New York artist Allen Frame, speaking for the 23 artists who are part of the "Witnesses" exhibition, said in a press conference statement that "it enrages, but does not surprise us that, by expressing ourselves on the subject of AIDS, we are now under attack. We refuse to allow the National Endowment for the Arts to become a vehicle for repression. We retain our right to self-expression and we hold [Frohnmayer] and our arts institutions accountable to our community."

The chairman of the National Endowment for the Arts, saying he needed time to "reflect" on the controversy created by his cancellation of a grant for an AIDS art show here, implied Wednesday that the federal arts agency may reconsider its position.

But John E. Frohnmayer declined to say whether the process of reflection might lead to restoration of part or all of a $10,000 grant approved last July for the show, which includes work by 23 artists.

The statement by Frohnmayer came at a press conference here after Frohnmayer met for more than two hours with a group of New York City artists and officials of Artists Space, a Manhattan gallery that plans to open the show, "Witnesses: Against Our Vanishing" tonight.

Source E

"Politics Is No Work of Art, America Is Getting Far Off-Track in Its Art Funding." *Los Angeles Times,* 3 Jul. 1990, home ed.: pg. 6.

The following article addresses who should make decisions regarding public art funding.

Over the past year, a small but vocal coalition of religious fundamentalists and conservative ideologues has subjected the National Endowment for the Arts to a campaign of vilification so intense that it has put the program's very existence in doubt.

According to these critics, the question at the root of this controversy involves obscenity, blasphemy and the obligations they believe artists should assume when they accept public subsidies. In fact, the central question is rather different and, in important respects, more fundamental. What is at issue here is who will decide what sort of publicly supported art the American people will be allowed to see.

Under the NEA's current system, that decision is made jointly by panels of artists, scholars and arts administrators—who allocate the endowment's grants—and, most important, by the people, who now are free to decide for themselves which art they will view and which they will ignore. Under the system proposed by the NEA's critics, that decision will be made by the politicians in Congress.

GO ON TO THE NEXT PAGE

Source F

Fact Sheet: Fiscal Year 2004 Funding. 30 Sep. 2004. National Endowment for the Arts. 1 Oct. 2005. Available at www.nea.gov/about/Facts/2004funding.html.

The following chart lists projects that were funded by the NEA in 2004.

Grant Category	Dollars Awarded
Challenge America	
Access to the Arts	$7,815,574
Reaching Every Community	1,280,000
State and Regional Partnerships	8,721,000
Leadership Initiatives	
Shakespeare in American Communities	2,953,975
Mayors' Institute on City Design	400,000
Access Ability initiatives	420,300
Other initiatives	1,234,000
Access to Artistic Excellence	
Grants to Organizations	
Creativity	19,960,000
Heritage/Preservation	4,231,000
Arts on Radio & Television	3,860,000
Services to Arts Organizations & Artists	2,525,000
Fellowships	
Literature Fellowships	1,000,000
National Heritage Fellowships	200,000
Jazz Masters Fellowships	125,000
Leadership Initiatives	
Folk & Traditional Arts Infrastructure Initiative	380,000
Arts Journalism Institutes	485,395
NEA Jazz Masters Initiative	574,709
Public Partnerships (including international programs)	1,038,300
Other initiatives	1,565,655
Learning in the Arts	
Learning in the Arts Grants to Organizations	9,672,680

Leadership Initiatives	
Shakespeare in American Communities	210,000
Arts Education Partnership	638,500
NEA Summer Institutes	250,000
Other initiatives	77,500
State & Regional Partnership Agreements	31,380,000
Save America's Treasures	1,362,000
TOTAL FUNDS OBLIGATED	$102,608,648

GO ON TO THE NEXT PAGE

Question 2

(Suggested time—40 minutes. This question counts one-third of the total essay section score.)

Directions: The following passages are comments on two places, M. F. K. Fisher on the French port of Marseille and Maya Angelou on the small town of Stamps, Arkansas. Read both carefully and write an essay on how the two passages are similar and different in their effect and in their authors' handling of the resources of language.

Passage I

One of the many tantalizing things about Marseille is that most people who describe it, whether or not they know much about either the place or the languages they are supposedly using, write the same things. For centuries this has been so, and a typically modern opinion could have been given in 1550 as well as 1977.

Not long ago I read one, mercifully unsigned, in a San Francisco paper. It was full of logistical errors, faulty syntax, misspelled French words, but it hewed true to the familiar line that Marseille is doing its best to live up to a legendary reputation as world capital for "dope, whores, and street violence." It then went on to discuss, often erroneously, the essential ingredients of a true bouill-abaisse! The familiar pitch had been made, and idle readers dreaming of a great seaport dedicated to heroin, prostitution, and rioting could easily skip the clumsy details of marketing for fresh fish. . . .

"Feature articles" like this one make it seem probable that many big newspapers, especially in English-reading countries, keep a few such mild shockers on hand in a back drawer, in case a few columns need filling on a rainy Sunday. Apparently people like to glance one more time at the same old words: evil, filthy, dangerous.

Sometimes such journalese is almost worth reading for its precociously obsolete views of a society too easy to forget. In 1929, for instance, shortly before the Wall Street Crash, a popular travel writer named Basil Woon published *A Guide to the Gay World of France: From Deauville to Monte Carlo* (Horace Liveright, New York). (By now even his use of the word "gay" is quaintly naïve enough for a small chuckle. . . .)

Of course Mr. Woon was most interested in the Côte d'Azur, in those far days teeming and staggering with rich English and even richer Americans, but while he could not actively recommend staying in Marseille, he did remain true to his journalistic background with an expectedly titillating mention of it.

***

If you are interested in how the other side of the world lives, a trip through old Marseilles—by daylight—cannot fail to thrill, but it is not wise to venture into this district at night unless dressed like a stevedore and well armed. Thieves, cutthroats, and other undesirables throng the narrow alleys, and sisters of scarlet sit in the doorways of their places of business, catching you by the sleeve as you pass by. The dregs of the world are here, unsifted. It is Port Said, Shanghai, Barcelona, and Sydney combined. Now that San Francisco has reformed, Marseilles is the world's wickedest port.

Passage II

There is a much-loved region in the American fantasy where pale white women float eternally under black magnolia trees, and white men with soft hands brush wisps of wisteria from the creamy shoulders of their lady loves. Harmonious black music drifts like perfume through this precious air, and nothing of a threatening nature intrudes.

The South I returned to, however, was flesh-real and swollen-belly poor. Stamps, Arkansas, a small hamlet, had subsisted for hundreds of years on the returns from cotton plantations, and until World War I, a creaking lumbermill. The town was halved by railroad tracks, the swift Red River and racial prejudice. Whites lived on the town's small rise (it couldn't be called a hill), while blacks lived in what had been known since slavery as "the Quarters." . . .

In my memory, Stamps is a place of light, shadow, sounds and entrancing odors. The earth smell was pungent, spiced with the odor of cattle manure, the yellowish acid of ponds and rivers, the deep pots of greens and beans cooking for hours with smoked or cured pork. Flowers added their heavy aroma. And above all, the atmosphere was pressed down with the smell of old fears, and hates, and guilt.

On this hot and moist landscape, passions clanged with the ferocity of armored knights colliding. Until I moved to California at thirteen I had known the town, and there had been no need to examine it. I took its being for granted and now, five years later, I was returning, expecting to find the shield of anonymity I had known as a child.

Question 3

(Suggested time—40 minutes. This question counts one-third of the total essay section score.)

Directions: Read the following excerpt from William Hazlitt's *Lectures on the English Comic Writers* (1819). Then write a well-developed essay analyzing the author's purpose by examining tone, point of view, and stylistic devices.

Man is the only animal that laughs and weeps; for he is the only animal that is struck with the difference between what things are, and what they ought to be. We weep at what thwarts or exceeds our desires in serious matters: we laugh at what only disappoints our expectations in trifles. We shed tears from sympathy with real and necessary distress; as we burst into laughter from want of sympathy with that which is unreasonable and unnecessary, the absurdity of which provokes our spleen or mirth, rather than any serious reflections on it.

To explain the nature of laughter and tears, is to account for the condition of human life; for it is in a manner compounded of these two! It is a tragedy or a comedy—sad or merry, as it happens. The crimes and misfortunes that are inseparable from it, shock and wound the mind when they once seize upon it, and when the pressure can no longer be borne, seek relief in tears: the follies and absurdities that men commit, or the odd accidents that befall them, afford us amusement from the very rejection of these false claims upon our sympathy, and end in laughter. If every thing that went wrong, if every vanity or weakness in another gave us a sensible pang, it would be hard indeed: but as long as the disagreeableness of the consequences of a sudden disaster is kept out of sight by the immediate oddity of the circumstances, and the absurdity or unaccountableness of a foolish action is the most striking thing in it, the ludicrous prevails over the pathetic, and we receive pleasure instead of pain from the farce of life which is played before us, and which discomposes our gravity as often as it fails to move our anger or our pity!

IF YOU FINISH BEFORE TIME IS CALLED, CHECK YOUR WORK ON THIS SECTION ONLY. DO NOT WORK ON ANY OTHER SECTION IN THE TEST.

Answer Key for Practice Test 2

Section I: Multiple-Choice Questions

First Passage

1. B
2. B
3. D
4. B
5. C
6. A
7. E
8. C
9. D
10. A
11. E
12. D
13. C
14. A

Second Passage

15. E
16. A
17. C
18. B
19. E
20. C
21. B
22. B
23. C
24. A
25. D
26. C

Third Passage

27. B
28. D
29. A
30. E
31. C
32. D
33. C
34. E
35. B
36. B
37. D
38. A
39. D
40. C
41. A

Fourth Passage

42. C
43. E
44. E
45. A
46. D
47. D
48. A
49. B
50. B
51. A
52. D
53. C
54. E
55. B

Section II: Essay Questions

Essay scoring guides, student essays, and analysis appear beginning on page 152.

Practice Test 2 Scoring Worksheet

Use the following worksheet to arrive at a probable final AP grade on Practice Test 2. Because being objective enough to estimate your own essay score is sometimes difficult, you might give your essays (along with the sample essays) to a teacher, friend, or relative to score if you feel confident that the individual has the knowledge necessary to make such a judgment and that he or she will feel comfortable doing so.

Section I: Multiple-Choice Questions

$$\underset{\substack{\text{right} \\ \text{answers}}}{\underline{\hspace{2cm}}} - (\tfrac{1}{4} \text{ or } .25 \times \underset{\substack{\text{wrong} \\ \text{answers}}}{\underline{\hspace{2cm}}}) = \underset{\substack{\text{multiple-choice} \\ \text{raw score}}}{\underline{\hspace{2cm}}}$$

$$\underset{\substack{\text{multiple-choice} \\ \text{raw score}}}{\underline{\hspace{2cm}}} \times 1.2272 = \underset{\substack{\text{multiple-choice} \\ \text{converted score}}}{\underline{\hspace{2cm}}} \text{ (of possible 67.5)}$$

Section II: Essay Questions

$$\underset{\substack{\text{question 1} \\ \text{raw score}}}{\underline{\hspace{2cm}}} + \underset{\substack{\text{question 2} \\ \text{raw score}}}{\underline{\hspace{2cm}}} + \underset{\substack{\text{question 3} \\ \text{raw score}}}{\underline{\hspace{2cm}}} = \underset{\substack{\text{essay} \\ \text{raw score}}}{\underline{\hspace{2cm}}}$$

$$\underset{\substack{\text{essay} \\ \text{raw score}}}{\underline{\hspace{2cm}}} \times 3.0556 = \underset{\substack{\text{essay} \\ \text{converted score}}}{\underline{\hspace{2cm}}} \text{ (of possible 82.5)}$$

Final Score

$$\underset{\substack{\text{multiple-choice} \\ \text{converted score}}}{\underline{\hspace{2cm}}} + \underset{\substack{\text{essay} \\ \text{converted score}}}{\underline{\hspace{2cm}}} = \underset{\substack{\text{final} \\ \text{converted score}}}{\underline{\hspace{2cm}}} \text{ (of possible 150)}$$

Probable Final AP Score

Final Converted Score	Probable AP Score
150–104	5
103–92	4
91–76	3
75–50	2
49–0	1

Answers and Explanations for Practice Test 2

Section I: Multiple-Choice Questions

First Passage

From Virginia Woolf's *A Room of One's Own*

1. **B.** The phrase that follows the list of names explains this answer: "call me . . . by any name you please—it is <u>not a matter of any importance</u>."

2. **B.** The speaker uses a metaphor as she describes her thought, imagining it to be on a fishing line that "swayed . . . among the reflections." The thought becomes a metaphorical fish that she hauls to shore on the line. The device is not personification (C) because in this case an abstract idea is given animal characteristics rather than human (her thought is compared to a fish caught on a line). The remaining choices are not used in this part of the passage.

3. **D.** The phrase that follows the quotation clearly identifies the answer: "the sudden conglomeration of an idea at the end of one's line." Choice A names not the abstract meaning but the literal meaning on which the metaphor is based. Choices B and C mention later occurrences unrelated to this "tug." There is no suggestion that the author has a guilty conscience (E).

4. **B.** Being made aware that she is in an area in which only "Fellows and Scholars" are allowed to walk sends her metaphorical "fish into hiding." The Beadle doesn't encourage, direct, or ask her questions—A, C, and E. The women's movement (D) is not addressed in the passage.

5. **C.** In the fish metaphor, the author points out "how small, how insignificant" her thought is when examined. There is no evidence that the thought passes very quickly (A) or is carefully thought out (E) or that either has to do with her forgetting. Notice of the rower (B) occurs before mention of the thought and does not cause her to forget.

6. **A.** The lawn that the author may not walk on and the library that she may not enter are symbols of the obstructions all women face. Choice D contradicts the purpose of the passage—to point out inequality. Choice E is incorrect because these two symbols reinforce, and do not distract from, the author's point.

7. **E.** There is no *allegory* (the use of characters to symbolize truths about humanity) in this passage. The passage does use personification ("willows wept in perpetual lamentation"), metaphor (the "fish" sequence), simile ("like a guardian angel"), and literary allusion (to Esmond).

8. **C.** The vignettes demonstrate how men have told women where they may and may not go; on a deeper level, they suggest that men's attitudes inhibit women in their intellectual pursuits. The author is angry (A) and touches on nature (B), but neither fact states the purpose of the essay. Choice D contradicts the passage; women have been *kept away* from university study. Choice E overstates. The author neither preaches nor discusses society and women's roles in general.

9. **D.** The passage presents external reality, such as the descriptions of the environs of the university and the actions of the Beadle and the doorman, while interspersing the author's thoughts about the events. The passage is too logical and grammatical to be classified as a stream of consciousness (A) (which is a narrative technique not a structural element). The passage doesn't compare or contrast the two events (B) or address the women's movement (C). Although choice E might be a method of organization, it is not used here.

10. **A.** The sentence accelerates as do her thoughts—"it became at once very exciting, and important; . . . it darted and sank . . . flashed hither and thither . . . tumult of ideas . . . impossible to sit still."

11. **E.** The description of the men, of their pompous behavior and dress, satirically emphasizes how trifling are the author's supposed crimes, walking on the grass and attempting to enter the library, and how foolish is the men's self-important enforcement of discriminating rules. Choices A and B contradict the passage. The author doesn't consider what she's done a "horror" nor would she intend to frighten women away from universities. Choice C is not addressed. Choice D is incorrect because the men's manners are similar, not contrasting.

12. **D.** The description of the gentleman is realistic but also takes a humorous turn in describing a simple doorman as "like a guardian angel barring the way with a flutter of black gown instead of white wings . . . deprecating" as he bars the author from entering the library. The doorman is not confused (A), and the reference is not to a jailer (B), but to a guardian angel.

13. **C.** It is highly unlikely that the events described produced a feeling of delight.

14. **A.** The author blends a presentation of her thoughts as she walks with description of external reality, such as the Beadle and the library doorman. Choice B is incorrect because there is no resolution to her problem. Choices C, D, and E are not accurate descriptions of the passage's pattern.

Second Passage

From *The Lives of the English Poets* by Samuel Johnson

15. **E.** The essay compares and contrasts the two authors, Dryden and Pope. Johnson begins by explaining that Dryden was a strong influence on Pope. Hence, Johnson sets out to "compare [Pope] with his master." The second paragraph explains Dryden's method of writing; the two following paragraphs discuss the care Pope took in writing and editing. The fifth paragraph explains the differences in the authors' educational backgrounds, and the sixth compares their prose skills. The essay's concluding paragraph continues to draw comparisons and contrasts, ultimately calling Dryden the better poet, while acknowledging both men's strengths. The essay is primarily one of opinion. There is no thesis given and no extensive use of illustrations (A) (other than mention of the *Iliad* and the *Essay on Criticism*). Both choices B and C are inaccurate. Johnson does not present a different argument in each paragraph (D) or strictly present arguments at all. The passage is an analysis of their styles.

16. **A.** In the 18th century, the word "candor" meant kindness, a meaning that fits in context here. Pope did not court his readers' kindness, but "dared [their] judgment." Because the sentence sets up an opposition, "criticism," "excellence," "sincerity" (the modern meaning of "candor"), and "indifference" make little sense, as they are not good opposites of "judgment."

17. **C.** In the sixth paragraph (lines 59–70), Dryden's prose style is described as "capricious," obeying "the motions of his own mind," sometimes "vehement and rapid," producing prose that is a "natural field, rising into inequalities . . . diversified"—that is, unsystematic, written quickly and without a preconceived order. Pope's prose, on the other hand, is described as "uniform," while he "constrains his mind to . . . rules of composition." Pope's prose is "smooth, uniform, and gentle," a "velvet lawn." If you check the first word of each answer pair, you will see that choices A, D, and E can be quickly eliminated as they are not suggested or inappropriate to refer to Dryden's prose. Finally, you can eliminate Choice B. While Dryden might be considered passionate, there is no suggestion that Pope is lyrical. (**Note:** In answering questions of this sort, you can also begin by checking the second term of each pair.)

18. **B.** Pope's attitude toward his own writing is best seen in "His parental attention never abandoned them," which suggests a nurturing attitude toward his work. Choice A shows not so much an attitude toward his writing as it does an attitude toward his audience. While a possible answer, Choice C deals with the outcome of Pope's editing and is not as clearly an attitude as is Choice B. Choices D and E are primarily Johnson's opinions of Pope's work.

19. **E.** A reader might be more convinced that Johnson's opinions are valid if presented with some evidence, some examples. He mentions Pope's editing of the *Iliad* but never explains exactly what was changed. He calls Dryden's prose "vehement and rapid" but, again, offers no proof. A reader might be left to wonder what Johnson had read of Pope's and Dryden's works that led him to reach these conclusions, and some examples would help. Choice A is incorrect because less emphasis would hardly provide a more convincing argument. The language of the passage is direct (B), and point-by-point comparisons (D) are made; more of the same is unlikely to more thoroughly convince the reader. Dryden, it seems, did little editing (C), so additional discussion here would not be helpful either.

20. C. Johnson makes no definitive claim about the superiority of either author's prose. In the sixth paragraph, they are presented as different in style but not necessarily in quality. It is Dryden's poetry that Johnson says is superior (although with some hesitation).

21. B. Johnson explains how quickly Dryden wrote: "He spent no time in struggles to rouse latent powers," and "He wrote, as he tells us, with very little consideration." Choice A deals with Dryden's lack of rewriting, not his method of writing—what he did not do rather than what he did.

22. B. Johnson claims that even though Pope did not have the same education opportunities that Dryden enjoyed, Pope gave his subjects his "minute attention"; he had "more certainty" than Dryden, suggesting that Pope knew his subjects well.

23. C. Genius invigorates judgments (without which it is cold) and knowledge (without which it is inert). Genius is not said to invigorate power, rather it *is* power.

24. A. The author suggests Dryden's ease in writing as a component of his genius. The fact that Dryden could produce great poetry and admirable prose so quickly and without laborious rewriting and editing attests to Dryden's genius. The quotation given in Choice B refers to Pope, not to Dryden. Choice C may be an apt description of Dryden's prose, but Johnson claims Dryden is genius in his poetry. Although Dryden had a strong educational foundation (D), Johnson does not address Dryden's education in relation to his genius.

25. D. Johnson uses an effective pair of metaphors to summarize his opinion of the two authors' prose: Dryden's is a "natural field," while Pope's is a "velvet lawn." The remaining choices are not used in this sentence.

26. C. Johnson clearly acknowledges that both authors are gifted, skillful, and talented; he levels little criticism of either writer. All other distinctions given are addressed in the essay.

Third Passage

From Henry David Thoreau's "Life Without Principle"

27. B. Thoreau insists that "getting a living" should be "not merely honest and honorable" (ethical), "but altogether inviting and glorious" (admirable).

28. D. Thoreau explains that "the lesson of value which money teaches . . . we are inclined to skip altogether" (lines 9–12).

29. A. A major assertion of the essay is that people no longer understand the proper value of money. The author claims that people get money in the wrong way and use it based on the wrong principles. Thoreau never addresses what will "save mankind" (B). And while he acknowledges that gold-digging may be "hard work," "gold thus obtained is not the same thing with the wages of honest toil" and "society is the loser." Although Thoreau believes that gold-diggers rely on luck to find gold, he doesn't believe that the entire world operates this way (C). Neither D nor E is suggested in the essay.

30. E. The "Author of the Universe" to Thoreau is God. None of the other choices is a reasonable answer.

31. C. The author wonders if Plato had to face the same dilemmas that others do, if Plato lived his life more admirably than did his contemporaries. The author's points about gold-digging—A and B—are not addressed in the discussion of Plato. Thoreau doesn't mention Plato's premises about morality (D). Mentioning Plato does nothing to change the tone of the essay (E), and it is highly unlikely that the author uses Plato merely to impress his readers.

32. D. Thoreau claims that he would not raise a finger for all the wealth of the world.

33. C. An aphorism, a brief, pointed statement of fundamental truth, is similar to a proverb. Choice C fits this definition.

34. E. Thoreau suggests that, although gold-digging may appear to be an honest way to earn "food and raiment" to some, it harms society in the same way that gambling does; it "is not the same thing with the wages of honest toil." The author never implies that philosophers should work harder (A), that society is improving (C), or that hard work produces wisdom (D). In fact, he suggests the opposite. Hard work can be the "enemy." Choice B is not an unstated assumption, but a paraphrase of an explicit statement.

35. B. The California gold rush, which some saw as an example of hard-working men diligently trying to get ahead, is used by this author as an example of immorality, of gambling in life. Thoreau doesn't compare gold-diggers to Greeks (A), explore relations of Orientals and Occidentals (C) (that relationship is only touched on), sensationalize (D), or criticize those who saw the gold rush as romantic (E) (he directly criticizes those who participate in the gold-digging).

36. B. Thoreau states that "cold and hunger seem more <u>friendly</u> to my nature." Cold and hunger, generally undesirable states, are here seen as better than man's methods of warding them off.

37. D. There is no syllogistic reasoning in this essay. The author does use simile ("The gold-digger . . . is as much gambler as his fellow in the saloons," lines 81–82), historical allusion (to Plato and to the gold rush), rhetorical question (for example, "Does Wisdom work in a tread-mill?"), and religious reference (for example, mention of Mahomet and God).

38. A. Knowledge is more valuable than gold; wisdom will metaphorically gild more surface than gold.

39. D. The author is angry, indignant at mankind's unseemly pursuit of money.

40. C. This quotation is not part of the argument against gold-digging. It simply states a fact about gold.

41. A. Thoreau doesn't directly address man's improving his lot in life, although one can infer that he probably believes man should do so.

Fourth Passage

From *Taking Flight* by Richard P. Hallion

42. C. The speaker walks a fine line; he includes dangerous elements in his narrative, but he concludes with praise for the overall success of this milestone flight. Choice A is incorrect because aviation had not yet become mass transportation. Choices B, D, and E do restate some of the speaker's negative points, but they all take his points to an extreme.

43. E. The sudden change in cadence focuses the reader's attention on the dramatic change of mood. Choices B and C are incorrect; these words are not a quote from Sikorsky or from an earlier work. Choice A is incorrect because the short sentence is a departure from both the content and the style of the preceding sentences.

44. E. The inclusion of this incident indicates that the speaker places a high value on the crewmen's actions, which, indeed, saved the lives of everyone on board. Choices A, B, C, and D are all negative reactions to the incident, which is a reversal of the speaker's true position.

45. A. The idea that the speaker wishes to emphasize is not Jules Verne, per se. Rather, the speaker's purpose is to dramatically juxtapose Verne's writing, in which human flight was purely fictional, with this true-life "flight of fantasy," which occurred only a few years later. Although Sikorsky was a Jules Verne fan, establishing this idea is not the speaker's rhetorical purpose; Choice B also includes the incorrect phrase "who lived in fantasy."

46. D. The effect that the speaker wishes to impart is Sikorsky's amazement at this unprecedented view, a sight that no man had ever beheld. Choice A also appears to have merit; the quotation does provide strong imagery, but that is not the speaker's intended rhetorical effect.

47. D. In this context, the speaker's use of the word "faithful" personifies the engines; he wishes to impart a sense of Sikorsky's empathy with, and gratitude for, these untiring, helpful servants.

48. A. The speaker wishes to emphasize Princip's unsavory physical appearance, thus, in note #4, he elevates Clark's brief description to an "evocative reflection" and he also includes odious comparisons to later murderous terrorists. The other choices include information that does not appear in note #4; Choice C refers to note #1 and Choice E refers to note # 5.

49. B. The speaker implies that Sikorsky is truly insulated in his fantastic world of flight, but only for a very brief time, because the coming Great War will wash away all vestiges of the naiveté of these early aviators. Choice E also seems to have merit; however, in the end, it is not Sikorsky's *choice* to turn his back on the old world, but rather, that the old world will disappear soon enough in flames and chaos of its own making.

50. B. The intent of the speaker's metaphor is to emphasize the *success* of this unprecedented flight, and in retrospect, to encapsulate the seeming naiveté of the early aviators. Although choices C and D do apply to Sikorsky, they are not the most important message. The quotes in choices A and E are off-topic since they do not refer to this specific flight.

51. A. Character development requires a more lengthy narrative than is provided by the format of this brief, yet wide ranging, passage. The other choices all indicate literary devises that *are* utilized in this work.

52. D. This phrase merely describes Gavrillo Princip's appearance; it is *not* one of the speaker's many examples of the pathetic security on that fateful day. On the other hand, choices A, B, C, and E *do* explore the inadequate security.

53. C. The details revealed in Sikorsky's own flight log in note #1 are neither well-known nor readily available, and they overturn the conventional wisdom. The fact that the speaker has uncovered these illuminating details clearly indicates the breadth of his research and the depth of his understanding.

54. E. On the contrary, rather than being stringent, the speaker emphasizes that security precautions were particularly *lax* that day. However, all of the other facts and inferences in choices A, B, C, and D *are* appropriately drawn from note #5.

55. B. The speaker's rhetorical purpose is well-served by his juxtaposition of two seemingly unrelated, yet concurrent events, each in its own way both exhilarating and terrifying, each with great perils and great bravery, each finally reaching a dramatic history-making resolution. All of the other answer choices are not global enough to address the speaker's *primary* purpose.

Section II: Essay Questions

Question 1

Scoring Guide for Question 1 (NEA Grant Funding)

9 Essays that earn a score of 9 meet the criteria for essays that receive a score of 8; in addition, they are especially sophisticated in their explanation and argument. They may also present particularly remarkable control of language.

8 Successful

Essays that receive a score of 8 respond to the prompt **successfully,** using at least three sources from the prompts. They take a position that defends, challenges, or qualifies the claim that the government should continue to fund NEA grants to artists. They effectively argue their position and support the argument with appropriate and convincing evidence. The prose demonstrates an ability to control an extensive range of the elements of effective writing but may not be entirely flawless.

7 Essays that earn a score of 7 fit the description of the essays that score a 6 but provide more complexity in both argumentation and explanation and/or demonstrate more distinguished prose style.

6 Satisfactory

Essays that earn a score of 6 respond to the prompt **satisfactorily,** utilizing at least three of the sources from the prompt. They take a position that defends, challenges, or qualifies the claim that the government should continue to fund NEA grants to artists. They adequately argue their position and support it with appropriate evidence, although without the precision and depth of the top-scoring essays. The writing may contain minor errors in diction or syntax, but the prose is generally clear.

5 Essays that earn a score of 5 take a position that defends, challenges, or qualifies the claim that the government should continue to fund NEA grants to artists. They support the position with generally appropriate evidence, but they may not adequately use three sources from the prompt. These essays may be inconsistent, uneven, or limited in the development of the argument. While the writing usually conveys the writer's ideas, it may demonstrate lapses in diction or syntax or an overly simplistic style.

4 Inadequate

Essays that earn a score of 4 respond to the prompt **inadequately.** They may have difficulty taking a position that defends, challenges, or qualifies the claim that the government should continue to fund NEA grants. The evidence may be particularly insufficient or may not utilize enough sources from the prompt. The prose may basically convey the writer's ideas but suggests immature control over the elements of effective writing.

3 Essays that earn a score of 3 meet the criteria for a score of 4 but reveal less ability to take a position that defends, challenges, or qualifies the claim that the government should continue to fund NEA grants. The presentation of evidence and argumentation is likely to be unconvincing. The writing may show less control over the elements of effective writing.

2 Little Success

Essays that earn a 2 demonstrate **little success** at taking a position that defends, challenges, or qualifies the claim that the government should continue to fund NEA grants and show little ability to present it with appropriate evidence from the sources in the prompt. These essays may misunderstand the prompt, may fail to establish a position with supporting evidence, or may substitute a simpler task by replying tangentially with unrelated, erroneous, or unsuitable explanation, argument, and/or evidence. The prose frequently demonstrates consistent weaknesses in the conventions of effective writing.

1 Essays that earn a score of 1 meet the criteria for a score of 2 but are undeveloped, especially simplistic in their explanation, argument, and/or evidence, or weak in their control of writing.

High-Scoring Essay

Our world is far from that of Renaissance Florence where all was abuzz with the revival of humanitarian philosophy and a rapidly changing society. This was a time of radical development in art, coupled with major shifts in social values and views. However, much has changed in the five-hundred years since this re-birth. The twenty-first century is driven by technological advancement and rational thinking more than any time before; these priorities have the result, whether intended or not, of placing funding for the arts in jeopardy. However, at the heart of mankind lies an appreciation for the arts and all they do to improve our world. Thus, it is necessary for government spending, through the National Endowment for the Arts (NEA), to step in and help provide the arts to a society that has forgotten the importance of art in fostering self-discovery and the progression of mankind.

It is only natural for art to be controversial. Art is often an expression of internal strife, a stinging criticism of society, a challenge to what is accepted, or a dare to humanity to look at our everyday world with a new perspective. Indeed, art is at the very cusp of social change. When Praxiteles sculpted the first female nude sculpture in Ancient Greece it produced as much uproar as Chris Ofili's 'Holy Virgin Mary' that Giuliani objected to (Source B). Yet today we look back at the countless nude figures in art as beautiful, not scornful. Art is a necessity that is very rarely accepted without conflict. So it remains today. A well-seasoned artist represented in Visual AIDS admitted, after losing NEA funding, that "It enrages, but does not surprise us that, by expressing ourselves on the subject of AIDS, we are now under attack"(Source D). But, if artists have been under attack for hundreds of years and have continued to persist why must they still require the support of our government?

The answer is a complex one. Art and government have always been intertwined. Before cameras, television, or the internet, art was a main form of propaganda used by the government and even the church. From the Great Pyramids to the frescos in the Sistine Chapel, from the Nazi recruiting posters to the murals of Diego Rivera, leaders of all times and regions have employed art for political and social purposes. However government-sponsored propaganda-art was often more subdued, and thus more ethically acceptable, than was non-governmental propaganda-art of the time. No government needed to worry about issuing, "formal obscenity-control guidelines" (Source C), for the art it sponsored. However, what the NEA seeks to achieve is quite different than any previous government institution and it is this that concerns people. Instead of supporting art that benefits the government they are supporting art that supposedly benefits the people. The NEA claims to be protecting "freedom of expression" (Source B), and generating a "positive relationship between public funding and private philanthropy" (Source A).

What necessitates this fusion of art and government is the changing ethos of the American people. Nowadays, there is very little emphasis placed on the humanities, personal expression, or creativity. Our world is changing rapidly and many feel there is simply no time for these frivolous pursuits. Math, science, and reason are emphasized as the pathways to success, fortune, fame, and the advancement of humanity. However, while humans are making huge strides with their minds, they are leaving their hearts and emotions underdeveloped. Many seem as if they are mentally stuck in the Age of Enlightenment, a time when reason was emphasized as the solution to all problems over all other human capabilities. Today people are much more willing to invest their money in economic ventures than the more intangible experiments of artists. The government has perceived this change and, fortunately, has deemed the arts important enough to be saved. Clearly the NEA Grants help fulfill this need.

The NEA must continue to award grants to artists to support the social change we value so much. Perhaps some art works will be better received than others and perhaps some works will make people "sick" (Source B) while others delight them. But, no matter what, the work of artists will keep our society awake and changing. It is for this reason that the NEA allows "artists, scholars, and art administrators" (Source E), who are willing risk takers, to make decisions rather than politicians who tend to favor social stagnation as a means of self-preservation. If we lose our art, we will lose our ability to express ourselves and expand our minds and we will lose the essence of our humanity. In our bustling world, the art supported by the NEA is an essential connection back to our internal experience.

Analysis of the High-Scoring Essay

This thoughtful and insightful essay clearly addresses the prompt and thoroughly develops the idea that the NEA should continue to fund grants for public art. By using five of the six available sources, the writer efficiently integrates both implicit and explicit evidence to bolster his or her position. The introduction blends a historical perspective, noting the Florentine Renaissance, with an examination of 21st-century priorities. The writer's logic demonstrates that funding for the arts has become a lower priority than funding for technology. The concept that mankind has a fundamental need for the arts in order to make societal progress sets up the thesis that the NEA should, indeed, continue to fund grants in the arts.

The second paragraph explores the fact that art has always had a component of controversy, and it effectively utilizes an example from Ancient Greek art, comparing the public reception to Praxiteles's sculpture to the objection posed by Mayor Giuliani to a recent art exhibit. The writer accepts the fact that art will always entail controversy but acknowledges that art is necessary to bring social advancement. Leaving the reader with a thought-provoking question, the writer wonders why artists need governmental support, given that their work will be "under attack." This paragraph encourages the reader to pause and contemplate the answer. By demonstrating both the ability to engage the reader's intellect and to pose thought provoking questions, the writer truly earns a high score.

The third paragraph readily acknowledges that "the answer is a complex one" and proceeds to demonstrate how intricate the issue really is. The effective use of examples throughout art history, all of which involve some degree of controversy, demonstrates the writer's overall awareness of the world and of how its political history affects the art world; this skill will impress any AP reader. Although the writer acknowledges the role that governments have played in funding the arts, he or she also acknowledges that the arts have sometimes been misused by governments as effective tools of propaganda. The writer then rightfully differentiates NEA funding from previous government-sponsored art by specifying that NEA-funded projects are designed to "benefit the people," not to propagate government propaganda. This paragraph, although a bit rough in its construction, presents sound ideas while separating the purpose of NEA grants from previous government-sponsored art. Given that this essay was written under a limited time period, it is easy to overlook its minor wording issues that would likely be clarified with a more polished draft.

The next paragraph adds to the progress of the argument by exploring the contemporary need for arts funding. The comparison of our current society to the Age of Enlightenment demonstrates this writer's grasp of mankind's intellectual development and the similarities between today and an era hundreds of years ago. The idea that mankind is too ensconced in becoming successful at the expense of the arts is an interesting one; it causes the reader to ponder this philosophical issue. The writer's choice to end the paragraph by emphasizing the positive role the NEA can play is also effective.

Finally, the writer lobbies on behalf of all mankind by acknowledging that "we value" the social change that the arts represent. This application works well, as it utilizes the classical rhetorical appeal of ethos, an appeal that makes the reader appreciate the commonality. Overall, the essay earns its high score because it is specifically on topic, plus it demonstrates superior organizational skills and admirable development. The writer's command of language is also excellent; syntax is varied, and diction is accurate and concise. It would be hard to ask for more success than this in a timed essay.

Medium-Scoring Essay

The National Endowment for the Arts (NEA) must stop awarding grants to artists because it takes society out of the picture, allows the public no say in what is produced, and crowds out public investment.

For as long as art has existed so has the strenuous relationship between art and society. It is a natural part of the production of art—that artists must struggle and search out support in society. The NEA takes the place of society and ruins this relationship: "the sense of responsibility and public enthusiasm to support a social cause might be diminished if the government takes responsibility for its funding" (Source A). Government interference is only hurting the production of art by hindering the centuries-old method of artistic-production.

It is dangerous to let a bureaucracy control something as creative as art. This is clear with Mayor Rudolph Giuliani who relied on, "a none-too-distinguished line of government officials who decided to become art critics" (Source B), for advice. Our country was founded on the ideas of freedom of expression and no taxation without representation. It is not right that people's money is being used for projects they do not support. For this reason I agree with the critics of the NEA who propose that, "decisions will be made by the politicians in congress" (Source E), instead of a panel of artists. Politicians are representative of society and its interests. The NEA is headed down a slippery-slope towards too much government control.

Finally, the NEA discourages people to donate to the arts because they think it has already been taken care of by the government. The NEA donated $102,608,648 in funds to the arts in 2004 (Source F). Many might have thought that this was enough. It is not unreasonable to think that "public funds tend to 'crowd out' private donations" (Source A). People no longer feel the moral obligation to support the arts. This separates people from the art of our society therefore decreasing its power, meaning, and effectiveness.

The National Endowment for the Arts hinders the public's involvement in the development and production of art. Furthermore, it is systematizing a creative progress and allocating funds in an irresponsible manner. The government is responsible for regulating trade, waging war, passing laws, and collecting taxes—not supporting art. That is the job of the people.

Analysis of Medium-Scoring Essay

This essay makes a few good points, but it is inhibited by brevity and logical flaws. Simply put, it does not exhibit the development and clarity of thought required for a high score. The introductory paragraph takes a clear, albeit simplistic, stand, stating that the NEA should stop funding grants. Several of the assumptions underlying this one-sentence paragraph are questionable at best. One example is the assumption that the "public has no say" in NEA decisions; no evidence is presented to substantiate this claim. Another questionable assumption is that NEA funding will indeed "crowd out public investment," despite any potential evidence to the contrary. These statements indicate that the writer is not as aware of the world as one would hope, and they lead the reader to fear that the essay will merely present an oversimplified view of a complex issue. That fear comes true.

The second paragraph simplistically states that artists *must* struggle, another questionable assertion that is heavily laden with the writer's preconceived notions about artists, and then it claims that NEA funding somehow "ruins" this struggle. Presumably, this writer believes that, since the NEA helps an artist to some degree with some form of funding, the artist is free to create art without any other pressures. The writer's conclusion is questionable because the logic is full of holes. He or she offers neither concrete examples nor logical explanation; therefore, the paragraph fails to convince the reader.

The next paragraph is riddled with logical errors that distract a reader's attention from the writer's points. For example, the writer leaps from the idea that bureaucratic control is dangerous to the unrelated idea of "no taxation without representation." This jump in logic leaves the reader's head spinning, wondering how the writer is trying to connect these two ideas. It comes across as if the writer suddenly remembered the "no taxation without representation" phrase from a history class and tried to work it in, regardless of its relevance. Although it may be possible to construct a convincing argument for this writer's ideas, this oversimplified presentation does not work in the writer's favor. The writer seems to be composing without considering what he or she had previously stated. For instance, in this paragraph, the writer claims that "politicians are representative of society." If this were true, then it directly contradicts the writer's statements in the first paragraph, which claim that the NEA takes "society out of the picture." If politicians *are* representative of society, then society is indeed "in the picture." The writer's word choices need clarification and accuracy.

The fourth paragraph contains awkward wording, such as the phrase, "discourages people to donate." Perhaps with more time the writer might have improved this diction. In addition, the muddled thinking and leaps of logic that the writer demonstrated previously appear once again in this paragraph. For instance, the writer equates "moral obligation" with financial funding, which are not necessarily the same; a moral obligation to the arts does not necessarily include a financial obligation. Additionally, the writer never addresses the important questions of how a lack of funding will "separate people from the art of our society" or how a decrease in arts funding would bring a decrease in art's "power, meaning, and effectiveness." The writer does not seem to have thought through these positions well enough to understand their logical ramifications.

The concluding paragraph does present a very interesting opinion, that NEA funding of the arts may be "systematizing a creative progress." If the writer were to develop this idea more and explore its implications, the essay might be stronger. However, as the essay is presented, it appears that the writer thought of this new idea just as time was running out. Overall, this essay demonstrates how a writer can begin with potentially good ideas and arguments, but, unless they are thought through to their logical conclusions, they can fall short of a convincing argument. Finally, the repeated problems with diction and poor development hold this essay to a low score.

Question 2

Scoring Guide for Question 2 (M. F. K. Fisher and Maya Angelou)

9 Essays that earn a score of 9 meet the criteria for essays that receive a score of 8; in addition, they are especially sophisticated in their explanation and argument. They may also present particularly impressive control of language.

8 Successful

These well-written essays **successfully** demonstrate a clear understanding of the similarities and differences between the effects of the two passages and the authors' handling of the resources of language in producing these effects. These papers support their points with specific and cogently presented evidence from the passage. Although these essays may contain a few minor errors, they demonstrate the ability to communicate effectively and precisely.

7 Essays that earn a score of 7 fit the description of the essays that score a 6 but provide more sophistication in argumentation and explanation and/or demonstrate more distinguished prose style.

6 Satisfactory

These essays, also well written, **satisfactorily** identify the effects of the two passages but perhaps in a less convincing manner than do top-scoring essays. The discussion of the handling of resources of language may be less thorough and specific. Connection between the thesis and the evidence may not be as clear as that found in top-scoring papers. Some errors in mechanics may occur, but overall, these essays show satisfactory control over organization, development, and use of language.

5 These average essays show a general understanding of the effects of the passages but may not present as clear a thesis concerning those effects. The attempt to analyze the handling of resources of language may be simplistic, or evidence offered to support the essay's points may be insufficient and may not be clearly related to the author's use of the resources of language. These essays may be coherently organized but may show inconsistent control of diction.

4 Inadequate

Essays that earn a score of 4 respond to the prompt **inadequately.** They may have difficulty identifying and discussing the effects of the passages. The evidence may be particularly insufficient or simplistically presented. The prose may convey the writer's ideas but suggests immature control over the elements of effective writing.

3 These essays attempt to identify and discuss the effects of the passages but do so ineffectively perhaps because of an inaccurate reading or with presentation of inadequate evidence. They may fail to complete all of the tasks given. These essays may simply catalog the devices, the resources of language, without analysis or comment on the connection between effect and language use. Weak control of the essay format and/or language may be evident, and mechanical errors may be frequent.

2 Little Success

These essays fail to sufficiently respond to the question or the passage. It may fail to understand the effects of the passages, misreading them in a way that distorts those effects. Little or no attention may be given to resources of language used in the passages. These essays fail to convince the reader of their points, and the thesis may be shallow or nonexistent. These essays may substitute a simpler task by replying to the question with irrelevant information. Persistent weaknesses in grammar and organization may be evident. The prose often demonstrates consistent weaknesses in writing.

1 Essays earning a score of 1 meet the criteria for a score of 2 but are undeveloped, especially simplistic in their analysis, or weak control of the language. The evidence is insufficient or may not utilize many, if any, sources from the prompt.

High-Scoring Essay

Although M. F. K. Fisher's description of Marseille and Maya Angelou's description of Stamps both seek to dispel illusions of their places, they differ in the use of technique, tone, and diction. In the first passage, Fisher uses a satiric style to poke fun of Marseilles' misconceived reputation as "the world's wickedest port." In the other passage, Maya Angelou uses fantastic imagery to also reveal a faulty reputation, this time, of the South. Both authors are attempting to reform mistaken opinions of their places, but they both use extremely different techniques.

In her passage, M. F. K. Fisher seeks only to quell Marseilles' misrepresentation. By wryly examining articles describing Marseilles, Fisher never directly gives her impression of this French port, but instead she reveals the spurious nature of these descriptions. Throughout the passage, a satiric tone is employed. Before introducing Basil Woon's piece on Marseilles, Fisher writes "Sometimes such journalese is almost worth reading for its precociously obsolete views." This statement ridicules Woon's work even before it is introduced. Contributing to the tone of his piece, Fisher not only derides the descriptions of Marseille, but also the backgrounds of their writers. Although Woon did not recommend visiting Marseilles, "he did remain true to his journalistic background with an expectedly titillating mention of it." Fisher masks an otherwise intense diatribe with the light-hearted, humorous use of satire.

The use of precise and informal diction also contributes to the effects of the first passage. In describing newspaper descriptions of Marseilles, the words "mind shockers" are used. The concise image formed by these words contributes to the informal mood of the passage. Also, instead of employing the more conservative and respected word "journalism," Fisher chose to use the word "journalese." This simple substitution embodies the essence of the passage. Like the word journalese, the passage continually ridicules writers' misrepresentations of Marseilles.

Using an opposite style of attack, Maya Angelou does not mock the faulty representation of the South. Instead she contrasts both a description of the "American fantasy" of the South with her own vivid impressions. The dream-like tone of the first paragraph is aided by the rich choice of diction. "Women float eternally" among "wisps of wisteria." Like paradise, the word eternally allows this scene of gentle alliteration to last forever.

This fantasy is contrasted in the remaining paragraphs with an intense, passionate tone of life. The descriptions, like smells "spiced with the odor of cattle manure, the yellowish acid of the ponds and rivers, the deep pots of greens and beans," are all concrete. These concrete images sharply contrast the ethereal images of women floating eternally. The misrepresentation of the South is easily dispelled by the reality of Maya Angelou's observations. Furthermore, the choice of diction is superb. Angelou's South was "flesh-real and swollen-belly poor." These words easily bring to mind the harshness of black life in the South. Towards the end of the passage, a metaphor is used to change the direction of the passage from concreteness into memories ". . . passions clanged with the ferocity of armored knights colliding." After erasing the erroneous images of the South, the passage prepares to tell Angelou's story.

Though these passages are similar in their goals, their distinct uses of diction and tone drastically differ their methods of dispelling illusions.

Analysis of the High-Scoring Essay

The paper begins by directly addressing the topic with a relevant comparison of the essays, pointing out that each "seek[s] to dispel illusions" of the perception of a location. This student recognizes that, although the essays have the same purpose, their differences lie in their stylistic choices. Such interesting ideas as these engage the reader.

The next two paragraphs analyze the Fisher passage on Marseille and together demonstrate a clear understanding of Fisher's use of humor and satire to ridicule those who have painted Marseille as the world's "wickedest port." The student supports the point with appropriate quotations from the passage. The second paragraph specifically analyzes and gives evidence for Fisher's purpose—to dispel the myths about Marseille—while the third paragraph explores how the language of the passage contributes to the effect. The student here uses effective organization and sophisticated diction, making this a strong section.

The fourth and fifth paragraphs deal with the Angelou passage, again analyzing the author's effect and the language used to create it. The analysis begins with Angelou's first paragraph, noting its differences from the Fisher passage—specifically, that she "does not mock the faulty representation" as Fisher does and noting that Angelou creates a "dream-like tone" contrasting with her own impressions. The analysis continues with a discussion of diction, noting how effectively Angelou dispels the misrepresentation of the South with her use of concrete images, an exploration of Angelou's use of metaphor, and an explanation of the metaphor's effect in introducing the realistic treatment, which would follow in the work.

The paper concludes with a brief summary of its main point—that the authors have similar goals but differing techniques. Although the statement is not itself thought provoking, it is an adequate end to the essay. Overall, this student makes points clearly while demonstrating a competent command of language. The essay prompt asks specifically for a comparison and contrast of the "effect" of the two pieces, and this essay can be faulted because, to some degree, it confuses effect with purpose. The essay also misreads the tone of the Fisher passage as an "intense diatribe" and could benefit from additional evidence from the passages. On the whole, however, the paper is intelligent, articulate, and substantiated with enough evidence score in the upper-half range.

Medium-Scoring Essay

Although both passages describe places, their styles are very different. The first passage illustrates how most descriptions of Marseilles treat this city unfairly. This is accomplished through the author's humiliation of these articles. The second passage shows how most people's description of the South is wrong. But rather than through satire, this is accomplished through the use of imagery. Thus both pieces are similar in their effect, but are different in their author's handling of the resources of language.

The first piece by M. F. K. Fisher about the French port of Marseille succeeds in showing that writers about this place only tell the wrong side of the story. Although Marseille like all cities has its attractions and its good points, these writers unfairly give it "A legendary reputation as a world capital for 'dope, whores, and street violence.'" Thus this piece humiliates and satirizes those writers. The tone of this piece is very light and humorous, but it hides the meaning of the author's words. For instance, "The familiar pitch had been made, and idle readers dreaming of a great seaport dedicated to heroin, prostitution, and rioting could easily skip the clumsy detail of marketing for fresh fish." By including the talk of fresh fish in the sentence, this passage is making a parody of the article where dope, whores, and street violence are combined with how to make a true bouillabaisse. The other article that this passage also talks about says "Marseilles is the world's wickedest port." The passage ridicules this piece with the satiric sentence "Sometimes such journalese is almost worth reading for its precociously obsolete views of a society too easy to forget." This piece is sarcastically saying that readers should read this article because it is a great example of something

bad. Therefore, this passage is able to use sarcasm, satire, and humiliation to show how Marseille is improperly represented by writers.

The second piece by Maya Angelou about the small town of Stamps, Arkansas tries to show how this place is also improperly represented. This is done by using imagery. First, that passage describes the South as "a much-loved region in the American fantasy where pale white women float eternally under black magnolia trees." These images show that the American fantasy is a peaceful, relaxed South where white people linger around. In fact, this image is wrong. In the next part of the passage, the south is shown in the harsh light of reality. "The South I returned to, however, was flesh-real and swollen-belly poor." These images succeed in showing the harshness of life the African Americans led in the South. This sentence also shows this point. "And above all, the atmosphere was pressed down with the smell of old fears, and hates, and guilt." The use of atmosphere adds to the depressingly real tone created by these images. Also a metaphor is used "passions clanged with the ferocity of armored knights colliding." This adds to the electrical atmosphere of the passage. By using such strong images to create the electrical atmosphere or the passage, the illusion of the first paragraph is shown for with it truly is. Therefore, this passage is able to use images, words, and atmosphere to show how Stamps, Arkansas is improperly represented by the American Fantasy of the South. The style of this passage is different from the other which humiliates the improper representation. Therefore, both passages use their author's handling of the resources of language in a different way to talk about the same effect.

Analysis of the Medium-Scoring Essay

The essay's introduction accurately addresses the topic. However, the student's writing style and depth of thought do not demonstrate the sophistication needed for a high-scoring essay. To claim merely that the two passages are "similar in effect, but . . . different" in their use of language barely touches on the topic.

The second paragraph concentrates on Fisher's article and points out that Fisher humiliates (an inaccurate word in this context) and satirizes the authors who had presented Marseille as the "wickedest port." The student seems to recognize Fisher's effect but doesn't extend the observation, merely stating that Fisher is "making a parody" through use of sarcasm. Some examples from the passage are included but are treated perfunctorily and obviously, without depth or strong analysis.

The last paragraph also is accurate in its discussion, but the presentation is simplistic and uninteresting. For example, "This sentence also shows the point" fails to connect the two examples effectively, and the claim that the use of metaphor creates an "electrical atmosphere" doesn't explain in what way "armored knights colliding" does so. This paragraph, as those preceding, makes valid points but doesn't explore them in enough depth to engage or convince the reader. This essay could be greatly improved with the use of deeper analysis and more sophisticated presentation.

Question 3

Scoring Guide for Question 3 (William Hazlitt)

9 Essays that earn a score of 9 meet the criteria for essays that receive a score of 8; in addition, they are especially sophisticated in their explanation and argument. They may also present particularly impressive control of language.

8 Successful

These well-written essays **successfully** demonstrate an understanding of Hazlitt's purpose in his discussion of comedy and its nature. In addition, they reveal a thorough comprehension of how Hazlitt's tone, point of view, and use of stylistic devices reflect that purpose. The thesis is thoughtful and articulate. Strong and relevant evidence from Hazlitt's essay supports intelligent insights concerning Hazlitt's purpose. Thoroughly convincing, these essays show a clear command of essay writing skills. Although they need not be without errors, these papers show a mature style and use of language.

7 These essays fit the description of an essay that scored a 6, but they provide a more complete explanation and clarity of thought. Also, they demonstrate a more mature prose style.

6 Satisfactory

These essays **satisfactorily** comprehend Hazlitt's purpose, but the thesis may be less explicit than that of the top-scoring essay. The evidence offered may be less convincing, but these papers still demonstrate clear thinking. The connection between the evidence and Hazlitt's purpose may not be as clear as in the top-scoring essays. Although well written, these essays may show some errors while maintaining satisfactory control over diction and the essay's requirements.

5 These adequately written essays show some understanding of Hazlitt's purpose but may not clearly comprehend the relationship between his language and his purpose. The writer may merely list the devices Hazlitt uses without relating them to his purpose. The thesis may be simplistic and the evidence insufficient to prove the writer's assertions. Acceptable organization and development may be evident, but the style may not be as sophisticated as that of higher-scoring essays.

4 Inadequate

These low-scoring essays fail to convince the reader. The **inadequate** presentation may not demonstrate a clear understanding of Hazlitt's purpose. Comprehension of how Hazlitt's manipulation of language reflects his purpose may be lacking. The thesis may be unsubstantiated, paragraph development may be weak, and superficial thinking may be evident. Frequent errors in composition that distract the reader may be present.

3 These essays meet the criteria for a score of 4 but show more weakness in developing the thesis and supporting arguments with sufficient evidence. These essays may fail to complete all the tasks given. These essays may simply catalog the devices, the resources of language, without analysis or comment on the connection between the author's purpose and language use. Weak control of the essay format and/or language may be evident, and mechanical errors may be frequent.

2 Little Success

These poorly written essays lack coherence and clarity. They may attempt to state Hazlitt's purpose without any mention of how his language reflects his purpose. The thesis may be overly obvious or absent. Little or no evidence may be offered, and any connection between the evidence and the thesis may be shallow or nonexistent. These essays may substitute a simpler task by replying to the question with irrelevant information. Persistent weaknesses in grammar and organization may be evident. These papers may be unusually short.

1 These essays meet the criteria for an essay earning a score of a 2, but lack evidence and connections between the evidence and thesis. These essays show a weak control of language and weakness in understanding Hazlitt's purpose.

High-Scoring Essay

Two masks symbolize the theater, the one merry, joyful, the other weeping and forlorn. In its turn, the theater acts as a microcosm of life, its twin emblems representative of life's paramount elements: comedy coupled with tragedy.

William Hazlitt explores the relationship of comedy and tragedy, tears and laughter, in Lectures on the English Comic Writers. Hazlitt proposes that, like love and hate, mirth and sadness are not really the opposites that some assume them to be. Apathy is perhaps the true opposite of all four emotions. Both comedy and tragedy are intensely concerned with the human condition. Responses to comedy and tragedy are perhaps our most profound reflexive reactions to the world around us, so it is instructive to examine, as Hazlitt does, the similar foundations of the two.

Hazlitt's enthusiastic tone fits his purpose of persuasion. He writes as if he has just made an amazing discovery, and cannot wait to tell readers about his find. Exploring the nature of the two responses, comedy and tragedy, to the world, Hazlitt writes that both are spurred by man's perception of possibilities, and disappointment or joy results when these are not met, depending on the gravity or ludicrousness of the situation. Indeed comedy often issues from the wellsprings of tragedy and hurt. Laughter can be a defense mechanism, a protective response to the realities of the world and an opportunity to mock the frightening rather than cower before it.

Hazlitt's point of view has arguably become a part of the conventional wisdom these days. Comedy and tragedy are two sides of the same coin, he asserts. Comedy is made up of trifling tragedies. Not serious enough to wound, they instead inspire ridicule and heckling. Confusion can exist between the emotions: People often cry tears of joy on happy occasions or laugh inappropriately in the face of despair. Hazlitt successfully persuades readers of the inexorable relationship between the emotions.

Hazlitt's prose is brisk, almost breathless. Even though compounded with prepositional phrases and the like, the first paragraph of his essay speeds along with emphasized repetition: "We weep . . . we laugh . . . we shed tears . . . we burst into laughter." Hazlitt keeps the reader to a relentless pace with a series of phrases and clauses separated by commas and semicolons, filling long complex sentences. His last sentence in the essay effectively uses technique as it builds to a crescendo. The <u>eureka</u> tone of amazed discovery is in part achieved by a liberal smattering of exclamation points throughout the essay, such as "it is in a manner compounded of these two!" and "it fails to move our anger or our pity!" The <u>gee whiz!</u> tone which these literary techniques help to create does aid in persuading the reader that Hazlitt's conclusions are valid.

Hazlitt's skillful, rhythmic writing seems capable of lulling readers into believing anything he asserts. He accomplishes his purpose with an enthusiastic passage that clearly demonstrates the inseparable connection between laughter and tears. Understand that, and we are well on our way to understanding life.

Analysis of the High-Scoring Essay

This well-written essay begins with two paragraphs that immediately spark the reader's interest, mentioning the comic and tragic masks of the theater and then effectively relating the theater, as a "microcosm of life," to the essay's content and to the topic question. There is no thesis statement, but that isn't an absolute requirement. This student is definitely on the right track, addressing the issue of Hazlitt's purpose and his means of achieving it.

The next two paragraphs explore Hazlitt's point of view and his success in achieving his purpose and his perception of comedy and tragedy, relating that perception to contemporary society's. No strong evidence is presented in these paragraphs, but none is required in paragraphs that serve primarily to discuss Hazlitt's ideas.

The fifth paragraph presents an analysis of Hazlitt's technique and style, noting the use of repetition and aptly describing the essay's pace as "breathless . . . relentless." The student also notes that Hazlitt's use of exclamation points produces a "tone of amazed discovery." This writer demonstrates an accurate understanding of how a writer's technique can produce a specific effect on the reader.

The concluding paragraph reiterates the relationship of Hazlitt's "rhythmic writing" to his purpose but doesn't stop at mere summary. It points to the essay's wider implication—that through understanding laughter and tears, we can broaden our understanding of life. This student, like Hazlitt, demonstrates both lively style and discriminating diction.

Medium-Scoring Essay

William Hazlitt begins by describing the differences between humans and animals. He writes that man has the emotions of humor and sadness that animals don't because men see that things aren't always as good as they could be.

Sometimes people laugh, and sometimes people cry about life, depending on the situation. Through Hazlitt's use of tone and stylistic devices he achieves his purpose to convince the reader that comedy and tragedy spring from the same well of emotion and essentially help mankind to cope with the vicissitudes of life. People just react to life in different ways.

Depending on people and situations, this can be true. "It is a tragedy or a comedy—sad or merry, as it happens," Hazlitt wrote, showing that people can and do react in a different way to the same event. One of Hazlitt's reasons for writing is to prove that mankind needs different reactions; it is part of man's defense mechanism.

Hazlitt's tone tries to educate people about laughing and crying. Perhaps this is so people can feel less self conscious and work together better in the future without worrying whether their response is right or not, since there isn't a lot of difference between comedy and tragedy. So where one person might see one thing as tragic, the other person may not.

Hazlitt uses many literary devices so readers can picture the differing details of comedy and sadness he discusses. He says tragedy can "shock and wound the mind." He describes tears of relief about comedy or happy times without tragedy. He also uses repetition and exclamation to achieve his purpose. Readers now understand the relationship of comedy and tragedy, and agree with his conclusions.

Analysis of the Medium-Scoring Essay

This essay clearly demonstrates areas in which a student writing under time pressure can make mistakes. This paper has a variety of problems in coherence, organization, diction, and proof.

The first paragraph fails to elicit much excitement. A good AP essay doesn't necessarily have to grab attention, but this one is particularly uninteresting, merely paraphrasing Hazlitt's opening comment on humans and animals. The second paragraph improves somewhat. The student attempts to identify Hazlitt's purpose. But while the statement is well worded, it does not yet deal with one of the assigned tasks, a discussion of Hazlitt's technique.

The third and fourth paragraphs discuss Hazlitt's contentions, but perfunctorily and without great insight. Although Hazlitt's tone is mentioned at the beginning of the fourth paragraph, no analysis or examples follow. Weaknesses of this sort usually arise from inadequacies in planning and organization.

The last paragraph finally addresses literary devices and lists "repetition and exclamation," but once again, no evidence follows proving the connection between literary devices and purpose. Here, the student seems to be grasping for ideas and unsure of his or her point.

While this essay shows some understanding of Hazlitt's purpose, which is to be commended, attempts at proof, analysis, and discussion produce confused sentences with murky ideas. In addition, the student's language, while occasionally sophisticated, is more often than not simplistic. Overall, the essay fails to convince the reader.

Answer Sheet for Practice Test 3

Remove this sheet and use it to mark your answers.
Answer sheets for "Section II: Essays" can be found at the end of the book.

Section I
Multiple-Choice Questions

First Passage

1 Ⓐ Ⓑ Ⓒ Ⓓ Ⓔ
2 Ⓐ Ⓑ Ⓒ Ⓓ Ⓔ
3 Ⓐ Ⓑ Ⓒ Ⓓ Ⓔ
4 Ⓐ Ⓑ Ⓒ Ⓓ Ⓔ
5 Ⓐ Ⓑ Ⓒ Ⓓ Ⓔ
6 Ⓐ Ⓑ Ⓒ Ⓓ Ⓔ
7 Ⓐ Ⓑ Ⓒ Ⓓ Ⓔ
8 Ⓐ Ⓑ Ⓒ Ⓓ Ⓔ
9 Ⓐ Ⓑ Ⓒ Ⓓ Ⓔ
10 Ⓐ Ⓑ Ⓒ Ⓓ Ⓔ
11 Ⓐ Ⓑ Ⓒ Ⓓ Ⓔ
12 Ⓐ Ⓑ Ⓒ Ⓓ Ⓔ
13 Ⓐ Ⓑ Ⓒ Ⓓ Ⓔ
14 Ⓐ Ⓑ Ⓒ Ⓓ Ⓔ
15 Ⓐ Ⓑ Ⓒ Ⓓ Ⓔ

Second Passage

16 Ⓐ Ⓑ Ⓒ Ⓓ Ⓔ
17 Ⓐ Ⓑ Ⓒ Ⓓ Ⓔ
18 Ⓐ Ⓑ Ⓒ Ⓓ Ⓔ
19 Ⓐ Ⓑ Ⓒ Ⓓ Ⓔ
20 Ⓐ Ⓑ Ⓒ Ⓓ Ⓔ
21 Ⓐ Ⓑ Ⓒ Ⓓ Ⓔ
22 Ⓐ Ⓑ Ⓒ Ⓓ Ⓔ
23 Ⓐ Ⓑ Ⓒ Ⓓ Ⓔ
24 Ⓐ Ⓑ Ⓒ Ⓓ Ⓔ
25 Ⓐ Ⓑ Ⓒ Ⓓ Ⓔ
26 Ⓐ Ⓑ Ⓒ Ⓓ Ⓔ
27 Ⓐ Ⓑ Ⓒ Ⓓ Ⓔ
28 Ⓐ Ⓑ Ⓒ Ⓓ Ⓔ

Third Passage

29 Ⓐ Ⓑ Ⓒ Ⓓ Ⓔ
30 Ⓐ Ⓑ Ⓒ Ⓓ Ⓔ
31 Ⓐ Ⓑ Ⓒ Ⓓ Ⓔ
32 Ⓐ Ⓑ Ⓒ Ⓓ Ⓔ
33 Ⓐ Ⓑ Ⓒ Ⓓ Ⓔ
34 Ⓐ Ⓑ Ⓒ Ⓓ Ⓔ
35 Ⓐ Ⓑ Ⓒ Ⓓ Ⓔ
36 Ⓐ Ⓑ Ⓒ Ⓓ Ⓔ
37 Ⓐ Ⓑ Ⓒ Ⓓ Ⓔ
38 Ⓐ Ⓑ Ⓒ Ⓓ Ⓔ
39 Ⓐ Ⓓ Ⓑ Ⓞ Ⓒ
40 Ⓐ Ⓑ Ⓒ Ⓓ Ⓔ
41 Ⓐ Ⓑ Ⓒ Ⓓ Ⓔ
42 Ⓐ Ⓑ Ⓒ Ⓓ Ⓔ

Fourth Passage

43 Ⓐ Ⓑ Ⓒ Ⓓ Ⓔ
44 Ⓐ Ⓑ Ⓒ Ⓓ Ⓔ
45 Ⓐ Ⓑ Ⓒ Ⓓ Ⓔ
46 Ⓐ Ⓑ Ⓒ Ⓓ Ⓔ
47 Ⓐ Ⓑ Ⓒ Ⓓ Ⓔ
48 Ⓐ Ⓑ Ⓒ Ⓓ Ⓔ
49 Ⓐ Ⓑ Ⓒ Ⓓ Ⓔ
50 Ⓐ Ⓑ Ⓒ Ⓓ Ⓔ
51 Ⓐ Ⓑ Ⓒ Ⓓ Ⓔ
52 Ⓐ Ⓑ Ⓒ Ⓓ Ⓔ
53 Ⓐ Ⓓ Ⓞ Ⓒ
54 Ⓐ Ⓑ Ⓒ Ⓓ Ⓔ
55 Ⓐ Ⓑ Ⓒ Ⓓ Ⓔ

CUT HERE

Practice Test 3

Section I: Multiple-Choice Questions

Time: 60 minutes

55 questions

Directions: This section consists of selections from prose works and questions on their content, form, and style. Read each selection carefully. Choose the best answer of the five choices.

Questions 1–15. Read the following passage carefully before you begin to answer the questions.

First Passage

At Oxford in 1850 the contemporaries of young Robert Cecil agreed that he would end as Prime Minister either because or in spite of his remorselessly uncompromising opinions. Throughout life (5) he never bothered to restrain them. His youthful speeches were remarkable for their virulence and insolence; he was not, said Disraeli, "a man who measures his phrases." A "salisbury" became a synonym for a political imprudence. He once (10) compared the Irish in their incapacity for self-government to Hottentots and spoke of an Indian candidate for Parliament as "that black man." In the opinion of Lord Morley his speeches were always a pleasure to read because "they were sure to contain (15) one blazing indiscretion which it is a delight to remember." Whether these were altogether accidental is open to question, for though Lord Salisbury delivered his speeches without notes, they were worked out in his head beforehand and emerged (20) clear and perfect in sentence structure. In that time the art of oratory was considered part of the equipment of a statesman and anyone reading from a written speech would have been regarded as pitiable. When Lord Salisbury spoke, "every sentence," (25) said a fellow member, "seemed essential, as articulate, as vital to the argument as the members of his body to an athlete."

Appearing in public before an audience about whom he cared nothing, Salisbury was awkward; (30) but in the Upper House, where he addressed his equals, he was perfectly and strikingly at home. He spoke sonorously, with an occasional change of tone to icy mockery or withering sarcasm. When a recently ennobled Whig took the floor to lecture (35) the House of Lords in high-flown and solemn Whig sentiments, Salisbury asked a neighbor who the speaker was and on hearing the whispered identification, replied perfectly audibly, "I thought he was dead." When he listened to others he could become (40) easily bored, revealed by a telltale wagging of his leg which seemed to one observer to be saying, "When will all this be over?" Or sometimes, raising his heels off the floor, he would set up a sustained quivering of his knees and legs which could (45) last for half an hour at a time. At home, when made restless by visitors, it shook the floor and made the furniture rattle, and in the House his colleagues on the front bench complained it made them seasick. If his legs were at rest his long fingers would be in (50) motion, incessantly twisting and turning a paper knife or beating a tattoo on his knee or on the arm of his chair. . . .

Mr. Gladstone, though, in political philosophy his bitterest antagonist, acknowledged him "a great (55) gentleman in private society." In private life he was delightful and sympathetic and a complete contrast to his public self. In public acclaim, Salisbury was uninterested, for—since the populace was uninstructed—its opinions, as far as he was concerned, (60) were worthless. He ignored the public and neither possessed nor tried to cultivate the personal touch that makes a political leader a recognizable personality to the man in the street and earns him a nickname like "Pam" or "Dizzy" or the "Grand Old (65) Man." Not in the press, not even in *Punch*, was Lord Salisbury ever called anything but Lord

GO ON TO THE NEXT PAGE

Salisbury. He made no attempt to conceal his dis-like for mobs of all kinds, "not excluding the House of Commons." After moving to the Lords,
(70) he never returned to the Commons to listen to its debates from the Peers Gallery or chat with members in the Lobby, and if compelled to allude to them in his own House, would use a tone of airy contempt, to the amusement of visitors from the
(75) Commons who came to hear him. But this was merely an outward pose designed to underline his deep inner sense of the patrician. He was not rank-conscious; he was indifferent to honors or any other form of recognition. It was simply that as a
(80) Cecil, and a superior one, he was born with a consciousness in his bones and brain cells of ability to rule and saw no reason to make any concessions of this prescriptive right to anyone whatever.

Having entered the House of Commons in the
(85) customary manner for peers' sons, from a family-controlled borough in an uncontested election at the age of twenty-three, and, during his fifteen years in the House of Commons, having been returned unopposed five times from the same bor-
(90) ough, and having for the last twenty-seven years sat in the House of Lords, he had little personal experience of vote-getting. He regarded himself not as responsible *to* the people but as responsible *for* them. They were in his care. What reverence he felt for
(95) anyone was directed not down but up—to the monarchy. He revered Queen Victoria, who was some ten years his senior, both as her subject and, with chivalry toward her womanhood, as a man. For her he softened his brusqueness even if at
(100) Balmoral he could not conceal his boredom.

1. In relation to the passage as a whole, the first sentence of the first paragraph presents

    A. a paradox that reveals a dominant characteristic of Lord Salisbury's character
    B. a criticism of Lord Salisbury that the rest of the passage will withdraw
    C. a definition of the principles upon which Lord Salisbury was to base his life
    D. an exception to the ideas that make up the rest of the passage
    E. an amusing comment with no important relevance to the development of the rest of the passage

2. Disraeli's description of Lord Salisbury as not "a man who measures his phrases" (lines 7–8) is an example of

    A. simile
    B. understatement
    C. indirect discourse
    D. *ad hominem* argument
    E. diatribe

3. Compared to the second, third, and fourth paragraphs, the first paragraph makes more extensive use of

    A. direct quotations from Lord Salisbury himself
    B. direct quotations from Lord Salisbury's contemporaries
    C. cause-and-effect reasoning
    D. *ad hominem* argument
    E. abstract generalizations

4. Which of the following best describes the function of the second paragraph of the passage?

    A. It makes an assertion that is proven in the third paragraph.
    B. It defines more clearly the flaws of Lord Salisbury's character.
    C. It develops the ideas of Lord Salisbury's "political imprudence."
    D. It enlarges the characterization begun in the first paragraph.
    E. It refutes a common misconception about Lord Salisbury.

5. We can infer that Salisbury was awkward before
   an audience he cared little about (paragraph two)
   because he

   A. was speaking without notes
   B. lacked public-speaking skills
   C. had not bothered to prepare
   D. was nervous about appearing before an
      audience that he feared was unsympathetic to
      his ideas
   E. feared he would betray his real feelings of
      contempt

6. In line 51, the word "tattoo" can be best defined
   as a

   A. rhythm
   B. continuous drumming
   C. picture on the skin
   D. forbidden activity
   E. percussion instrument

7. In the first sentence of the third paragraph, the
   speaker cites Gladstone's words about Lord
   Salisbury because

   I. they have the special authority of words of
      praise from a political opponent
   II. they introduce a favorable presentation of
      Lord Salisbury's private life
   III. it would especially embarrass Lord Salisbury
      to be praised by a political enemy

   A. II only
   B. I and II only
   C. I and III only
   D. II and III only
   E. I, II, and III

8. From the phrase in the third paragraph "not in the
   press, not even in *Punch,* was Lord Salisbury ever
   called anything but Lord Salisbury," we can infer
   that *Punch* was probably a

   A. contemporary novel
   B. political report
   C. conservative magazine
   D. satirical publication
   E. daily newspaper

9. In the last sentence of the third paragraph, all of
   the following words or phrases function as
   intensifiers and could be omitted EXCEPT

   A. "simply"
   B. "and brain cells"
   C. "no reason"
   D. "any"
   E. "whatever"

10. Which of the following accurately describe(s) the
    long sentence which begins the last paragraph of
    the passage ("Having entered . . . vote-getting")?

    I. It is a sentence containing more than ten
       prepositional phrases.
    II. It is a sentence using parallel participial
        phrases.
    III. It is a periodic sentence.

    A. I only
    B. I and II only
    C. I and III only
    D. II and III only
    E. I, II, and III

11. To which of the following would Lord Salisbury
    have been most likely to have shown deference?

    A. the Prince of Wales
    B. the President of the United States
    C. the elderly female newspaper-seller
    D. the British Prime Minister
    E. a Scottish knight

12. The speaker of the passage may be best
    described as

    A. a skeptical biographer
    B. a political supporter
    C. a sympathetic observer
    D. a mordant satirist
    E. an objective commentator

13. In its presentation of the character of Lord Salisbury, the passage overtly employs all of the following sources EXCEPT the

    A. words of contemporary politicians

    B. author's interpretation of Lord Salisbury's actions

    C. words of Lord Salisbury himself

    D. judgments of other modern historians

    E. words of unnamed contemporaries of Lord Salisbury

14. Which of the following does the passage present as central to an understanding of Lord Salisbury?

    A. his deep-seated fear of the possibility of major social change

    B. his intense consciousness of his social rank

    C. his hypocrisy

    D. his genuine respect for men and women of all classes

    E. his firm belief in the native superiority of his family

15. The passage reveals all of the following biographical facts about Lord Salisbury EXCEPT that he

    A. served in the House of Commons

    B. was a contemporary of Queen Victoria and of Gladstone

    C. disapproved of home rule for Ireland

    D. served in the House of Lords

    E. became Prime Minister late in the 19th century

Questions 16–28. Read the following passage carefully before you begin to answer the questions.

Second Passage

To Archibald Forbes[1]

[20 January 1882] Arlington Hotel, Washington

Dear Mr. Forbes, I felt quite sure that your remarks on me had been misrepresented. I must however say that your remarks about me *in your lecture* may be regarded as giving *some* natural ground for the report. I feel bound to
(5)   say quite frankly to you that I do not consider them to be either in good taste or appropriate to your subject.

I have something to say to the American people, something that I know will be the beginning of a great movement here, and all foolish ridicule does a great deal of harm to the cause of art and refinement and civilisation here.

I do not think that your lecture will lose in brilliancy or interest by expunging the passage, which is, as you say yourself, poor fooling enough.

(10)   You have to speak of the life of action, I of the life of art. Our subjects are quite distinct and should be kept so. Believe me, yours truly, OSCAR WILDE

To Archibald Forbes

Monday [23 January 1882] Arlington Hotel, Washington

Dear Mr. Forbes, Colonel Morse[2], who kindly manages for me a somewhat bulky correspondence, tells me that
(15)   you feel yourself wronged by something I am supposed to have said of you in the papers, and that you have written to me in, natural I acknowledge, indignation on the subject. He has sent the letter to Mr Carte without my
reading it, as he considers that Mr Carte can best answer those parts of it relating to my intended visit to
Baltimore. In any case let me assure you that I have neither spoken of you to anyone except as I would speak of a
man whose chivalry, whose personal bravery, and whose pluck, have won him the respect and the admiration of
(20)   all honest men in Europe and in America, and who has given to English journalism the new lustre of action, of
adventure and of courage. I did not believe what I read in the papers about you, that you had spoken of me in a
sneering way behind my back. I in fact denied it to a reporter who came here with the story on *Thursday* night
late, I do not think you should have believed it of me. It is true you hardly know me at all personally, but at least
you know me well enough to come and ask me personally if, after your generous letter to me, I had said of you
(25)   things which seem to you ungenerous and unfair and untrue. The only papers I have seen about the subject are the
Herald and *World*. Miss Meigs whom I had the honour of meeting last night tells me that some garbled interview
appeared in the *Post* which contained certain foolish things supposed to have proceeded from me. I have not seen
the paper at all, or I would have written to you at once about it. [*The rest of this letter is missing.*]

Forbes had answered Wilde's letters of 20 and 23 January as follows:

(30)   26 January 1882 46 West 28 Street, New York

Dear Mr. Wilde, It has a tendency to create confusion when a man does not read important letters addressed to
himself, and there is yet greater risk of this when he essays to reply to them on a summary given him apparently
without a due realisation of their personal significance to him.

I accept your disclamation of the remarks in connection with me which your letter states to have been put into
(35)   your mouth without warrant.

GO ON TO THE NEXT PAGE

But it was not of these remarks which my letter complained. What the letter protested against was

First: the claim set up by you in your letter of Friday last, that I should trim a lecture of mine to suit your sensitiveness to an inoffensive effort at humour; and

(40) *Secondly* and *chiefly*—with the knowledge I have, and which you know I have, of the utterly mercenary aim of your visit to America, the possibility of my accepting your pretensions put forward in the same letter as follows: 'I have something to say to the American people, something that I know will be the beginning of a great movement; and all foolish ridicule does a great deal of harm to the cause of art, refinement and civilisation here.'

It is no affair of mine to whom else you may choose to advance these pretensions; but I must utterly decline to allow you to address them to me, for the reasons given at length in my letter which you have not thought proper to read.

(45) Your letter of Monday, with its irrelevant expressions of cordiality, cannot affect the situation. What I have to ask is that you withdraw, as obviously offensive to me, the whole of your letter of Friday, and that you do so categorically, and in so many words, with the exception of the first sentence of it.

As it is irksome to me that the matter should hang over, I must demand that you send me a letter containing the withdrawal specified, by Sunday next. In the event of my non-receipt thereof, I beg to intimate to you that I will
(50) print the whole correspondence in a New York paper of Monday morning. I am faithfully yours,

ARCHIBALD FORBES.

[1] *British war correspondent and author (1838–1900). He was also lecturing in the States at this time, wearing all his medals, and had small sympathy with Wilde's ideas on aesthetics and dress reform. It had been reported that Wilde would attend Forbes's lecture at Baltimore on 19 January, but the two men quarreled on the train from Philadelphia and Wilde went straight on to Washington without stopping at Baltimore. Both Forbes and the leaders of Baltimore Society were offended. The passage in Forbes's lecture to which Wilde objected described a visit to the Czar in war-torn Bulgaria: "I glanced down at my clothes, which I had not changed in a fortnight, and in which I had ridden 150 miles. Now I wish it understood that I am a follower, an humble follower, of the aesthetic ecstasy, but I did not look much like an art object then. I did not have my dogskin knee breeches with me, nor my velvet coat, and my black silk stockings were full of holes. Neither was the wild, barren waste of Bulgaria congenial to the growth of sunflowers and lilies."*

[2] *D'Oyly Carte's representative in America.*

16. Wilde's choice to italicize *"in your lecture"* (line 4) indicates that

   A. Wilde is willing to disregard Forbes's written correspondence
   B. formal presentations deserve accuracy
   C. Wilde is determined to retaliate in his own lectures
   D. Wilde capriciously decided to chastise Forbes
   E. chance meetings can instill misperceptions

17. Wilde suggests that Forbes do all of the following EXCEPT

   A. delete the offending passage from his lecture
   B. allow each man to speak to the American people
   C. use stronger discretion in his lecture remarks
   D. continue speaking on subjects he knows well
   E. reword the section of his lecture that discusses Wilde

18. Both letter writers employ all of the flowing devices EXCEPT

   A. parallel structure
   B. thinly veiled innuendo
   C. false praise
   D. direct reference to offending remarks
   E. a defiant tone

19. All of the following can be inferred about American journalism of the 1880s EXCEPT

   A. newspapers published libel
   B. newspapers were used as vehicles of personal correspondence
   C. journalistic integrity was paramount
   D. anyone could easily get something printed quickly
   E. the public believed what was published

20. The pronoun "it" in Wilde's remark "I do not think you should have believed *it* of me" (line 23) most likely refers to

    A. Forbes's talking about Wilde behind his back

    B. the paper's reporting the two men's argument

    C. Wilde's supposedly sneering remarks about Forbes

    D. Wilde's capacity for chivalry and personal bravery

    E. the harm done by "foolish ridicule" (line 7)

21. Forbes's use of the word "essays" as a verb (line 32) serves as a

    A. symbolic gesture of support for Wilde's writing

    B. hyperbolic display of Forbes's anger

    C. metaphor of Wilde's body of work

    D. play on words regarding Wilde's correspondence with Forbes

    E. demonstration of Forbes's linguistic prowess

22. The attitude of each author can best be described as

    A. condescending to the other and convinced of his own moral superiority

    B. hopeful that they can come to an agreement and put this past misunderstanding behind them

    C. fearful that their reputation will be permanently tarnished

    D. complacent about future encounters they may have

    E. sincere in their effort to mend past disagreements

23. Wilde would most likely object to the quotation from Forbes's lecture in note #1 because it

    A. is a direct attack on Wilde's pacifism

    B. is a poorly written description of the countryside

    C. denigrates Wilde's antiwar position

    D. presumes that Wilde would never participate in a war

    E. is a disguised attack on Wilde's notions of dress reform and aesthetics

24. Note #1 serves the rhetorical purpose of

    A. summarizing Forbes's argument about the need for war

    B. juxtaposing what Forbes perceives as serious issues, namely "war-torn Bulgaria" with trivial matters, namely Wilde's preoccupation with clothing

    C. providing a logical completion to Forbes's humorous anecdote

    D. serving as an incentive for Wilde to respond

    E. allowing Forbes a chance to repeat his criticism of Wilde

25. The series of letters display all of the following rhetorical techniques EXCEPT

    A. *ad hominem* argument

    B. direct references to perceived slights

    C. innuendo involving other acquaintances

    D. direct condescension regarding appearance

    E. apologetic rebuttal to previous accusations

26. Wilde's letter of January 23 and Forbes's reply differ in that

    A. Forbes is direct and confrontational; Wilde is conversational and explanatory

    B. Forbes is willing to forget their past disagreement; Wilde insists on bringing it up repeatedly

    C. Wilde takes responsibility for his actions while Forbes deflects the blame

    D. Wilde anticipates an amicable end to their dispute; Forbes believes it will continue

    E. Wilde makes logical, step-by-step assertions; Forbes meanders to his point

27. Wilde's second letter differs rhetorically from his first in that the second

    A. systematically outlines his points

    B. shows respect for Forbes's ideas

    C. attacks Forbes more directly

    D. becomes less assertive and aggressive

    E. condescends to flatter Forbes

GO ON TO THE NEXT PAGE

28. Which of the following phrases most clearly displays Wilde's intended ironic condescension?

    A. "I do not think your lecture will lose in brilliancy or interest by expunging the passage" (line 8).

    B. "You have to speak of the life of action, I of the life of art" (line 10).

    C. ". . . you feel yourself wronged by something I am supposed to have said of you in the papers" (line 15).

    D. "I would speak of a man whose chivalry, whose personal bravery, and whose pluck, have won him the respect and the admiration" (lines 18–19).

    E. "It is true you hardly know me at all personally" (line 23).

Questions 29–42. Read the following passage carefully before you begin to answer the questions.

Third Passage

This single stick, which you now behold ingloriously lying in that neglected corner, I once knew in a flourishing state in a forest; it was full of sap, full of leaves, and full of boughs; but now, in vain, does the
(5) busy art of man pretend to vie with nature, by tying that withered bundle of twigs to its sapless trunk; 'tis now, at best, but the reverse of what it was, a tree turned upside down, the branches on the earth, and the root in the air; 'tis now handled by every dirty
(10) wench, condemned to do her drudgery, and, by a capricious kind of fate, destined to make other things clean, and be nasty itself; at length, worn to the stumps in the service of the maids, either thrown out of doors, or condemned to the last use, of kindling a
(15) fire. When I beheld this, I sighed, and said within myself: *Surely Man is a Broomstick!* Nature sent him into the world strong and lusty, in a thriving condition, wearing his own hair on his head, the proper branches of this reasoning vegetable, until
(20) the axe of intemperance has lopped off his green boughs, and left him a withered trunk; he then flies to art, and puts on a periwig, valuing himself upon an unnatural bundle of hairs (all covered with powder) that never grew on his head; but now should
(25) this our broomstick pretend to enter the scene, proud of all those birchen spoils it never bore, and all covered with dust, though the sweepings of the finest lady's chamber, we should be apt to ridicule and despise its vanity. Partial judges that we are of our own
(30) excellences, and other men's defaults!

But a broomstick, perhaps you will say, is an emblem of a tree standing on its head; and pray, what is a man but a topsy-turvy creature, his animal faculties perpetually mounted on his rational, his head where
(35) his heels should be, groveling on the earth! And yet, with all his faults, he sets up to be a universal reformer and corrector of abuses, a remover of grievances, rakes into every slut's corner of nature, bringing hidden corruption to the light, and raises a
(40) mighty dust where there was none before; sharing deeply all the while in the very same pollutions he pretends to sweep away; his last days are spent in slavery to women, and generally the least deserving; till, worn out to the stumps, like his brother broom,
(45) he is either kicked out of doors, or made use of to kindle flames for others to warm themselves by.

29. All of the following are present in the opening sentence of the passage EXCEPT

A. syntactically complex structure
B. parallel construction
C. a pedantic tone
D. the narrative of a broomstick's life
E. subordinate clauses

30. According to the speaker, both a broomstick and a man

A. cleanse the world
B. become corrupted by the evil in society
C. can be proud of their humble accomplishments
D. symbolize integrity in the world
E. were untainted in their natural state

31. Which of the following does the speaker imply?

I. Man has the ability to return to a better state.
II. Man in his youthful, natural state is closer to perfection than when he is older.
III. Man misuses nature for his own needs.

A. I only
B. II only
C. I and II only
D. II and III only
E. I, II, and III

32. According to the passage, the broomstick symbolizes

A. society's corruption of the youth
B. the goodness in nature that man uses and discards
C. the triumph of nature over man's evil tendencies
D. the evil inherent in man's soul
E. the tremendous power of nature that man fears

GO ON TO THE NEXT PAGE

33. The "axe of intemperance" (line 20) can be interpreted as

   A. an understatement of man's dominance over nature

   B. a metaphor for nature's nourishing elements

   C. a simile comparing man and tree

   D. a hyperbole describing man's destruction

   E. a metaphor for man's excesses

34. The speaker's attitude toward mankind can best be described as

   A. disillusionment at man's deeds

   B. perplexed concern for man's future

   C. guarded optimism for man's soul

   D. anger at the society man has created

   E. sincere praise for man's use of nature

35. Which of the following does NOT demonstrate a negative attitude by this speaker?

   A. "a flourishing state in a forest" (lines 2–3)

   B. "the axe of intemperance" (line 20)

   C. "an unnatural bundle of hairs" (line 23)

   D. "sweepings of the finest lady's chamber" (lines 27–28)

   E. "sharing . . . the very same pollutions he pretends to sweep away" (lines 40–42)

36. According to the speaker, which of the following is NOT a similarity between man and the broomstick?

   A. Both endure the same fate.

   B. Both began life in a healthy state.

   C. Both are turned "topsy-turvy."

   D. Both accomplish magnificent achievements.

   E. Both attempt to cleanse while being dirty.

37. The word referred to by the phrase "this reasoning vegetable" (line 19) is

   A. "Man" (line 16)

   B. "hair" (line 18)

   C. "head" (line 18)

   D. "branches" (line 19)

   E. "green boughs" (lines 20–21)

38. In the essay, the speaker uses all of the following literary devices EXCEPT

   A. metaphor

   B. parallel syntax

   C. oxymoron

   D. analogy

   E. symbolism

39. In context, "this our broomstick" (line 25) is a

   A. symbol for the thriving forest

   B. metaphor for man's pretentious character

   C. link between nature and society

   D. demonstration of nature's control

   E. representation of man's intelligence

40. What does the speaker imply about man's ability to be a "corrector of abuses" (line 37)?

   A. Man easily solves his own problems.

   B. Man effectively improves society.

   C. Man can act as a fair arbitrator in disputes.

   D. Man readily accepts his role as a social reformer.

   E. Man causes problems where none previously existed.

41. The tone of the passage can best be described as

   A. neutral toward society

   B. condescending toward nature

   C. cynical toward mankind

   D. bellicose toward mankind

   E. dogmatic toward society

42. Which of the following represents the strongest statement of the speaker's theme?

   A. "condemned to do her drudgery" (line 10)

   B. "destined to make other things clean" (lines 11–12)

   C. "the axe of intemperance has lopped off his green boughs" (lines 20–21)

   D. "Partial judges that we are of our own excellences" (lines 29–30)

   E. "his last days are spent in slavery" (lines 42–43)

Questions 43–55. Read the following passage carefully before you begin to answer the questions.

Fourth Passage

The time is coming, I hope, when each new author, each new artist, will be considered, not in his proportion to any other author or artist, but in his relation to the human nature, known to us all, which is
(5) his privilege, his high duty, to interpret. "The true standard of the artist is in every man's power" already, as [Edmund] Burke says; Michelangelo's "light of the piazza," the glance of the common eye, is and always was the best light on a statue; . . . but
(10) hitherto the mass of common men have been afraid to apply their own simplicity, naturalness, and honesty to the appreciation of the beautiful. They have always cast about for the instruction of some one who professed to know better, and who browbeat
(15) wholesome common-sense into the self-distrust that ends in sophistication. . . . They have been taught to compare what they see and what they read, not with the things that they have observed and known, but with the things that some other artist or writer has
(20) done. Especially if they have themselves the artistic impulse in any direction they are taught to form themselves, not upon life, but upon the masters who became masters only by forming themselves upon life. The seeds of death are planted in them, and they
(25) can only produce the still-born, the academic. They are not told to take their work into the public square and see if it seems true to the chance passer, but to test it by the work of the very men who refused and decried any other test of their won work. The young
(30) writer who attempts to report the phrase and carriage of every-day life, who tries to tell just how he has heard men talk and seen them look, is made to feel guilty of something low and unworthy by the stupid people who would like to have him show how
(35) Shakespeare's men talked and looked, or Scott's, or Thackeray's, or Balzac's, or Hawthorne's, or Dickens's; he is instructed to idealize his personages, that is, to take the life-likeness out of them, and put the book-likeness into them. He is approached in
(40) the spirit of the wretched pedantry into which learning . . . always decays when it withdraws itself and stands apart from experience in an attitude of imagined superiority, and which would say with the same confidence to the scientist: "I see that you are look
(45) ing at a grasshopper there which you have found in the grass, and I suppose you intend to describe it.

Now don't waste your time and sin against culture in that way. I've got a grasshopper here, which has been evolved at considerable pains and expense out
(50) of the grasshopper in general; in fact, it's a type. It's made up of wire and cardboard, very prettily painted in a conventional tint, and it's perfectly indestructible. It isn't very much like a real grasshopper, but it's a great deal nicer, and it's served to represent the
(55) notion of a grasshopper ever since man emerged from barbarianism. You may say that it's artificial. Well, it is artificial; but then it's ideal too; and what you want to do is to cultivate the ideal. You'll find the books full of my kind of grasshopper, and
(60) scarcely a trace of yours in any of them. The thing that you are proposing to do is commonplace; but if you say that it isn't commonplace, for the very reason that it hasn't been done before, you'll have to admit that it's photographic."
(65) I hope the time is coming when not only the artist, but the common, average man, who always "has the standard of the arts in his power," will have also the courage to apply it, and will reject the ideal grasshopper wherever he finds it, in science, in liter
(70) ature, in art, because it is not "simple, natural, and honest," because it is not like a real grasshopper. But . . . I think the time is yet far off, and that the people who have been brought up on the ideal grasshopper, the heroic grasshopper, the impas
(75) sioned grasshopper, the self-devoted, adventureful, good old romantic cardboard grasshopper, must die out before the simple, honest, and natural grasshopper can have a fair field. I am in no haste to compass the end of these good people, whom I find in the
(80) meantime very amusing. It is delightful to meet one of them, either in print or out of it some sweet elderly lady or excellent gentleman whose youth was pastured on the literature of thirty or forty years ago—and to witness the confidence with which they
(85) preach their favorite authors as all the law and the prophets. They have commonly read little or nothing since or, if they have, they have judged it by a standard taken from these authors, and never dreamed of judging it by nature; they are destitute of the docu
(90) ments in the case of the later writers; they suppose that Balzac was the beginning of realism, and that Zola is its wicked end; they are quite ignorant, but

GO ON TO THE NEXT PAGE

they are ready to talk you down, if you differ from them, with an assumption of knowledge sufficient

(95) for any occasion. The horror, the resentment, with which they receive any question of their literary saints is genuine; you descend at once very far in the

moral and social scale, anything short of offensive personality is too good for you; it is expressed to you

(100) that you are one to be avoided, and put down even a little lower than you have naturally fallen.

43. The tone of the passage could best be described as

    A. somber

    B. ornate

    C. didactic

    D. critical

    E. formal

44. The speaker feels common people make which of the following mistakes?

    A. judging a work of art too quickly

    B. letting their own interpretation interfere with their reading

    C. letting authorities tell them how to interpret literature

    D. basing their judgments on appearances only

    E. not modeling their tastes after their neighbors'

45. The phrase "The seeds of death" (line 24) is a

    A. metaphor for imitative art

    B. symbol for the destruction of art

    C. metaphor for the art of an older age

    D. reference to Michelangelo's art

    E. symbol of artistic immaturity

46. In context, which of the following does NOT represent an object of the speaker's criticism?

    A. "some one . . . who browbeat wholesome common-sense" (lines 13–15)

    B. "are taught to form themselves, not upon life" (lines 21–22)

    C. "he is instructed to idealize his personages" (lines 37–38)

    D. "put the book-likeness into them" (line 39)

    E. "will reject the ideal grasshopper" (lines 68–69)

47. The speaker's criticism of those who read only older literature is tempered by the fact that he

    A. is certain their ideas will die out quickly

    B. finds them entertaining and delightful

    C. dismiss them as unimportant

    D. alleges they do little harm to the average reader

    E. acknowledges that they have great knowledge

48. The idealized grasshopper is a symbol for

    A. the quest to merge art and science

    B. the human search for perfection

    C. art that lasts through the ages

    D. artificial rather than realistic art

    E. the scientist's folly in trying to describe nature

49. According to the speaker, the irony of the idealized grasshopper is that

    A. it ceases to be realistic

    B. scientists will find it useful

    C. it blends science and art into one

    D. it cannot be distinguished from a real grasshopper

    E. it has not been created

50. Which of the following types of grasshopper does the speaker feel will be the slowest to become integrated into mainstream literature?

    A. the heroic grasshopper

    B. the ideal grasshopper

    C. the simple, honest, natural grasshopper

    D. the impassioned grasshopper

    E. the good old romantic cardboard grasshopper

51. Which of the following would the speaker recommend for modern readers?

    I.   Read only classical literature.

    II.   Read literature from all ages.

    III.   Read with your own interpretation.

    A. I only

    B. II only

    C. III only

    D. I and II only

    E. II and III only

52. The story of the grasshopper contains

    A. hidden hyperbole

    B. satiric humor

    C. overstated oxymoron

    D. ruthless criticism

    E. remarkable realism

53. In context, which of the following best represents the speaker's main idea about art appreciation?

    A. "simplicity, naturalness, and honesty" (lines 11–12)

    B. "people who would like to have him show how Shakespeare's men talked" (lines 34–35)

    C. "an attitude of imagined superiority" (lines 42–43)

    D. "it is artificial; but then it's ideal too" (line 57)

    E. "witness the confidence with which they preach their favorite authors" (lines 84–85)

54. What similarity is suggested between the scientist and artist who discuss the grasshopper?

    A. The models of their studies will both be artificial.

    B. They both love to observe nature.

    C. They both look to old masters for inspiration.

    D. Both of their methods will become obsolete.

    E. They both spend too much time on research.

55. Which of the following devices is NOT used in the passage?

    A. irony

    B. metaphor

    C. motif

    D. allusion

    E. analogy

IF YOU FINISH BEFORE TIME IS CALLED, CHECK YOUR WORK ON THIS SECTION ONLY. DO NOT WORK ON ANY OTHER SECTION IN THE TEST.

Practice Test 3

Section II: Essay Questions

Time: 2 hours, 15 minutes

3 questions

Question 1

(Reading time—15 minutes. Suggested writing time—40 minutes. This question counts one-third of the total essay section score.)

Directions: The prompt that follows is based on six accompanying sources. This essay requires you to integrate a variety of sources into a coherent, well-written essay. Refer to the sources, both directly and indirectly, to support your position. Avoid mere paraphrasing or summarizing. Your argument should be the central focus; the use of the sources should support your argument.

Introduction

Polling has become an integral part of the United States election process. The media, as well as the voting population, take into great consideration the results of various political polls. But are these polls truly accurate? Has the United States been relying too heavily on the inaccurate data of political polling?

Assignment

Read the following sources (including any introductory information) carefully. **Then, in an essay that synthesizes at least three of the sources for support, take a position that defends, challenges, or qualifies the claim that political polls do not accurately represent the views of a population.**

Refer to the sources as Source A, Source B, and so on; authors' names or titles are included for your convenience.

Source A (Chart)

Source B (Triola)

Source C (Fund)

Source D ("All Polls")

Source E (Greenberg)

Source F (Ponnuru)

Source A

Wilson, James Q., and John J. DiIulio, Jr. *American Government: Institutions and Policies,* 7th ed. Boston: Houghton Mifflin Company, 1998. 114.

RESPONSE STABILITY OVER REPEATED INTERVIEWS: TWO EXAMPLES

American Relations with Russia [a]

Some people feel it is important for us to try very hard to get along with Russia. Others feel it is a big mistake to try too hard to get along with Russia. Where would you place yourself on this scale, or haven't you thought about this?

	Attitudes in **January** 1980			
Attitudes in **June** 1980	Cooperate	Middle	Tougher	Unsure
Cooperate	**52%**	25%	13%	19%
Middle	14	**24**	17	16
Tougher	23	41	**60**	18
Unsure	10	11	11	**47**
Number	338	153	266	74

Level of Government Services [aa]

Some people think the government should provide fewer services, even in areas such as health and education, in order to reduce spending. Other people feel it is important for the government to continue the services it now provides even if it means no reduction in spending. Where would you place yourself on this scale, or haven't you thought about this?

	Attitudes in **January** 1980			
Attitudes in **June** 1980	Cut	Middle	Keep Same	Unsure
Cut	**54%**	38%	18%	34%
Middle	18	**24**	10	10
Keep Same	11	25	**59**	15
Unsure	17	14	13	**41**
Number	362	122	208	138

[a] *Respondents were asked to place themselves on a 7-point scale. In this table, points 1, 2, and 3 have been counted as "cooperate"; 4 is counted as "middle"; 5, 6, and 7 have been counted as "tougher." [aa] Points 1, 2, and 3 have been counted as "cut"; 4 is counted as "middle"; 5, 6, and 7 have been counted as "keep same." SOURCE: National Election Studies, 1980 panel study. Reprinted from* The American Enterprise, *a Washington-based magazine of politics, business, and culture.*

GO ON TO THE NEXT PAGE

Source B

Triola, Mario F. *Elementary Statistics,* 7th ed. Reading: Addison Wesley Longman, Inc., 1998. 11–12.

The following passage is taken from a statistics textbook that examines the uses and abuses of statistics.

Abuses of statistics have occurred for some time. For example, about a century ago, statesman Benjamin Disraeli famously said, "there are three kinds of lies: lies, damned lies, and statistics." It has also been said that "figures don't lie; liars figure," and that "if you torture the data long enough, they'll admit to anything." Historian Andrew Lang said that some people use statistics "as a drunken man uses lampposts—for support rather than illumination." These statements refer to abuses of statistics in which data are presented in ways that may be misleading. Some abusers of statistics are simply ignorant or careless, whereas others have personal objectives and are willing to suppress unfavorable data while emphasizing supportive data. We will now present a few examples of the many ways in which data can be distorted.

Loaded Questions: Survey questions can be worded to elicit a desired response. A famous case involves presidential candidate Ross Perot, who asked this question in a mail survey: "Should the president have the line item veto to eliminate waste?" The results included 97% "yes" responses. However, 57% said "yes" when subjects were randomly selected and asked this question: "Should the President have the line item veto, or not?" Sometimes questions are unintentionally loaded by such factors as the order of the items being considered. For example, one German poll asked these two questions:

- Would you say that traffic contributes more or less to air pollution than industry?
- Would you say that industry contributes more or less to air pollution than traffic?

When traffic was presented first, 45% blamed traffic and 32% blamed industry; when industry was presented first, those percentages changed dramatically to 24% and 57%, respectively.

Source C

Fund, John. "Polling Isn't Perfect." *The Wall Street Journal* 14 Nov. 2002: n. pag.

The following passage is excerpted from an article about the current problems facing pollsters.

America has too many political polls, and Americans pay too much attention to them. Many people have believed that for a long time. What's different now is that some pollsters are starting to agree.

"We have falsely raised expectations about polling," says John Zogby, who is famous for having called Bill Clinton's margin in the 1996 presidential race almost exactly and having been virtually the only pollster to give Al Gore a slight popular-vote edge on election eve in 2000. But this year Mr. Zogby saw three of his final 11 statewide polls indicate the wrong winner. He says it would be helpful if people discovered the limitations of polling. In a speech and interview in Washington yesterday he described some of the problems his profession faces:

- The nightly tracking polls that both candidates and reporters fixate on are less reliable than larger polls taken over a longer period of time. "I probably should have used larger samples," admits Mr. Zogby, who thought that Democrat Jeanne Shaheen would win an open New Hampshire Senate seat and that Republican Jim Ryan was tied for the governor's race in Illinois. (She lost by four points and he by seven.)

Dave Winston, a Republican pollster, says one problem with nightly tracking polls is that a pollster doing them doesn't have the time to make innumerable repeat calls to people who won't pick up the phone. Mr. Zogby says that he now has to make an average of seven calls to get just one person willing to spend the 20 minutes or so it takes to answer his polling questions.

- *Pollsters can't poll on Election Day.* Surveys this year found that between 4% and 12% of voters in key states made up their mind who to vote for on Election Day. Although challengers tend to pick up most of the undecided vote, it doesn't always work out that way—making last-minute votes impossible to predict.
- *Answering machines, caller ID and other screening devices make pollsters easier to avoid.* Some phones won't even ring unless they recognize the number of the caller. Scott Adler, University of Colorado political scientist, says pollsters are now concerned that the people who do finally agree to answer a pollster's questions are no longer representative of the voters as a whole.

Whit Ayres, a GOP pollster, told the *Atlanta Journal-Constitution* that "I can't fathom 20 years from now the telephone remaining the primary means of data collection. This industry is in a transition from telephone data collection to Internet data collection." In the meantime, look for polls to be more variable and less reliable than ever. Perhaps it's time that we spend more time listening to the candidates and having people make up their own mind who's doing well.

GO ON TO THE NEXT PAGE

Source D

"All Polls are Not Created Equal." *U.S. News & World Report* 28 Sept. 1992: 24–25.

The following passage is excerpted from an article containing the comments of former Perot pollster, Frank Luntz, on the problems with polls.

There is a variety of ways in which polls that seem identical on the surface can lead to shockingly different results, including:

Order bias. The order in which polling questions are asked can have a significant impact on the results. Pollsters have learned that responses to emotional questions will influence responses to later questions. When respondents are asked whether they themselves are better off today than four years ago, then asked to rate George Bush's handling of the economy and only then asked whom they want for president, Bush's support will be several points lower than if the ballot question is asked first.

Interview bias. Most national polls are conducted from one site by interviewers with similar accents. Respondents from one region can recognize and may respond differently to interviewers who sound as if they are from a different region.

Sampling bias. Typically, to avoid completing too many interviews with individuals of the same age or gender, the person who first answers the phone (disproportionately male and younger) is often not the person who should be interviewed. When the designated interviewee—usually the registered voter with the next birthday—is not home, the interviewer should schedule a call-back—an expensive and time-consuming practice that few media pollsters conduct.

Repetition bias. Some media polls use long questionnaires asking whether respondents hold a "favorable" impression or "agree" to a series of similar questions. Respondents tend not to consider each question on its own merits before answering or will give any answer just to get the interview over with.

Wording bias. Political polls have been conducted for more than 50 years, yet there are still only half a dozen industry-accepted ways to ask whom people prefer for president. The problem is that different wordings do not yield the same result and so aren't exactly comparable. For example, asking people whom they will "vote for" will draw a slightly higher undecided or refusal rate than asking whom they "support." Some people who respond to the "support" question will not respond to "vote for" because they feel their vote is confidential but that their opinion is not.

Timing bias. The 1984 Reagan campaign discovered that Republicans are slightly more likely than Democrats to go out on Friday evenings; Friday polling tends to over represent Democrats. Most campaign pollsters try not to poll on Friday, but media polls still interview on Friday to publish fresh results in the Sunday newspapers.

A properly conducted media poll can provide tremendous insight into the electorate. But too often media polls fail to put the results in context or explain why some data may be misleading.

Source E

Greenberg, Anna. "Why the Polls Were Wrong." *The Nation* 1 Jan. 2001: 26.

The following passage is excerpted from an article that provides an example of inaccurate polling from the 2000 presidential election.

Polls play an increasingly central part in election coverage as the horse race becomes a greater and greater media preoccupation. With survey results, the press can breathlessly report the impact of events and gaffes, like Gore's performance in the debates or Bush's abuse of the English language. The twists and turns of the race are cloaked in the scientific mantle of survey research, like the results of the Gallup tracking poll used by CNN and USA Today, which once showed an eighteen-point shift in the electorate in the course of a couple of nights.

Although we understand a great deal about the science of polling, the methodology of these surveys relies on a set of debatable assumptions about who is most likely to turn out and vote on Election Day. This year most experts predicted low turnout, meaning that only the most motivated voters—normally the most highly educated and affluent citizens—would find their way to the polls. Generally, low turnout favors the Republicans, since high socio-economic status is associated with both political participation and conservative political preferences.

To accommodate these predictions, the polls screened tightly for those most likely to vote, adjusted for predicted turnout and in some cases "weighted up" the GOP share in the sample. All those adjustments meant that most of the national polls going into Election Day showed a 2- to 5-point Bush lead, even when individual state polls showed Gore performing much better. In fact, one of the great mysteries during the campaign was how Gore could hold leads or remain tied in so many battleground states and trail Bush so consistently in the national polls. One answer was simply that those polls were wrong. In fact, internal Gore polling showed the race tied and stable for the last two weeks of the campaign.

GO ON TO THE NEXT PAGE

Source F

Ponnuru, Ramesh. "Margin of Error." Rev. of Mobocracy: *How the Media's Obsession with Polling Twists the News, Alters Elections, and Undermines Democracy,* by Matthew Robinson. *National Review* 6 May 2002: 49.

The following passage is excerpted from a book review of Mobocracy: How the Media's Obsession with Polling Twists the News, Alters Elections, and Undermines Democracy, *by Matthew Robinson.*

Reporters lean on polls because they provide the illusion of numerical certainty amid all the spin. In political campaigns, reporters are torn between the conflicting desires to stay with the herd and to write a new story: Changes in the poll numbers provide the pivot point that lets everyone know when to make the switch together. Now the candidate whose campaign was brilliant last week is revealed as a sad-sack loser. His initiative on health care has bombed. How do we know that? Because he's down in the polls. Why is he down in the polls? Because his health-care initiative has bombed.

The over reliance on polls has the effect of overestimating public support for small policies that seem innocuous to voters. But it kills big ideas in the crib. Voters' initial reaction to any sweeping change is likely to be negative, so the first polls on it will show that it is unpopular. From then on, the idea can be dismissed as such. Polls can interfere with the formation of public opinion.

They can also create the illusion that public opinion exists when it does not. Reports that discuss what the public thinks about stem-cell research, or the Middle East peace process, are pointless because the public has no coherent, consolidated view on these matters, at least at the level of specificity needed to guide action. Polls, and media summaries of them, routinely gloss over the vast public ignorance and apathy that makes them so fluid.

Question 2

(Suggested time—40 minutes. This question counts one-third of the total essay section score.)

Directions: The following passage is the opening of Susan Sontag's book *Illness as Metaphor*. Read the passage carefully, and write a cohesive essay in which you discuss Sontag's attitudes toward and use of metaphor in this excerpt.

Illness is the night-side effect of life, a more onerous citizenship. Everyone who is born holds dual citizenship, in the kingdom of the well and in the kingdom of the sick. Although we all prefer to use only the good passport, sooner or later each of us is obliged, at least for a spell, to identify ourselves as citizens of that other place.

I want to describe, not what it is really like to emigrate to the kingdom of the ill and live there, but the punitive or sentimental fantasies concocted about that situation: not real geography, but stereotypes of national character. My subject is not physical illness itself but the uses of illness as a figure of metaphor. My point is that illness is *not* a metaphor, and that the most truthful way of regarding illness—and the healthiest way of being ill—is one most purified of, most resistant to, metaphoric thinking. Yet it is hardly possible to take up one's residence in the kingdom of the ill unprejudiced by the lurid metaphors with which it has been landscaped. It is toward an elucidation of those metaphors, and a liberation from them, that I dedicate this enquiry.

GO ON TO THE NEXT PAGE

Question 3

(Suggested time—40 minutes. This question counts one-third of the total essay section score.)

Henry David Thoreau wrote, "Many men go fishing all of their lives without knowing that it is not fish they are after."

Directions: In a well thought out essay, examine the accuracy of this aphorism in modern society. Concentrate on examples from your observations, reading, and experiences to develop your ideas.

IF YOU FINISH BEFORE TIME IS CALLED, CHECK YOUR WORK ON THIS SECTION ONLY. DO NOT WORK ON ANY OTHER SECTION IN THE TEST.

Answer Key for Practice Test 3

Section I: Multiple-Choice Questions

First Passage

1. A
2. B
3. B
4. D
5. C
6. B
7. B
8. D
9. C
10. E
11. A
12. E
13. D
14. E
15. E

Second Passage

16. B
17. E
18. A
19. C
20. C
21. D
22. A
23. E
24. B
25. E
26. A
27. D
28. D

Third Passage

29. C
30. E
31. D
32. B
33. E
34. A
35. A
36. D
37. A
38. C
39. B
40. E
41. C
42. D

Fourth Passage

43. D
44. C
45. A
46. E
47. B
48. D
49. A
50. C
51. E
52. B
53. A
54. A
55. C

Section II: Essay Questions

Essay scoring guides, student essays, and analysis appear beginning on page 196.

Practice Test 3 Scoring Worksheet

Use the following worksheet to arrive at a probable final AP grade on Practice Test 3. Because being objective enough to estimate your own essay score is sometimes difficult, you might give your essays (along with the sample essays) to a teacher, friend, or relative to score if you feel confident that the individual has the knowledge necessary to make such a judgment and that he or she will feel comfortable doing so.

Section I: Multiple-Choice Questions

_____ – (¼ or .25 × _____) = _____
right   wrong   multiple-choice
answers   answers   raw score

_____ × 1.2272 = _____ (of possible 67.5)
multiple-choice   multiple-choice
raw score   converted score

Section II: Essay Questions

_____ + _____ + _____ = _____
question 1 question 2 question 3   essay
raw score   raw score   raw score   raw score

_____ × 3.0556 = _____ (of possible 82.5)
essay   essay
raw score   converted score

Final Score

_____ + _____ = _____ (of possible 150)
multiple-choice   essay   final
converted score   converted score   converted score

Probable Final AP Score

Final Converted Score	Probable AP Score
150–104	5
103–92	4
91–76	3
75–50	2
49–0	1

Answers and Explanations for Practice Test 3

Section I: Multiple-Choice Questions

First Passage

From *The Proud Tower* by Barbara Tuchman

1. **A.** The first sentence speaks of the "remorselessly uncompromising opinions" of Robert Cecil (Lord Salisbury), which paradoxically are to be the means of making him prime minister or the obstacle that must be overcome. The freedom with which Lord Salisbury expresses and acts on his opinions is a central issue in the rest of the passage. The notion is not retracted (B or D), and although the comment is amusing, it is also relevant (E).

2. **B.** The remark is an understatement expressed by using the negative and, in the restraint of its expression, at odds with a phrase like "remarkable for their virulence and insolence." Disraeli's phrase could be called a metaphor ("measures") but not a simile (A). It is directly quoted (C). Although the remark is "to the man" *(ad hominem),* that is, a personal comment, it is not an *ad hominem* argument (D) or a diatribe (E), an abusive attack.

3. **B.** There are direct quotations from Disraeli, Lord Morley, and an unnamed fellow member in the first paragraph. The later paragraphs have fewer quotations, although at least one can be found in each of the two following paragraphs. Neither the first paragraph nor the rest of the passage makes noteworthy use of cause-and-effect reasoning, *ad hominem* arguments, or abstract generalizations.

4. **D.** The second paragraph and the remainder of the passage enlarge the characterization of Lord Salisbury. The second paragraph provides examples of his rudeness and his short attention span but also discusses his attitudes toward the public and his oratorical skills, so B and C are not quite as accurate as D. Choices A and E are untrue.

5. **C.** Although he spoke without notes, we know from the first paragraph that his speeches could be "clear and perfect." Choices A and B cannot be correct. The characterization of Lord Salisbury makes it clear that he didn't fear any audience and wasn't at all reluctant to reveal his real feelings. If his speeches in public were awkward, they were so because he was indifferent to what the public thought and didn't, as he saw it, waste his time in preparation for them.

6. **B.** As it is used here, a "tattoo" is a continuous drumming, not an ink picture on skin. A student who chooses answer D probably has the word "taboo" in mind.

7. **B.** The praise of an enemy is praise that is untainted by prejudice so (I) is certainly true. The paragraph goes on to discuss Lord Salisbury's "sympathetic" private self (II). Given Lord Salisbury's indifference to the opinions of others, especially those of the opposing political party, it is far more likely that Salisbury would be equally unconcerned by Gladstone's praise or blame.

8. **D.** Since the phrase says "not in the press," there would be no point in adding "not even in *Punch*" even if *Punch* was a mainstream newspaper (E). We can infer that *Punch* must be some kind of publication even more likely to take liberties with a public figure than the press, pointing to a satirical publication rather than a conservative one.

9. **C.** The sentence is loaded with intensifiers: "simple," "in his bones and brain cells," "any," "anyone whatever." If the phrase "no reason" were omitted, the sentence would lack a direct object and make no sense.

10. **E.** The sentence contains 12 prepositional phrases. It uses three parallel participial phrases ("having entered . . . ," "having been returned . . . ," and "having . . . sat . . ."). The sentence is periodic, reaching its subject, verb, and object only at the end.

11. **A.** The last paragraph says that Lord Salisbury revered "up—to the monarchy." The only member of the royal family among these choices is the Prince of Wales, the son of the king or queen.

12. E. The speaker or author here is a biographer but not a skeptical one. She is not a political supporter or a mordant satirist, the latter phrase being far too strong. The adjective "objective" is more appropriate than "sympathetic," since the passage presents both the strengths and the limitations of its subject.

13. D. There is no overt use of the judgments of other modern historians, although the author, no doubt, has studied them. An example of Choice A can be found in the Disraeli quotation; Choice C can be found in the Gladstone quotation in the second paragraph; and an example of Choice E is in the last sentence in the first paragraph. The conclusion of the third paragraph demonstrates a good example of Choice B.

14. E. There is no mention of Lord Salisbury's fearing social change (A). He is anything but a hypocrite (C), and although "he was not rank-conscious," he was uninterested in the general populace. The final sentence of the third paragraph insists upon the importance of his consciousness of himself as a Cecil, a distinguished family for centuries.

15. E. Although the passage implies that Lord Salisbury became prime minister and implies that this happened sometime after 1850, it doesn't necessarily place the event late in the 19th century. The other options can be easily demonstrated by closely reading the passage.

Second Passage

From *The Complete Letters of Oscar Wilde*

16. B. Wilde's italicizing the phrase *"in your lecture"* specifies that his strong reaction to Forbes's negative remarks is due to the fact that they were made in a public speaking forum, a formal setting that deserves accuracy. The remaining answer choices are not reasonable inferences one can draw from this italicized phrase.

17. E. Wilde states that he believes Forbes's lecture will not suffer "by expunging the passage" that Wilde finds so offensive. Therefore, Wilde will *not* settle for Forbes's merely rewording it (Choice E). Wilde does suggest all of the other answer choices.

18. A. Wilde uses parallel structure in line 10, "You have to speak of the life of action; I of the life of art" and in lines 20–21, "the lustre of action, of adventure and of courage." However, Forbes does not display any parallel structure. Both writers do demonstrate all other devices.

19. C. One can infer that in American journalism in the 1880s, journalistic integrity was a virtue not yet generally practiced, since both writers' libelous accusations toward each other were published in newspapers. All other answers are reasonable inferences.

20. C. Wilde's phrase, "I do not think you should have believed *it* of me," is an attempt to persuade Forbes that Wilde did not actually utter the alleged negative remarks about the war correspondent. Choice A is a contradiction; Choice D refers to something Wilde said about Forbes, not about himself. Choice E is inaccurate because the word "it" does not refer to *harm* done, and in context the phrase "foolish ridicule" refers to the world of "art and refinement," not Wilde's actions or remarks.

21. D. Using the word "essays" as a verb is a play on words; Wilde is writing personal letters to Forbes, not essays, but perhaps his letters come across with the formality of an essay. Choice E is unreasonable; Forbes hardly exhibits any linguistic prowess but instead uses a straightforward, logical presentation.

22. A. Each writer's tone is rife with condescension and a feeling that he is morally above the other. Each man feels certain that he has been socially snubbed and accordingly displays a snobbish and patronizing attitude. The passage does not include any evidence for any of the other answer choices.

23. E. Note #1 states that Forbes had "small sympathy with Wilde's ideas on aesthetics and dress reform." Most of the direct quotation details Forbes's own disheveled dress as he arrived in Bulgaria, yet Forbes insists on describing himself as a follower of "aesthetic ecstasy." This becomes a thinly veiled attack on Wilde's ideals of aesthetics and dress reform. None of the incorrect answer choices address clothing or aesthetics.

24. B. Forbes points out in his quotation that his reporting is serious; after all, he *is* meeting with the czar of war-torn Bulgaria. In aiming his slight at Wilde, he points out that his own subpar clothing after hard and long travel was inconsequential to his purpose; in contrast, Forbes implies that Wilde is only interested in appearances and the trivial fluff of life. Choice C is incorrect because Forbes is not drawing a logical conclusion. The passage does not suggest that Forbes is trying to bait Wilde into retaliating (Choice D). Although Forbes may indeed repeat his criticism of Wilde (Choice E), it is not the *purpose* of the note.

25. E. Although Wilde does rebut Forbes's accusations, the word "apologetic" makes this exception the correct answer; Wilde never directly apologizes in his letter. Both letter writers use *ad hominem* argumentation, directly attacking the man (Choice A). All other answer choices are evidenced in the exchange of letters.

26. A. Forbes's letter is very direct, listing his grievances toward Wilde in an itemized list. Wilde's reply explains how innocent he feels he is in this matter, and he rambles on in a conversational tone. Choice B is inaccurate because both ideas are direct contradictions to the men's letters. Choice C states wrongly that Wilde takes responsibility when he instead claims his innocence. Choice E reverses the two men's approach.

27. D. Wilde's first letter begins the fray with a direct attack, stating specifically that Forbes's remarks were not "in good taste or appropriate" (line 5). However, in the second letter Wilde tries to appease Forbes, claiming that he did not and would not say negative remarks about Forbes, and hopes Forbes knows him well enough to believe this claim. Therefore, Wilde becomes more conciliatory and less aggressive in his second letter. Choice A is inaccurate because Wilde never "systematically outlines" his points. He never mentions Forbes's ideas, making Choice B wrong, and he definitely does not attack Forbes at all in the second letter (Choice C). Wilde does not flatter Forbes in either letter (Choice E).

28. D. Wilde's use of the word "chivalry" shows cutting irony as he satirizes Forbes for living in an idealized past. In addition, his phrases such as "personal bravery" and "pluck" are actually tongue-in-cheek comments about Forbes's experience as a war correspondent. The remaining answer choices are sincere, not ironic.

Third Passage

From "Meditations upon a Broomstick" by Jonathan Swift

29. C. The sentence is not pedantic (overly scholarly). All of the remaining answer choices can be found in this sentence.

30. E. The broomstick began life in nature in a "flourishing state . . . full of sap, full of leaves, and full of boughs." Man began life in youth "strong and lusty, in a thriving condition." Choices A, C, and D contradict the passage. B is not addressed.

31. D. The author feels that man, as a youth, is closer to perfection. The older a man gets, the more mistakes he makes. The author also believes that man misuses nature, as he misuses the broomstick, out of selfishness. The author does not believe it is likely that man will take a turn for the better.

32. B. The broomstick starts life as a flourishing tree, but after man uses it up, he throws it away or burns it. Choices C and E contradict the passage. Nature does not triumph over man's evil tendencies, and man does not fear nature, but rather destroys it. The evil inherent in man's soul (D) is not addressed.

33. E. Intemperance is a lack of moderation in behavior, and the "axe of intemperance" is a metaphor for those excesses. It is the "axe" that chops man down like a tree. Before that, man had "green boughs"; after, he has but a "withered trunk." The phrase does not refer to "man's dominance over nature" (A). Nature is not shown as providing much nourishment (B); rather, it is destroyed. "Axe of intemperance" is neither a simile (C) nor a hyperbole (D).

34. A. The author is saddened and disillusioned at man's behavior. Choice B is incorrect because man's future is not addressed. Choices C and E contradict the tone of the passage—there is no optimism or praise here. This author is angry with man and his nature, not the society man has created (D).

35. A. The phrase "a flourishing state in a forest" refers to pure, untouched nature (before man chops down trees) and has positive connotations.

36. D. Swift never suggests that man accomplishes anything magnificent; obviously, a broomstick can't claim such an accomplishment.

37. A. "Man" is the antecedent: "man" is a reasoning vegetable to this author.

38. C. No oxymorons (the juxtaposition of two contradictory terms) appear. All the other literary devices are used.

39. B. Man pretends to solve the problems of the world but only makes them worse. Choice A is inaccurate—the broomstick represents decline, not thriving. Choice C is also inaccurate; the broomstick is a metaphor for man, not society. There is no evidence for Choice D; nature doesn't exert control in this author's world, man does. E is obviously incorrect: The broomstick is an analogy for man's physical state, not his intellectual state.

40. E. It is only man's presentation that allows him to believe that he can correct abuses; in fact, he "raises a mighty dust where there was none before."

41. C. Swift is cynical toward mankind and all of man's works, believing that mankind is motivated wholly by self-interest and therefore not to be trusted. This author takes a strong position, not a neutral one (A), and while he may be condescending, the condescension is directed toward man, not nature (B). "Bellicose" (D) means quarrelsome and warlike and is too strong a term to accurately describe the tone here.

42. D. Swift appears to concentrate on how inappropriate it is for man to try to reform nature while thinking of himself in such grand terms and, in reality, being the corrupter of nature.

Fourth Passage

From "Criticism and Fiction" by William Dean Howells

43. D. The best term is "critical." The author's purpose is to criticize those who do not think for themselves, imitating older works in pursuit of art. Some examples of this critical tone: "men have been afraid to apply their won simplicity," "seeds of death are planted," "spirit of the wretched pedantry," "decays when it withdraws itself," "they are destitute of the documents," "they are quite ignorant," "you descend . . . in the moral social scale," and "you are one to be avoided." "Somber" (A) is too strong, as evidenced by the playful grasshopper analogy and fun the author pokes at old readers. The sentences are not complex enough or the diction flamboyant enough to be called "ornate" (B). The author's purpose is not "didactic" (C), that is, he does not mean to teach, and his diction is not pedantic. Choice E, "formal," like "ornate," is too strong. The tone is more conversational than formal.

44. C. Howells feels that the common people don't place enough trust in their own abilities to interpret literature, but rather rely on "some one who professed to know better and who browbeat wholesome common-sense" into them (lines 13–15). Choices A and C are not mentioned. Choices B and E contradict the passage. Howells feels that common people should attempt to make their own judgments rather than copy anyone's taste.

45. A. "The seeds of death" is a metaphor for imitative art, art formed from studying older masters who themselves imitated the life of their time. According to Howells, this practice produces dead art, imitative art. The author doesn't deal with the destruction of art (B), but with the imitation of art. The "seeds of death" do not represent the art of an older age (C), but the tendency to mimic the art.

46. E. Howells hopes the artist and common person will reject the ideal grasshopper in favor of a more natural form of art.

47. B. While Howells feels that readers who restrict their reading to older literature are narrow-minded, he also finds them "very amusing . . . delightful." The author claims that these old ideas will die out slowly, not quickly (A), that "the time is yet far off," and doesn't dismiss these readers as unimportant, suggesting only that they are far too limited in their approach. Howells does attribute harm to them (D), in their narrow approach, and characterizes their knowledge as assumed rather than great (E).

48. D. The idealized grasshopper, made of cardboard and wire, is symbolic of the artificial. No quest to merge art and science is mentioned (A); the passage presents only an artist talking to a scientist, and no reference is made to the search for perfection—the cardboard grasshopper is far from perfection. Although this cardboard grasshopper is said by the artist to be indestructible, it will not last through the ages of art (C) because it is divorced from reality (although the artist seems to think that it will). Choice E is incorrect because the scientist doesn't produce the idealized grasshopper; the artist does.

49. A. In the quest for the ideal, the grasshopper is created out of wire, cardboard, and paint, ironically becoming in the process a lesser thing because it does not resemble reality. Even if true (and there is no evidence that they are), choices B and C are not ironic. Common sense tells us that everyone can tell a cardboard grasshopper from a real one (D), and the passage suggests that the cardboard grasshopper has, indeed, been created (E).

50. C. In lines 65–78, Howells claims that the natural, simple grasshopper will eventually be recognized. The remaining choices are types of grasshoppers that he hopes will disappear as the natural one emerges.

51. E. Howells urges his readers to read widely from all literary periods and to reach an individual interpretation that is not based on some pedantic notion. Conversely, he feels that it is a mistake to read only classical literature.

52. B. Howells's satire makes fun of those who believe that they can create an idealized copy of nature when, obviously, nature's product is alive, real, and superior. It is also humorous to think of this silly cardboard grasshopper as realistic imitation of life. The other answer choices are either stated too strongly or not evident in the passage.

53. A. The author believes that one should use simplicity, naturalness, and honesty in art and in its appreciation. The remaining answers involve attitudes that Howells criticizes.

54. A. Although the artist creates an idealized version of the grasshopper and the scientist's description (version) of the grasshopper will be based on reality, both of their creations remain artificial, both representations rather than reality. It is true that Howells presents the scientist's creation as preferable because it approaches reality more closely, but the fact remains that neither creation is itself reality. There is no evidence in the passage for the remaining answer choices.

55. C. A motif is a conventional or recurring element in a narrative, a device not found in the passage. The remaining devices are present. Some examples: Irony: the grasshopper analogy (while the artist professes that the cardboard grasshopper is to be preferred to the real, Howells would have the reader understand that the opposite is true). Metaphor: "The seeds of death" (line 24). Allusion: to Shakespeare, Thackeray, Hawthorne, and others. Analogy: extended analogy in the grasshopper segment.

Section II: Essay Questions

Question 1

Scoring Guide for Question 1 (Political Polls)

9 Essays that earn a score of 9 meet the criteria for essays that receive a score of 8. In addition, they are especially sophisticated in the use of language, explanation, and argument.

8 Successful

These essays respond to the prompt **successfully,** employing ideas from at least three of the sources from the prompt. They take a position that defends, challenges, or qualifies the claim that political polls do not accurately represent the views of a population. They effectively argue the position and support the argument with appropriate evidence. The control of language is extensive and the writing errors are minimal.

7 These essays meet the criteria for essays that receive a score a 6 but provide more depth and strength to the argument and evidence. The prose style is mature and shows a wide control over language.

6 Satisfactory

These essays respond to the prompt **satisfactorily.** Using at least three of the sources from the prompt, these essays take a position that defends, challenges, or qualifies the claim that political polls do not accurately represent the views of a population. The position is adequately argued with support from appropriate evidence, although without the precision and depth of top-scoring essays. The writing may contain minor errors in diction or in syntax, but the prose is generally clear.

5 These essays take a position that defends, challenges, or qualifies the claim that political polls do not accurately represent the views of a population. It supports the position with generally appropriate evidence but may not adequately quote, either directly or indirectly, from three sources in the prompt. These essays may be inconsistent, uneven, or limited in the development of their argument. Although the writing usually conveys the writer's ideas and perspectives, it may demonstrate lapses in diction or syntax or an overly simplistic style.

4 Inadequate

These essays respond to the prompt **inadequately.** They have difficulty taking a clear position that defends, challenges, or qualifies the claim that political polls do not accurately represent the views of a population. The evidence may be insufficient, or may not utilize enough sources from the prompt. The prose conveys the writer's ideas but suggests immature control over the elements of effective writing.

3 These essays meet the criteria for a score of 4 but reveal less success in taking a position that defends, challenges, or qualifies the claim that political polls do not accurately represent the views of a population. The presentation of evidence and arguments is unconvincing. These writers show little or no control over the elements of effective writing.

2 Little Success

These essays demonstrate **little success** at taking a position that defends, challenges, or qualifies the claim that political polls do not accurately represent the views of a population and show little success in presenting it clearly and with appropriate evidence from the sources in the prompt. These essays may misunderstand the prompt, fail to establish a position with supporting evidence, or substitute a simpler task by replying tangentially with unrelated, erroneous, or unsuitable explanation, argument, and/or evidence. The prose frequently demonstrates consistent weaknesses in the conventions of effective writing.

1 These essays meet the criteria for a score of 2 but are undeveloped, especially simplistic in their explanation, argument, and/or evidence, or weak in their control of writing.

High-Scoring Essay

In modern elections, candidates are under constant pressure to stay in the public eye. Long gone are the days when candidates would traverse the country by train, for instance, visiting city after city on a pre-set itinerary. To be competitive today, candidates for national office must crisscross the country many times; their image must be seen and heard relentlessly. One factor that helps modern candidates and their managers decide what route to travel and which issues to highlight is the modern political poll. Recall the 2004 presidential election: in the final weeks and days before the voting, John Kerry and George W. Bush traversed the country, showing up at carefully planned rallies to muster more support. Both the locations and attendees were carefully chosen, based on the most up-to-date poll information about likely voters and their ballot choices. Attaining success in any close political contest is difficult; candidates must utilize many voting tactics, and no tactic is more prevalent, albeit less precise, than political polls. These polls theoretically provide candidates with an accurate assessment of public opinion. Unfortunately, political polls tend to be unreliable; their results are sometimes intentionally skewed; they yield inaccurate information and provide a poor indicator of public opinion.

Designed to ascertain general public opinion by querying a small number of individuals, then multiplying the individual's answers to project a population's opinion, polls inherently rely upon statistics. However, Benjamin Disraeli, the famous British Prime Minister succinctly stated, "'there are three kinds of lies: lies, damned lies, and statistics'" (Source B). Common sense indicates that polls should be taken with the proverbial grain of salt; polls often display a specific margin of error, an explicit admission of fallibility. Unfortunately, far too many rely on the results of polls while ignoring their potential inaccuracies. Perhaps this stems from mankind's tendency to "trust numbers" as if they are facts that are actually true. Ramesh Ponnuru, in a book review, commented that "reporters lean on polls because they provide the illusion of numerical certainty" (Source F). Indeed, this "illusion" also persuades the public to rely on and trust in polls, simply because they appear to be so accurate. But when the logic behind any political poll is faulty, the integrity of the poll's results is compromised.

Often a poll's accuracy is compromised by its authors. The intentional skewing of questions and audiences is a significant factor that adversely affects a poll's results. For example, identical questions pertaining to Ross Perot's platform resulted in a 40 percent variance between answers when the questions were subtly reworded (Source B). Unfortunately, polls suffer from a "variety of [problems] that . . . can lead to shockingly different results" (Source D). According to Source D, polls' accuracy falls prey to deliberate manipulation of question order, interview bias, sample audiences, repetition, wording bias, and timing bias. Naturally, those who conduct and write polls are extremely aware of these ways to skew the results and use these techniques to their advantage. Polls exhibiting the aforementioned faults provide inaccurate information for a variety of reasons, only one of which is antagonizing the respondent who will in turn "give any answer just to get the interview over with" (Source D). While the published poll results attempt to appear "fair and balanced," for instance, by revealing the number of people polled and what part of the country they live in, etc., the public rarely thinks about the important questions one needs to know about any given poll before judging its accuracy. The public needs to question who wrote the poll, who administered it and under what conditions, how many people were sampled at what time of day, how many questions the poll had, what order they were given in, etc. Regrettably, we do not take the time to even think of these questions, yet alone search out the answers; we just accept the numbers.

The advent of modern technology has increasingly enabled target audiences to elude pollsters. Caller ID and answering machines enable people to circumvent time consuming political polls (Source C), therefore reducing the potential variety of opinions from those who do respond. Even when a pollster does manage to contact an individual, "a significant number of people refuse to finish poll questions" (Source C) thus further compromising a poll's accuracy. Similar to the number of people who have opinions about governmental matters but do not take the time to write letters to the editor in their local newspaper, those who do not answer the phone when approached by a pollster can add to the inaccuracy of a poll merely by keeping their opinions to themselves.

Polls are ubiquitous in national publications; however, their value is debatable. For example, in the 2000 Presidential Election, certainly a crucial event for poll authors, only two of eleven national polls correctly predicted the outcome (Source E).

Perhaps the promise and pitfalls of polling are most aptly summarized by *U.S. News & World Report:* "A properly conducted poll can provide tremendous insight . . . but too often polls fail to put the results in context or explain why some data is misleading" (Source D). This long track record of unreliability, perpetuated by inherent flaws in the creation and administration of polls, has consistently yielded inaccurate data, thus making polls a poor representation of a population's opinion.

Analysis of the High-Scoring Essay

This essay is praiseworthy for its development and its thoughtful discussion of the role that political polls play in American elections. The introductory paragraph successfully juxtaposes the campaigns of "long gone" elections with the tactics of contemporary politicians. Although this comparison is apt, the presentation could be a bit stronger in drawing connections; as it is, the reader must implicitly understand the writer's point. The thesis follows: Although candidates in modern elections must rely heavily on political polls, these polls do not provide an accurate assessment of the populace's opinions.

Next, in discussing the reliability of polls, the essay skillfully includes both the humorous quotation from Disraeli and the interesting notion that numbers *seem* so trustworthy to humanity. This idea is a fascinating one that helps to capture the reader's attention. This idea points out one of the underlying reasons why polls are trusted by politicians and the public alike, which demonstrates that this writer is incorporating more than just the information in the sources. This paragraph synthesizes the sources well, presenting more than one reference in the same paragraph to advance the writer's points.

The third paragraph discusses the ways in which polls can elicit inaccurate information, based on examples from the sources. Clearly this writer understands the problematic nature of polls and data gathering. The writer also uses appropriate presentation of information and logical reasoning to demonstrate a good grasp of human psychology.

Next, the essay explores an additional factor that contributes to inaccurate poll results. This paragraph focuses on the fact that many people simply avoid responding to polls; this factor alone indicates that polls cannot represent all people's opinions. With the example of those who never write letters to the editor, the writer makes an appropriate analogy to those who have opinions but never share them. Then the writer extends this logic to show that the accuracy of polls diminishes with fewer respondents. The thinking is sound and the presentation valid.

By the fifth paragraph, this essay seems to lose some of the energy and forcefulness of the beginning paragraphs, almost as if the writer is both running out of steam and running out of time to develop ideas thoroughly. This paragraph only has two sentences, and it's hard to understand how they connect. The reader wonders where the writer got the idea about polls being "ubiquitous" in national publications and what connection that has to the inaccurate poll predictions in the 2000 election. If the writer were to have expanded this paragraph and explored the controversies of the 2000 election in more depth, this paragraph would have more to offer. As written, it falls flat.

The sixth and concluding paragraph neatly summarizes the essay. Adding the quotation from Source D works well, as it precisely fits the writer's thesis. The reader can hope the essay's conclusion would have had more to offer than a recapitulation of the essay's main ideas, but again, this issue is most likely due to the limited time, not the writer's ability to think. However, overall, the essay is consistently on topic, decently organized, well developed, and appropriate in its use of language. It does deserve a high score.

Low-Medium-Scoring Essay

In the United States, where politics is heavily bankrolled, political races are tight, and (in the presidential election) the victor becomes the world's most powerful man, so candidates seek every advantage. Polls are regarded as a source of information regarding potential voters. After subscribing to a political poll, parties will attempt to tailor their campaigns to reach voters who indicated they were disaffected on the poll. Thus, political campaigns consider polls to be valuable assets that indicate a population's opinion. Unfortunately for the political parties, polls have proved to be unreliable indicators of opinion; effectively rendering them useless.

One major fault of the polls is that they are misleading. According to Source B, a statistics textbook, "survey questions can be worded to elicit . . . desired response[s]." Important factors such as diction and the order of the statements in the question can heavily affect the response. For example, Ross Perot asked, "'should the president have the line item veto to eliminate waste?'" 97 percent of respondents said "yes" (Source B). Conversely when the same question was rephrased to "'should the president have a line item veto, or not?'" only 57 percent of respondents indicated "yes" (Source B). The big difference between the first poll's results and the second's (which asked essentially the same question) indicate that polls are unreliable because of their intentional loaded questions.

Polls are designed by experts in order establish accurate information. According to Source D, polls suffer from interview, sampling, wording, order, and repetition bias. "Many national polls are conducted from one site with interviewers with a similar accent" (Source D) so regional bias undoubtedly affects a poll's results. Long questionnaires intimidate subjects so much that they "will give any answer just to get the interview over with" (Source D). Another problem is that many of the people surveyed are "disproportionately male and younger" (Source D) which is not indicative of the general voting population.

Rather than providing a public service, polls actually limit the infusion of new ideas into society. Source F states that because initial reactions to reform are almost always negative, early polls will present reform as "unpopular" and ultimately "interfere with the formation of public opinion."

Polls do not accurately reflect a population's views for a variety of reasons. First, polls are filled with loaded questions designed to trick the participant and elicit a wrong answer. Secondly, polls suffer from a variety of handicaps such as sampling bias, interview bias, and wording bias. Finally, polls are often used improperly, clouding the true intentions of the poll's subject. Thus, it is fair to conclude that polls do not provide an accurate representation of the population's opinions.

Analysis of the Low-Medium-Scoring Essay

This essay attempts to present an adequate response to the prompt but suffers from simplistic thinking and presentation. In the first paragraph, the writer establishes a thesis, namely that political polls are "useless" and "unreliable indicators of public opinion." However, the writing demonstrates numerous errors that begin to distract the reader. The first sentence contains a subject-verb error: "politics *is* bankrolled." The second sentence includes odd and repetitive diction that essentially says nothing, such as, "Polls are regarded as a source of information regarding potential voters." The third sentence displays additional problems with diction: First, political parties do not "subscribe" to polls; second, the phrase "disaffected on the poll" is simply inaccurate and inexact language. The fourth sentence has no grammatical or diction errors, but the final sentence uses the semicolon inappropriately. The reader is left with a fairly disappointing introduction, so the first impression from this essay is not a strong one. The writer has taken a stand, claiming that political polls are "useless" but that's about all.

The second paragraph is adequate, but only in restating the facts in Source B. Basically, this paragraph paraphrases Source B but offers no strong ideas that help prove the thesis. It does make the point that diction and the order of questions can affect responses to polls, but that information is already in the source. The paragraph would be stronger if the writer were to integrate more sources and develop more analytical ideas. Unfortunately, as it reads now, the paragraph is undeveloped and overly simplistic.

The third paragraph gets off to a bad start with an unwarranted assumption, that the goal of polls is, in fact, to design ones that do elicit "accurate information." However, this idea contradicts this essay's overall point, that polls are "useless." The writer seems to ignore the first sentence in this paragraph and continues to paraphrase Source D, pointing out the many ways in which polls can be misleading. This paragraph, just like the previous one, would be much stronger were it to contain additional ideas, incorporated from more sources, and stronger analysis from the writer.

The fourth paragraph, containing only two sentences, presents an underdeveloped idea: that polls tend to limit the spread of new ideas in a society. The writer basically copies the information in Source F and the paragraph ends clumsily. The reader cannot avoid the impression that the writer felt compelled to produce five paragraphs, focusing a body paragraph on one of the sources, but by now was running out of time.

The essay finishes with simplistic summary of the three body paragraphs; it displays no new insights. Overall, the entire essay is held back from a higher score by the continual lack of analytical depth. The essay would be more impressive if the writer were to actually *synthesize* the information in the sources and then present a more engaging argument. This essay clearly demonstrates the oversimplification that is typical of low- to medium-scoring essays. Remember the synthesis essay offers writers an open opportunity to truly demonstrate how they think and how well they interact with the world; every writer should try to seize this opportunity and present well-developed ideas in a sophisticated manner. The extra effort will be rewarded with a higher score than this sample essay earns.

Question 2

Scoring Guide for Question 2 (Susan Sontag)

9 Essays that earn a score of 9 meet the criteria for essays that receive a score of 8; in addition, they are especially sophisticated in demonstrating the clear understanding of the author's attitudes toward metaphors and her use of metaphors. They may also present a particularly remarkable control of language.

8 Successful

These well-written essays show **successful** understanding of both Sontag's attitudes toward metaphor and use of metaphor. The thesis is thoughtful and articulate. Strong and relevant evidence from the passage combines with intelligent insights connecting the evidence to Sontag's attitudes toward metaphor and use of metaphor. Successfully convincing, this essay demonstrates a command of essay-writing skills. Although it need not be without errors, these essays are written with mature style and diction.

7 These essays meet the requirements for essays that score a 6 and, in addition, demonstrate a thorough understanding of the author's attitudes, while providing stronger and more relevant insights. The prose style is generally more mature.

6 Satisfactory

These essays demonstrate a **satisfactory** comprehension of Sontag's attitudes toward metaphor and use of metaphor, but its thesis may be less explicit than that of the top-scoring essays. The evidence offered may be less convincing, but the paper still demonstrates clear thinking. The connection between the evidence and Sontag's attitudes toward metaphor and use of metaphor may not be as clear as that of the top-scoring essays. Although well written, these papers may show some errors, while maintaining satisfactory control over diction and the essay's requirements.

5 These adequately written essays show some understanding of Sontag's attitudes toward metaphor and use of metaphor but may not clearly demonstrate the relationship between details of the passage and those attitudes and use. These essays may merely identify the attitudes without effectively discussing them or may not effectively deal with the author's use of metaphor. The thesis may be simplistic and the evidence insufficient to prove the essay's points. Acceptable organization and development may be evident, but the style may not be as sophisticated as that of higher-scoring essays.

4 Inadequate

These low-scoring essays fail to convince. The weak and **inadequate** presentation may not demonstrate a clear understanding of either Sontag's attitudes toward metaphor or her use of metaphor. The thesis may be unsubstantiated, paragraph development may be weak, and superficial thinking may be evident. Frequent errors in composition that distract the reader may be present.

3 Essays earning a score of 3 meet the criteria for a score of 4 but demonstrate less understanding of the attitudes and show a lack of depth to the insights. These essays may show little control over the elements of writing.

2 Little Success

These poorly written essays lack coherence and clarity. They may attempt with **little success** to identify an attitude or attitudes without mention of the use of metaphor in the passage. The thesis may be overly obvious or absent. Little or no evidence may be offered, and any connection between the evidence and the thesis may be shallow or nonexistent. These essays may be unusually short, and persistent grammatical problems may exist.

1 These poorly written essays meet the criteria for a score of 2 but are undeveloped, especially shallow in insights, and weak in the control of language.

High-Scoring Essay

In this passage, Sontag uses the metaphor of illness as a nation in which we all must eventually reside. In the face of this inevitability, she suggests that it is best to confront illness face to face rather than through a façade of preconceived ideas. Sontag ironically uses this metaphor to express her dismay with the prevalence of such stereotypes regarding the nature of illness.

The paragraph sequence itself helps to illuminate the insidious nature of the metaphor. The passage begins with such a metaphor, equating illness with a detestable nation. With such descriptions as "the night-side of life" and "onerous citizenship," Sontag firmly implants illness' negative connotations in the reader's mind. Yet the very next paragraph opens up with her intent to describe "not what it is really like to emigrate to the kingdom of the ill . . . but the punitive and sentimental fantasies concocted about that situation: not real geography, but stereotypes of national character." In this statement she establishes the fallacy of the metaphor in general, and specifically of her own opening metaphor by referring to it as, "not real geography." In so doing, Sontag alerts the reader to his or her own unquestioning acceptance of such parallels.

Throughout the passage, she continues the use of the geographical metaphor to ironically and effectively show the suggestive power of this literary tool. In her claim "it is hardly possible to take up one's residence in the kingdom of the ill unprejudiced by the lurid metaphors with which it has been landscaped," she subtly weaves in such irony. Her reference to "the kingdom of the ill" is indeed one of the very same "lurid metaphors" against which she cautions the reader. This technique of interweaving irony is very powerful in that the reader, not expecting an author to contradict herself, is forced to reexamine the sentence in closer detail, only to discover the clever subtlety of the author. This forcefully drives home Sontag's implication that the danger in metaphors lies in their unchallenged acceptance.

Sontag's perception of illness metaphors is effectively revealed in the concluding sentence, "It is toward an elucidation of those metaphors that I dedicate this inquiry." By joining the elucidation of metaphor with the liberation from those metaphors, Sontag suggests that close examination will reveal their inaccuracy, thus allowing them to be abandoned by the newly enlightened and astute reader.

Susan Sontag's suspicion of metaphorical approaches to illness is subtly yet clearly conveyed in this passage through irony and implication. The strongest statements are often written between the lines, as Sontag's work clearly demonstrates.

Analysis of the High-Scoring Essay

The essay's introduction effectively addresses the topic: the analysis of Sontag's attitudes toward and use of the metaphor. The writer notes that Sontag uses the metaphor as a tool of irony to "express her dismay" at the use of stereotypes. The writer's language is sophisticated, inviting the reader to follow the essay's engaging ideas.

The writer then analyzes Sontag's sequence of ideas, noting how she effectively presents the concept of illness as metaphor only to dash it to pieces in her following paragraph. The essay's presentation is intelligent, and the writing style is strong. Such paraphrasing as "helps to illuminate the insidious nature" demonstrates an impressive command of language. The writer also includes relevant and sufficient evidence from Sontag's writing to prove the essay's points.

The essay continues the effective discussion in the next paragraph by analyzing Sontag's use of metaphor, noting that Sontag contradicts herself and explaining the effect of that contradiction on the reader—that it forces one to reexamine preconceived notions about both illness and metaphor. This awareness demonstrates why the essay receives its high score; less adept writers tend to ignore such ambivalence entirely and instead only address that which they can easily explain from a given passage.

The third paragraph begins the conclusion by analyzing Sontag's last sentence, suggesting that Sontag's real purpose is to reveal the inaccuracy of metaphors and, thus, to enlighten her readers. Though this paragraph is not as well developed as the previous ones, it is necessary as it addresses an important part of the topic: Sontag's attitudes toward metaphor. The paragraph could be improved, however, by mention of more than one attitude; the topic specifies "attitudes," plural, which should suggest to the writer that there will be some subtle nuances in the passage.

The essay concludes with a summary statement about Sontag's use of metaphor and includes a perceptive comment that readers must read between the lines in order to glean the meaning of an author's writing. Given the essay's thoughtful analysis and sophisticated presentation, it deserves a high score.

Medium-Scoring Essay

In the introduction to Susan Sontag's book, <u>Illness as Metaphor</u>, she talks about using metaphors to compare illness to something else. She believes that metaphors are too limiting to be used to generalize all illness and that they don't allow for a clear view of sickness itself. This attitude is reflected not only in her direct comments, but also through her own use of metaphor.

Her negative attitude about metaphors for illness is stated at various places in the excerpt. She very strongly states that "illness is <u>not</u> a metaphor, and that the most truthful way of regarding illness . . . is one most purified of, most resistant to, metaphoric thinking." This shows that since illness isn't a metaphor, people shouldn't try to treat it like one. Sontag feels that using a metaphor to define illness is not truthful because it doesn't necessarily reveal the whole story. Another example where her attitude about metaphors can be seen is in her comment that, "It is toward . . . a liberation from them, that I dedicate this inquiry." Her whole purpose in the book, then, is to draw people away from the metaphor. She wants to get people to confront illness as it is, without a confining metaphor, to be "liberated" from it.

Sontag shows her dislike for metaphor indirectly by in fact using one herself. She describes "the kingdom of the sick" as "the night-side of life." This establishes a clearly defined view of illness. Then she later seems to point out the invalidity of her own metaphor, when she implies that the "kingdom" is "not real geography but stereotypes." This implies that it is not based on reality, but rather ideas. She is referring to metaphors as stereotypes, which expresses her view that they are prejudiced and consequently not very accurate. In a roundabout way, by insulting her own metaphor as a mere stereotype, Susan Sontag conveys the error of metaphors.

In this passage, she claims that metaphors should not be used to describe illness. The reasons she gives are that it is not "the most truthful way" of looking at it, and that they are just stereotypes. She even uses one herself to show you that you can't always trust them to be right. What's true for one person may not necessarily be true for another.

Analysis of the Medium-Scoring Essay

This average-scoring essay demonstrates the faults so often seen in medium-scoring essays: It makes some accurate points but without sufficient thoughtful analysis. In addition, the presentation lacks the sophistication seen in high-scoring essays. Both the points presented and the style of presentation do not rise above the mundane.

The second paragraph is primarily summary, not analysis. While correct in acknowledging that Sontag has a "negative attitude" toward illness metaphors, the writer has nothing more important to say than "since illness isn't a metaphor, people shouldn't treat it like one." The writer acknowledges Sontag's purpose (which wasn't asked for in the topic), "to draw people away from the metaphor," but shows no deeper perception and continues to write mere summary.

The third paragraph is more thoughtful but, once again, lacks strong analysis. The writer suggests that Sontag herself makes use of a metaphor, that of the kingdom, but sees only that she is trying to "convey the error of metaphors." This essay points out only what is obvious to most readers.

The conclusion summarizes the essay's main points about Sontag's attitude toward and use of metaphor, but unfortunately, no new points are presented. Overall, this essay attempts to address the topic, but its ideas are shallow and its presentation simplistic.

Question 3

Scoring Guide for Question 3 (Henry David Thoreau)

9 These essays meet the criteria for essays that receive a score of 8, and in addition, they are deeper in their analysis and frequently reveal an exquisite use of language.

8 Successful

These well-written essays thoroughly explore the accuracy of Thoreau's aphorism in modern society. They **successfully** and clearly substantiate their points with relevant evidence from contemporary life, connecting that evidence to the thesis with meaningful insight about human nature. Although these essays may contain a few flaws, they demonstrate a command of language, sentence structure, and conventions of essay form.

7 These essays meet the requirements for essays scored as a 6 and, in addition, demonstrate a thorough understanding of the author's aphorism, while providing stronger and more relevant evidence. The prose style is generally more mature.

6 Satisfactory

These essays **satisfactorily** explore Thoreau's aphorism but produce a less explicit thesis than that of top-scoring essays. Evidence offered is perhaps less specific or not as clearly connected to the thesis. These essays' ideas may not be as crisply articulated as those in top-scoring essays. Although there may be some errors, these papers are well written and demonstrate mature style and satisfactory command of language.

5 These adequately presented essays have an acceptable thesis and present some evidence concerning the applicability of the aphorism in modern society but may exhibit flaws in organization, number of examples, or discussion of ideas. In general, these essays are not as effective or convincing because of a pedestrian treatment of the topic, producing commonplace, predictable reading. Inconsistent control of language and sentence structure may be present.

4 Inadequate

These essays fail to convince because of their **inadequate** presentation. Superficial thinking and weak evidence may be combined with an uninteresting or obvious thesis. Confused or contradictory thinking may be present, and these essays may lack adequate support to prove their points. Weak organization and paragraph development may be present. Frequent grammatical problems may distract the reader.

3 Essays earning a score of 3 meet the criteria for a score of 4 but demonstrate little understanding of the ideas, frequently coupled with a lack of evidence to support the arguments made. These essays may show little control over the elements of writing.

2 Little Success

These essays frequently lack coherence and clarity of thought and may produce an unclear thesis concerning the accuracy of the aphorism. Little or no evidence may be presented for the thesis, and the connection between the evidence and the thesis may be shallow or nonexistent. These essays may exhibit poor organization and paragraph development. Weak syntax and persistent grammatical errors may be present.

1 Essays that earn a score of 1 meet the criteria for a score of 2 but are undeveloped; especially simplistic in their explanation, argument, and/or evidence; or weak in their control of writing.

High-Scoring Essay

Henry David Thoreau aptly described the nature of mankind by expressing man's tendency to become lost in unimportant pursuits in today's society. Using fish as a symbol for what people believe they are searching for, Thoreau describes a problem of human nature which is seen in all of society: the problem of continually searching while not recognizing what one truly desires in life.

This problem is clouded by the confusing mist of appearances. This shroud hangs over what society has taught one to see as success: money, fancy cars, large houses, to name a few. In the pursuit of what society deems symbolic of success, one is trapped in the conflict of appearance versus reality. All too often someone craves a material object, only to find it boring shortly after it was acquired. This, of course, causes the person to want more possessions, always with the same result. This endless cycle continues, the result being dissatisfaction; as Thoreau might note, this person looks for still more fish, not knowing that fish will not satisfy.

This conflict leads only to the greater problem of getting lost in the race for success and losing sight of life's full meaning. In a society such as America, it is easy to forget that inner happiness cannot to be bought with material goods. With so many opportunities for one to flaunt wealth, it is not difficult to understand how people get caught up in trivial pursuits which do not satisfy their actual desire for success. The necessity to discern between needs and wants then becomes apparent within society. Today this confusion of true desire and false success is seen as the divorce rate increases, as drug abuse rises, as people continue to look for permanent happiness and inner success in temporary feelings and actions. Thoreau was accurate as he used this aphorism to describe human tendencies. Sad yet true, Thoreau's comment is still truthful in regard to the earnest search for false success.

Analysis of the High-Scoring Essay

This essay is concisely articulate in its exploration of Thoreau's aphorism in relation to modern society. It clearly takes a stand and buttresses it with discussion and examples. The student is not side-tracked into irrelevance and keeps the commentary specific.

The second paragraph presents its insights with a nice flair. Phrases like "clouded by the confusing mist of appearance" and the "shroud [that] hangs over" are negative images appropriate to the writer's assertions, and reinforce the theme of the deceit of "success" as our society defines it. By returning to Thoreau's symbol of fish, the writer completes the paragraph logically and effectively links it to the topic.

The third paragraph continues the philosophical discussion, adding additional relevant, contemporary examples and expanding the notion that people are never satisfied with what they have. Divorce and drugs are especially apt illustrations. The essay would be stronger if it included more such examples, but those used are convincing.

Overall, the essay deserves a fairly high score because it is clearly on topic, is well organized, shows sufficient paragraph development, and demonstrates maturity in style, even if only sporadically. It would earn a higher score if it offered stronger evidence and development and used more precise language. The repetition of ideas is a problem but one sometimes seen when writing upon philosophical topics under time pressure.

Low-Scoring Essay

Thoreau's quote relating to man's futile search for fish is applicable to modern society today. I think this quote especially relates to materialism, which is rampant within our greedy, American, self-centered society. Many values today revolve around selfishness and instant gratification, and the big picture of life isn't really seen. This drive for ownership and power and wealth often materializes itself in the mad rush to buy things. Credit cards only encourage this behavior, and the trip for the fish is not what they need. Materialism is a perfect example of this behavior, since many people feel the need to fill their lives with something, whether it's love or money or things. Thoreau sums up this observation about human nature so well, and this statement related not only to Thoreau's society, but to our society in modern America as well. The difference between needs and wants are easily confused, and those who are consumed by materialism cannot see the forest for the trees. I think Thoreau was reminding people not to forget what the important things in life are, and to express the importance of searching for what really matters in life, not settling for temporary things like material goods.

Analysis of the Low-Scoring Essay

This essay has some merit: It attempts to discuss the topic. The paragraph is acceptable and some of the points relevant, but the paper falls short of thoroughly convincing a reader. The writer's one-paragraph format leads to a rambling, unfocused result. It isn't necessarily the essay's ideas alone that lower the score, but the presentation. The writer uses pertinent examples from contemporary life, such as the use of credit cards and "materialism," but lapses into vague terms like "things."

The writer should be commended for trying to connect the essay to Thoreau's "fish" aphorism, but that important connection should be incorporated more smoothly. For example, the sudden jump from "credit cards" to "fish" in the fifth sentence needs a transitional phrase so that the reader can follow the writer's argument. In addition, demonstrating more sophisticated skills in the fundamentals of the essay form and more effective diction would significantly improve this essay.

Answer Sheet for Practice Test 4

Section I
Multiple-Choice Questions

First Passage

1 Ⓐ Ⓑ Ⓒ Ⓓ Ⓔ
2 Ⓐ Ⓑ Ⓒ Ⓓ Ⓔ
3 Ⓐ Ⓑ Ⓒ Ⓓ Ⓔ
4 Ⓐ Ⓑ Ⓒ Ⓓ Ⓔ
5 Ⓐ Ⓑ Ⓒ Ⓓ Ⓔ
6 Ⓐ Ⓑ Ⓒ Ⓓ Ⓔ
7 Ⓐ Ⓑ Ⓒ Ⓓ Ⓔ
8 Ⓐ Ⓑ Ⓒ Ⓓ Ⓔ
9 Ⓐ Ⓑ Ⓒ Ⓓ Ⓔ
10 Ⓐ Ⓑ Ⓒ Ⓓ Ⓔ
11 Ⓐ Ⓑ Ⓒ Ⓓ Ⓔ
12 Ⓐ Ⓑ Ⓒ Ⓓ Ⓔ
13 Ⓐ Ⓑ Ⓒ Ⓓ Ⓔ
14 Ⓐ Ⓑ Ⓒ Ⓓ Ⓔ
15 Ⓐ Ⓑ Ⓒ Ⓓ Ⓔ

Second Passage

16 Ⓐ Ⓑ Ⓒ Ⓓ Ⓔ
17 Ⓐ Ⓑ Ⓒ Ⓓ Ⓔ
18 Ⓐ Ⓑ Ⓒ Ⓓ Ⓔ
19 Ⓐ Ⓑ Ⓒ Ⓓ Ⓔ
20 Ⓐ Ⓑ Ⓒ Ⓓ Ⓔ
21 Ⓐ Ⓑ Ⓒ Ⓓ Ⓔ
22 Ⓐ Ⓑ Ⓒ Ⓓ Ⓔ
23 Ⓐ Ⓑ Ⓒ Ⓓ Ⓔ
24 Ⓐ Ⓑ Ⓒ Ⓓ Ⓔ
25 Ⓐ Ⓑ Ⓒ Ⓓ Ⓔ
26 Ⓐ Ⓑ Ⓒ Ⓓ Ⓔ
27 Ⓐ Ⓑ Ⓒ Ⓓ Ⓔ
28 Ⓐ Ⓑ Ⓒ Ⓓ Ⓔ

Third Passage

29 Ⓐ Ⓑ Ⓒ Ⓓ Ⓔ
30 Ⓐ Ⓑ Ⓒ Ⓓ Ⓔ
31 Ⓐ Ⓑ Ⓒ Ⓓ Ⓔ
32 Ⓐ Ⓑ Ⓒ Ⓓ Ⓔ
33 Ⓐ Ⓑ Ⓒ Ⓓ Ⓔ
34 Ⓐ Ⓑ Ⓒ Ⓓ Ⓔ
35 Ⓐ Ⓑ Ⓒ Ⓓ Ⓔ
36 Ⓐ Ⓑ Ⓒ Ⓓ Ⓔ
37 Ⓐ Ⓑ Ⓒ Ⓓ Ⓔ
38 Ⓐ Ⓑ Ⓒ Ⓓ Ⓔ
39 Ⓐ Ⓑ Ⓒ Ⓓ Ⓔ
40 Ⓐ Ⓑ Ⓒ Ⓓ Ⓔ
41 Ⓐ Ⓑ Ⓒ Ⓓ Ⓔ
42 Ⓐ Ⓑ Ⓒ Ⓓ Ⓔ

Fourth Passage

43 Ⓐ Ⓑ Ⓒ Ⓓ Ⓔ
44 Ⓐ Ⓑ Ⓒ Ⓓ Ⓔ
45 Ⓐ Ⓑ Ⓒ Ⓓ Ⓔ
46 Ⓐ Ⓑ Ⓒ Ⓓ Ⓔ
47 Ⓐ Ⓑ Ⓒ Ⓓ Ⓔ
48 Ⓐ Ⓑ Ⓒ Ⓓ Ⓔ
49 Ⓐ Ⓑ Ⓒ Ⓓ Ⓔ
50 Ⓐ Ⓑ Ⓒ Ⓓ Ⓔ
51 Ⓐ Ⓑ Ⓒ Ⓓ Ⓔ
52 Ⓐ Ⓑ Ⓒ Ⓓ Ⓔ
53 Ⓐ Ⓑ Ⓒ Ⓓ Ⓔ
54 Ⓐ Ⓑ Ⓒ Ⓓ Ⓔ
55 Ⓐ Ⓑ Ⓒ Ⓓ Ⓔ

CUT HERE

CUT HERE

Practice Test 4

Section I: Multiple-Choice Questions

Time: 60 minutes

55 questions

Directions: This section consists of selections from prose works and questions on their content, style, and form. Read each selection carefully. Choose the best answer of the five choices.

Questions 1–15. Read the following passage carefully before you begin to answer the questions.

First Passage

Even though he had finished *The School of Athens* more than a year earlier, Raphael returned to this work in the early autumn of 1511. Using a piece of red chalk, he sketched a single figure in
(5) freehand onto the painted plaster beneath Plato and Aristotle. . . . Raphael then proceeded to paint, in a single *giornata,* the slumped, solitary philosopher known as the *pensieroso,* or "the thinker."[1]

This figure—the fresco's fifty-sixth—is gener-
(10) ally thought to represent Heraclitus of Ephesus. Heraclitus was one of the few philosophers in *The School of Athens* to remain outside the teacher-student groups through which, in Raphael's view, knowledge was transmitted. No eager philosophi-
(15) cal apprentices huddle around Heraclitus. A self-absorbed, downcast figure with black hair and a beard, he rests his head on his fist as he scribbles distractedly on a piece of paper, utterly oblivious to the philosophical debates raging about him. With
(20) leather boots and a shirt cinched at the waist, he is dressed in considerably more modern garb than his fellow philosophers, all of whom are barefoot and wrapped in flowing robes. Most interesting of all, his nose is broad and flattened—a feature that has
(25) convinced a number of art historians that the model for him was none other than Michelangelo, whom Raphael added to the fresco as an act of homage af-ter seeing the Sistine ceiling.[2]

If Michelangelo was in fact the model for
(30) Heraclitus, the compliment was double-edged. Heraclitus of Ephesus, known as both Heraclitus the Obscure and "the Weeping Philosopher," believed the world to be in a state on constant flux, a proposi-tion summed up in his two most famous sayings:

(35) "You cannot step into the same river twice" and "The sun is new every day." But it is not this philos-ophy of universal change that seems to have inclined Raphael to lend him the features of Michelangelo; more likely it was Heraclitus's legendary sour tem-
(40) per and bitter scorn for all rivals. He heaped derision on predecessors such as Pythagoras, Xenophanes, and Hecataeus. He even abused Homer, claiming the blind poet should have been horse-whipped. The cit-izens of Ephesus were no more popular with the
(45) cantankerous philosopher. Every last one of them, he wrote, ought to be hanged.

The appearance of Heraclitus in *The School of Athens* was, therefore, perhaps both a tip of the hat to an artist whom Raphael greatly admired and a joke at
(50) the expense of the surly, remote Michelangelo. Its ad-dition also possibly carried the implication that the grandeur and majesty of Michelangelo's style on the Sistine ceiling—with its robust physiques, athletic posturings, and vibrant colors—had somewhat over-
(55) shadowed Raphael's own work in the Stanza della Segnatura. Put another way, Michelangelo's individ-ualistic and isolated figures from the Old Testament had eclipsed the elegant and congenial classical worlds of Parnassus and the "new Athens."

(60) One way to understand the differing styles of the two artists is through a pair of aesthetic categories developed two and a half centuries later by the Irish statesman and writer Edmund Burke in his *Philosophical Enquiry into the Origin of Our Ideas*
(65) *of the Sublime and Beautiful,* published in 1756. For Burke, those things we call beautiful have the prop-erties of smoothness, delicacy, softness of color, and elegance of movement. The sublime, on the other

GO ON TO THE NEXT PAGE

(70) hand, comprehends the vast, the obscure, the powerful, the rugged, the difficult—attributes which produce in the spectator a kind of astonished wonder and even terror.[3] For the people of Rome in 1511, Raphael was beautiful but Michelangelo sublime.

[1] For Raphael's technique in adding the pensieroso, see Nesselrath, Raphael's "School of Athens," p.20. The pensieroso is known to be a later addition because it does not appear in Raphael's cartoon for The School of Athens, and because examination of the plaster has proved that it was painted on intonaco added to the wall at a later date. The exact timing of this addition is speculative, but it seems most likely that Raphael painted it as he finished work in the Stella della Segnatura, that is, sometime in the summer or autumn of 1511 (ibid., p.21).

[2] This intriguing theory was fist suggested by Deoclecio Redig de Campos in Michelangelo Buonarroti nel IV centenario del "Giudizio universale" and repeated in his Raffaello nelle Stanze. Roger Jones and Nicolas Penny find the argument "implausible" without, however, offering strong counterarguments; see their Raphael. Ingrid D. Rowland, on the other hand, states that Heraclitus "presents a simultaneous portrait of Michelangelo's face and Michelangelo's artistic style" in her essay "The Intellectual Background" to Hall's book, Raphael's "School of Athens," and Frederick Hartt claims that his features are "clearly those of Michelangelo" in his History of Italian Renaissance Art.

[3] Edmund Burke, A Philosophical Enquiry into the Origin of Our Ideas of the Sublime and Beautiful, ed. James T. Boulton (Notre Dame, Ind.: University of Notre Dame Press, 1986), esp. pp. 57–125.

1. What can one infer about Raphael's decision to modify his masterpiece, the School of Athens, by adding the "solitary philosopher" at a later date?

   A. He was experimenting with new techniques in figure painting.
   B. He realized the painting needed at least one contemporary figure.
   C. He realized the painting was unbalanced before its addition.
   D. He added it after realizing his admiration for his rival, Michelangelo.
   E. He wanted to show the variety of personalities in the ancient Athenian school.

2. The rhetorical purpose behind the speaker's description of "the thinker" is to emphasize that it

   A. integrates the philosophers by placing them in the same picture
   B. visually distinguishes the lone figure by distancing him from the other Athenians
   C. shows how Heraclitus was held in disdain by his fellow Athenian philosophers
   D. causes one to ponder Raphael's motive for including the philosopher
   E. demonstrates the author's knowledge of art history

3. All of the following can be inferred from the description of the solitary figure EXCEPT:

   A. The figure is alienated physically and intellectually from the other philosophers.
   B. The figure is a dark, foreboding character.
   C. The figure does not invite empathy in the viewer.
   D. The figure rests in a languid pose.
   E. The figure may be a self-portrait by Raphael.

4. The use of the word "double-edged" (line 30) implies that the speaker feels

   A. the comparison was a compliment to both Michelangelo and Heraclitus
   B. Michelangelo should feel doubly-honored to receive the compliment from Raphael
   C. Raphael's comparison to the disputatious Heraclitus was actually a cutting retort to Michelangelo
   D. the comparison of Michelangelo to Heraclitus is beyond the edge of reason
   E. Raphael was conflicted in his opinion of Michelangelo

5. In his description of Heraclitus, the speaker includes all of the following ideas EXCEPT:

   A. He was respected for his philosophy by the citizens of Ephesus.
   B. He was known for being difficult to understand.
   C. He was known as "the Weeping Philosopher."
   D. He had a legendary sour temper and displayed bitter scorn for his rivals.
   E. He ridiculed his predecessors such as Pythagoras and Homer.

6. In considering the structure of the essay as a whole, the most important rhetorical function of paragraph 5 is to

A. present new information regarding how the two artists were regarded in their own time

B. analyze the styles of the two artists vis-à-vis modern artistic styles

C. analyze the styles of the two artists using aesthetic categories developed two and a half centuries earlier

D. reconcile the various positions on the artists; they were equally invaluable because "Raphael was beautiful but Michelangelo sublime"

E. utilize Edmund Burke's description of the two artists as his closing line

7. All of the following describe the *pensieroso* EXCEPT:

A. His garb is less modern than his fellow philosophers.

B. He wears leather boots and a shirt cinched at the waist.

C. He has black hair and a beard.

D. He is a self-absorbed, downcast figure.

E. He rests his head on his fist as he scribbles distractedly.

8. From the lengthy description of Heraclitus, a logical conclusion is that the speaker

A. greatly admires Heraclitus for his many contributions to the field of philosophy

B. considers Heraclitus a great teacher to other philosophers

C. reveals Heraclitus was really "the laughing philosopher."

D. believes Heraclitus's dictum "You cannot avoid stepping into the same river twice."

E. concentrates on Heraclitus's foul disposition and acidic derision for all rivals

9. The speaker's inclusion of not just one but two direct quotes from Heraclitus (lines 35–36) reveals that

A. Raphael followed Heraclitus's teachings

B. Michelangelo followed Heraclitus's teachings

C. the speaker followed Heraclitus's teachings

D. the speaker understands little of Heraclitus's teachings

E. Heraclitus's own words add depth and humanity to his portrait

10. The original *School of Athens* does NOT portray philosophers who are

A. engaged in philosophical debates with one another

B. engaged in philosophical debates with Heraclitus

C. surrounded by enthusiastic novices

D. dressed in open, flowing robes

E. gathered in teacher-student groupings

11. From his use of metaphorical language in the closing line, one can conclude that the speaker

A. confuses the subtle differences between Raphael and Michelangelo

B. feels the need to properly explain and illuminate his positions

C. uses the metaphors to provide a powerful summation of his position

D. believes that these metaphors provide the best summary of Edmund Burke's views regarding Raphael versus Michelangelo

E. believes that the metaphors add new facts to his argument

12. Based on the final comments, including "Raphael was beautiful but Michelangelo sublime," one can infer all of the following EXCEPT that

A. Raphael's painting style has elegance of movement

B. Michelangelo's style delved into mysteries that are vast, obscure, and powerful

C. their differing styles and personalities led to conflict between these two artists

D. Michelangelo was obviously a superior artist

E. the people of Rome in 1511 held both artists in high regard

GO ON TO THE NEXT PAGE

13. The most important rhetorical purpose for the addition of note #1 is that it provides

   A. conclusive evidence about the timing of the addition to the *School of Athens*

   B. a reference for the *pensieroso* appearing in Raphael's cartoon of *The School of Athens*

   C. credibility to the speaker's views by referencing another source

   D. examples of similar works by Raphael in the Stella della Segnatura

   E. additional space for the speaker to express his own conclusions regarding the *pensieroso*

14. As to the question of whether Michelangelo was the model for the *pensieroso,* the information presented in note #2 implies that the speaker's conclusion is

   A. probable agreement; he dismisses the only contrary quote as "without . . . offering strong counterarguments"

   B. strong agreement; he feels the *pensieroso* must be Michelangelo, because Raphael identified him as such in his cartoon of *The School of Athens*

   C. complete neutrality; he quotes an equal number of experts on both sides of the issue

   D. strong disagreement; he feels the timing is not correct

   E. probable disagreement; he feels that the figure does not look like Michelangelo

15. The structure of the two sentences in lines 65–72 ("For Burke . . . even terror.") includes which of the following?

   A. simple sentences with substantial imagery

   B. complex sentences with parallel construction

   C. compound sentences with descriptive appositives

   D. varied sentence constructions with participial phrases

   E. compound-complex sentences with adverbial clauses

Questions 16–28. Read the following passage carefully before you begin to answer the questions.

Second Passage

When I was first aware that I had been laid low by the disease, I felt a need, among other things, to register a strong protest against the word "depres-sion." Depression, most people know, used to be
(5) termed "melancholia," a word which appears in English as early as the year 1303 and crops up more than once in Chaucer, who in his usage seemed to be aware of its pathological nuances. "Melancholia" would still appear to be a far more
(10) apt and evocative word for the blacker forms of the disorder, but it was usurped by a noun with a bland tonality and lacking any magisterial presence, used indifferently to describe an economic decline or a rut in the ground, a true wimp of a word for such a
(15) major illness. It may be that the scientist generally held responsible for its currency in modern times, a Johns Hopkins Medical School faculty member justly venerated—the Swiss-born psychiatrist Adolf Meyer—had a tin ear for the finer rhythms of
(20) English and therefore was unaware of the semantic damage he had inflicted by offering "depression" as a descriptive noun for such a dreadful and raging disease. Nonetheless, for over seventy-five years

the word has slithered innocuously through the lan-
(25) guage like a slug, leaving little trace of its intrinsic malevolence and preventing, by its very insipidity, a general awareness of the horrible intensity of the disease when out of control.

As one who has suffered from the malady in ex-
(30) tremis yet returned to tell the tale, I would lobby for a truly arresting designation. "Brainstorm," for in-stance, has unfortunately been preempted to de-scribe somewhat jocularly, intellectual inspiration. But something along these lines is needed. Told that
(35) someone's mood disorder has evolved into a storm—a veritable howling tempest in the brain, which is indeed what a clinical depression resem-bles like nothing else—even the uninformed layman might display sympathy rather than the standard re-
(40) action that "depression" evokes, something akin to "So what?" or "You'll pull out of it" or "We all have bad days." The phrase "nervous breakdown" seems to be on its way out, certainly deservedly so, owing to its insinuation of a vague spinelessness, but we
(45) still seem destined to be saddled with "depression" until a better, sturdier name is created.

16. For which of the following reasons would the speaker prefer to use the word "melancholia" instead of the word "depression"?

 I. It has been used to refer to the disease for a much longer time.

 II. Its meaning is limited to its reference to mental condition.

 III. It suggests the severity of the disease more effectively.

 A. II only
 B. I and II only
 C. I and III only
 D. II and III only
 E. I, II, and III

17. In line 13, the word "indifferently" can be best defined as

 A. apathetically
 B. neither particularly well nor badly
 C. indiscriminately
 D. disinterestedly
 E. with no understanding

18. The speaker objects to the word "depression" to describe the disease because

 I. its other meanings are nondescript.

 II. it is too euphemistic.

 III. it has been used for only about seventy-five years.

 A. II only
 B. I and II only
 C. I and III only
 D. II and III only
 E. I, II, and III.

19. The phrases "wimp of a word" (line 14) and "tin ear" (line 19) are examples of

 A. paradox
 B. colloquialism
 C. euphemism
 D. mixed metaphor
 E. parody

GO ON TO THE NEXT PAGE

20. All of the following words or phrases contribute to creating the same meaning and effect EXCEPT

- **A.** "semantic damage" (lines 20–21)
- **B.** "dreadful and raging disease" (lines 22–23)
- **C.** "intrinsic malevolence" (lines 25–26)
- **D.** "horrible intensity" (line 27)
- **E.** "howling tempest in the brain" (line 36)

21. The word "Brainstorm" (line 31) can probably not be used to replace the word "depression" because

- I. it does not adequately suggest what depression is like.
- II. it already has another very different meaning.
- III. it has comic overtones.

- **A.** II only
- **B.** I and II only
- **C.** I and III only
- **D.** II and III only
- **E.** I, II, and III

22. In the sentence in lines 34–42 ("Told that someone's . . . have bad days."), the speaker

- I. suggests a possible way of changing the conventional response to a victim of depression.
- II. exaggerates the unsympathetic response in order to increase the sympathy for the mentally ill.
- III. exaggerates the suffering of the victim of depression in order to increase the sympathetic response.

- **A.** I only
- **B.** II only
- **C.** I and II only
- **D.** I and III only
- **E.** I, II, and III

23. In line 42, the speaker refers to the phrase "nervous breakdown" in order to

- **A.** suggest that the phrase is more evocative that the word "depression"
- **B.** give an example of an inadequate phrase that is losing its currency
- **C.** offer a second example of a bland and unevocative phrase
- **D.** contrast a well-chosen name for mental illness with the ill-chosen word "depression"
- **E.** show that the uninformed layman is unsympathetic to mental illness

24. Of the following, which would the speaker probably prefer to use to describe a man suffering from acute depression?

- **A.** dispirited
- **B.** down-at-the-mouth
- **C.** utterly desolated
- **D.** gloomy
- **E.** low

25. The passage makes use of all of the following EXCEPT

- **A.** metaphor
- **B.** direct quotation
- **C.** literary citation
- **D.** hyperbole
- **E.** simile

26. Of the following, which best describes the speaker's attitude toward the use of the word "depression"?

- **A.** resigned acceptance
- **B.** amused disapproval
- **C.** casual disinterestedness
- **D.** cool dislike
- **E.** strong resentment

27. Which of the following best describes the rhetorical purpose of the passage?

    A. to record the history of the word "depression"

    B. to criticize the inadequacy of the word "depression"

    C. to explain the multiple meanings of the word "depression"

    D. to demonstrate the shortcomings of medical language

    E. to argue for the use of the word "melancholia" in place of the word "depression"

28. Which of the following is a central idea of this passage?

    A. The connotation of a word may be just as important as its denotation.

    B. The healthy do not properly sympathize with victims of mental illness.

    C. The changes in meanings of words over time are unpredictable.

    D. The scientific understanding of depression is incomplete.

    E. Words are an inadequate means of describing reality.

GO ON TO THE NEXT PAGE

Questions 29–42. Read the following passage carefully before you begin to answer the questions.

Third Passage

First, he that hath words of any language, without distinct ideas in his mind to which he applies them, does, so far as he uses them in discourse, only make a noise without any sense or signification; and how
(5) learned soever he may seem by the use of hard words, or learned terms, is not much more advanced thereby in knowledge than he would be in learning, who had nothing in his study but the bare titles of books, without possessing the contents of them. For
(10) all such words, however put into discourse, according to the right construction of grammatical rules, or the harmony of well turned periods, do yet amount to nothing but bare sounds, and nothing else.

Secondly, he that has complex ideas, without par-
(15) ticular names for them, would be in no better case than a bookseller, who had in his warehouse volumes that lay there unbound, and without titles; which he could therefore make known to others only by showing the loose sheets, and communicating
(20) them only by tale. This man is hindered in his discourse for want of words to communicate his complex ideas, which he is therefore forced to make known by an enumeration of the simple ones that compose them; and so is fain often to use twenty
(25) words to express what another man signifies in one.

Thirdly, he that puts not constantly the same sign for the same idea, but uses the same words sometimes in one, and sometimes in another signification, ought to pass in the schools and conversation for as
(30) fair a man as he does in the market and exchange, who sells several things under the same name.

Fourthly, he that applies the words of any language to ideas different from those to which the common use of that country applies them, however
(35) his own understanding may be filled with truth and light, will not by such words be able to convey much of it to others, without defining his terms. For however the sounds are such as are familiarly known, and easily enter the ears of those who are accus-
(40) tomed to them; yet standing for other ideas than those they usually are annexed to, and are wont to excite in the mind of the hearers, they cannot make known the thoughts of him who thus uses them.

Fifthly, he that imagined to himself substances
(45) such as never have been, and filled his head with ideas which have not any correspondence with the real nature of things, to which yet he gives settled and defined names, may fill his discourse, and perhaps another man's head, with the fantastical
(50) imaginations of his own brain, but will be very far from advancing thereby one jot in real and true knowledge.

He that hath names without ideas, wants meaning in his words, and speaks only empty sounds. He
(55) that hath complex ideas without names for them, wants liberty and dispatch in his expressions, and is necessitated to use periphrases. He that uses his words loosely and unsteadily, will either be not minded, or not understood. He that applies his
(60) names to ideas different from their common use, wants propriety in his language, and speaks gibberish. And he that hath the ideas of substances disagreeing with the real existence of things, so far wants the materials of true knowledge in his under-
(65) standing, and hath instead thereof chimeras.

29. As it is used in line 12 the word "periods" may be best defined as

A. conclusions
B. sentences
C. musical measures
D. marks of punctuation
E. times

30. In line 23, the word "ones" refers to

A. words
B. books
C. ideas
D. discourse
E. names

31. In the second paragraph, the shift from the first sentence (lines 14–20) to the second sentence (lines 20–25) can be best described as one from

   A. objective to subjective
   B. indicative to interrogative
   C. analytical to discursive
   D. figurative to literal
   E. speculative to assertive

32. The comparison of lines 14–20 likens words to

   A. the pages of a book
   B. the contents of a warehouse
   C. complex ideas
   D. booksellers
   E. the binding of a book

33. In the first and second paragraphs, the speaker supports his arguments by the use of

   A. analogies
   B. personifications
   C. understatements
   D. rhetorical questions
   E. hyperboles

34. In line 30, the word "fair" is best understood to mean

   A. equitable
   B. attractive
   C. clement
   D. unblemished
   E. average

35. The third paragraph of the passage (lines 26–31) is an example of

   A. an extended metaphor
   B. a loose sentence
   C. a periodic sentence
   D. an antithesis
   E. an *ad hominem* argument

36. In line 44, "substances" are contrasted with

   A. shadows
   B. ideas
   C. imaginings
   D. realities
   E. names

37. Which of the following best categorizes the organizational coherence of the first five of the six paragraphs in the passage?

   A. paragraph 1; paragraphs 2 and 3; paragraphs 4 and 5
   B. paragraph 1; paragraphs 2, 3, and 4; paragraph 5
   C. paragraphs 1, 2, and 3; paragraphs 4 and 5
   D. paragraphs 1 and 2; paragraph 3; paragraphs 4 and 5
   E. paragraphs 1 and 2; paragraphs 3 and 4; paragraph 5

38. Which of the following best describes the relation of the last paragraph to the rest of the passage?

   A. It comments upon and develops the arguments of the first five paragraphs.
   B. It calls into question the arguments of the preceding paragraphs.
   C. It raises new issues about language that the preceding paragraphs have not addressed.
   D. It sums up the contents of the first five paragraphs.
   E. It develops the ideas raised in the fourth and fifth paragraphs.

39. Which of the following is the meaning of the word "chimeras" that can be inferred from its use in the last sentence of the passage (line 65)?

   A. fabulous monsters
   B. oriental potentates
   C. religious revelations
   D. logical conclusions
   E. philosophical distinctions

40. In which paragraph is a person who misunderstands the meaning of the word "refuse" and frequently uses it to mean "agree" described?

   A. the first (lines 1 13)
   B. the second (lines 14–25)
   C. the third (lines 26–31)
   D. the fourth (lines 32–43)
   E. the fifth (lines 44–52)

GO ON TO THE NEXT PAGE

41. In which paragraph does the passage deal with a speaker or writer who would use the word "apple" to denote a fruit, an animal, and an article of footwear?

    A. the first (lines 1–13)
    B. the second (lines 14–25)
    C. the third (lines 26–31)
    D. the fourth (lines 32–43)
    E. the fifth (lines 44–52)

42. Which of the following does the passage use as a synonym for "word"?

    I.   term
    II. name
    III. sign

    A. III only
    B. I and II only
    C. I and III only
    D. II and III only
    E. I, II, and III

Questions 43–55. Read the following passage carefully before you begin to answer the questions.

Fourth Passage

Wyoming has no true cities. Every hundred miles or so there's a small town. Some, like Moneta, Arminto, Emblem, Morton, and Bill, boast populations as minuscule as five or ten. A boomtown I
(5) drove through in the eastern part of the state consists of two trailer houses. One is the cafe post office, the other is the school. Some Wyoming towns are a brief miscellany of log buildings whose central focus is the bar. When you walk in, everyone is sure to turn
(10) and stare at you. Others have shoals of untended pickups, rusting balers, and new backhoes behind which lurk a grocery store and a town hall.

Elsewhere, the environments Americans have fashioned for themselves are aswim in paradox.
(15) Being both pragmatists and idealists, we've adopted all kinds of high-minded utopian ideas, from the Greek revivalist to the International style, but upended them so completely they now stand for opposite ideals. Walter Gropius's antibourgeois, socialist
(20) housing has been transformed into the icy, machined skyscrapers in which the corporate creme de la creme hold court; the Greek columned portico, which Jefferson loved because it symbolized human uprightness and dignity within the Greek polis, ap-
(25) peared on the mansions of slave owners and came to symbolize their beleaguered era.

Wyoming has no architectural legacy except for the trapper's cabin and homesteader's shack: dark, smoky, often windowless, and papered with the clas-
(30) sifieds from the weekly newspaper. Yet I like to think that those who landed here during Wyoming's territorial days had been exposed to the ideals of Jefferson and Thoreau. Both men distrusted cities, but Thoreau was disdainful of most social gatherings
(35) while Jefferson promoted a local participatory democracy in which each person had a farmable plot and an active citizenship to go with it. They sought out the opposite kinds of freedom. Thoreau's had to do with personal privacy, unencumbered by foot-
(40) ball games and town meetings, while Jefferson's implied a busyness—citizens having a voice in every proceeding.

Wyoming attracted people of both minds. The first trappers and cattlemen, like Osborne Russell
(45) and Henry Lovell, thrived on the expanse and solitude of the state. They claimed territory the way geographers would—on the basis of water, vegetation, the contour of the land, not by the Jeffersonian grid.

The Mormons stretched Jefferson fair-minded-
(50) ness into a socialistic regime under the guidance of Brigham Young. Each "colonist" was allotted a town plot, arranged on streets of specific length and width, while farmland and pasturing of livestock remained communal.

(55) The word "building" is both a noun and a verb and implies two contradictory things Americans love: security and movement. We want a firm tie to a place but to remain footloose and fancy free. Native Americans rolled up their skins and followed the
(60) game through the seasons (now they go on the pow-wow circuit in smoky colored vans); trappers and mountain men commuted between cities like St. Louis and the Tetons, the Wind Rivers, the Absaroka Mountains. Even now, cowboys and sheepherders
(65) move from job to job, ranch to ranch, and it's no wonder so many of the manmade structures here have a temporary feel.

But back to politics. It's one thing to construct shelter and quite another to announce with the
(70) grandness of one's architecture a hierarchical intention. Take medieval Europe, for example, whose first cities were built out of fear. They started as stone walls behind which herdsmen and their families huddled and fought off invaders. Temporary walls
(75) became permanent. People built houses behind them, and itinerant merchants set up shop there. Then the priests came and the governors, and the buildings they erected became physical signs of their authority. You can go anywhere in Europe and see
(80) how they did this. Castles and churches were built on hills. Everyone else had to use their dirty water.

GO ON TO THE NEXT PAGE

43. In lines 7–8, the phrase "brief miscellany" is best defined as a

    A. concise collection of verse

    B. short-lived confusion

    C. small hodgepodge

    D. little circle

    E. short, varied street

44. In the phrase "shoals of untended pickups, rusting balers, and new backhoes" (lines 10–11), the speaker compares vehicles and farm equipment with

    A. shallow places

    B. bundles of grain

    C. large groups of fish

    D. camouflaged soldiers

    E. coral reefs

45. The third paragraph (lines 27–42) contains an example of

    A. overstatement

    B. parallel construction in a periodic sentence

    C. literary allusion

    D. apostrophe

    E. first-person commentary

46. From the third and fourth paragraphs, we can infer that Wyoming would have appealed to Thoreau because of its

    A. natural beauty

    B. solitude

    C. fur-bearing animals

    D. natural resources

    E. vegetation

47. In their context in this passage, the fourth and fifth paragraphs function to

    A. introduce a new theory about the settlers of Wyoming

    B. prepare for the definitions of "building" in the sixth paragraph

    C. demonstrate the range of the occupations of early Wyoming settlers

    D. develop two ideas presented in the third paragraph

    E. question traditional ideas about the western expansion

48. The passage suggests that Thoreau rather than Jefferson has more in common with all of the following EXCEPT

    A. cowboys

    B. Brigham Young

    C. Osborne Russell

    D. Native American hunters

    E. sheepherders

49. The effect of the parenthetical remark "now they go on the powwow circuit in smoky colored vans" in lines 60–61 is to

    I. comment on the mechanization of 20th-century America

    II. establish the close relationship between the "powwow circuit" and the "game" of the 19th century

    III. stress the importance of the preservation of ancient customs in Native American culture

    A. I only

    B. III only

    C. I and III only

    D. II and III only

    E. I, II, and III

50. The rhetorical function of the last paragraph of the passage (lines 68–81) is to

    A. present the European historical precedent of American architecture

    B. sum up the first six paragraphs of the passage

    C. contrast the ideal (America) with the historical (Europe)

    D. introduce another paradox in the history of building

    E. introduce new ideas about the relation of architecture and politics

51. All of the following could be called examples of what the passage defines as an architecture built with a "hierarchical intention" (lines 70–71) EXCEPT

    A. European castles

    B. corporate skyscrapers

    C. the towns of Mormon "colonists"

    D. European cathedrals

    E. the Greek revival mansions of the Old South

52. The passage suggests that all of the following are paradoxical pairs EXCEPT

    A. pragmatism and idealism

    B. international-style architecture and American corporate executives

    C. the American love of security and of movement

    D. Thomas Jefferson and Brigham Young

    E. "building" as a noun and as a verb

53. Of the following paragraphs in the passage, which one is NOT concerned with the architecture of Wyoming or its designers?

    A. the first (lines 1–12)

    B. the second (lines 13–26)

    C. the third (lines 27–42)

    D. the fourth (lines 43–48)

    E. the fifth (lines 49–54)

54. The passage contrasts all of the following EXCEPT

    A. society and solitude

    B. movement and rootedness

    C. the Greek polis and the slave-owning South

    D. freedom and security

    E. the priests and the rulers of the Middle Ages

55. Which of the following best describes this passage?

    A. a carefully developed logical argument with a focus on a central point

    B. an examination of the values reflected by the buildings of Wyoming

    C. a discursive discussion of the architecture of Wyoming, America, and Europe

    D. an unresolved questioning of the materialism of American values

    E. a brief survey of American architectural history in the 19th and 20th centuries

IF YOU FINISH BEFORE TIME IS CALLED, CHECK YOUR WORK ON THIS SECTION ONLY. DO NOT WORK ON ANY OTHER SECTION IN THE TEST.

Section II: Essay Questions

Time: 2 hours, 15 minutes

3 questions

Question 1

(Reading time—15 minutes. Suggested writing time—40 minutes. This question counts one-third of the total essay section score.)

Directions: The prompt that follows is based on six accompanying sources. This essay requires you to integrate a variety of sources into a coherent, well-written essay. Refer to the sources, both directly and indirectly, to support your position. Avoid mere paraphrasing or summarizing. Your argument should be the central focus; the use of the sources should support your argument.

Introduction

Throughout recent years, professional athletes' salaries have skyrocketed. Do you find that today's athletes are overpaid? Or are professional athletes paid an appropriate amount for their physical talents?

Assignment

Read the following sources (including any introductory information) carefully. **Then, in an essay that synthesizes at least three of the sources for support, take a position that defends, challenges, or qualifies the claim that athletes are overpaid.**

Refer to the sources as Source A, Source B, and so on. For your convenience, a description or authors' names are included.

Source A (Simmons)

Source B *(Salt Lake Tribune)*

Source C (Looney)

Source D *(USA Today)*

Source E *(USA Today)*

Source F (Halloway)

Source A

Simmons, Mark. "Most Paid Salaries." *Ask Men.* 2 Oct. 2005. www.askmen.com/sports/business/23_sports_business.html.

This article examines the recent history of professional sports salaries.

Economics theory would suggest that with expansion comes increased supply, which would decrease the price that people would pay for a good or service. What happened was the opposite. Why?

As the number of teams increased, so did the number of jobs. As the number of jobs increased, so did the demand for players.

While the early owners had taken Business 101 and knew that fighting for players would rapidly escalate prices (the not-so-nice term is collusion), the more recent club owners knew that signing the marquee players would not only attract more fans, but also the premium advertisers that end up financing new stadiums and subsidizing players' salaries.

In 1988, the highest earning basketball player was the Los Angeles Lakers' Earvin "Magic" Johnson at $3 million. Ten years later, Shaquille was making $17.14 million, a 472% increase.

In baseball, Ozzie Smith earned $2.34 million from the St. Louis Cardinals for pounding his frame into the dirt and fetching all of those grounders. Ten years later, Pedro Martinez (part of that 1994 Expos team) was getting $11 million from the Boston Red Sox, a 370% increase.

Football was no different. The Denver Broncos' John Elway was paid $1.96 million in 1988. A decade later, Dallas Cowboys Troy Aikman's compensation was $5.87 million, a 200% increase.

Something has got to give. Players making millions is fine by me. Really. No, not because I make millions. I think that players sacrifice a lot to make it to the big show. So many players end up as road kill, as their careers fail to take them to the pros.

Perhaps 1 player out of 100 makes it to the college squad, and 1 college player out of 100 gets drafted. And as you may know, just because you get drafted, that doesn't mean you will make it. It takes an insane amount of dedication, sacrifice, aversion to pain, tenacity, and determination to get to be the king of the hill. If you make it, then you deserve every penny.

My only fear is what will happen when players want $100 million per year. Think it's funny? While the BoSox were paying Martinez $11 million in 1998, the Dodgers are currently paying $15 million for Kevin Brown, a 36% increase within two years. Eleven million would not even crack the top ten.

All in all, this is scary in a time when people are finding it harder and harder to cough up the dough to go to ballgames. Yet corporations are scooping up tickets at high prices, writing off the cost as business expenses. They are increasing ticket demand, thus increasing prices. If that weren't enough, they are simultaneously paying premium dollars to get stadium naming rights and advertising spots, adding to the teams' wallets and allowing them to pay the multi-million-dollar contracts that are increasingly out of whack.

For an idea of baseball players' salaries, check this out:

Player and Team	Yearly Salary
Kevin Brown, L.A. Dodgers	$15,000,000
Shawn Green, L.A. Dodgers	$14,000,000
Mo Vaughn, Anaheim Angels	$13,333,333
Randy Johnson, Arizona Diamondbacks	$13,100,000
Mike Piazza, N.Y. Mets	$13,000,000
Albert Belle, Baltimore Orioles	$13,000,000
Pedro Martinez, Boston Red Sox	$12,500,000
Bernie Williams, N.Y. Yankees	$12,500,000
Larry Walker, Colorado Rockies	$12,500,000
David Cone, N.Y. Yankees	$12,000,000

GO ON TO THE NEXT PAGE

Source B

Letter. *Salt Lake Tribune* 19 May 1999: A10.

This letter to the editor argues that NBA players are overpaid.

Hey, all you sport fans out there. Our favorite NBA athletes are playing their hearts out, but should they really be getting all these millions of dollars? I think not. Even though they are the best at what they do, they are in fact overpaid.

Kevin Garnett is just one of the many overpaid athletes. Kevin gets $126 million over a short six-year period, and he just signed this contract only last season. Kevin is one of the top players at his position (which is power forward), but he does not deserve more money that players like Scottie Pippen, Grant Hill, and David Robinson, to name a few, who have been around longer.

Stephon Marbury is probably the best point guard playing the game today. Marbury in March signed a $70.9 million contract for six years. It isn't as much as Garrett's but it will have to do.

Salary caps have helped this problem greatly. The salary cap for the 1998–1999 season is $30 million. Along with the salary cap there is the collective bargaining agreement. For 0–6 years you get 25% of salary cap but not less than $9 million, for 7–9 years you get 30% of the salary cap but not less than $11 million, and for 10 or more years you get 35% of the salary cap but not less than $14 million.

NBA players, although they are the best at what they do, are still overpaid.

Source C

Looney, Douglas S. "Overpaid athletes? It's fans that make them so." *Christian Science Monitor* [Boston] 30 July 1999: 12.

This article presents the idea that high salaries in professional sports are an effect of sports' popularity.

Arguably the easiest thing in the world to do, with the possible exception of pulling the covers over our heads in the morning, is to rail against others who make way more money than they deserve and, worse, don't work nearly as hard as we do.

Nowhere do we see this phenomenon so clearly at work as in sports.

Talk about obscenely and grossly overpaid. *Forbes* magazine has reported that Michael Jordan made the most money of any athlete in a single year, $78.3 million, more than half of it in endorsements. Three questions: How does *Forbes* know? Is it really secure in its numbers? And does anybody know save Michael Jordan—or perhaps Michael Jackson or Oprah Winfrey—how much $78.3 mil really is?

Outfielder Bernie Williams of the Yankees and catcher Mike Piazza of the Mets each make about $90 million over seven years. Albert Belle, perhaps baseball's most misbehaved player (six suspensions), gets $65 million over five years to play for the Orioles. For this, he thinks he will be able to improve his deportment.

The average hockey goalie, for puck's sake, is making more than $1.3 mil per frosty season.

Guess what? These guys are underpaid.

Ditto every other professional athlete. In a just world, the case easily can be made that Jordan, when he was playing, should have hauled in closer to $500 mil annually, or a lot more. Multiply every pro salary by 10 and they all remain bargains worthy of Filene's Basement.

The reasons are simple. These athletes have skills, amazing skills, that are incredibly rare. They do things routinely that we can't do in our dreams. Look and marvel at Tiger Woods, Pete Sampras, Wayne Gretzky, Barry Sanders, Dennis Rodman. Well, OK, marvel at four of the five.

When there is only one or possibly just a few of a kind, the worth is incalculable. That's why it does no good, ultimately, to insure a Picasso or Monet. After all, we want the paintings, not the cash. Deep in your honest heart, what was Joe DiMaggio's value to baseball and was he ever fairly compensated? Chris Evert earned millions, a pittance compared with her contributions to tennis.

So the shame is when the *Dallas Morning News* and Associated Press report that 317 baseball players earn $1 million or more this year. Why so few? Not fair.

Conversely, almost all the rest of us have no special skill. Or, at the most, we have skills that easily are replicated. It's true that sometimes we get to thinking our office can't run without us. Then we leave, and it runs fine.

Latest figures show there are nearly 3 million cashiers in the country, making an average of $11,388 a year. (That sounds about right for the skill involved.) Same for office clerks who average about $18,500. There are almost 4.5 million handlers, equipment cleaners, helpers, and laborers; they make $15,600.

Further bolstering the case for athletes is that we, as a society, put value on sports. Can't pay the athletes like this if we don't watch. If people really liked opera, instead of just pretending to, sopranos and baritones would be high on various *Forbes*'s lists.

Yup, a free and open market is a wondrous thing. The National Education Association says the average teacher makes $38,611 a year. Many grouse this isn't enough considering we entrust our 45 million public-school students to them daily. But it must be or else we'd pay them more. Sacramento, Calif., tries to hire police officers for as low as $23,904 a year, a plumber in the U.S. averages $27,000, a long-haul trucker $33,580, a firefighter in the Northwest starts around $36,000, a lawyer with no specialty averages $69,804, a doctor $150,000.

Who among these can be replaced with no sweat? All of them. (Stunning, but even a newspaper columnist could be replaced. Doubtful, of course, but remotely possible.) However, replacing Mark McGwire can't happen since only one was minted.

Make out your checks to Star Athletes Miserably Underpaid, Inc., Mike Piazza, Treasurer. Please be generous. They're counting on you. Thank you.

GO ON TO THE NEXT PAGE

Source D

"Before crying foul, consider reasons behind ballplayer pay." Letter. *USA Today* 2 Aug. 2002: A08.

This letter to the editor supports NBA players' salaries.

As a former pro athlete and team representative of a player union, I am tired of hearing complaints about "overpaid athletes" ("Ballplayers cry all the way to the bank," Letters, July 8; "Salaries mirror market forces," Letters, July 11).

People are paid for what they collectively produce. No salary is based on a job's intrinsic value. Is an advertising executive really "worth" $100,000 a year? What is the worth of a CEO who runs a company that goes bankrupt, causing thousands of workers to lose compensation?

I am only familiar with the NFL collective bargaining agreement. I do know that NFL salaries are based on what the league brings in from revenues—which is predominantly TV revenue.

If Americans didn't spend so much time watching and reading about sports, athletes wouldn't be paid as much. It's a shame, but I'm sure more Americans can identify the center for the Los Angeles Lakers than the Senate majority leader.

True, there are other professions that should get better compensation, such as teachers. But let's not forget that, for the most part, they're paid by the taxpayers—and high-income athletes contribute a great share.

The myopic view that any highly paid individual should accept any working terms that management implements is ridiculous. Get real, people.

That said, I'm not asking anyone to shed tears for athletes who face labor problems. But the public should try to understand the real issues at hand before it whines about athletes' salaries.

Maybe critics of athlete salaries should put down their sports pages and pick up an economics book—or any book for that matter.

Source E

"Ballplayers cry all the way to the bank." Letter. *USA Today* 2 Aug. 2002: A11.

This letter to the editor criticizes baseball players' salaries.

Here we go again. Do the poor, starving millionaires of Major League Baseball really feel they need to go on strike? Please, somebody say it ain't so ("Owners tell players they won't back down," Sports, Wednesday).

What is it with these people? Don't they make enough money for throwing a ball or swinging a bat? They can't be serious. The owners should wake up and stop being held hostage by these overpaid and pampered players.

They are athletes, for goodness' sakes. They are not saving people's lives, and the owners should stop paying them the money they do.

Some sense of sanity has to return to the salary structure of professional sports. It's absurd that a ballplayer makes millions of dollars while research analysts at places such as the Centers for Disease Control and Prevention get peanuts by comparison for doing work that saves lives. And look at what a small salary a schoolteacher makes.

Athletes are just not worth the big bucks they get when they continually whine about collective bargaining and the other silly things that occupy their spoiled lives.

Can anybody feel sorry for someone who drives to the picket line in a Ferrari?

GO ON TO THE NEXT PAGE

Source F

Hallway, Cameron. "Bargain Or Bust?" *St. Louis Post-Dispatch* 3 Aug. 2005: D2.

This article questions the validity of professional sports salaries.

Since Bobby Hull became the first reported million-dollar man in 1972, salaries in professional sports have escalated to out-of-control proportions. Tuesday, Shaquille O'Neal's restructured contract worth $100 million over five years was barely a blip on the radar screen in the NBA, where $100 million deals are common. Bryant Reeves makes $7.8 million a year and LeBron James pockets $90 million for wearing Nike skids.

Athlete contracts have become more about "respect" and one-upping a rival player than about the money—seriously, besides Mike Tyson, who can really spend $100 million? Tiger Woods might actually be worth his reported $1-billion-plus bank account, but are any of the other milestone millionaires deserving of their loot?

From Hull to O'Neal, we take a look at a few big-money payouts and whether they were worth the risk.

Alex Rodriguez (baseball)

The money: A-Rod's 10-year, $252-million contract delivered by Texas in December 2000 is the richest in professional sports history. In January, Carlos Beltran became the 10th big-league player to sign a $100 million contract.

Bust: Babe Ruth's $50,000 contract in 1922 was a record that took 25 years to double (Hank Greenberg, $100K, 1947). After Mike Piazza signed for $13 million annually in 1998, it took only two years for A-Rod to pull in more than double at $27 million.

Shaquille O'Neal (NBA)

The money: The game's most dominant big man opted out of his one-year contract for $30.6 million, saying through his agent that he preferred the "stability" of a long-term deal. Five years, $100 million buys a stable of stability.

Bust: Remember when Magic Johnson signed a 25-year deal for $25 million in 1984? Shaq Daddy is too fat, too injury-prone and too dramatic to draw $20 million per, even if he is the most physically dominant player in NBA history.

Question 2

Suggested time—40 minutes. This question counts one-third of the total essay score.

In the following excerpt, John Updike, in his essay titled "The First Kiss," describes the opening of a new baseball season, including reflecting on the past season and the attitude of the fans as the new season begins.

Directions: Read the following narrative carefully. Then, in a well-developed essay, analyze the author's use of metaphor and other rhetorical devices to convey an audience's attitude toward a sporting event.

The many-headed monster called the Fenway Faithful yesterday resumed its romance with twenty-five youngish men in red socks who last year broke its monstrous big heart. Just showing up on so dank an Opening Day was an act of faith. But the wet sky dried to a mottled pewter, the tarpaulin was rolled off the infield and stuffed into a mailing tube, and we Faithful braced for the first kiss of another prolonged entanglement.

Who can forget the ups and downs of last year's fling? First, the Supersox; then, the unraveling. Our eyeballs grew calluses, watching Boomer swing from the heels and Hobson throw to the stars. Dismal nights watching the Royals play pinball with our heroes on that plastic prairie in Kansas City. Dreadful days losing count of Yankee singles in the four-game massacre. Fisk standing ever more erect and stoic at the plate, looking more and more like a Civil War memorial financed with Confederate dollars. The Noble Lost Cause.

In September, the mini-resurrection, Zimmer's last stand, the miraculous last week of no losses, waiting for the Yankees to drop one. Which they did. And then, the cruelest tease, the playoff game surrendered to a shoestring catch and a shortstop's cheap home run. Enough. You'll never get us to care again, Red Sox.

But monsters have short memories, elastic hearts, and very foolable faculties, as many an epic attests. From natty-looking to nasty-looking, the fans turned out. "We Miss Louis and Bill," one large cardboard complained. "Windsor Locks Loves the Sox!" a bedsheet benignly rhymed. Some fellow behind us exhaled a sweetish smell, but the dragon's breath was primarily flavored with malt.

Governor King was booed royally. Power may or may not corrupt, but it does not win friends. A lady from Dedham not only sang all the high notes in "The Star-Spangled Banner" but put in an extra one of her own, taking "free" up and out of the ballpark. We loved it. Monsters love high notes and hoards of gold.

The two teams squared off against each other in a state of statistical virginity. Every man in both lineups was batting .000. On the other hand, both pitchers had earned-run averages of 0.00. And every fielder there had thus far played errorless ball.

Eckersley looked quick. A moment of sun made some of the windows of the Prudential Center sparkle. The new Red Sox uniforms appeared tight as outfits for trapeze artists but otherwise struck the proper conservative note, for a team of millionaires: buttons on the shirt and a single red pinstripe. Eckersley yielded a double and then struck out two. The first nicks in statistical virginity had been taken. The season had begun.

We witnessed a little by-play at the beginning that may tell it all. After the Cleveland lineup had been called out, the Red Sox roll began with Zimmer. Out he trotted, last year's anti-hero, the manager who watched ninety-nine victories be not quite enough, with his lopsided cheeks and squint, like a Popeye who has let the spinach settle to his middle. The many-headed monster booed furiously, and Zimmer laughed, shaking hands with his opposite manager, Torborg.

That laugh said a strange thing. It said, *This is fun*. Baseball is meant to be fun, and not all the solemn money men in fur-collared greatcoats, not all the scruffy media cameramen and sour-faced reporters that crowd around the dugouts can quite smother the exhilarating spaciousness and grace of this impudently relaxed sport, a game of innumerable potential redemptions and curious disappointments. This is fun.

A hard lesson for a hungry monster to master, but he has six months to work on it. So let's play ball.

GO ON TO THE NEXT PAGE

Question 3

Suggested time—40 minutes. This question counts one-third of the total essay score.

Directions: Read carefully the following excerpt from Cynthia Ozick's "Portrait of the Essay as a Warm Body." Then, in a well-organized essay, examine how the author distinguishes an essay from an article. Analyze how she employs rhetorical strategies (perhaps considering such elements as syntax, diction, irony, and paradox) to convey her opinions.

An essay is a thing of the imagination. If there is information in an essay, it is by-the-by, and if there is an opinion in it, you need not trust it for the long run. A genuine essay has no educational, polemical, or sociopolitical use; it is the movement of a free mind at play. Though it is written in prose, it is closer in kind to poetry than to any other form. Like a poem, a genuine essay is made out of language and character and mood and temperament and pluck and chance.

And if I speak of a genuine essay, it is because fakes abound. Here the old-fashioned term poetaster may apply, if only obliquely. As the poetaster is to the poet—a lesser aspirant—so the article is to the essay: a look-alike knockoff guaranteed not to wear well. An article is gossip. An essay is reflection and insight. An article has the temporary advantage of social heat—what's hot out there right now. An essay's heat is interior. An article is timely, topical, engaged in the issues and personalities of the moment; it is likely to be stale within the month. In five years it will have acquired the quaint aura of a rotary phone. An article is Siamese-twinned to its date of birth. An essay defies its date of birth, and ours too.

A small historical experiment. Who are the classical essayists who come at once to mind? Montaigne, obviously.

Among the nineteenth-century English masters, the long row of Hazlitt, Lamb, De Quincey, Stevenson, Carlyle, Ruskin, Newman, Martineau, Arnold. Of the Americans, Emerson. It may be argued that nowadays these are read only by specialists and literature majors, and by the latter only when they are compelled to. However accurate the claim, it is irrelevant to the experiment, which has to do with beginnings and their disclosures.

So the essay is ancient and various: but this is a commonplace. There is something else, and it is more striking yet—the essay's power. By "power" I mean precisely the capacity to do what force always does: coerce assent. Never mind that the shape and intent of any essay is against coercion or persuasion, or that the essay neither proposes nor purposes to get you to think like its author. A genuine essay is not a doctrinaire tract or a propaganda effort or a broadside. Thomas Paine's "Common Sense" and Emile Zola's "J'Accuse" are heroic landmark writings; but to call them essays, though they may resemble the form, is to misunderstand. The essay is not meant for the barricades; it is a stroll through someone's mazy mind. All the same, the essay turns out to be a force for agreement. It co-opts agreement; it courts agreement; it seduces agreement.

IF YOU FINISH BEFORE TIME IS CALLED, CHECK YOUR WORK ON THIS SECTION ONLY. DO NOT WORK ON ANY OTHER SECTION IN THE TEST.

Answer Key for Practice Test 4

Section I: Multiple-Choice Questions

First Passage

1. D
2. B
3. E
4. C
5. A
6. D
7. A
8. E
9. E
10. B
11. C
12. D
13. C
14. A
15. B

Second Passage

16. E
17. C
18. B
19. B
20. A
21. D
22. A
23. B
24. C
25. D
26. E
27. B
28. A

Third Passage

29. B
30. A
31. D
32. E
33. A
34. A
35. C
36. D
37. E
38. D
39. A
40. D
41. C
42. E

Fourth Passage

43. C
44. A
45. E
46. B
47. D
48. B
49. A
50. E
51. C
52. D
53. B
54. E
55. C

Section II: Essay Questions

Essay scoring guides, student essays, and analysis appear beginning on page 239.

Practice Test 4 Scoring Worksheet

Use the following worksheet to arrive at a probable final AP grade on Practice Test 4. Because being objective enough to estimate your own essay score is sometimes difficult, you might give your essays (along with the sample essays) to a teacher, friend, or relative to score if you feel confident that the individual has the knowledge necessary to make such a judgment and that he or she will feel comfortable doing so.

Section I: Multiple-Choice Questions

_____ – (¼ or .25 × _____) = _____
right   wrong   multiple-choice
answers   answers   raw score

_____ × 1.2272 = _____ (of possible 67.5)
multiple-choice   multiple-choice
raw score   converted score

Section II: Essay Questions

_____ + _____ + _____ = _____
question 1   question 2   question 3   essay
raw score   raw score   raw score   raw score

_____ × 3.0556 = _____ (of possible 82.5)
essay   essay
raw score   converted score

Final Score

_____ + _____ = _____ (of possible 150)
multiple-choice   essay   final
converted score converted score converted score

Probable Final AP Score

Final Converted Score	Probable AP Score
150–104	5
103–92	4
91–76	3
75–50	2
49–0	1

Answers and Explanations for Practice Test 4

Section I: Multiple-Choice Questions

First Passage

From *Michelangelo & the Pope's Ceiling* by Ross King

1. **D.** The speaker states that an examination of the painting ". . . convinced a number of art historians that the model was none other than Michelangelo, whom Raphael added to the fresco as an act of homage after seeing the Sistine ceiling."

2. **B.** The visual details demonstrate the intent of the artist to set the solitary figure apart in every way; his mode of dress, his expression, his self-absorbed, downcast pose all help to show his lack of connection to his fellow philosophers. No other answer choice addresses the speaker's rhetorical purpose.

3. **E.** Although the figure does appear to be modeled after a great artist of the day, the likely model is Michelangelo, *not* Raphael.

4. **C.** The addition of the *pensieroso* figure to *The School of Athens* was both a great compliment to Michelangelo and also a somewhat insulting joke at his expense. Raphael's addition of Michelangelo to his own masterwork was "an act of homage after seeing the Sistine ceiling," but his comparison of Michelangelo to a disputatious, sour-tempered old philosopher was certainly not complimentary. Choice E is incorrect because "conflicted" is too strong; Raphael knew his opinion of Michelangelo.

5. **A.** The passage offers no evidence of Heraclitus's being respected by the citizens of Ephesus. All other answer choices *do* have evidence in the passage.

6. **D.** The speaker resolves the disparate portraits of the two artists that he has presented in the preceding paragraphs. He demonstrates that both artists, while quite different from each other, each present an artistic vision of inestimable value. Choice A is incorrect because this paragraph does not address how the artists were regarded in their own time. Choice B is incorrect; the paragraph does not address contemporary artistic styles. Choice C is incorrect because it does not reflect the "most important rhetorical purpose"; the speaker does not analyze the two artists' styles but merely labels them. Choice E is incorrect; the closing line is written by the speaker, not Edmund Burke.

7. **A.** The passage states that the figure "is dressed in considerably *more* modern garb than his fellow philosophers . . ." not less-modern garb. Choices B, C, D, and E all *do* describe the figure.

8. **E.** The passage indicates that Raphael portrayed Heraclitus as Michelangelo because ". . . more likely it was Heraclitus's legendary sour temper and bitter scorn for all rivals." Choices A and B are incorrect because the speaker neither admires Heraclitus nor considers him a great teacher. Choice C is incorrect; he was known as "the Weeping Philosopher." Choice D is incorrect; it misquotes Heraclitus's famous aphorism.

9. **E.** The speaker makes good use of the two quotes, as they help to "humanize" and balance the negativity with which he portrays Heraclitus. Choices A, B, and C are all incorrect because none of these individuals followed the teachings of Heraclitus. Choice D is incorrect because the inclusion of the quotes demonstrates that the speaker *does* understand Heraclitus's true nature.

10. **B.** The other philosophers are *not* engaging Heraclitus in discussion; he appears solitary, self-absorbed and ". . . utterly oblivious to the philosophical debates raging around him." All other answer choices *are* demonstrated in the picture.

11. **C.** In his final line, the speaker succinctly presents his position through the use of metaphor. Choices A and B are both incorrect; the speaker is quite secure in his conclusions, and he reveals them clearly. Choice D is incorrect; these metaphors give voice to the speaker's words, not those of Edmund Burke.

12. **D.** This is the exception because the speaker holds both artists in equally high esteem. Choice A is incorrect because "elegance of movement" is part of the definition of "beautiful." For Choice B, the speaker claims Michelangelo is sublime, after defining "sublime" as something which "comprehends the vast, the obscure, the powerful." Choice C is incorrect because the speaker provides ample evidence of conflict between the two high-strung artists. For Choice E, his final metaphor rests on seeing the artists as would "the people of Rome in 1511."

13. **C.** The footnote adds credibility to the speaker's assertion that the figure was a later addition to the already-completed *School of Athens* by providing additional documentation. Choice A is incorrect because the footnote states, "The exact timing of this addition is speculative." B is incorrect; the speaker cites the cartoon to show that the figure was not originally in *The School of Athens*. Choice D is incorrect; the speaker does not indicate that Raphael's painting in Stella della Segnatura is *similar,* only contemporaneous.

14. **A.** It is very likely that the speaker agrees. Throughout his overview of the scholarly writings regarding the identity of the *pensieroso*, it is clear that the majority concludes that Michelangelo was, indeed, the model. Choice B is incorrect; the *pensieroso* was not in the original cartoon of *The School of Athens*. Choice C is incorrect; the speaker is not neutral and does not present a balanced number of arguments pro and con. Choice D is incorrect; the *pensieroso* does not appear in the cartoon. Choice E is incorrect because the figure does look like Michelangelo.

15. **B.** The two sentences in lines 65–72 are both complex sentences and each contains parallel construction. All other answer choices misidentify the sentences' construction.

Second Passage

The passage is from the American novelist William Styron's *Darkness Visible,* an autobiographical account of his suffering from clinical depression.

16. **E.** The first paragraph of the passage gives all three of these reasons for preferring "melancholia" to the less "apt and evocative" word "depression."

17. **C.** Though "indifferent" can mean "apathetic" (A) or "average"(C), in this context the word has another of its several meanings, "showing no preference or bias, indiscriminate." The author's point is that a word that can be equally well used to denote a rut or financial hard times should not be used to describe a disease as terrible as depression.

18. **B.** The passage objects to using a word with two other commonplace meanings, and to its "bland tonality," its euphemistic effect; the author believes the word is less expressive, less shocking than is necessary to denote the condition accurately. Because the passage suggests the replacement of "depression" with another word, the length of time the word has been used cannot be held against it. The 75 years are too long rather than too short a time.

19. **B.** Both "wimp" and "tin ear" are colloquialisms, that is, a word, phrase, or idiom used in conversation or informal writing. The phrase "wimp of a word" is metaphorical, the word compared to a type of person, but it is not a mixed metaphor, which might compare a word to a person and to a tree at the same time, for example.

20. **A.** The phrases in the last four options all refer to the fierce power of depression, the disease. The phrase "semantic damage" refers to harm done by the use of the word "depression," but not to the effect of the illness.

21. **D.** The passage says that "brainstorm" describes the disease well, but that it cannot be used because it already has a different established meaning, and one with comic ("jocular") overtones.

22. **A.** The sentence argues that a better word than depression might change the conventional response to the illness. The author insists that he is not exaggerating ("veritable," "indeed," "like nothing else") what the victim suffers, and we have no reason to assume his examples of the "standard reaction" are inaccurate.

23. **B.** The author alludes to "nervous breakdown" as a phrase that like "depression" is ill-chosen, but, unlike it, is passing out of use. His objection to "nervous breakdown" is not because it is "bland," but because it appears to blame the victims for their illness.

24. **C.** Because the author presents depression as "dreadful and raging," as horrible and malevolent, we can assume he would choose the most powerful adjective of the five, and reject the four other choices as too weak to describe its "horrible intensity."

25. **D.** The passage uses metaphor ("wimp of a word"), simile ("like a slug"), direct quotation ("So what?"), and literary citation (Chaucer), but does not use hyperbole. Its point is that the word "depression" is too understated, the opposite of hyperbole.

26. **E.** The passage uses the phrase "strong protest" in its first sentence, and this position does not change.

27. **B.** Though the passage does incidentally give the history of the word (A) and some of its meanings (C), its central idea is to protest the "bland tonality" of "depression." The author does reveal his dislike of the phrase, "nervous breakdown," but the passage is focused on the word "depression," not on the shortcomings of medical language in general.

28. **A.** Though the author would probably agree with B, C, and D, the real issue here is the misleading connotation of the word "depression," when it refers to the illness. The passage complains about the one word, not about all words. Those who genuinely believe that words are an inadequate means of describing reality (E) probably do not become professional writers.

Third Passage

The passage is from John Locke's *An Essay Concerning Human Understanding* (1690).

29. **B.** Any of these five choices can define the word "periods," but in this context, the best choice is "sentences." In most multiple-choice exams, a question calling for the definition of a word will ask about a word with several legitimate meanings, and you must look carefully at the context in the passage to determine your answer.

30. **A.** The antecedent of "ones" is "words" in line 21. The "them" that follows ("that compose them") refers to "ideas."

31. **D.** The first sentence employs a figure of speech (a simile) while the second sentence is literal.

32. **E.** The simile compares the man who lacks the words to express his complex ideas to the bookseller whose books are only loose sheets of paper, with no means of binding them together.

33. **A.** The author uses analogies (comparisons) to support his arguments.

34. **A.** In this context, the word "fair" means equitable or honest.

35. **C.** The paragraph is a single periodic sentence, that is, a sentence that is not grammatically complete until its end.

36. **D.** Here the "substances" are imagined and are contrasted with realities. In other usages, the word "substance" denotes reality as opposed to "shadow."

37. **E.** Paragraphs one and two are related; the first presents the speaker who has words but no ideas, and the second one with ideas but no words. Paragraphs three and four describe two related misuses of words: using one word to mean many things, and using words with meanings different from those that are commonly accepted. The fifth paragraph is about imaginary notions.

38. **D.** The sixth paragraph recapitulates the contents of the first five.

39. **A.** In classical myth, a chimera was a monster with the head of a lion, the body of a goat, and the tail of a serpent. The word has come to mean an impossible fantasy, and the adjective "chimerical" means imaginary, unreal, or absurd.

40. **D.** The fourth paragraph describes the man who uses familiar words to mean something different from what everyone else understands them to mean.

41. **C.** The third paragraph describes the man who uses a word "sometimes in one, sometimes in another signification."

42. **E.** All three of these are used interchangeably for "word."

Fourth Passage

The passage is from "Letters to an Architect," by Gretel Ehrlich.

43. C. A "miscellany" (the noun form of the adjective "miscellaneous") can be a collection of verse, but in this context, it has its more familiar meaning, a varied collection or medley.

44. A. A "shoal" is a shallow or sandbar in the sea or a river, a place that is difficult to navigate. The word that B defines is "sheaves."

45. E. In fact, the whole passage, as part of a letter, has a first-person speaker, but it is not clear in this excerpt until the writer uses the "I" in line 30.

46. B. The third paragraph refers to Thoreau's search for a freedom with "personal privacy." The fourth paragraph describes men like Thoreau who thrived in the "expanse and solitude of the state."

47. D. The third paragraph suggests some differences between Thoreau and Jefferson. The fourth paragraph describes the settlers who resemble Thoreau, while the fifth paragraph presents those with more in common with Jefferson.

48. B. The fifth paragraph associates Brigham Young with Jeffersonian ideas. The four other options are associated with Thoreau in the fourth paragraph.

49. A. Option II is simply untrue, and Option III sounds good and makes a point that is true in another context, but it has no connection at all with the passage at hand.

50. E. The last paragraph is about architecture, but it is not closely related to what has preceded it. It is about medieval Europe, not the Wyoming of the 19th and 20th centuries.

51. C. The last paragraph refers to priests and governors as buildings to demonstrate their authority. The same may be said of slave owners and businessmen described in the second paragraph. The Mormons, on the other hand, had a "socialist regime."

52. D. Choices A and B are presented as paradoxical in the second paragraph. The fifth paragraph describes the paradox of Choices C and E, and presents Brigham Young as extending Jeffersonian ideals.

53. B. The second paragraph is about the architecture "elsewhere." The last paragraph is also about other places.

54. E. The priests and governors of the Middle Ages are alike in their use of architecture with "hierarchical intentions." The other four pairs are contrasts in the passage.

55. C. Of the five choices, C is the best. The passage is discursive, and not at all a carefully developed argument. It does not survey American architecture, and it does not examine the values reflected by the buildings of Wyoming. The second paragraph glances at American materialism, but this is not the subject of the passage.

Section II: Essay Questions

Question 1

Scoring Guide for Question 1 (Sports Salaries)

9 Essays that earn a score of 9 meet the criteria for essays that receive a score of 8; in addition, they are especially sophisticated in their explanation and argument. They may also present particularly remarkable control of language.

8 Successful

Essays that receive a score of 8 respond to the prompt **successfully,** using at least three sources from the prompts. They take a position that defends, challenges, or qualifies the claim that professional athletes are overpaid. They effectively argue their position and support the argument with appropriate and convincing evidence. The prose demonstrates an ability to control an extensive range of the elements of effective writing but may not be entirely flawless.

7 Essays that earn a score of 7 fit the description of the essays that score a 6 but provide more complexity in both argumentation and explanation and/or demonstrate more distinguished prose style.

6 Satisfactory

Essays that earn a score of 6 respond to the prompt **satisfactorily,** utilizing at least three of the sources from the prompt. They take a position that defends, challenges, or qualifies the claim that professional athletes are over-paid. They adequately argue their position and support it with appropriate evidence, although without the precision and depth of the top-scoring essays. The writing may contain minor errors in diction or syntax, but the prose is generally clear.

5 Essays that earn a score of 5 take a position that defends, challenges, or qualifies the claim that professional athletes are overpaid. They support the position with generally appropriate evidence, but they may not adequately use three sources from the prompt. These essays may be inconsistent, uneven, or limited in the development of the argument. Although the writing usually conveys the writer's ideas, it may demonstrate lapses in diction or syntax or an overly simplistic style.

4 Inadequate

Essays that earn a score of 4 respond to the prompt **inadequately.** They may have difficulty taking a position that defends, challenges, or qualifies the claim that professional athletes are overpaid. The evidence may be particu-larly insufficient, or may not utilize enough sources from the prompt. The prose may basically convey the writer's ideas but suggests immature control over the elements of effective writing.

3 Essays that earn a score of 3 meet the criteria for a score of 4 but reveal less ability to take a position. The presen-tation of evidence and argumentation is likely to be unconvincing. The writing may show less control over the elements of effective writing.

2 Little Success

Essays that earn a 2 demonstrate **little success** at taking a position that defends, challenges, or qualifies the claim that professional athletes are overpaid and show little ability to present it with appropriate evidence from the sources in the prompt. These essays may misunderstand the prompt, fail to establish a position with supporting evidence, or substitute a simpler task by replying tangentially with unrelated, erroneous, or unsuitable explana-tion, argument, and/or evidence. The prose frequently demonstrates consistent weaknesses in the conventions of effective writing.

1 Essays that earn a score of 1 meet the criteria for a score of 2 but are undeveloped, especially simplistic in their explanation, argument and/or evidence, or weak in their control of writing.

High-Scoring Essay

In recent decades, athletes' salaries have soared, allowing them to collect millions in yearly earnings for merely displaying their physical gifts. Although athletes are arguably the world's most physically gifted individuals, their preposterous salaries are unjustifiable when their jobs are limited to seasonal games intended for purely entertainment purposes. Magnified by the allure of extravagant wealth, athletes become sedated by the extrinsic value of playing their respective sports, which in turn negatively affects society's younger generation. Salaries that run in the ten-millions and even in the hundred-millions are not only excessive, but also unwarranted for individuals who simply play a game for their jobs.

While some sports such as tennis and golf entail all-year-round games, most of the mainstream and high-paying sports, such as basketball, baseball and football are limited to seasons that are played over the course of several months. Especially when athletes are paid on the basis of their performance over a fraction of the year, their absurd salaries do not properly reflect their job's length. And although some may argue that athletes must train in the off-season to maintain their peak-condition, it is no different than the unpaid preparation that teachers must sacrifice before each school year. Furthermore, the games in which athletes participate last for an average of three hours per game. It is illogical that athletes are paid in the millions for their performances for a couple of hours per game, when other professions judge individuals' production over the compilation of full day's work. Once again, the preparation that athletes must endure is not a relevant argument, since it is ultimately during the games that fans are entertained. People do not pay for preparation; people pay for the action and pleasure of games.

While society may "put value on sports," which reflects one of the reasons for the rich salaries that athletes receive, this fact does not fully account for all of the reasons that athletes' salaries are as such (Source C). Many goods in society are vastly overpriced and although individuals continue to succumb to outrageous prices by giving in, it may be that society is simply at the receiving end of corruption and inflation. Humans are naturally drawn to what is portrayed as rich and wealthy. It is evident that exorbitant prices for sports venues do not have a proper effect on individuals' decision making, which leads to the fact that society is ultimately submitting to the immoral standards of sports entertainment. And, while "NFL salaries are based on what the league brings in from revenues," this does not serve as proper basis for the uncontrollable upward trend in athletes' salaries (Source D).

The argument that "players sacrifice a lot to make it to the big show," is faulted in the fact that athletes sacrifice no more than other professionals who aspire to become teachers and researchers (Source A). Many professions require intense "sacrifice" and yet do not offer the outrageous remuneration professional sports offers. Why should the basketball player's "sacrifice" be worth more than any other professional's? Athletes' salaries are climbing at unprecedented rates, as over a ten-year period, some salaries in the NBA skyrocketed by 472%, which resulted in about a $14 million increase (Source A). Meanwhile, teachers are paid on average of $38,611 a year; however, their salaries remain basically static, even though they are entrusted with the education of 45 million public-school students (Source C). Although athletes may boast "amazing skills, that are incredibly rare," million dollar salaries are definitely not reasonable, when their productivity level lies entirely in entertainment purposes (Source C). Although athletes encompass elite physical skills, it is nearly impossible to compare their gifts with those of others. Furthermore, athletes are "not saving people's lives," and while they are continually paid as if they were, it elicits a problem of unequal and unethical balance (Source E). Firefighters who are "saving people's lives," are receiving a humble $36,000 per year (Source C). Although societal attitudes may be at the root of this imbalance, in which the value of entertainment may supersede the value of life, the disparity in athletes' salaries as compared to most other professional salaries illustrates a self-evident problem. Regardless of deciding where to place the blame for allowing such overpriced salaries, it is clear that athletes receive too much for their supposed sacrifice and production year in and year out.

As athletes continue to receive more than what they are worth, youngsters who delve their interest in modeling their lives after sports superstars are negatively influenced by greed and discontent. The questionable plight of players' unions seeking even greater salaries for athletes combined with the instances in which athletes "opt out of contracts" only to sign bigger and better ones for "stability" purposes, elicits a message of insatiability and pure greed (Source F). Youngsters begin with the innocent passion of playing sports—similar to how professional athletes began—but when they are exposed to the attempts of athletes and agents in receiving more and more millions of dollars, they can become corrupted. Athletes who boast contracts that reach up to $252 million dollars are unconditionally blinded by the allure of money (Source F). While their gross incomes are unfair and unjust, their commitment to negotiating for millions of dollars adds an immoral image that unavoidably plagues the rest of society and the younger generation.

Amidst the façade of athletic talent and physical stature, athletes' ridiculous earnings have reached excessive and unprecedented levels that are not warranted, given their limited entertainment-driven performances. The myopia of athletes in merely attempting to find the longest and richest contract further illustrates the pathos of outrageous and disproportionate salaries in the world of sports. After all, it's only a game.

Analysis of High-Scoring Essay

This essay earns a high score because it is on topic and thoroughly developed. The writer begins with an understanding that athletes are indeed "physically gifted individuals" but acknowledges that this gift, coupled with athletes' limited season does not warrant their multi-million-dollar salaries. The introduction sets up the content and organization of the essay well, demonstrating that the writer has planned his or her ideas successfully in advance.

The second paragraph focuses on the aspect that most highly paid athletes only perform for a limited time in a limited season, and, therefore, should not receive such exorbitant salaries. Comparing the time athletes train to the time teachers prepare brings the argument to the level of everyman and draws an apt analogy. Certainly an AP reader can relate to working long hours, but so can every other person who works as hard. By extension, wouldn't all professionals prefer to be paid so handsomely for their preparation? Although this logic demonstrates clear thinking on the writer's part, the idea that fans only pay for action and not preparation is not as convincing as it could be. The writer would be better served to expand this argument by considering counterarguments and then logically dismissing them.

The next paragraph discusses society's value system and acknowledges the truth that many people in society are willing to pay dearly for those things they deem worthy. The writer makes the point even more forceful by discussing that "humans are naturally drawn to what is *portrayed* as rich and wealthy," intimating that humans do not always know the true value of things; rather, we are influenced by the value judgments of others. This level of analysis demonstrates the maturity of the writer.

The following paragraph uses multiple sources from the prompt to compare the actual salaries of many professions. It is as thorough an examination of the data as one could expect in a timed essay. The writer continues by discussing the value of certain professions, namely firefighters who actually save lives, and makes the point that the value of athletes' jobs pales in comparison. This paragraph is particularly convincing in its logical and fact-based presentation and helps earn the essay's high score.

The writer then explores the effect that athletes have on the young, pointing out how young people are so easily influenced by the glitz and glamour of professional athletes. Then, by discussing the example of how an athlete can opt out of a contract in order to sign an even more lucrative one, the writer makes a logical connection between the corrupting power of money triumphing over the intrinsic fun of playing a game and how easily a youth's belief system can be swayed by this self-centered behavior. This point is important to all of society, as this writer clearly proves.

The concluding paragraph shows that this writer does not run out of steam, but rather ends the essay forcefully, using striking phrases such as "the myopia of athletes," and "the pathos of outrageous and disproportionate salaries." The last sentence, concise and pithy, reminds us to place sports into the big picture of society: after all, it *is* only a game. This concludes the essay with finality, with conviction.

Although this essay does have some flaws, both in minor wording issues and minor lapses in logic, they are not serious enough to keep this essay from receiving a high score. Its intelligent presentation and well-developed discussion clearly demonstrate that the writer's efforts are worthy of a high score.

Medium-Scoring Essay

With the general trend of popularity in sports, athletes have signed contracts worth a lot of money. However, many argue how fair this is despite the fact that athletes have irreplaceable talents and are ultimately paid for the amount of attention they receive. America's emphasis on sports makes the million dollar contracts of athletes just and necessary.

Although there is a disparity in the incomes that athletes earn with the incomes of professionals such as teachers, firefighters and truckers, there are only a limited number of athletes represented in the professional ranks compared to the many individuals in relatively common professions. Given the minority of athletes, the amount of money that they are paid is warranted, if there were as many professional athletes as there were teachers, then it would be vastly unjust, but this is not the case. Furthermore, athletes' talents that they display in their respective sports are unique and unmatchable. After honing their skills for countless years, only a few select individuals who display exceptional athletic abilities are rewarded for their training. On the other hand, the common man has "skills that are easily replicated." Which is not so with athletes (Source C). The reasoning behind the rich contracts of athletes is ultimately the valuable God-given talents that athletes have over other individuals. Athletes who grace the covers of magazines and serve as role models for many youngsters are arguably the fittest and most disciplined individuals in society, the achievements that they reach in sports are historically unique and therefore are met with fanatical acceptance through enthusiastic fanfare. People may argue that other professions should receive more incentive for their work, but the fact is that "we, as a society, put value on sports," (Source C). Many individuals display insurmountable passion for sports and in turn are willing to pay the money to see their favorite athletes.

Additionally, unlike most other professions, athletics is distinctive in the fact that athletes are constantly under the scrutiny of the press and the opinions of fans. Athletes are human, they are plagued with a flow of attention. Although attention may have beneficial outcomes, it can also be excruciating and undesirable. Athletes living under this spotlight, sacrifice their personal lives as they continue to perform at high-caliber levels of competition. In turn, the incomes that athletes earn are not merely represented through their accomplishments on the field, but also serve as compensation for the loss of privacy in becoming an athlete.

Given the excitement and exuberance for sports throughout society, athletes are given salaries based on their popular demand. Ultimately, athletes are paid "based on what the league brings in from revenues," (Source D). With money coming from television, ticket sales and other outlets, athletes' salaries are not generated from nothingness, but in actuality in terms of what fans pay to see these athletes perform. Rather than continuing to deem sports as overpriced, individuals must realize that athletes are simply earning what they are given. Athletes are in reality like every other individual in society and should be given the same rights. When individuals cry afoul regarding contract disputes, athletes are merely exercising the exact rights that other individuals exercise when they seek signing bonuses and other incentives. While the blame continues to revolve around athletes and their supposed extorted earnings, the reality is that athletes are for the most part earning every dollar that they receive. For many individuals, sports is everything, and amidst that fervor, fans are willing to put in the money to watch athletes in action. If people are willing to support athletes, yet criticize them, then the problem lies within the populous of society. The true difference between sports and many other professions is that sports entails a large fan-base. In turn, the revenues coming from sports are immense. Just as any front-office executive, team owners merely reward their players with what the organization earns from yearly revenues.

Inevitably through the uniqueness of athletes' skills and achievements in their respective sports, their grossing salaries that consistently run in the million dollar ranges are both just and reasonable. Professional athletes are rare and given their incredible talents, their rich contracts are merely substantiated from the amount of work that they put in and the passionate fanfare they encounter.

Analysis of Medium-Scoring Essay

This essay, while deceptively lengthy, does not construct a convincing argument, nor does it utilize the minimum of three sources from the prompt as directed. Ultimately, this essay demonstrates how a writer can write a long essay but basically go nowhere. The language is not particularly striking, and it displays a disturbing number of grammatical and mechanical errors.

The essay begins with a simplistic thesis: that professional athletes justly deserve a large salary merely because America emphasizes sports. The reader is left wondering where this logic will lead.

The first body paragraph displays organizational problems, beginning with a discussion of the disparity in the ratio of professional athletes to other professions, then moving into the skills an athlete must hone to succeed. The writer also displays gaps in logic, for example, claiming that athletes deserve more money simply because they make up a minority of the workforce. This illogical claim is followed by the equally puzzling remark that if there were as many professional athletes as teachers, "then it would be vastly unjust." Many of the writer's phrases seem hollow and do not help to propel the essay forward. For instance, some statements such as "athletes' talents . . . are unique and unmatchable" are simply untrue and really say nothing. The writer does include one source from the prompt, but merely uses it to make the point that society values sports without a deeper analysis of how this affects athletes' incomes.

The next brief paragraph does not make a strong argument, merely asserting the claim that, because athletes are "under scrutiny," they deserve more money to compensate for their loss of privacy. However, if the writer were to take this argument to its logical conclusion, then many professions would also deserve multi-million-dollar salaries simply because the jobs propel one into the public's eye.

The following paragraph presents contradictory ideas. The writer previously declared that athletes are unique, and therefore deserve their high salary, but now claims that athletes are "in reality like every other individual in society." Self-contradictory thinking like this cannot help an essay's score.

The conclusion repeats the essay's main idea, that athletes deserve their salary because of their "rare and incredible talent." But it's a sentiment the reader has heard before, and so the conclusion offers no food for thought, merely summary.

Finally, take note of how the sentence fragments, run-on sentences, punctuation errors, and frequent verb mistakes distract the reader from the essay's content.

Question 2

Scoring Guide for Question 2 (John Updike)

9 Essays earning a score of 9 meet the criteria for essays that are scored an 8 and, in addition, are especially full or apt in their analysis or reveal particularly remarkable control of language.

8 Successful

Essays that score at the top perceptively and **successfully** analyze how Updike's metaphors and other rhetorical devices help establish the love-hate relationship an audience has toward sports. These essays appreciate how Updike's language works and wisely use appropriate examples from the text, both implicit and explicit, to support the writer's ideas. Top-scoring essays offer thorough development and superior organization. Although these essays may have a few minor flaws, the writing demonstrates a suave command of written English and the ability to write with syntactic variety.

7 Essays earning a score of 7 fit the description of essays that are scored a 6 but provide more complete analysis, and a more mature prose style.

6 Satisfactory

Upper-level essays correctly understand how Updike's metaphors work and explore other rhetorical devices as well, using this understanding in the service of **satisfactorily** explaining how these devices convey attitude. Characteristically, these essays use the text well, implicitly or explicitly, to support the writer's thoughts, although these ideas may not be as perceptive or as sophisticated as those of the top-scoring essays. Usually these essays are well developed and organized. Minor errors in writing may be present, but the writer's meaning is clear and coherent.

5 Essays that score in the middle range attempt to analyze the topic, but frequently do not understand how figurative language connects to meaning. Their insights are quite often obvious and pedestrian. Paraphrasing the excerpt instead of analyzing it may be evident. Development and organization may be too brief, illogical, or unfulfilled. Although the writing style itself may be adequate to convey meaning, inconsistencies in controlling written English may be present.

4 Inadequate

Lower-scoring essays **inadequately** respond to the prompt. They may concentrate solely on what the audience feels during a sporting event, or perhaps only discuss the use of metaphor, without connecting figurative language to the audience's attitude. Paraphrasing is frequently employed instead of analysis. Development and organization of ideas is often inconsistent and limited. Although the writing may communicate ideas, the writing may have serious or persistent flaws that distract the reader. These low-scoring essays offer simple ideas that are presented in a simple manner.

3 Essays earning a score of 3 meet the criteria for a score of 4 but demonstrate less understanding of how metaphor and figurative language connects to attitude. These essays may show less control over the elements of writing.

2 Little Success

The lowest-scoring essays demonstrate **little** or no **success** at analyzing how Updike's language creates attitude. They may pay scant attention to structural or rhetorical techniques or misunderstand their use. These essays may misunderstand the task, fail to articulate any connection between language and attitude, or substitute a simpler task. These essays may be unusually short and exhibit poor fundamental essay skills. Weak sentence construction may persist, and persistent weaknesses in mechanics may be present.

1 These poorly written essays meet the criteria for a score of 2 but are undeveloped, especially simplistic in their analysis, and weak in their control of language.

High-Scoring Essay

In this passage, John Updike's juxtaposition of two central metaphors, combined with his occasional bellicose diction, allows him to emphasize the vicissitudes and the simple grandeur of baseball and the game's ability to reveal our humanity. Symbolic of our life and love, baseball offers prospective liberation along with possible disillusionment.

Both the monster and romance metaphors are used throughout the passage, creating a sense of continuity and allowing the author to thematically connect all the elements—from opening day to the action of the field to the real significance of the passage. Phrases like "its monstrous big heart," "act of faith," and "the first kiss of another prolonged entanglement" sustain imagery that the monster is altogether human and thus forgiving and loving. The contrast of the typical monster and the one portrayed as the "Fenway Faithful" not only adds interest to the piece, but also mirrors the roller coaster ride experienced by the fans. From "Supersox" to "dreadful days," the metaphors' inherent contrasts allow Updike to emphasize the same in the hearts of the fans. The author relies on us to draw upon our own life experiences, as we know romance, too, is full of disagreements and perfect moments, of triumphs and disappointments, truly a "hard lesson for a hungry monster to master." And yet, by the end of the passage, the author recognizes the simple beauty of baseball. Updike implies the innocent joy and magnificence in the way these "twenty-five youngish men" manipulate the hearts of fans. Indeed, it is so much like a romance, with its simplicity and complexity, perfectly summed up in the words, "You'll never get us to care again." However, Updike's voice clearly implies the opposite, that this game of love and hate will continue.

Indeed, the author seems to use the game of baseball as a microcosm of the outside world. His use of warlike diction elevates the game to a near life or death struggle. A four game sweep by the Yankees becomes a "massacre;" a winning streak becomes a "mini-resurrection;" and players seem to be "Civil War memorials" who are fighting for a "Noble Lost Cause" in "Zimmer's last stand." Interestingly enough, this supposed struggle between life and death that is fought out on the baseball diamond ultimately turns into Updike's commentary on life itself. For, in reality, it is not war, but instead, to quote the manager Zimmer, "This is fun." Ultimately, his metaphors using the monster and romance only seek to simplify the relationship between the game and the fans. Like baseball, life, the author implies, should be fun at its core element, stripped of "solemn money men . . . scruffy media cameramen and sour-faced reporters." It is, in the end, a game of "innumerable potential redemptions and curious disappointments." In our attempts to understand, influence, and record these vicissitudes, perhaps Updike's intention is to leave us with some sense of the here and now. Perhaps it's best that we just jeer, holler, boo, and cheer as we enjoy ourselves in the sun. Perhaps that special moment is a little of what that "many-headed monster" feels that makes it come back again and again.

Analysis of the High-Scoring Essay

This essay does an excellent job of addressing the topic; it thoroughly explores metaphors and the connotation of Updike's "warlike diction," showing in the process how these elements create not only Updike's attitude toward baseball, but toward life itself. The introduction clearly tells the reader what to expect and ends with a graceful statement of how baseball symbolizes life. Updike would agree that this student truly comprehends his point.

The first body paragraph examines the monster and romance metaphors, showing how the two are intricately tied. The student offers ample examples of each and then connects them together with appropriate logic and interesting ideas. The student makes noteworthy points about how Updike relies on his audience to connect his ideas about baseball to their own life experiences, which we will find to be "full of disagreements and perfect moments, of triumphs and disappointments. . . ." The student's poise in using parallelism in this sentence also demonstrates his or her polish as a writer, which an AP reader will certainly notice and appreciate. The student's final idea in this paragraph, that baseball is a "game of love and hate" that "will continue," serves effectively not only as a clinching sentence to this paragraph, but also as a transition to the next paragraph, which explores the author's diction.

The second body paragraph scrutinizes how Updike's diction, especially the references to war, emphasizes the "life or death struggle" of the game. The student presents virtually every example of "warlike diction" that the excerpt offers, but does not stop at merely listing them. He or she makes a larger point about how this diction helps establish Updike's attitude: that although it may seem like war on the baseball diamond, it is really just a game played for fun. The student has a good perspective on language analysis and on life itself.

Overall, this essay covers the topic very well; it is organized logically and develops ideas substantially. The student also demonstrates a very nice flair for language use, as witnessed in the use of parallelism (notice it not only in the first body paragraph as previously noted, but also in the closing two sentences with the repetition on the word "Perhaps . . ."). The student's sentence structure is varied, vocabulary is sophisticated, and a sense of rhythm is present. This essay indeed deserves a high score.

Medium-Scoring Essay

The author's use of the monster metaphor allows him to paint the fans as having similar hopes and reactions to the Boston Red Sox's at times rocky season.

By incorporating the monster metaphor throughout the passage, the author calls the fans both hopeful and disappointed. He writes that last year's had broken its "monstrous big heart," and that showing up was "an act of faith." Clearly, the fans cannot help but come back and watch the Boston Red Sox, despite the multitude of horrifying disappointments, often at the hands of the Yankees. "Monsters," the author writes, "have short memories, elastic hearts, and very foolable faculties." The fans, interestingly, in all their differences, have a singular attitude and wish that unites them. It is this wish for the Boston Red Sox to win that enables the author to group these people into an entity, what he calls the "many-headed monster." What is the focus of much of the passage, however, is a description of the fundamental essence of the game of baseball.

It is decidedly from a baseball fans point of view. It is focused on the fun of baseball, how little things within the game bring so much enjoyment and pleasure. It is, to this author, more than just a game of baseball, but rather a celebration of life and an atmosphere. As the author writes, "Monsters love high notes and hoards of gold," referring to "The Star-Spangled Banner" performance and the governor's appearance. The fans, represented as a whole by the monster, love everything about the atmosphere of baseball. From the pure essence of "statistical virginity" to the manager, "last year's anti-hero," the fans love the effect it has on their lives. They keep coming back, it makes no difference because of the elevation of baseball to a more important level—a staple of their lives. The author may be saying to us that the wonderfulness of baseball is, in itself, good enough.

Analysis of the Medium-Scoring Essay

This essay essentially attempts to tackle the topic, but does not accomplish much more than paraphrasing the original excerpt. The student recognizes that Updike uses a metaphor, but there is little else in this essay that is praiseworthy. The introduction/thesis is somewhat vague. For example, when the student writes that the fans have "similar hopes and reactions" the reader wonders exactly *what* they are similar to; are they similar to the "rocky season"? A clearer thesis statement would certainly help this essay.

The first body paragraph identifies the monster metaphor and correctly identifies that it represents the baseball audience, but the student offers no strong analysis of that metaphor. Instead, the student paraphrases Updike: Yes, the fans are "both hopeful and disappointed"; yes, the fans come back to watch over and over; yes, the fans have a "singular . . . wish that unites them," but the student merely lists these ideas and never analyzes *how* Updike's metaphor establishes his attitude. It is not convincing to merely state the attitude and drop a quotation or two from the author.

The second body paragraph, too, is basically accurate in its paraphrasing of Updike; indeed, to Updike the game *is* a "celebration of life." However, once again, the student offers little more than a string of quotations and examples of the behavior and attitude of fans from the passage. For a stronger essay, the student needs to have a *reason* for presenting all of this information, an analytical point about *how* these examples work in this excerpt.

Also compounding the student's weak analytical skills is his or her weak command of written English. Apostrophe errors abound ("last year's had broken . . ." and "a baseball fans point of view" to name two), plus run-on sentences ("They keep coming back, it makes no difference. . . .") and weak wording ("things," "the author writes," and so on) do not help demonstrate sophistication in this writer. Top-scoring essays answer the topic, have clear organization, develop ideas thoroughly, and demonstrate strong control over written English. This essay simply does not show those traits.

Question 3

Scoring Guide for Question 3 (Cynthia Ozick)

9 Essays earning a score of 9 meet the criteria for essays that are scored an 8 and, in addition, are especially full or apt in their analysis or reveal particularly remarkable control of language.

8 Successful

Essays earning a top score astutely and **successfully** understand the differences between Ozick's attitudes toward essays and articles, while demonstrating a strong appreciation of how her language and style establish those attitudes. These essays are thoroughly developed and refer to the text frequently, both implicitly and explicitly, demonstrating the ability to explore the subtleties of Ozick's language and syntax. Not necessarily without flaws, these essays still show mastery over the conventions of written English and sophisticated style.

7 Essays earning a score of 7 fit the description of essays that are scored a 6 but provide more complete analysis, and a more mature prose style.

6 Satisfactory

Well-written, these essays accurately reflect the different attitudes Ozick presents and **satisfactorily** attempt to connect her style to her attitude. These essays refer to the text and recognize important features of rhetorical development. While these essays might comprehend some of the subtleties of Ozick's language, awareness might not be as far-reaching as the top-scoring essays. Well-developed ideas and clear diction show strong control over the elements of written English, although minor errors may be present.

5 Average essays may not explore the deep differences that the author presents between essays and articles, or may dwell on obvious or superficial differences. Instead of analyzing how the author's style and language create attitude, these essays may rely on paraphrasing the author's points. Development and organization may be clear but not as effective as that of higher-scoring essays. Inconsistencies in the command of language may be present, but the prose in these essays usually is sufficient to convey the writer's ideas.

4 Inadequate

These lower-scoring essays **inadequately** discuss the author's differences or may only write on Ozick's views of either an essay or an article. They frequently paraphrase without making a connection between the author's point and how her language conveys her attitude. Insights may be inaccurate or trite. The writing may convey some ideas, but weak control over language holds the ideas back. Frequent mechanical errors may be present, suggesting immature control over organization of ideas, diction, or syntax.

3 Essays earning a score of 3 meet the criteria for a score of 4 but demonstrate less understanding of how metaphor and figurative language connects to attitude. These essays may show less control over the elements of writing.

2 Little Success

Essays earning a low score show **little success** in responding sufficiently to the prompt or the passage. They may try to present a discussion of the author's attitude, but may provide insufficient evidence from the passage, or may misread the passage and present erroneous ideas. These essays may misunderstand the task, fail to articulate any connection between language and attitude, or may substitute a simpler task. These essays may be unusually short and exhibit poor fundamental essay skills. Weak sentence construction may persist, and persistent weaknesses in mechanics may be present.

1 These poorly written essays meet the criteria for a score of 2 but are undeveloped, especially simplistic in their analysis, and weak in their control of language.

High-Scoring Essay

Exploiting metaphorical portraitures of the essay, mellifluous syntax, and painstakingly precise paradox, Ozick conveys the intellectual curiosity towards the pulsating, artistically ageless essay, while dismissing the "lookalike knock off" temporary article.

Claiming at first that the essay represents "a thing of the imagination" Ozick's survey of the essay deepens into a three-dimensional, fleshed, elusive body. By first enumerating the metaphorical characteristics of the essay to an artistic perspective, reveling its form akin to poetry, "made out of language and character and mood and temperament and pluck and change," Ozick humanizes the essay's composite personality. Skillfully, the author juxtaposes the ersatz article with the genuine essay to emphasize the inimitable soul of the essay's essence. Indeed, unlike the spurious version, an article, the essay represents a super-mortal, whose blood burns with infinite "reflection and insight," whose skin emanates internal heat, a body whose very being "defies its date of birth." In a sense, Ozick elevates the essay from an ephemeral phantasmagoria to an immortal god, each time tracing its evolution with awe because the essay cannot be hinged or yoked to one static form. Ozick delineates how an essay traverses the landscape of our imagination, piquing in the reader a plaguing sense of direction begot by the various and ancient metaphorical molds assumed by the essay; the lesser article, meanwhile, lies flat, something that "will be stale within the month."

Inculcating the ebb and flow of a harmoniously question-inciting essay upon which it expounds, Ozick's syntax in the second paragraph parallels the challenges posed in a "genuine" essay. Employing imperative adjurations and if-then clauses, the voice carries an edifying, instruction-giving objectivity efficacious in structuring a cohesive conviction that "a genuine essay has no education, polemical or sociopolitical use; it is the movement of a free mind at play." The syntax attempts no moralizing fables, instead bent upon the repetitive construction of contrasting the article with the essay. The Spartan noun-linking verb sequence demonstrates the unaffected,

unshielded investigative temerity of "an essay [that] is reflection and insight . . . an essay [whose] heat is interior . . . an essay [that] defies its date of birth" while the article remains merely "gossip" that will last no longer than "a rotary phone." Ozick's disdainful tone when describing an article starkly contrasts with her lofty tone toward essays. Perhaps, Ozick construes, it is the disarming simplicity permeating the essay that renders it captivatingly mysterious. Here is one form, aptly embellished with an armory of rhetorical tricks—such as fragmentation and allusion—to engage the reader into responding to proffered pivotal conjectures like "Who are the classical essayists who come at once to mind?" Curiously enough, despite the segmented nuances of its syntax, the cumulative effect of the essay is to simply "coerce assent."

Paradoxically, the implication of this essay leans toward persuasion. However, like any work of art, the irony herein lies that, as Oscar Wilde noted, "all art is quite useless," and any manifestation of art masquerading with a purpose clearly cannot belong to its high aesthetic class. Thus, Ozick leaves us to question whether the essay can indeed be construed as an artistic form or merely an inveigling penny-tract. Eliminating the possibility that "Paine's 'Common Sense' and Zola's 'J'Accuse'" mirror the essay, Ozick suggests again that the essay is something we cannot conceptualize—a form without formal form. The ultimate paradox that the essay engenders is that, akin to an article, it represents an amorphous form, as well as an art that "co-opts agreement . . . courts agreement . . . seduces agreement."

Analysis of the High-Scoring Essay

This writer addresses the topic in a pleasing fashion. Instead of relying on a traditional format, the writer weaves ideas together skillfully and builds to a last, climactic paragraph. This thought-provoking response succeeds by intelligently articulating the differences between an article and an essay. The thesis is relevant and stimulating and makes a reader want to continue, hoping to find out what the student will have to discuss about paradox and "mellifluous syntax."

The first body paragraph establishes the vitality of the essay form, which is surely one of Ozick's strong opinions. By elevating an essay to "artistic perspective" this student shows how Ozick gives animation and sparkle to the concept of an essay. This student's phrasing, for instance in describing an essay as a "super-mortal whose blood burns . . . whose skin emanates . . . heat," unquestionably demonstrates the student's command over figurative language. Then, most appropriately, he or she swiftly classifies an article as something that "lies flat." When discussing an essay, this student's words are as lofty as Ozick's ideas; when discussing an article, this student's words are as simple and concise as Ozick's.

The second body paragraph begins to analyze Ozick's style and syntax in greater detail, aptly exploring Ozick's second paragraph as a way to show the student's understanding of how language works. In evaluating the linking verb pattern, the implied "if . . . then" concepts, and the author's tone, the student quite aptly demonstrates skillful comprehension of Ozick's sentence patterns, artistic choices, and their effect.

The final paragraph analyzes the inherent paradox hidden within Ozick's essay: namely that it actually does "lean toward persuasion" even though Ozick herself claims the contrary. This student demonstrates greater awareness than most, and this paragraph on paradox completes the essay with strong analytical skills; this paragraph truly builds to a crescendo.

Taken as a whole, this student's depth of understanding is impressive, as is his or her vocabulary and carefully reasoned presentation. The essay might be improved with additional examples from the text to back up some of its ideas, but its development is admirable. However, it cannot be denied that the student clearly understands how Ozick's language conveys her attitude. While diction can occasionally get away from the student, the ideas, awareness, and overall style are first rate.

Medium-Scoring Essay

Not many people think very often about the difference between an article and an essay. Cynthia Ozick, however, detachedly describes the essay as a force of the imagination using diction, structure, and imagery, but she claims the article is not as imaginative.

With adjectives precisely depicting the genuine essay, the author conjures how the essay cannot be duplicated by a article, how it defies time, shape, and form. The essay's body is "reflection and insight", not wreathed in the social heat of what's popular like an article, yet its heat is "inferior", and it defies its date of birth. In contrast, the article is its opposite, something stuck in a specific era, "Siamese-twinned to its date of birth" and in 5 years, "guaranteed not to wear well." The word "genuine" compellingly connotes the force of a true essay—it bears the stamp of strong essayists like "Montaigne . . . Hazlitt, Lamb, De Quincey, Carlyle . . . Emerson." Yet, it possesses a power outside this authorship "to coerce assent." The phrase "stroll through someone's mazy mind" also tells us how the essay functions—it allows us to see into a person's mind and be informed by this person's ideas. Also, the essay is made "out of the character & mood & temperament" of the author's imagination.

The structure of this selection also presents the essay as an imaginative force, which an article can't do. Using parallel structure, the author shows us how the essay can persuade with language its conviction. The succession of "an essay is", and "an article is" comparisons also contrast how the essay cannot be duplicated outside the imagination. The author relies upon adjectives and passive voice to convey the essay's picture.

The imagery in this selection also renders the essay a mysterious power. It paints the essay as something unreliable. It says that the essay "represents the movement of a free mind at play", and a "stroll through someone's mazy mind". The essay seems to be portrayed as a journey rather than an entity—something that is not a form that can be categorized but instead a direction that tries to persuade us in some way.

Analysis of the Medium-Scoring Essay

This essay earns a medium score because it demonstrates adequate understanding of Ozick's attitude, but it truly fails to analyze the passage. Indeed, it relies more on paraphrasing than on analyzing. The introduction begins with a fairly bland sentence that implies the writer has never before considered the thrust of Ozick's ideas about articles and essays, which is not an impressive opening. The thesis is not terribly insightful, and it remains at the surface level.

The body paragraphs may appear to present the student's ideas, but a closer examination shows that the writer instead merely paraphrases Ozick; the analysis is either simplistic or nonexistent. The length of the body paragraphs may be deceiving, but they get stuck by simply presenting what Ozick *says,* not *how* her language establishes her attitude. The body paragraphs do distinguish that Ozick thinks essays superior to articles, but that obvious idea can only go so far. In particular, the second body paragraph is weak, promising to discuss the "structure of [the] selection" but never fulfilling that promise. It provides no examples of parallel structure to back up its assertion about that rhetorical device. This paragraph is disorganized, jumping from one idea to another, and its development is subsequently flawed. Notice, for instance, the simplistic last sentence of the paragraph; it merely states that the author uses adjectives and passive voice. Neither device has any backing, nor does the student do anything with this information. High-scoring essays analyze *how* these devices work; medium- and lower-scoring essays merely list what devices appear in the passage.

In addition, this essay demonstrates some errors in mechanics and wording that compound its simplistic thinking. The punctuation error of placing a comma or period outside of quotation marks persists. Some phrasing is unclear, imprecise, or cumbersome; for example, reread the phrases "the author shows us how the essay can persuade with language its conviction," and "it allows us to see into a person's mind and be informed by this person's ideas." Perhaps with a better job of proofreading, the student may have clarified these sentences.

The positive elements in this essay are hidden by its weak presentation, which combines limited development, weak organization, poor word choice, and simplistic ideas.

Answer Sheet for Practice Test 5

Remove this sheet and use it to mark your answers.
Answer sheets for "Section II: Essays" can be found at the end of the book.

Section I
Multiple-Choice Questions

First Passage

1 Ⓐ Ⓑ Ⓒ Ⓓ Ⓔ
2 Ⓐ Ⓑ Ⓒ Ⓓ Ⓔ
3 Ⓐ Ⓑ Ⓒ Ⓓ Ⓔ
4 Ⓐ Ⓑ Ⓒ Ⓓ Ⓔ
5 Ⓐ Ⓑ Ⓒ Ⓓ Ⓔ
6 Ⓐ Ⓑ Ⓒ Ⓓ Ⓔ
7 Ⓐ Ⓑ Ⓒ Ⓓ Ⓔ
8 Ⓐ Ⓑ Ⓒ Ⓓ Ⓔ
9 Ⓐ Ⓑ Ⓒ Ⓓ Ⓔ
10 Ⓐ Ⓑ Ⓒ Ⓓ Ⓔ
11 Ⓐ Ⓑ Ⓒ Ⓓ Ⓔ
12 Ⓐ Ⓑ Ⓒ Ⓓ Ⓔ
13 Ⓐ Ⓑ Ⓒ Ⓓ Ⓔ
14 Ⓐ Ⓑ Ⓒ Ⓓ Ⓔ

Second Passage

15 Ⓐ Ⓑ Ⓒ Ⓓ Ⓔ
16 Ⓐ Ⓑ Ⓒ Ⓓ Ⓔ
17 Ⓐ Ⓑ Ⓒ Ⓓ Ⓔ
18 Ⓐ Ⓑ Ⓒ Ⓓ Ⓔ
19 Ⓐ Ⓑ Ⓒ Ⓓ Ⓔ
20 Ⓐ Ⓑ Ⓒ Ⓓ Ⓔ
21 Ⓐ Ⓑ Ⓒ Ⓓ Ⓔ
22 Ⓐ Ⓑ Ⓒ Ⓓ Ⓔ
23 Ⓐ Ⓑ Ⓒ Ⓓ Ⓔ
24 Ⓐ Ⓑ Ⓒ Ⓓ Ⓔ
25 Ⓐ Ⓑ Ⓒ Ⓓ Ⓔ
26 Ⓐ Ⓑ Ⓒ Ⓓ Ⓔ
27 Ⓐ Ⓑ Ⓒ Ⓓ Ⓔ
28 Ⓐ Ⓑ Ⓒ Ⓓ Ⓔ
29 Ⓐ Ⓑ Ⓒ Ⓓ Ⓔ

Third Passage

30 Ⓐ Ⓑ Ⓒ Ⓓ Ⓔ
31 Ⓐ Ⓑ Ⓒ Ⓓ Ⓔ
32 Ⓐ Ⓑ Ⓒ Ⓓ Ⓔ
33 Ⓐ Ⓑ Ⓒ Ⓓ Ⓔ
34 Ⓐ Ⓑ Ⓒ Ⓓ Ⓔ
35 Ⓐ Ⓑ Ⓒ Ⓓ Ⓔ
36 Ⓐ Ⓑ Ⓒ Ⓓ Ⓔ
37 Ⓐ Ⓑ Ⓒ Ⓓ Ⓔ
38 Ⓐ Ⓑ Ⓒ Ⓓ Ⓔ
39 Ⓐ Ⓑ Ⓒ Ⓓ Ⓔ
40 Ⓐ Ⓑ Ⓒ Ⓓ Ⓔ
41 Ⓐ Ⓑ Ⓒ Ⓓ Ⓔ
42 Ⓐ Ⓑ Ⓒ Ⓓ Ⓔ
43 Ⓐ Ⓑ Ⓒ Ⓓ Ⓔ

Fourth Passage

44 Ⓐ Ⓑ Ⓒ Ⓓ Ⓔ
45 Ⓐ Ⓑ Ⓒ Ⓓ Ⓔ
46 Ⓐ Ⓑ Ⓒ Ⓓ Ⓔ
47 Ⓐ Ⓑ Ⓒ Ⓓ Ⓔ
48 Ⓐ Ⓑ Ⓒ Ⓓ Ⓔ
49 Ⓐ Ⓑ Ⓒ Ⓓ Ⓔ
50 Ⓐ Ⓑ Ⓒ Ⓓ Ⓔ
51 Ⓐ Ⓑ Ⓒ Ⓓ Ⓔ
52 Ⓐ Ⓑ Ⓒ Ⓓ Ⓔ
53 Ⓐ Ⓑ Ⓒ Ⓓ Ⓔ
54 Ⓐ Ⓑ Ⓒ Ⓓ Ⓔ
55 Ⓐ Ⓑ Ⓒ Ⓓ Ⓔ

CUT HERE

Practice Test 5

Section I: Multiple-Choice Questions

Time: 60 minutes

55 questions

Directions: This section consists of selections from prose works and questions on their content, style, and form. Read each selection carefully. Choose the best answer of the five choices.

Questions 1–14. Read the following passage carefully before you begin to answer the questions.

First Passage

Good and evil we know in the field of this world grow up together almost inseparably; and the knowledge of good is so involved and interwoven with the knowledge of evil, and in so many cunning resem-
(5) blances hardly to be discerned, that those confused seeds which were imposed upon Psyche[1] as an incessant labour to cull out, and sort asunder, were not more intermixed. It was from out the rind of one apple tasted, that the knowledge of good and evil, as
(10) two twins cleaving together, leaped forth into the world. And perhaps this is that doom which Adam fell into of knowing good and evil, that is to say, of knowing good by evil.

As therefore the state of man now is, what wis-
(15) dom can there be to choose, what continence to forbear without the knowledge of evil? He that can apprehend and consider vice with all her baits and seeming pleasures, and yet abstain, and yet distinguish, and yet prefer that which is truly better, he
(20) is the true wayfaring Christian. I cannot praise a fugitive[2] and cloistered virtue, unexercised and unbreathed, that never sallies out and sees her adversary, but slinks out of the race where that immortal garland is to be run for, not without dust and heat.
(25) Assuredly we bring not innocence into the world, we bring impurity much rather: that which purifies us is trial, and trial is by what is contrary. That virtue which is but a youngling in the contemplation of evil, and knows not the utmost that vice promises to
(30) her followers, and rejects it, is but a blank virtue, not a pure; her whiteness is but an excremental[3] whiteness; which was the reason that our sage and serious poet Spenser, whom I dare be known to think a better teacher than Scotus or Aquinas[4], describing true
(35) temperance under the person of Guion[5], brings him in with his palmer[6] through the cave of Mammon[7] and the bower[8] of earthly bliss, that he might see and know, and yet abstain.

[1] Lines 6–7, Psyche = Venus set Psyche the task of sorting out the different kinds of grain in a large mixed heap.
[2] Line 21, fugitive = that which flees from life.
[3] Line 31, excremental = superficial, on the surface.
[4] Line 34, Scotus, Aquinas = two great scholastic philosophers.
[5] Line 35, Guion is the knight of temperance in Spenser's "Faerie Queene."
[6] Line 36, palmer = an itinerant monk under a vow of poverty.
[7] Line 36, the cave of Mammon = the temptation of wealth.
[8] Line, 37, bower = temptation of sensual pleasure.

1. In the first sentence of the passage, the speaker compares good and evil to

   A. children
   B. light and darkness
   C. plants
   D. this world and the next
   E. fibers

2. In lines 12–13, "of knowing good and evil, that is to say, of knowing good by evil" is suggesting that

   A. we cannot distinguish between good and evil
   B. we can understand good by avoiding evil
   C. good and evil are simultaneously alike and opposites
   D. we can know evil only by knowing good
   E. we can know good only by knowing evil

GO ON TO THE NEXT PAGE

3. The first sentence of the second paragraph (lines 14–16) is an example of

    A. an indirect question
    B. an analogy
    C. personification
    D. syllogism
    E. a rhetorical question

4. In lines 22–23, "adversary" refers to

    A. monasticism
    B. vice
    C. hypocrisy
    D. virtue
    E. trial

5. In lines 20–24, all of the following words contribute to the same metaphor EXCEPT

    A. "cloistered" (line 21)
    B. "race" (line 23)
    C. "garland" (line 24)
    D. "run for" (line 24)
    E. "dust" (line 24)

6. The "garland" of line 24 may be best understood to mean

    A. an elective office
    B. the prize of immortality
    C. a circlet of laurel
    D. a collection of poems
    E. a fantastic ornament

7. The argument of lines 25–27 ("Assuredly we . . . is contrary.") is that

    A. no human is ever completely free of guilt
    B. no human is wholly unfamiliar with vice and its temptations
    C. the experience of life is like a trial in a court of law
    D. it is experience, not innocence, which purifies humans
    E. a child is innocent until he or she has experienced evil

8. In line 27, the phrase "trial is by what is contrary" can best be paraphrased as

    A. by refusing to fight, we may achieve victory
    B. a true verdict can be reached only after the careful study of evidence on both sides
    C. before we can win a victory, we must first be defeated
    D. humans are tested by their experience of conflict
    E. what a court determines may well be wrong

9. The implication of the comment on Spenser in lines 32–34 is that

    A. philosophers are unqualified to teach morality
    B. literature may teach better than philosophy
    C. comedy may be as effective a teacher as serious writing
    D. the first function of literature is to teach temperance
    E. literature cannot take the place of revealed religion

10. The passage refers to the "bower of earthly bliss" (line 37) as an example of

    A. an evil recognized and resisted
    B. the heavenly rewards of the temperate
    C. the sensual pleasure of literature
    D. a state of pure innocence
    E. the Garden of Eden before Adam

11. The central argument of this passage is that

    A. true virtue must avoid evil
    B. good and evil are interdependent
    C. we must understand evil to be able to resist it
    D. if we can avoid occasions of sin, we can overcome temptations
    E. all men and women are equally susceptible to good and evil

12. The style of the passage is characterized by the use of all of the following EXCEPT

    A. colloquial diction
    B. literary allusion
    C. first-person pronouns
    D. metaphor and simile
    E. balanced compound sentences

13. In developing its thesis, the passage relies on all of the following EXCEPT

    A. ethical argument

    B. personal anecdote

    C. extended definition

    D. abstract generalization

    E. reference to authority

14. Which of the following best describes the speaker of the passage?

    A. an impartial observer

    B. a cautious advisor

    C. a skeptical commentator

    D. a wry reporter

    E. a dedicated partisan

GO ON TO THE NEXT PAGE

Questions 15–29. Read the following passage carefully before you begin to answer the questions.

Second Passage

A greater inducement to folly is excess of power. After he had conceived his wonderful vision of philosopher-kings in the *Republic,* Plato began to have doubts and reached the conclusion that
(5) laws were the only safeguard. Too much power given to anything, like too large a sail on a vessel, he believed, is dangerous; moderation is overthrown. Excess leads on the one hand to disorder and on the other to injustice. No soul of man is able
(10) to resist the temptation of arbitrary power, and there is "No one who will not under such circumstances become filled with folly, the worst of diseases."[1] His kingdom will be undermined and "all his power will vanish from him." Such indeed was
(15) the fate that overtook the Renaissance Papacy to the point of half, if not all, of its power; and Louis XIV, although not until after his death; and—if we consider the American Presidency to confer excess of power—Lyndon Johnson, who was given to
(20) speaking of "*my* air force" and thought his position entitled him to lie and deceive; and, most obviously, Richard Nixon.

Mental standstill or stagnation—the maintenance intact by rulers and policy-makers of the ideas they
(25) started with—is fertile ground for folly. Montezuma is a fatal and tragic example. Leaders in government, on the authority of Henry Kissinger, do not learn beyond the convictions they bring with them; these are "the intellectual capital they will consume as long as
(30) they are in office."[2] Learning from experience is a faculty almost never practiced. Why did American experience of supporting the unpopular party in China supply no analogy to Vietnam? And the experience of Vietnam none for Iran? And why has none of
(35) the above conveyed any inference to preserve the present government of the United States from imbecility in El Salvador? "If men could learn from history, what lessons it might teach us!" lamented Samuel Coleridge. "But passion and party blind our
(40) eyes, and the light which experience gives us is a lantern on the stern which shines only on the waves behind us."[3] The image is beautiful but the message misleading, for the light on the waves we have passed through should enable us to infer the nature
(45) of the waves ahead. . . .

Aware of the controlling power of ambition, corruption and emotion, it may be that in the search for wiser government we should look for the test of character first. And the test should be moral
(50) courage. Montaigne adds, "Resolution and valor, not that which is sharpened by ambition but that which wisdom and reason may implant in a well-ordered soul."[4] The Lilliputians in choosing persons for public employment had similar criteria.
(55) "They have more regard for good morals than for great abilities," reported Gulliver, "for, since government is necessary to mankind, they believe . . . that Providence never intended to make management of publick affairs a mystery, to be compre-
(60) hended only by a few persons of sublime genius, of which there are seldom three born in an age. They suppose truth, justice, temperance and the like to be in every man's power: the practice of which virtues, assisted by experience and a good intention, would
(65) qualify any man for service of his country, except where a course of study is required."[5]

While such virtues may in truth be in every man's power, they have less chance in our system than money and ruthless ambition to prevail at the
(70) ballot box. The problem may be not so much a matter of educating officials for government as educating the electorate to recognize and reward integrity of character and to reject the ersatz. Perhaps better men flourish in better times, and wiser government
(75) requires the nourishment of a dynamic rather than a troubled and bewildered society. If John Adams was right, and government is "little better practiced now than three or four thousand years ago," we cannot reasonably expect much improvement. We
(80) can only muddle on as we have done in those same three or four thousand years, through patches of brilliance and decline, great endeavor and shadow.

[1] *Plato, "The worst of diseases": Laws, III, 691D.*

[2] *"Intellectual Capital": Kissinger, 54.*

[3] *Coleridge, "If men could learn": Oxford Dictionary of Quotations, 157, no. 20.*

[4] *Montaigne, "Resolution and Valor": Complete Essays, trans. Donald M. Frame, Stanford, 1965, II, 36.*

[5] *Lilliputians "Have more regard": Jonathan Swift, Gulliver's Travels, Part One, chap. 6.*

15. In the discussion of Plato's idea that "laws were the only safeguard" (lines 2–5), the speaker implies that

    A. Plato's original vision of philosopher-kings is valid

    B. excess always leads to injustice

    C. excess always leads to disorder

    D. rulers can never be trusted with too much power

    E. Plato believed that one should not put too large a sail on a vessel

16. One can infer that Plato would most likely disagree with the idea that

    A. no man can resist totalitarian authority

    B. intellectual idleness causes folly

    C. successful leaders can be trained

    D. good rulers need to have superior ethics

    E. governing effectively will not improve in the future

17. The passage employs all of following figurative devices EXCEPT

    A. simile

    B. allegory

    C. historical allusions

    D. metaphors

    E. literary quotations

18. The rhetorical effect of the use of italics in the quotation "*my* air force" (line 20) is that it

    A. emphasizes the corruption of Richard Nixon

    B. emphasizes the heartfelt attention paid by Lyndon Johnson to the war effort

    C. depersonalizes Johnson's use of power

    D. is just another example of the use of power; the italics add nothing

    E. gives depth to Johnson's excesses; his use of power was *personal*

19. The third paragraph can be distinguished from the others because it

    A. discusses traits that are valuable in an effective leader

    B. shifts the emphasis of the essay to literary analysis

    C. explores the positive and the negative aspects of government

    D. questions the practicality of finding a successful ruler

    E. sends a strong message, thus connecting literature to daily life

20. The series of questions posed in lines 31–37 serve the rhetorical purpose of

    A. demonstrating a few contrary examples that modify the speaker's position

    B. introducing the reference to *Gulliver's Travels*

    C. proving that "Learning from experience is a faculty almost never practiced" (lines 30–31)

    D. exploring 19th-century examples of mankind's folly

    E. exhorting antiwar protestors to rethink their position

21. Which of the following most clearly enunciates the speaker's position vis-à-vis Coleridge's "lantern on the stern" metaphor (lines 37–42)?

    A. The speaker believes that Coleridge misstates the importance of the "light of history."

    B. The speaker believes that shining a light on the past is an excellent method for divining future events.

    C. The speaker believes that Coleridge is blinded by "passion and party."

    D. The speaker believes that the image of the lantern on the stern is visually terrifying.

    E. The speaker believes Coleridge's metaphor is a powerful summation of the misuse of historical precedents by men blinded by "passion and party."

GO ON TO THE NEXT PAGE

22. The speaker's rhetorical purpose in citing Montezuma (lines 25–26) is to provide a concrete historical example of

    A. an effective ruler who successfully changed with the times

    B. a tragic ruler who gave his own life to save his people

    C. an autocratic ruler who was destroyed by his excesses of power

    D. a stubborn ruler who failed to change with the times and thus failed to save his people.

    E. a mendacious ruler who thought that "his position entitled him to lie and deceive"

23. According to this passage, all of the following can contribute to political folly EXCEPT

    A. extreme use of authority

    B. an investigation of honorable character

    C. mental languishing

    D. excesses that lead to disarray or to injustice

    E. the electorate being easily misled by ersatz integrity

24. A comparison of the speaker's description of Plato's philosopher-king to the Lilliputians' ideas about selecting public servants leads to the conclusion that

    A. Plato's vision is a more practical idea than the Lilliputians'

    B. the Lilliputians believed that all power should reside in one individual

    C. Plato's original idea was too fanciful; the Lilliputians' idea was much more pragmatic

    D. the Lilliputians believed that many people who are well-suited to be rulers were born in every age

    E. Plato's ideal of a philosopher-king was one he carried throughout his life

25. Based on the inclusion of such diverse historical examples as Plato, the Renaissance Papacy, Montezuma, and American presidents, one can infer that the speaker is

    A. demonstrating that the same factors arise repeatedly throughout history and always result in the folly of power

    B. searching far and wide to find any examples that fit her preconceived notions

    C. throwing in everything that she can find, hoping that the reader will be able to relate to at least one of the examples

    D. showing the diverse methods these individuals used successfully to wield great power

    E. trying to tie these examples together into a coherent narrative, although she ultimately fails

26. What is the primary rhetorical purpose of the third paragraph?

    A. It details the folly of the excess of power.

    B. It details the folly of mental stagnation.

    C. It explains the significance of the "lantern on the stern" metaphor.

    D. It clarifies what kind of man actually governs best.

    E. It clarifies what type of man governs worst.

27. Considering the passage as a whole, the best description of the speaker's tone is that it is

    A. tentatively optimistic about mankind's future

    B. cynical about mankind's inability to overcome the same mistakes

    C. reverent toward 19th-century authors

    D. credible as to the successful examples of governance

    E. hagiographical in its exultation of successful rulers

28. Collectively, the five footnotes demonstrate that the speaker

    A. synthesizes ideas culled from a wide variety of sources

    B. specializes in 19th-century philosophers

    C. chooses to ignore any author who disagrees with her position

    D. admires great philosophers

    E. disagrees with Coleridge's positions

29. The speaker would most likely agree with which of the following ideas?

    A. Mankind's predilections are unalterable; the public should never be allowed a direct vote in the selection of their leaders.

    B. Although brutal, excesses of power can sometimes be used for the public good and the betterment of mankind.

    C. Through proper training, even unsuitable political leaders can govern effectively.

    D. It is likely that mankind will manage to overcome their illogical propensities and select better leaders in the future.

    E. History provides numerous examples of the folly of political leaders who succumbed to the excesses of power.

GO ON TO THE NEXT PAGE

Questions 30–43. Read the following passage carefully before you begin to answer the questions.

Third Passage

It is a familiar example of irony in the degradation of words that "what a man is worth" has come to mean how much money he possesses; but there seems a deeper and more melancholy irony in the
(5) shrunken meaning that popular or polite speech assigns to "morality" and "morals." The poor part these words are made to play recalls the fate of those pagan divinities who, after being understood to rule the powers of the air and the destinies of men, came
(10) down to the level of insignificant demons, or were even made a farcical show for the amusement of the multitude.

I find even respectable historians of our own and of foreign countries, after showing that a king was
(15) treacherous, rapacious, and ready to sanction gross breaches in the administration of justice, end by praising him for his pure moral character; by which one must suppose them to mean that he was not lewd nor debauched, not the European twin of the
(20) typical Indian potentate whom Macaulay describes as passing his life in chewing bang[1] and fondling dancing girls. And since we are sometimes told of such maleficent kings that they were religious, we arrive at the curious result, that the most serious
(25) wide-reaching duties of man lie quite outside both morality and religion—the one of these consisting in not keeping mistresses (and perhaps not drinking too much), and the other in certain ritual and spiritual transactions with God, which can be carried on
(30) equally well side by side with the basest conduct toward men. With such a classification as this it is no wonder, considering the strong reaction of language on thought, that many minds, dizzy with indigestion of recent science and philosophy, are far
(35) to seek for the grounds of social duty, and without entertaining any private intention of committing a perjury which would ruin an innocent man, or seeking gain by supplying bad preserved meats to our navy, feel themselves speculatively obliged to
(40) inquire why they should not do so, and are inclined to measure their intellectual subtlety by their dissatisfaction with all the answers to this "Why?" It is of little use to theorize in ethics while our habitual phraseology stamps the larger part of our social du-
(45) ties as something that lies aloof from the deepest needs and affections of our nature. The informal definitions of popular language are the only medium through which theory really affects the mass of minds, even among the nominally educated; and
(50) when a man whose business hours, the solid part of every day, are spent in an unscrupulous course of private or public action which has every calculable chance of causing wide-spread injury and misery, can be called moral because he comes home to dine
(55) with his wife and children and cherishes the happiness of his own hearth, the augury is not good for the use of high ethical and theological disputation.

[1] Line 21, bang = marijuana

---

30. In the opening sentence, the speaker calls the interpretation of the phrase "what a man is worth" a "degradation of words" because she believes that

A. "worth" should refer to material value
B. the phrase refers only to a man, not to both men and women
C. "worth" should refer to what a specific sum can purchase
D. the example, ironically, is not "familiar"
E. "worth" should refer to merit

31. In lines 6–7, the phrase "the poor part these words are made to play" is

A. part of a parallel construction
B. a theatrical metaphor
C. a paradox
D. an understatement
E. a colloquialism

32. In line 5, "popular or polite speech" refers to language that is

A. common and refined
B. inexpressive and courteous
C. universally admired and cultured
D. ungrammatical and correct
E. rude and polished

33. The extended figure in lines 6–12 compares

    A. words and actors
    B. rulers and demons
    C. words and gods
    D. tragedy and farce
    E. words and entertainers

34. In lines 20–22, the speaker includes the allusion to Macaulay in order to

    A. refer to a well-known historian who exemplifies the fault she is exposing
    B. demonstrate the superiority of European kings
    C. strengthen her argument by referring to another writer who supports her position
    D. satirize historians by the use of overstatement
    E. attack the licentious behavior of Asian rulers

35. In the phrase "the one of these consisting in not keeping mistresses" in lines 26–27, "the one" refers to

    A. "twin" (line 19)
    B. "Macaulay" (line 20)
    C. "result" (line 24)
    D. "morality" (line 26)
    E. "religion" (line 26)

36. According to the "respectable historians" of the second paragraph, a king could be described as "moral" so long as he is not guilty of

    A. injustice
    B. treachery
    C. indecency
    D. greed
    E. deceit

37. The idea of the phrase "the strong reaction of language on thought" (lines 32–33) is repeated in

    A. "without entertaining any private intention of committing a perjury" (lines 35–37)
    B. "seeking gain by supplying bad preserved meats to our navy" (lines 38–39)
    C. "measure their intellectual subtlety by their dissatisfaction with all the answers" (lines 41–42)
    D. "our habitual phraseology stamps the larger part of our social duties as something that lies aloof from the deepest needs and affections of our nature" (lines 43–46)
    E. "the informal definitions of popular language are the only medium through which theory really affects the mass of minds" (lines 46–49)

38. In its context in lines 34–35, the idiom "are far to seek for" means

    A. have difficulty finding
    B. refuse to look for
    C. stumble upon
    D. go to any lengths in search of
    E. try to avoid

39. Lines 46–57 conclude the passage with the argument that

    A. the moral values of the modern world are in decline
    B. the degeneration of language will erode philosophical discussion
    C. private life and public life are at odds with one another
    D. a good husband and father is not necessarily a moral man
    E. it is easy to predict a general decline in religion and thought

40. The concluding clause of the passage ("the augury is not good for the use of high ethical and theological disputation") is an example of

    A. understatement
    B. overstatement
    C. parallel construction
    D. *ad hominem* argument
    E. paradox

GO ON TO THE NEXT PAGE

41. All of the following words or phrases are examples of what the speaker calls the "degradation" of language EXCEPT

    A. "what a man is worth" (line 2)
    B. "morality" (line 6)
    C. "morals" (line 6)
    D. "religious" (line 23)
    E. "perjury" (line 37)

42. The primary objective of the passage is to

    A. comment on a popular misconception
    B. encourage more carefully researched historical writing
    C. characterize a specific historical period
    D. deplore the abasement of language
    E. encourage a more religious view of life

43. Which of the following current events would best support the argument of the passage?

    A. A rating system evaluates films on the basis of their language and sexual content, but not on their content of violence.
    B. A state senator convicted of fraud is praised for his support of family values.
    C. An accused swindler is acquitted after an eight-month-long trial.
    D. A politician with a criminal record is elected mayor of a large city.
    E. A television evangelist is accused of embezzling church funds.

Questions 44–55. Read the following passage carefully before you begin to answer the questions.

Fourth Passage

The talent of turning men into ridicule, and exposing to laughter those one converses with, is the qualification of little ungenerous tempers. A young man with this cast of mind cuts himself off from all
(5) manner of improvement. Everyone has his flaws and weaknesses; nay, the greatest blemishes are often found in the most shining characters; but what an absurd thing it is to pass over all the valuable parts of a man and fix our attention on his infirmi-
(10) ties; to observe his imperfections more than his virtues; and to make use of him for the sport of others, rather than for our own improvement.

We therefore very often find that persons the most accomplished in ridicule, are those who are
(15) very shrewd at hitting a blot, without exerting anything masterly in themselves. As there are many eminent critics who never writ a good line, there are many admirable buffoons that animadvert upon every single defect in another, without ever discov-
(20) ering the least beauty of their own. By this means these unlucky little wits often gain reputation in the esteem of vulgar minds and raise themselves above persons of much more laudable characters.

If the talent of ridicule were employed to laugh
(25) men out of vice and folly, it might be of some use to the world; but instead of this, we find that it is generally made use of to laugh men out of virtue and good sense, by attacking everything that is solemn and serious, decent and praiseworthy in hu-
(30) man life.

We may observe, that in the first ages of the world, when the great souls and masterpieces of human nature were produced, men shined by a noble simplicity of behaviour, and were strangers to those
(35) little embellishments which are so fashionable in our present conversation. And it is very remarkable, that notwithstanding we fall short at present of the ancients in poetry, painting, oratory, history, architecture, and all the noble arts and sciences which de-
(40) pend more upon genius than experience, we exceed them as much in doggerel, humour, burlesque, and all the trivial arts of ridicule. We meet with more raillery among the moderns, but more good sense among the ancients.

44. Lines 7–12 ("but what an absurd . . . our own improvement") are an example of a(n)

A. periodic sentence
B. parallel construction
C. conditional sentence
D. extended metaphor
E. indirect question

45. In lines 19–20, the word "discovering" can be best understood to mean

A. hoping to realize
B. understanding
C. concealing
D. being the first to find
E. revealing

46. The simile of the second paragraph compares

A. defects and beauties
B. weakness and blot
C. critics and buffoons
D. fault-finders and archers
E. height and reputation

47. The function of the second paragraph is to

A. develop the idea of the opening sentence of the passage
B. suggest exceptions to the ideas of the opening paragraph
C. shift the focus from personal opinion to a widely held view
D. provide a comic interlude in an otherwise serious passage
E. introduce the ideas to be developed in the third paragraph

48. In lines 27–28, the phrase "virtue and good sense" is contrasted with

A. "vulgar minds" (line 22)
B. "persons of much more laudable characters" (line 23)
C. "vice and folly" (line 25)
D. "solemn and serious" (line 29)
E. "decent and praiseworthy" (line 29)

GO ON TO THE NEXT PAGE

263

49. In lines 29–30, the phrase "solemn and serious, decent and praiseworthy in human life" is used to

A. suggest the speaker's uncertainty about condemning ridicule

B. clarify what the speaker means by "vice and folly" (line 25)

C. provide an example of the proper use of ridicule

D. clarify what the speaker means by "virtue and good sense" (lines 27–28)

E. introduce the central idea of the paragraph that follows

50. We can infer from the third paragraph that the speaker would approve of ridicule if it were directed against

A. youth

B. foolishness

C. human weakness

D. solemnity

E. raillery

51. In line 40, the contrast between "genius" and "experience" can be best understood as the contrast between

A. spiritual values and physical realities

B. praise and ridicule

C. natural aptitude and active participation

D. instinctive capacity and acquired knowledge

E. uniqueness and familiarity

52. In the fourth paragraph, all of the following refer to kinds of comic speech or writing EXCEPT

A. "embellishments" (line 35)

B. "doggerel" (line 41)

C. "humour" (line 41)

D. "burlesque" (line 41)

E. "raillery" (line 43)

53. According to the passage, in which of the following forms would the modern writer be most likely to surpass the ancient?

A. lyric poetry

B. tragedy

C. satire

D. epic

E. prose fiction

54. The author of this passage would be likely to agree with all of the following EXCEPT

A. No one is perfect.

B. The fine arts of the moderns are inferior to those of the ancients.

C. The best of men often have the worst of faults.

D. There are proper and improper uses of ridicule.

E. The history of the world is a record of very slow improvement.

55. Of the following literary works, which one would the author of this passage probably regard most highly?

A. ancient epics

B. drama of the Middle Ages

C. religious lyrics of the Renaissance

D. Elizabethan tragedy

E. contemporary comedy

IF YOU FINISH BEFORE TIME IS CALLED, CHECK YOUR WORK ON THIS SECTION ONLY. DO NOT WORK ON ANY OTHER SECTION IN THE TEST.

Section II: Essay Questions

Time: 2 hours, 15 minutes

3 questions

Question 1

(Reading time—15 minutes. Suggested writing time—40 minutes. This question counts one-third of the total essay section score.)

Directions: The prompt that follows is based on six accompanying sources. This essay requires you to integrate a variety of sources into a coherent, well-written essay. Refer to the sources, both directly and indirectly, to support your position. Avoid mere paraphrasing or summarizing. Your argument should be the central focus; the use of the sources should support your argument.

Introduction

After Title IX was implemented by the federal government, many colleges fielded additional women's sports teams to fulfill the requirement for more equality between men's and women's collegiate sports. How has Title IX been beneficial to women in sports? Has Title IX created equality in sports between men and women or has it furthered the inequalities?

Assignment

Read the following sources (including any introductory information) carefully. **Then, in an essay that synthesizes at least three of the sources for support, take a position that defends, challenges, or qualifies the claim that Title IX has allowed for more equality in the world of sports.**

Refer to the sources as Source A, Source B, and so on; authors' names or titles are included for your convenience.

Source A (Clayton)

Source B (Zucker)

Source C (United States of America)

Source D (Rosania)

Source E (Schwartz)

Source F (Lancaster)

GO ON TO THE NEXT PAGE

Source A

Clayton, Mark. "Has Equality in Sports Gone too Far?" *The Christian Science Monitor,* 22 December 2002.

The following passage is excerpted from an article about how Title IX has changed women's sports.

There's little argument that the impact of Title IX has been enormous. In the decades since it was enacted, the law has transformed opportunities for women at all levels, but particularly in college. Without the law, there might not have been a Mia Hamm, the world-famous soccer star, who honed her skills in college. Women's college soccer has soared from just 1,855 participants in 1981–1982 to 18,548 in 2000–2001, a 10-fold leap.

Meanwhile, some argue that many men's teams have been dropped in recent decades to meet the proportionality test—which they see as a form of reverse discrimination. Indeed, a group of college wrestling coaches is suing the DOE to change its proportionality requirement—even if the commission doesn't ultimately recommend such change. While many of these critics support the progress of women's and girls' sports, they believe Title IX is being unfairly enforced. "We've lost over 434 college wrestling programs since the early 1970s, not all to Title IX, but a good number of programs have been," says Michael Moyer, executive director of the National Wrestling Coaches Association.

Women's groups counter that Title IX isn't to blame for the cuts. Instead, they point to big-money college sports, like football, that often squeeze small-scale men's sports like swimming and gymnastics. Just what is behind the elimination of athletic programs is often difficult to determine and draws differing views from even the athletes themselves. Take the University of Minnesota in Minneapolis. In April, the school announced it would axe its trophy-winning men's gymnastics team as well as its men's and women's golf programs. University officials cited an out-of-control athletic budget as the culprit. But even though Title IX was not officially mentioned, many athletes blame the law anyway, including William Callahan, a junior who competes on floor exercise, parallel bars, and the high bar. It was tough for him to hear that his team would get cut, in part because his girlfriend is a female gymnast whose team survived. "It seems like we have stupid sports up here just to compensate for Title IX requirement," he says. "We have women's crew up here where the lakes freeze over. We recently built a women's hockey rink right next to the men's. I don't understand it."

Source B

Zucker, Brad. "Women Merit Equality in Sports." *Daily Bruin,* 24 April 1997.

The following passage is excerpted from a college newspaper that discusses the differences between men and women in sports.

Many college officials will argue that there are more male athletes at their respective schools because more men want to participate. It is unfair, they argue, to discriminate against these athletes simply because a quota needs to be met. I don't believe there is equality of opportunity between men and women in terms of participation in college athletics, regardless of whether or not there are an equal number of teams. When there are so far fewer athletes of one gender than the other, it is likely the social structure is to blame.

The reason there are fewer female athletes out there is not because they can't compete effectively with men on the playing field. At the higher levels of competition, men and women don't even square off against one another. There are fewer women involved in college athletics because women in general have historically been discouraged from participating in sports. Parallel to the basis of arguments on behalf of affirmative action in terms of race, women today face a legacy of sexism in the world of athletics. Whereas proponents of racial affirmative action would argue that the history of racism in this country must be overcome by a forceful hand, advocates of a gendered quota system in college athletic programs would argue that bringing about equality in this sense entails more than simply providing access to a team. Combined with a long history of unequal access and a lack of encouragement toward athletic participation, the social-psychological effects of being told by one's culture that it is "unfeminine" to play sports has kept growth in the world of women's sports from rising above a certain level. The court ruling on the suit filed against Brown University is an example of what it will take to give generations of women the same opportunity to benefit from the wonderful experience of playing sports that men have.

At the professional level, it is ultimately the consumer who will determine how many women will compete. But college athletics should not be run according to the laws of supply and demand. Men and women do not compete against each other on the athletic field in college, but they do compete in terms of resources. If one believes that part of the purpose of higher education is to produce positive social change, then it makes sense for the law to allow this to occur.

GO ON TO THE NEXT PAGE

Source C

United States of America. Office of the Assistant Secretary for Administration and Management. Department of Labor. *Title IX, Education Amendments of 1972*. Washington DC, 1972.

The following passage is excerpted from the Education Amendments of 1972.

Section 1681. Sex

(a) Prohibition against discrimination; exceptions. No person in the United States shall, on the basis of sex, be excluded from participation in, be denied the benefits of, or be subjected to discrimination under any education program or activity receiving Federal financial assistance, except that:

> **(1) Classes of educational institutions subject to prohibition** in regard to admissions to educational institutions, this section shall apply only to institutions of vocational education, professional education, and graduate higher education, and to public institutions of undergraduate higher education;

(b) Preferential or disparate treatment because of imbalance in participation or receipt of Federal benefits; statistical evidence of imbalance. Nothing contained in subsection (a) of this section shall be interpreted to require any educational institution to grant preferential or disparate treatment to the members of one sex on account of an imbalance which may exist with respect to the total number or percentage of persons of that sex participating in or receiving the benefits of any federally supported program or activity, in comparison with the total number or percentage of persons of that sex in any community, State, section, or other area: *Provided,* that this subsection shall not be construed to prevent the consideration in any hearing or proceeding under this chapter of statistical evidence tending to show that such an imbalance exists with respect to the participation in, or receipt of the benefits of, any such program or activity by the members of one sex.

Source D

Rosania, Jenna. "Women vs. Their Society." Editorial. *Serendip,* 2003.

The following excerpt discusses the images of women in sport and how they are affected by today's cultural ideal of women.

Women in sports have definitely come a long way from the barriers and prejudices of previous times. Only recently have women been able to compete in a very public way, with established leagues, payrolls and plenty of endorsement opportunities. Title IX has allowed teams of girls for almost every sport as well as better opportunities for sports scholarships to college and many other privileges only given to boys for their talents in sports. Under all these legal provisions and establishments for the encouragement of women in sports, women should now really be able to do any kind of sport they want in as much freedom as is afforded to men in sports.

Although women have been given so many freedoms in this field, it is the social aspect, the audiences of sports, the people of our biased culture that is now hindering women who wish to be known as athletes and competitors. Our culture is filled with deeply imbedded ideas about power and strength and competition being masculine qualities, and for women to want to embody these things is confusing and goes against our unconscious stereotypes about the abilities and attributes of men versus women. The acceptance of women in sports becomes not a matter of ability or talent in their field, but rather is based on ways women can be what is considered by our culture to be feminine while they play their sport. If a woman can still be what the average person thinks of as a woman while also displaying talent, her "masculine" attributes can be more accepted by the audience and so the woman is more accepted.

GO ON TO THE NEXT PAGE

Source E

Schwartz, Larry. "Billie Jean Won for all Women." *ESPN,* 29 Aug. 2000.

The following excerpt is from a Sportscentury Biography about Billie Jean King and her role in sports and the fight for women's equality.

Billie Jean King won a dozen Grand Slam singles titles, including six Wimbledon championships and four U.S. crowns. She was ranked No. 1 in the world five years. She defeated such magnificent players as Martina Navratilova, Chris Evert and Margaret Court. Yet of all her victories, the one that is remembered most is her beating a 55-year-old man.

History has recorded all she has accomplished in furthering the cause of women's struggle for equality in the 1970s. She was instrumental in making it acceptable for American women to exert themselves in pursuits other than childbirth. She was the lightning rod in starting a professional women's tour. She started a women's sports magazine and a women's sports foundation. Navratilova said, "She was a crusader fighting a battle for all of us. She was carrying the flag; it was all right to be a jock."

It was for King's crusading that *Life* magazine in 1990 named her one of the "100 Most Important Americans of the 20th Century." Not sports figures, but Americans. She was the only female athlete on the list, and one of only four athletes (Babe Ruth, Jackie Robinson and Muhammad Ali were the others).

She convinced her colleagues to form a players' union, and the Women's Tennis Association was born. King was its first president in 1973. King, who received $15,000 less than Ilie Nastase did for winning the U.S. Open in 1972, said if the prize money wasn't equal by the next year, she wouldn't play, and she didn't think the other women would either. In 1973, the U.S. Open became the first major tournament to offer equal prize money for men and women. The next year, King founded *WomenSports* magazine, started the Women's Sports Foundation, an organization dedication to promoting and enhancing athletic opportunities for females, and with her husband, formed World Team Tennis.

King believes that she was born with a destiny to work for gender equity in sports and to continue until it's achieved. "In the seventies we had to make it acceptable for people to accept girls and women as athletes," she said. "We had to make it okay for them to be active. Those were much scarier times for females in sports." Pop star Helen Reddy may have sung the words, but it is King who is best living them, "I am woman, hear me roar, in numbers too big to ignore."

Source F

Lancaster, Mike. "Title IX and its Effects on College Athletic Programs." *Athletic Scholarships,* 2000. 30 Sept. 2005. Available at http://athleticscholarships.net/title-ix-college-athletics-3.htm.

Year	Men	Male Percent of Total	Women	Female Percent of Total	Total
1988–89	120	48.6	127	51.4	247
1989–90	129	41.6	181	58.4	310
1990–91	157	48.8	165	51.2	322
1991–92	185	46.8	210	53.2	395
1992–93	139	45.3	168	54.7	307
1993–94	133	34.5	253	65.5	386
1994–95	90	29.3	217	70.7	307
1995–96*	119	27.6	312	72.4	431
1996–97*	112	29.1	273	70.9	385
1997–98*	122	33.1	247	66.9	369
1998–99*	116	32.5	241	67.5	357
1999–00*	198	39.2	307	60.8	505
2000–01*	167	43.2	220	56.8	387
2001–02*	161	43.4	210	56.6	371
2002–03*	136	45.9	160	54.1	296
2003–04*	119	45.6	142	54.4	261
Total	2,203	39.1	3,433	60.9	5,636

* Provisional members are included in these numbers

GO ON TO THE NEXT PAGE

Question 2

Suggested time—40 minutes. This question counts one-third of the total essay score.

Directions: Read the following excerpt from Mary Oliver, called "Building the House," in which she draws an analogy between constructing poetry and constructing a house. In a well-organized essay, analyze how the author uses metaphor and other rhetorical devices to express her attitude toward writing poetry.

I know a young man who can build almost anything—a boat, a fence, kitchen cabinets, a table, a barn, a house. And so serenely, and in so assured and right a manner, that it is a joy to watch him. All the same, what he seems to care for best—what he seems positively to desire—is the hour of interruption, of hammerless quiet, in which he will sit and write down poems or stories that have come into his mind with clambering and colorful force. Truly he is not very good at the puzzle of words—not nearly as good as he is with a mallet and the measuring tape—but this in no way lessens his pleasure. Moreover, he is in no hurry. Everything he learned, he learned at a careful pace—will not the use of words come easier at last, though he begin at the slowest amble? Also, in these intervals, he is happy. In building things, he is his familiar self, which he does not overvalue. But in the act of writing he is a grander man, a surprise to us, and even more to himself. He is beyond what he believed himself to be.

I understand his pleasure. I also know the enclosure of my skills, and am no less pert than he when some flow takes me over the edge of it. Usually, as it happens, this is toward the work in which he is so capable. There appears in my mind a form; I imagine it from boards of a certain breadth and length, and nails, and all in cheerful response to some need I have or think I have, aligned with a space I see as opportunistic. I would not pry my own tooth, or cobble my own shoes, but I deliberate unfazed the niceties of woodworking—nothing, all my life, has checked me. At my side at this moment is a small table with one leg turned in slightly. For I have never built anything perfectly, or even very well, in spite of the pleasure such labor gives me. Nor am I done yet, though time has brought obstacles and spread them before me—a stiffness of the fingers, a refusal of the eyes to follow the aim of the hammer toward the nail head, which yearly grows smaller, and smaller.

The labor of writing poems, of working with thought and emotion in the encasement (or is it the wings?) of language is strange to nature, for we are first of all creatures of motion. Only secondly—only oddly, and not naturally, at moments of contemplation, joy, grief, prayer, or terror—are we found, while awake, in the posture of deliberate or hapless inaction. But such is the posture of the poet, poor laborer. The dancer dances, the painter dips and lifts and lays on the oils; the composer reaches at least across the octaves. The poet sits. The architect draws and measures, and travels to the quarry to tramp among the gleaming stones. The poet sits, or, if it is a fluid moment, he scribbles some words upon the page. The body, under this pressure of nonexisting, begins to draw up like a muscle, and complain. An unsolvable disharmony of such work—the mind so hotly fired and the body so long quiescent—will come sooner or later to revolution, will demand action! For many years, in a place I call Blackwater Woods, I wrote while I walked. That motion, hardly more than a dreamy sauntering, worked for me; it kept my body happy while I scribbled. But sometimes it wasn't at all enough. I wanted to build, in the other way, with the teeth of the saw, and the explosions of the hammer, and the little shrieks of the screws winding down into their perfect nests.

Question 3

Suggested time—40 minutes. This question counts one-third of the total essay score.

The following excerpt comes from Anwar F. Accawi's reflective essay titled "The Telephone," in which he looks back at his childhood in Lebanon before the first telephone had been installed and before the concept of clock-time had much meaning to him.

Directions: Read the excerpt carefully. Then, in a well-organized essay, examine the rhetorical devices that the author employs as he expresses his attitude toward time.

When I was growing up in Magdaluna, a small Lebanese village in the terraced, rocky mountains east of Sidon, time didn't mean much to anybody, except maybe to those who were dying, or those waiting to appear in court because they had tampered with the boundary markers on their land. In those days, there was no real need for a calendar or a watch to keep track of the hours, days, months, and years. We knew what to do, just as the Iraqi geese knew when to fly north, driven by the hot wind that blew in from the desert, and the ewes knew when to give birth to wet lambs that stood on long, shaky legs in the chilly March wind and baaed hesitantly, because they were small and cold and did not know where they were or what to do now they were here. The only timepiece we had need of then was the sun. It rose and set, and the seasons rolled by, and we sowed seed and harvested and ate and played and married our cousins and had babies who got whooping cough and chickenpox—and those children who survived grew up and married *their* cousins and had babies who got whooping cough and chickenpox. We lived and loved and toiled and died without ever needing to know what year it was, or even the time of day.

It wasn't that we had no system for keeping track of time and of the important events in our lives. But ours was a natural—or, rather, a divine—calendar, because it was framed by acts of God. Allah himself set down the milestones with earthquakes and droughts and floods and locusts and pestilences. Simple as our calendar was, it worked just fine for us.

Take, for example, the birth date of Teta Im Khalil, the oldest woman in Magdaluna and all the surrounding villages. When I first met her, we had just returned home from Syria at the end of the Big War and were living with Grandma Mariam. Im Khahlil came by to welcome my father home and to take a long, myopic look at his foreign-born wife, my mother. Im Khahlil was so old that the skin of her cheeks looked like my father's grimy tobacco pouch, and when I kissed her (because Grandma insisted that I show her old friend affection), it was like kissing a soft suede glove that had been soaked with sweat and then left in a dark closet for a season. Im Khahlil's face got me to wondering how old one had to be to look and taste the way she did. So, soon as she had hobbled off on her cane, I asked Grandma, "How old is Teta Im Khahlil?"

Grandma had to think for a moment; then she said, "I've been told that Teta was born shortly after the big snow that caused the roof on the mayor's house to cave in."

"And when was that?" I asked.

"Oh, about the time we had the big earthquake that cracked the wall in the east room."

Well, that was enough for me. You couldn't be more accurate than that, now, could you? Satisfied with her answer, I went back to playing with a ball made from an old sock stuffed with other, much older socks.

And that's the way it was in our little village for as far back as anybody could remember: people were born so many years before or after an earthquake or a flood; they got married or died so many years before or after a long drought or a big snow or some other disaster. One of the most unusual of these dates was when Antoinette the seamstress and Saeed the barber (and tooth puller) got married. That was the year of the whirlwind during which fish and oranges fell from the sky. Incredible as it may sound, the story of the fish and the oranges was true, because men—respectable men, like Abu George the blacksmith and Abu Asaad the mule skinner, men who would not lie even to save their own souls—told and retold that story until it was incorporated into Magdaluna's calendar, just like the year of the black moon and the year of the locusts before it. My father, too, confirmed the story for me. He told me that he had been a small boy himself when it had rained fish and oranges from heaven. He'd gotten up one morning after a stormy night and walked out into the yard to find fish as long as his forearm still flopping here and there among the wet navel oranges.

IF YOU FINISH BEFORE TIME IS CALLED, CHECK YOUR WORK ON THIS SECTION ONLY. DO NOT WORK ON ANY OTHER SECTION IN THE TEST.

Answer Key for Practice Test 5

Section I: Multiple-Choice Questions

First Passage

1. C
2. E
3. E
4. B
5. A
6. B
7. D
8. D
9. B
10. A
11. C
12. A
13. B
14. E

Second Passage

15. D
16. C
17. B
18. E
19. A
20. C
21. E
22. D
23. B
24. C
25. A
26. D
27. B
28. A
29. E

Third Passage

30. E
31. B
32. A
33. C
34. D
35. D
36. C
37. E
38. A
39. B
40. A
41. E
42. D
43. B

Fourth Passage

44. B
45. E
46. C
47. A
48. C
49. D
50. B
51. D
52. A
53. C
54. E
55. A

Section II: Essay Questions

Essay scoring guides, student essays, and analysis appear beginning on page 281.

Practice Test 5 Scoring Worksheet

Use the following worksheet to arrive at a probable final AP grade on Practice Test 5. Because being objective enough to estimate your own essay score is sometimes difficult, you might give your essays (along with the sample essays) to a teacher, friend, or relative to score if you feel confident that the individual has the knowledge necessary to make such a judgment and that he or she will feel comfortable doing so.

Section I: Multiple-Choice Questions

$$\underline{\hspace{2cm}} - (\frac{1}{4} \text{ or } .25 \times \underline{\hspace{2cm}}) = \underline{\hspace{2cm}}$$

right	wrong	multiple-choice
answers	answers	raw score

$$\underline{\hspace{3cm}} \times 1.2272 = \underline{\hspace{3cm}} \text{ (of possible 67.5)}$$

multiple-choice	multiple-choice
raw score	converted score

Section II: Essay Questions

$$\underline{\hspace{1.5cm}} + \underline{\hspace{1.5cm}} + \underline{\hspace{1.5cm}} = \underline{\hspace{1.5cm}}$$

question 1	question 2	question 3	essay
raw score	raw score	raw score	raw score

$$\underline{\hspace{3cm}} \times 3.0556 = \underline{\hspace{3cm}} \text{ (of possible 82.5)}$$

essay	essay
raw score	converted score

Final Score

$$\underline{\hspace{2.5cm}} + \underline{\hspace{2.5cm}} = \underline{\hspace{2.5cm}} \text{(of possible 150)}$$

multiple-choice	essay	final
converted score	converted score	converted score

Probable Final AP Score

Final Converted Score	Probable AP Score
150–104	5
103–92	4
91–76	3
75–50	2
49–0	1

Section I: Multiple-Choice Questions

First Passage

The passage is from John Milton's *Areopagitica* (1644) in which the poet argues for printing without governmental restraints.

1. **C.** The metaphor is in the words "in the field" and "grow up." Of the five choices, only plants grow up in a field.

2. **E.** The lines are arguing that we cannot know or recognize good without knowing evil also. This idea is the central point of the passage. If we cannot recognize evil, we cannot understand good.

3. **E.** The sentence is a rhetorical question (that is, a question used for rhetorical effect, to emphasize a point with no expectation of an answer). Due to the way the question is worded in the passage, the only reply is, "none."

4. **B.** The "adversary" of virtue is vice. The argument here is that virtue must not hide from its enemy but must contend with evil directly.

5. **A.** The developed figure in the lines is a comparison of life to a footrace between good and evil, a contest to be run for the garland (prize) of immortality. The race will be hot and dusty, but true virtue will not shirk the contest.

6. **B.** The "garland" is "immortal," the reward of immortality for those who struggle in life's race and defeat evil.

7. **D.** These lines argue that we are born impure ("we bring not innocence into the world"), but we can be purified by facing evil and overcoming it. This "trial" is an inner contest, not a judicial proceeding.

8. **D.** Of the five choices, D is the best paraphrase. The phrase "by what is contrary" means by its opposite, because evil is the contrary of virtue. This passage comes from a defense of the freedom of the press, an argument against the suppression of the contrary viewpoint.

9. **B.** The passage claims that the "sage and serious poet Spenser" is a better teacher than philosophers like Scotus or Aquinas.

10. **A.** In Spenser's "Faerie Queene," the knight of temperance, Guion, visits the cave of Mammon and the bower of earthly bliss. The cave is the temptation of wealth; the bower, the temptation of sensual pleasures. To be truly temperate, Guion must be exposed to, understand, and resist these temptations.

11. **C.** The central point of the passage is that to learn to resist evil properly, we must be exposed to it. A "cloistered virtue" (that is, a virtue that never faces evil directly) is inadequate.

12. **A.** The passage uses literary allusion (the references to Spenser, for example); both the singular and the plural first person ("we know," line 1; "I cannot," line 20); metaphor ("field of this world," line 1) and simile ("as two twins," lines 9–10); and balanced sentences (lines 25–27). The language of the passage, however, is not colloquial.

13. **B.** The passage does not employ any personal anecdotes. As a whole, the piece is an ethical argument, which employs extended definition, abstract generalization, and reference to authority.

14. **E.** The speaker is by no means impartial, cautious, skeptical, or wry. He is a committed believer in his argument.

Second Passage

From *The March of Folly* by Barbara Tuchman

15. D. The speaker juxtaposes Plato's early optimistic vision of an all-powerful yet benevolent philosopher-king with his later jaded conclusion that "laws were the only safeguard." This implies that Plato eventually realized rulers with too much power cannot be trusted. Choices B and C are incorrect because they are stated as facts, not implications. Choice E is Plato's metaphor, not the author's implication. Choice A contradicts the key point of this paragraph.

16. C. The speaker states that Plato "began to have doubts" about the ability to select and nurture a philosopher-king who is carefully chosen and trained in the art of rational decision-making for the good of the community. All other answer choices, although they do appear in the excerpt, *are* ideas with which one can reasonably infer Plato would agree.

17. B. Allegory is not utilized in the passage; the author *does* effectively use all of the other literary devices.

18. E. The speaker's use of italics in "*my* air force" helps to demonstrate the very personal connection that President Johnson felt in his use of power. Choice A is incorrect; the quote is not from Richard Nixon. Choice B is incorrect; the author's intent is not to *praise* Johnson's personal attention to the war.

19. A. Paragraph 3 provides many examples of both valuable leadership traits and effective selection methods that can combine to produce a successful leader. Choices C and D are both incorrect because they are too negative to describe this optimistic paragraph. Choices B and E do not accurately relate to the content of this paragraph.

20. C. Recognizing the context of the series of queries is essential to understanding their impact, which derives power from placement. These probing questions provide vigorous reinforcement for the preceding statement, "Learning from experience is a faculty almost never practiced."

21. E. The speaker utilizes Coleridge's quotation eloquently to state her own conclusions that history and experience can be misleading when attempting "to infer the nature of the waves ahead. . . ." Choices A and C are incorrect; the speaker does not hint that Coleridge misspoke or was blinded. Choice B is actually a reversal of the speaker's conclusion about the worth of shining a light on the past. Choice D is incorrect; the speaker states, "The image is beautiful. . . ."

22. D. The statement regarding Montezuma is very brief; this shorthand approach expects that readers have some familiarity with the fall of the Aztec empire. The allusion to Montezuma is a powerful statement, emphasizing how a ruler who fails to change with the times can bring the downfall of his own people.

23. B. Choice B is the exception; in lines 47–49, the speaker states ". . . in the search for wiser government we should look for the test of character first." Choices A, C, D, and E are all issues that *can* contribute to the abuse of power.

24. C. Because even Plato himself finally discarded the idea of a benevolent philosopher-king, the speaker gives greater credence to the Lilliputians, as "They have more regard for good morals than for great abilities." Choice A is a contradiction. Choice E is incorrect; Plato changed his mind and decided his idea of a philosopher-king was impractical. Additionally, Choices B, D, and E are incorrect because they do not answer the question; they do not *compare* Plato to the Lilliputians.

25. A. The speaker successfully integrates these disparate historical examples to help illustrate how man's folly throughout the ages displays that the same factors repeatedly lead to abuses of power.

26. D. The speaker's purpose in comparing the ideas espoused by such diverse thinkers as Montaigne and the fictional Lilliputians is to illustrate her belief that the *morally righteous* man is best suited to govern. Choice A is simply incorrect; the folly of the abuse of power is discussed in the first paragraph. Choices B and C are likewise incorrect; both mental stagnation and the "lantern on the stern" metaphor are in the second paragraph. Choice E is incorrect; the third paragraph deals exclusively with men who govern best.

27. B. The speaker indicates specific ways in which men *can* govern wisely, but she appears unconvinced that this will actually happen. She ends on a sad, cynical note: ". . . we cannot reasonably expect much improvement."

28. A. Taken collectively, the five footnotes clearly demonstrate both the breadth of the speaker's research, as well as the depth of her analysis; they reveal her to be a truly-qualified expert in this field of study. Choice C is incorrect; she does not dismiss contradictory ideas out of hand. Choices B, D, and E are incorrect because these facts do not appear in the footnotes.

29. E. The passage's main theme is the oft-repeated story of political leaders who do not avoid excesses of power and, thus, they fail to avoid folly. Choices B and C are incorrect because the speaker believes that unsuitable leaders will, in the end, remain unsuitable, and that excesses of power are never justified. Choice D is inaccurate; the speaker does not expect improvement in mankind's skill in the selection of leaders. Choice A exaggerates the speaker's position; she has little faith in the public's ability to select successful leaders, but she never intimates that direct elections should be abolished.

Third Passage

The passage is from an essay by the 19th-century novelist George Eliot (Mary Ann Evans).

30. E. The author's complaint here is the replacement of what she believes ought to be a moral meaning of the word "worth" with a financial one. The noun "worth" can mean either material value or moral excellence; George Eliot regards the loss of the second meaning as an example of the "degradation of words."

31. B. The phrase is a metaphor that compares words to an actor in a play. The use of "part" (that is, the actor's role) and the verb "play" (that is, to perform) make the theatrical reference of the figure clear.

32. A. The root meaning of the word "popular" is "of the people," "common" or "in general use." The root meaning of "polite" is "polished"; "refined" is the best choice here.

33. C. Though the lines contain a metaphor in line 6 and describe the pagan gods as players in a farce in line 11, the extended figure in lines 6–11 compares the words, which have fallen to low uses, with the once-revered pagan gods, who have been trivialized. This figure of speech is a simile, since the phrase "recalls the fate" makes the comparison explicit.

34. D. The allusion to Macaulay does not tell us that he was guilty of (A) or even aware of (C) the misuse of "moral." George Eliot's use of this extravagant comment ridicules the historians' calling anyone who does not fit this description a "pure moral character."

35. D. The antecedent of "the one" is "morality" in line 26, while "the other" in line 28 refers to "religion" in line 26.

36. C. The historians may call a king guilty of injustice, treachery, greed, or deceit a "moral" man, so long as he is neither "lewd nor debauched."

37. E. In this phrase, the word "reaction" means "influence" or "effect." The central idea of the passage is that a debased language will lead to a debased way of thinking. Of the five choices, only D and E deal with language. Choice D complains of the degeneration of language ("our habitual phraseology") but does not, like E, deal with the effect of language ("affects") on thought ("the mass of minds").

38. A. The best choice here is "have difficulty finding." This sentence describes the difficulties of a mind already confused by contemporary science and philosophy (the passage was written at the time of the publication of the works of Darwin) undermined further by the loss of clear definitions of words like "moral" or "religious."

39. B. The point of the closing sentence is not that the businessman is immoral, but that the decline of language indicated by his being called "moral" points to an upcoming decline in ethical and religious discussion.

40. A. The best of the five choices is understatement. The use of "the augury is" and "not good," and the obvious error in the use of "moral" in lines 54–57 set against a phrase like "high ethical and theological disputation" make it clear that George Eliot is not really uncertain. None of the other four options is correct.

41. E. The word "perjury" (oath-breaking) is not an example of the weakened use of language.

42. D. The author states her thesis in the first sentence, and makes clear her disapproval ("a more melancholy irony").

43. B. The passage attacks the "shrunken meaning" of the words "morals" and "morality" so that dishonesty in the business world can be seen as irrelevant to "morals" or "morality." The example suggests that family values are more important than honesty.

Fourth Passage

The passage is from an 18th-century essay written by Joseph Addison.

44. B. The lines are an example of parallel construction; they employ a series of infinitive phrases, all dependent on the phrase "what an absurd thing it is . . . to pass . . . to observe . . . to make use." ‑

45. E. Though several of the answers are meanings that "discover" may have in other contexts, here the word means to disclose or reveal. The prefix "dis–" often means "not" or "un–." This 18th-century usage is similar to "uncover."

46. C. The sentence begins with a simile, introduced by "As." The figure compares "many eminent critics" and "many admirable buffoons." There is only one simile in the paragraph.

47. A. The passage begins with the criticism of the "ungenerous tempers" that are given to ridicule. The second paragraph further develops this idea.

48. C. The single long sentence in this paragraph contrasts and deplores the infrequent use of ridicule to mock "vice and folly" with the more common practice of jesting at the expense of "virtue and good sense."

49. D. The phrase makes clear what the author sees as the significance of the earlier phrase, "virtue and good sense."

50. B. The paragraph argues that ridicule would be useful if it were directed against "vice and folly," that is, immoral conduct and foolishness.

51. D. The best choice here is "instinctive capacity and acquired knowledge." The passage is contrasting the arts of the ancients that depend upon "genius" rather than "experience," the source of the inferior productions of the modern world.

52. A. In this sentence, "doggerel," "humour," "burlesque," and "raillery" are forms of comic speech or writing, but "embellishments" are not necessarily comic.

53. C. Since modern writers surpass the ancient in the "arts of ridicule," they should be more accomplished in satire, the only one of these forms that depends chiefly upon ridicule.

54. E. The passage supports the first four ideas, but it suggests that men and man's productions have declined since the "first ages of the world" produced "great souls and masterpieces of human nature."

55. A. Given his praise of the "first ages," the author would probably value the ancient epics more highly than the literary works of later periods.

Section II: Essay Questions

Question 1

Scoring Guide for Question 1 (Title IX Influence on Sports)

9 Essays that earn a score of 9 meet the criteria for essays that receive a score of 8. In addition, they are especially sophisticated in their use of language, explanation, and argument.

8 Successful

These essays respond to the prompt **successfully,** employing ideas from at least three of the sources from the prompt. They take a position that defends, challenges, or qualifies the claim that Title IX has allowed for more equality in the world of sports. They effectively argue the position and support the argument with appropriate evidence. The control of language is extensive and the writing errors are minimal.

7 These essays meet the criteria for essays that receive a score of 6 but provide more depth and strength to the argument and evidence. The prose style is mature and shows a wide control over language.

6 Satisfactory

These essays respond to the prompt **satisfactorily.** Using at least three of the sources from the prompt, these essays take a position that defends, challenges, or qualifies the claim that Title IX has allowed for more equality in the world of sports. The position is adequately argued with support from appropriate evidence, although without the precision and depth of top-scoring essays. The writing may contain minor errors in diction or in syntax, but the prose is generally clear.

5 These essays take a position that defends, challenges, or qualifies the claim that Title IX has allowed for more equality in the world of sports. It supports the position with generally appropriate evidence but may not adequately quote, either directly or indirectly, from three sources in the prompt. These essays may be inconsistent, uneven, or limited in the development of their argument. Although the writing usually conveys the writer's ideas and perspectives, it may demonstrate lapses in diction or syntax or an overly-simplistic style.

4 Inadequate

These essays respond to the prompt **inadequately.** They have difficulty taking a clear position that defends, challenges, or qualifies the claim that Title IX has allowed for more equality in the world of sports. The evidence may be insufficient, or may not utilize enough sources from the prompt. The prose conveys the writer's ideas but suggests immature control over the elements of effective writing.

3 These essays meet the criteria for a score of 4 but reveal less success in taking a position that defends, challenges, or qualifies the claim that Title IX has allowed for more equality in the world of sports. The presentation of evidence and arguments is unconvincing. These writers show little or no control over the elements of effective writing.

2 Little Success

These essays demonstrate **little success** at taking a position that defends, challenges, or qualifies the claim that Title IX has allowed for more equality in the world of sports and show little success in presenting it clearly and with appropriate evidence from the sources in the prompt. These essays may misunderstand the prompt, fail to establish a position with supporting evidence, or substitute a simpler task by replying tangentially with unrelated, erroneous, or unsuitable explanation, argument, and/or evidence. The prose frequently demonstrates consistent weaknesses in the conventions of effective writing.

1 These essays meet the criteria for a score of 2 but are undeveloped, especially simplistic in their explanation, argument, and/or evidence, or weak in their control of writing.

High-Scoring Essay

There is no doubt the United States is a great nation based on liberty and opportunity for the common man. Yet the survival of our nation owes much to the unrecognized work of countless enslaved Africans, struggling immigrants, and silently supportive wives and daughters. Fortunately, we have progressed much as a people since 1776 and now realize the debt we owe to these demographic groups. The United States, a country of liberty and equality, will lose its greatness if it fails to recognize and act upon the inequalities of the past. While not a perfect solution, Title IX is necessary because limited female participation in sports, like all social stereotypes, is rooted in cultural misconceptions that can be changed by giving individuals the opportunity to fight for themselves and prove their ability to succeed.

The "legacy of sexism" (Source A) hinders females in sports just as it does in education or business. Striving for equality in sports may be one step towards combating sexism. After all, it is easier to initiate cultural changes in the world of sports than the cut-throat business arena. Title IX is especially affective because, within this world of sports, colleges are the ideal place to begin change. Besides not having to worry about the pressures of supply and demand (Source B), colleges offer an atmosphere that is generally accepting of change. From the Civil Rights Movement to the Vietnam War protests, colleges have frequently been at the root of reform. But will these cultural changes come to be accepted on a larger scale? How will a society that holds "deeply imbedded ideas about power and strength and competition being masculine qualities" (Source D) ever come to fully support women's sports?

Many hope our society, through extended exposure to talented female athletes, will experience a gradual shift in values. This will take much time and patience, but it is possible. Fortunately, the human spirit is resilient and determined. As long as there is an opportunity to do so, women like Billie Jean King (Source E) will continue to fight for their rights. Title IX gives these women the ability to fight, to persevere, to succeed—without this law and its quotas there would be little hope. Because of Title IX, "only recently have women been able to compete in a

very public way, with established leagues, payrolls and plenty of endorsement opportunities" (Source D). Title IX has given women's athletics the credibility they need to attract attention and initiate change. With enough exposure people will begin to see that it is acceptable for a woman to show "her 'masculine' attributes" (Source D). Less than a century ago the Irish were banned from many local buildings. Yet today we pay no attention to whether someone is of Irish descent or not—we have assimilated them into our culture and have come to value the diversity they bring to it. While it may be harder to end gender stereotypes, for they are as old as the ages, it is possible. In fact things are looking up with women's soccer participation increasing ten-fold in under twenty years (Source A) and 3,433 new women's college teams since 1988 (Source F). The social norms which say, "that it is 'unfeminine' to play sports" (Source B), cannot long withstand the achievements of these young vibrant female athletes who are daily proving these stereotypes false.

The gradual dismantling of gender stereotypes will take dedication, patience, and hard work. Young women are largely responsible for their own advancement in this respect. However, they can be assured that Title IX will at least give them an opportunity to express their views and show their strengths. Blacks may have been given freedom and the right to vote shortly after the civil war but it was not until the Civil Rights Movement a hundred years later that real equality began to emerge. We must not let another injustice go unchallenged for so long. Let us hope that someday, "no person in the United States shall, on the basis of sex, be excluded from participation in, be denied the benefits of, or be subjected to discrimination under any program or activity" (Source C).

Analysis of High-Scoring Essay

This intelligent essay immediately engages the reader with an introduction that provides a historical perspective of the many demographic groups whose diversity adds to America's greatness in underappreciated ways. The writer takes a clear stand that Title IX is necessary to provide opportunities for women to succeed. It may be too grandiose for the writer to claim that "the United States . . . will lose its greatness if it fails to recognize and act upon the inequalities of the past." Although the wording is perhaps questionable, the sentiment is valid. In addition, the writer effectively utilizes a pleasing turn of phrase with the alliterative "silently supporting" diction.

The next paragraph begins an astute and in-depth discussion of the issue, avoiding the overly idealistic or simplistic approaches that lower-scoring essays all too frequently take. Acknowledging that colleges traditionally serve as vehicles of societal change, the writer establishes that Title IX legislation sets into motion the modifications that can provide increased opportunities for women in the very institutions that can nurture such changes. The writer ends this paragraph well, with two thought-provoking questions as a setup for the discussion in the next paragraph.

The essay next displays its strongest paragraph, based on the universal truth that "the human spirit is resilient and determined," a notion that elevates the essay's ideas to a realm far beyond mere sports. This paragraph focuses on the idea that increased exposure to women's sports will in turn progressively help change society's views about women in many of life's arenas. Citing several sources from the prompt, this writer effectively documents many concrete examples of positive change in women's sports that are a direct result of Title IX legislation. However, the writer's statement that the

Irish were "banned from many local buildings" is open to a degree of criticism; the example is a bit too vague and not as clearly related to this topic as one might hope. At the same time, one can praise the writer for trying to bring in more historical references that relate to repressed groups in America. It would have been more successful if the writer had explained the context of this example and related it to women's sports more clearly, but let's not criticize too harshly!

The essay concludes with a mature outlook, the understanding that young females are still responsible for their own advancement, and that Title IX certainly gives them opportunities to succeed. While some may feel that Civil Rights issues have had more historical significance in our society than women's issues, the writer's claim that women still face "injustice" certainly brings credibility to the essay's position. In concluding with a direct reference to Source C, the actual words of the Title IX legislation, the writer finishes with a voice of authority and optimism. Overall, this essay is impressive with its comprehensive use of all six sources in the prompt, thus demonstrating that this writer can successfully absorb many different viewpoints, synthesize them, and then produce a coherent and convincing argument. The writer's style, crisp and clear, occasionally displays some delightful parallel structure that adds a pleasant rhythm to the essay. It clearly deserves its high score.

Medium to Low-Scoring

Title IX creates an inefficient bureaucracy that fails to address the real causes of sexism and instead creates problems in regulations and further inequalities.

Title IX provides opportunities to female athletes but at the expense of less well known male sports teams. Title IX, like so many laws, has good intentions but lacks the resources to back them up. It is not right that the University of Minnesota "axed its trophy winning men's gymnastic team (Source A)," simply because it needed to spend more money on women's sports to fulfill the quotas established by Title IX (Source B). If the government is going to require female sports quotas for all institutions "receiving Federal financial assistance (Source C)," it is going to have to fork up enough funds to support both men and women's sports alike. In 1994–5, two-hundred and seventeen new women's teams were created nation wide while only ninety male teams were (Source F). It is not right to try to improve the status of one group if it is detrimental to another.

Furthermore, it does no good for women to play sports if no one supports them. "There are fewer women involved in college athletics because women in general have historically been discouraged from participating in sports (Source B)." Government programs like Title IX are ineffective in changing our "legacy of sexism (Source B)." Instead, we must rely on the work of a dedicated few like famous woman professional tennis player, Billie Jean King (Source E). Motivated individuals and organizations are always more effective than government programs. For example, Martin Luther King Junior and the efforts of churches and community organizations accomplished much more in the fight for civil rights than did any government program since Reconstruction. There is no way that an impersonal bureaucracy can possibly, "produce positive social change (Source B)." These gender stereotypes are deeply rooted but will fade with time as more and more women make their way into the business world and prove themselves equal to men. The fight for gender equality in sports goes way beyond simply how many sports teams there are for women.

Title IX was created to fight sexism in sports yet it fails to address why this sexism exists. Meanwhile it is creating further divisions in sports between popular sports, like football, and lesser-known sports, such as gymnastics, by cutting funding for men's sports. Title IX is creating more complicated problems than effective solutions.

Analysis of Medium to Low-Scoring Essay

This essay tries to present an argument opposing Title IX, but because of its poor organization, simplistic thinking, and lapses in logic, it does not convince the reader. The introduction is undeveloped, simply stating the writer's thesis that Title IX creates regulation problems that result in more inequalities. The writer's phrasing also presents problems. The idea that Title IX's bureaucracy "fails to address the real causes of sexism," assumes that, in this specific Title IX legislation, the government *should* address the causes of sexism, which is certainly a questionable assertion. The reader is forced to wonder why the writer thinks the legislation itself is the proper venue to address the causes of sexism, or question whether these causes can, indeed, be clarified.

The second paragraph suffers from a continued lack of clear organization. The writer attempts to discuss two diverse ideas but ends up muddling them together. The writer tries to connect (1) the losses in men's sports caused by Title IX with (2) the lack of federal funding for this legislation. The first example, that the University of Minnesota dropped its men's gymnastics programs, could provide support for the writer's argument, but instead it is left dangling, as the writer all-too-quickly moves on to the next claim, that the government must "fork up enough funds" for both men's and women's sports programs. The writer appears unaware of the logical implications of this simplistic argument and how little relation it bears to the original intent of this legislation. Such one-dimensional thinking appears frequently in medium- to low-scoring essays. The final sentence of this paragraph also displays flawed logic. The oversimplified statement that "it is not right to try to improve the status of one group if it is detrimental to another" seems to show that the writer is confused at a very basic level. The logical conclusion of this idea is that progress itself is impossible, because the writer insists that no group can *ever* suffer detriment even for the greater good of society.

The third paragraph begins with two unrelated sentences. The first contains the already questionable idea that women should not play in sports "if no one supports them." Next, the writer drops in a quotation from one of the sources, a quotation indicating that an important rationale for Title IX is that women have historically been dissuaded from sports participation. But without integrating this quotation into the surrounding ideas, the writer leaves it isolated and unexplained. The Billy Jean King example has merit and potential, but it is used in such a vague and unsuccessful manner that it provides only negligible support for the writer's point that Title IX is ineffective. The writer next makes an absolute claim, that individuals and organizations are *always* more effective than governments at accomplishing change. Surely this black-or-white statement cannot be accurate, and demonstrates a common verbal fallacy, the use of absolute words such as "always," "all," "never," and "only," which are imprecise and so frequently misused. Instead of an absolute, the use of a qualifying word like "frequently," or "often" is generally more accurate. Next, the writer's example of Martin Luther King is one that could perhaps provide support for the thesis, but it is presented in an unconvincing manner. Arguable as the writer's claim is, the writer never explains how the Civil Rights Movement is related to Title IX. While the writer earns praise for trying to show a greater awareness of the world, this idea's presentation limits its persuasion. Notice that the writer asserts yet another implausible absolute phrase in the next sentence: "There is no way that an impersonal bureaucracy can possibly, 'produce positive social change.'" These statements are riddled with logical flaws, such as assuming bureaucracies are "impersonal" and cannot possibly produce any good. This writer needs to devote much more time to considering the ramifications of the essay's ideas and the accuracy of its phrasing. The paragraph ends with a completely unwarranted conclusion. After discussing inequities in women's sports, the paragraph jumps to the assertion that "these gender stereotypes . . . will fade" as women prove themselves in the workplace. The reader is left wondering how the writer reached this unjustified conclusion.

The final paragraph continues the faults of the essay, bringing up new ideas that seem unrelated to what has been stated previously and making claims that are not substantiated. Overall, this writer needs to focus on the topic much more clearly and then think through his or her ideas and logical conclusions before writing. The logical flaws and gaps reveal muddled thinking and result in an unconvincing argument. This is typical in lower-scoring essays; writers too often jump to a conclusion and then spend the entire essay trying to defend it without pausing to consider if their examples are indeed supporting the conclusions they are trying to prove. This essay would benefit greatly from clearer thinking and stronger organization.

Question 2

Scoring Guide for Question 2 (Mary Oliver)

9 Essays earning a score of 9 meet the criteria for essays that are scored an 8 and, in addition, are especially full or apt in their analysis. They frequently reveal particularly remarkable control of language.

8 Successful

Top-scoring essays **successfully** analyze how Oliver uses metaphor to create her opinion about writing poetry. These high-quality essays refer to the text concretely or abstractly and show a clear understanding of how Oliver's rhetorical devices combine to create effect. These essays are well-developed in their presentation of ideas and show outstanding organization. Although these essays may contain minor errors, the prose demonstrates an ability to control a wide range of writing elements and a flair for sophistication.

7 Essays earning a score of 7 fit the description of essays that are scored a 6 but provide more complete analysis and a more mature prose style.

6 Satisfactory

Essays that score in the upper level **satisfactorily** analyze Oliver's language and how it generates effect. Typically, these essays use the text well, either directly or indirectly, to help develop ideas, and they clearly and logically connect any textual evidence to the writer's thoughts. While these high-scoring essays explore Oliver's rhetoric and attitude about writing poetry well, they may not be as perceptive or thorough as the top-scoring essays. They are effectively developed and clearly organized. A few minor lapses in diction or syntax may be evident; however, the prose is well written enough to convey the ideas well.

5 Essays earning a score of 5 adequately analyze the rhetoric Oliver uses, and may attempt to connect her language to her attitude, but their insights may be more pedestrian, more obvious. Quite often their development is limited by weak textual evidence, simplistic ideas, over-reliance on paraphrasing, or a combination of all three. The focus may be superficial. While the writing may generally convey ideas decently, lapses in written English may be present or persistent.

4 Inadequate

Lower-scoring essays **inadequately** respond to the topic. Their analysis of Oliver's rhetorical strategies is usually too brief. They may misunderstand or misrepresent Oliver's metaphor, or merely paraphrase her ideas. Development and/or organization may be flawed. The prose may convey ideas but may hint at immaturity in control of written English. Simplistic ideas coupled with a simplistic style may characterize low-scoring essays.

3 Essays earning a score of 3 meet the criteria for a score of 4 but demonstrate less understanding of how the metaphor connects to attitude. These essays may show less control over the elements of writing.

2 Little Success

The lowest-scoring essays demonstrate **little success** in analyzing Oliver's central metaphor or any other rhetorical devices. They may ignore or pay limited attention to her techniques. They may try to discuss her attitude about writing poetry, but may not demonstrate how her language presents that attitude. Often these essays rely on paraphrasing throughout. The prose frequently reveals consistent weaknesses in writing, severely limited development and organization, and poor control over mechanics.

1 These poorly written essays meet the criteria for a score of 2 but are undeveloped, especially simplistic in their analysis, weak in their control of language.

High-Scoring Essay

Mechanistic diction, a tautly constructed metaphor of linguistic carpentry, and the powerlessness of personification convey how the author's instinctive impulse to write poetry paralyzes her.

In a self-deprecating way, the author foils her adept, nimble-fingered handyman wunderkind's mysterious ambition and underlying impetus "in building things," which, for her, is analogous to the fabrication of a physical entity, an act that renders her ". . . a grander [human being]; a surprise to us and even more to [her]self." For holding together this desire to hammer, glue, and yoke her yearning to create houses of concrete and not just

285

abodes of fiction are subtle rivets of mechanistic diction. Indeed, what the author does in forming fiction approximates the figure and shape of a plot, plied from "boards of a certain breadth and length and nails." The word "boards" connotes manufacturing of predestined materials, existentially directed toward a larger purpose than their unadorned, plank-wood form. As "board," "measuring tape," and "mallets" hearken visions of splinter-carrying, unhewed resources, so too is writing representative of potential constructs, pregnant with the possibility of imperfection, equally possibly a "small table with one leg turned in slightly" or a miraculous model house. Yet the promise of "contemplation, joy, grief, prayer, or terror" pushes the author to pursue woodworking with a fervor unchecked by her mediocrity. The "stiffness" of the fingers that the author depicts suggests the inflexible nature of writing poetry that possesses her; it stuns her senses into submission, makes her eye refuse to "switch easily from near to far," fatigues and ossifies her fingers. The alliterative descriptive "clamoring and colorful" force of searching for words depicts how noisy the process of writing is internally, how it acts like a tool, a hammer, in untapping the visions inside. Indeed, the imagery of the whole passage fills the senses with mechanical sounds and sensations, emphasizing the central metaphor of construction.

For Oliver, poetry writing translates into a metaphor of carpentry that is intrinsically intellectual. The implements needed for its internal foundation are understanding the perspicacity to know "the enclosure of my skills." Comparing herself to other artistic laymen, the author elucidates the unique challenge of writing poetry. Instead of fermenting external activity through introspective investigation, it begets "at moments of contemplation, joy, grief, prayer, or terror . . . the posture of deliberate or hapless inaction." Likening herself metaphorically to a carpenter, "a poor poet laborer," she mimics in the reader the sentiment of unjust powerlessness by glorifying the ecstasy of how "the dancer dances, the painter dips and

lifts . . . the composer reaches . . . across the octaves." As this exultative action occurs, the poet "sits . . . scribbles some words," condemned to condense the mind's excitement to the twitching of three fingers. In this way, the author hints that writing poetry engenders this unspoken torment—the impatience of a "mind so hotly fired and . . . body so long quiescent." No matter what the poetry constructs externally, internally it ferments the disharmony of being dream-ridden, of being inactive—a state contrary to the carpenter's impulsive action.

But what can the author stymie her linguistic frustration with but with a physical reaction—building a tangible construct with nails and hammers, pounding out affirmation of her intrinsic intellectual insights, translating an image into something like a "small table." Surprisingly, what the author insinuates is that for all of its paralysis, the act of writing poetry itself wrests a personificative power over us, making for us an ephemeral flash "beyond what [we] believed [ourselves] to be." Personifying writing as a conquering agent, the writer depicts how writing invades the writer's mind like a phantom, appearing "on my mind a form," causing physical symptoms of its visitation, "stiffness . . . a refusal of my eyes to switch easily." For a small physical price, the act of writing unleashes the possibilities of bypassing a human state—instead of being consumed with action, we transcend it into mystifying lethargy. The author even endues writing "with wings" of language, making the labor of composition a figure like a bird. At the same time, writing is metaphorically painted in the screaming of the "teeth of the saw . . . explosions of the hammer . . . shrieks of screws" because the poet can be paralyzed into poetic creation by monstrous clamor of her own imagination. However, the ultimate form that writing poetry assumes is one of inner peace; it takes the form of "a flow," a stream that "appears in my mind" and ultimately one that "will demand action." Just as a carpenter will build a house of beauty, a poet will create a work of art.

Analysis of the High-Scoring Essay

The writer of this high-scoring essay clearly articulates his or her understanding of how Oliver's metaphor and other rhetorical devices combine to create her attitude about writing poetry. It begins with a thesis, one that is promising. The reader is intrigued to discover what the writer will have to say about "mechanistic diction" and "the powerlessness of personification."

The first body paragraph centers on the mechanical imagery of the passage. The writer shows good insight into the sights and sounds, indeed the very feel, of housing construction and how these images connect to Oliver's metaphor about constructing poetry. The writer includes apt examples from the text and explains them unambiguously. This writer also shows promise in sentence construction, pleasing the reader with such creations as, "For holding together this desire to hammer, glue, and yoke her yearning to create houses of concrete and not just abodes of fiction are subtle rivets of mechanistic diction." The alliteration is pleasing to the ear, as is the connotation of "rivets" holding diction together.

The second body paragraph explores Oliver's metaphor that connects carpentry and poetry writing. The writer's insights are sophisticated and well founded in the text. As in the previous paragraph, this writer continues to demonstrate a sense of style, for example, beginning one sentence with "Comparing herself" and another with "Likening herself." This parallelism will not go unnoticed by an experienced reader.

The final paragraph explores the thesis idea of "the powerlessness of personification," perhaps the most interesting idea in the thesis. The student understands the subtleties of Oliver's language and how the personification not only, by definition, gives life to inanimate objects, but also adds to the poet's feeling of mediocrity or paralysis. The ideas are not only intriguing, but also convincing to the reader.

Ultimately, this essay deserves a high score. It is on topic throughout, and it shows superior organization and development. The writer indeed demonstrates the kind of thorough and thoughtful essay that can be produced in 40 minutes. Additionally, the writer's ability to present ideas with panache demonstrates the elegance that is often seen in top-scoring essays.

Medium-Scoring Essay

When somebody thinks a bit about the comparison, "building" a poem can be a lot like "building" a house. They both need to start with an idea and then "build" from there. In Mary Oliver's essay, "Building the House," she uses precise diction, varied syntax, and metaphor to liken writing poetry to constructing a house.

At first, the atmosphere of tranquility builds as Oliver uses careful-connoting sounding words to describe the effort of constructing "a boat, fence, kitchen cabinets, a table, a house." Words like "serene", "assured", "right", and "careful" show the measured, articulate labor in constructing poetry "at the slowest amble" initially. There persists an attitude of awe in these adjectives, the sense that the builder of compositions "is a surprise to himself" because he knows "the enclosure of (his) skills", and metes out his motions with his limitations marked in his mind. "Unfazed" and "aligned" also dwell upon the writer's instinct to rely on his own clear-minded, lucid independence, to envision "a form in his mind . . . to boards of a certain length" unmoved by the outside factors, "the niceties of woodworking" or the fact that he "has never built anything perfectly." The diction blueprints how Oliver explains her motivation for writing poetry as an effort that "surprises" herself, that she meticulously learns "at a careful place" and constructs painstakingly with each word.

The varied syntax deepens the imagery of Oliver's effort of writing poetry to the construction of a house. At the beginning, the sentences are interrupted by dashes; thoughts interrupted by personal insight and detail that inform us about "—what (the builder) cares for best—"

and challenging questions "—will not the use of words come easier at last . . . ?" Oliver forces the reader to break a train of thought, and the author suggests that the process of writing parallels this pause-ridden path, one that is roughened by breaths and time, one slowed down by the need to begin at a slow pace and form a firm foundation. Next, the essay evolves, into a first person commentary with a more conventional subject-verb flow, but still interlaced with intruding alien subject-verb phrases like "there appeared in my mind a form." These abrupt cadences in a sense nail together the flowing narrative walls by offering an objective sense of the author's powerlessness to the "form" imagined and "time" that brings "obstacles and spread them" before her.

The clever metaphorical construction of essay writing evolves through simple syntactic progression and the meticulous diction from the simple boards of the words to the "small table" of furniture of a completed phrase. The imagery in this selection filters through how the poet's mentally acts like an architect. The poet's internal labor sensually evokes the ruckus of constructing an edifice, "the teeth of the saw, explosions of the hammer, and the little shrieks of the screws" indivisible from woodworking. The pencil is compared to a hammer "which yearly grows smaller and smaller" as the poet "sits . . . scribbles . . . words upon a page." The essay-writing process is something that originates of "a form" like a house, miraculously of "boards of a certain breadth and length and nails," a form taut and mysteriously that possesses an essence that the poet employs the hammer and tools of language to realize.

Analysis of the Medium-Scoring Essay

This essay presents some interesting insights and it attempts to offer ideas in an analytical fashion, but it basically falls flat in both its presentation and its wording. The introductory sentences are fairly bland, and the thesis merely restates what the essay topic does; namely, it "uses . . . diction . . . syntax, and metaphor" to show how writing poetry parallels building a house. The thesis ignores the author's *attitude* about writing poetry, an important aspect of the original topic question.

The first body paragraph offers some good ideas from the writer, and it attempts to clarify that the author's attitude toward writing poetry is ambiguous or negative. However, the student's analysis is fairly superficial. The writer explains the obvious connotations of words that are listed from the essay. Also disconcerting is the fact that the thesis claims the essay will analyze "precise" diction, but this particular adjective is largely ignored.

The next paragraph contains some good insights about Oliver's syntax and provides some pleasing syntax in turn (for instance, in the sentence in which the writer explores Oliver's use of the dash). Similarly, the last sentence in this paragraph has a delightful play on words with the phrasing ". . . cadences . . . nail together . . . the narrative walls," but the rest of the sentence falls apart, both in its cadence and in its simplistic analysis.

The last paragraph of this essay turns into mere paraphrasing that simply does not fulfill the requirements of the topic. By this point, the writer should be addressing *how* Oliver's metaphor expresses her attitude; unfortunately, the writer seems to have forgotten that task.

Compounding the lapses in addressing the topic, this writer's command of English is flawed. Excessive diction and errors in mechanics become disconcerting. Unidiomatic expressions, such as "something that originates *of* a form" or using the wrong part of speech, such as "a form taut and *mysteriously*" both distract the reader and diminish the writer's force. The many punctuation errors in quotation usage and apostrophes also divert the reader's attention. Ultimately, the writer's insightful ideas deserve a stronger, clearer presentation.

Question 3

Scoring Guide for Question 3 (Anwar Accawi)

9 Essays earning a score of 9 meet the criteria for essays that are scored an 8 and, in addition, are especially full or apt in their understanding of how rhetorical devices connect to Accawi's opinion about time. They frequently reveal particularly remarkable control of language.

8 Successful

Astute and discerning essays earn the top score. These perceptive essays **successfully** understand the rhetorical devices that Accawi uses as he develops his opinion about how irrelevant the concept of time, as we understand it in the Western world, can be. These essays use the text well, both in a direct and indirect fashion, and they succinctly explain how Accawi's language establishes his attitude. Development and organization are outstanding in top-scoring essays. The writer's ability to use language effectively is demonstrated by a sophisticated style and vocabulary, although the essay may not be without minor flaws.

7 Essays earning a score of 7 fit the description of essays that are scored a 6 but provide more complete and clear connections supported with strong evidence. Often, they exhibit a more mature prose style.

6 Satisfactory

Upper-level essays **satisfactorily** understand how Accawi's language creates meaning and attitude. These essays refer to text frequently and understand how to connect textual examples to the writer's ideas; however, those connections or insights may not be as deep or perceptive as the top-scoring essays. Upper-level essays usually show strong development and organization of ideas. While minor errors in the command of written English may be present, they do not cloud the writer's ability to make meaning clear.

5 These adequate essays may attempt to complete the topic, but fall short of analysis. The essays may paraphrase the action in the excerpt instead of connecting rhetorical devices to attitude. Ideas are frequently superficial and obvious in mid-scoring essays. Development and organization may be reasonable, but not as successful as in higher-scoring essays; too often the mid-level essays are simply too brief. The writing may be sufficient enough to convey meaning, but immature command of English conventions may be demonstrated.

4 Inadequate

These lower-half essays **inadequately** discuss the author's attitude or may only paraphrase the passage. These writers may miss the author's implied attitude about time or may not understand how to connect language to attitude. Inconsistent control over language may be visible, distracting the reader from the essay's ideas. Frequently, low-scoring essays wrap simple ideas in a simple package, and development and organization are equally unsophisticated.

3 Essays earning a score of 3 meet the criteria for a score of 4 but demonstrate less understanding of the author's attitude. These essays may show less control over the elements of writing.

2 Little Success

Essays earning the lowest score have **little success** in responding to the topic. They may misread the passage or misconstrue it to the reader. They may pay limited attention to Accawi's language or offer nothing but paraphrasing. Quite often, these lowest-scoring essays are unacceptably brief; ideas are not explored, and examples are not provided. Continual weaknesses in grammar and mechanics may demonstrate a lack of control over the conventions of written English, and vocabulary usage may be overly simplistic.

1 These poorly written essays meet the criteria for a score of 2 but are undeveloped, especially simplistic in their ideas and evidence, and weak in their control of language.

High-Scoring Essay

Time, as a human invention, a theoretical concept, may not be deemed as significant a creation to some as it is to others. In the excerpt from Anwar Accawi's "The Telephone," the narrator's attitude towards time encompasses the accumulated influences of his society and cultural background, an attitude which views time as a spiritual entity and a representation of the ever-present past. This attitude is displayed through the author's implementation of contrasting imagery, forceful connotation, and the repetition of ideas.

Accawi contrasts manmade and natural imagery to express the disparity between his personal understanding of seasons and cycles and the modern idea of time. He creates a parallel between himself and the natural world by comparing his understanding of time with that of Iraqi geese and ewes. Additionally, Accawi describes the natural "rocky mountains of Sidon" as being "terraced," obviously by man. The narrator's reaction to time is an innate, primitive perception, an almost primal behavior developed from an intuition of the cycles of life and the passing of seasons. The manmade and natural world are also juxtaposed as he pits such massive natural events (that he ironically classifies mildly as "milestones") as "earthquakes and droughts and floods and locusts and pestilences" against minute manmade objects like a suede glove or a tobacco pouch. Nature obviously takes a much larger role in the passage of time as man's puny gloves and pouches will not stand the test of time. The imagery of the "old sock stuffed with other, much older socks" further develops the relationship of the individual with time. The ball of socks represents the intertwining of time; the past is the present, and there is no differentiation between the two except that one may feel that which is in the present. Even though it is intangible, the past remains always in existence.

This basic association with the passage of time is again displayed through Accawi's employment of powerful and religious connotation, such as the narrator's use of the sun and God to determine time's passage. The narrator asserts that "the only timepiece [they] had need of then was the sun" and that theirs was a "natural—or, rather, a divine—calendar in God. The sun not only may be used to establish the passage of hours in the day but also carries with it the connotation of warmth, contentedness, and spirituality.

The sun possesses a sense of power that the mechanical precision of the watch cannot. Furthermore, the religious, spiritual connotation of God overshadows the limited capability of the calendar. The passage of time is portrayed as spiritual and symbolic, not to be quantified by technological advances, after all, "Allah himself set down the milestones. . . ." In the measurement of time, the emotional qualities of past and present seem disregarded.

Accawi again represents this relationship between the past and the present in his repetition of phrases, demonstrating the repetitious pervasiveness of time. The narrator himself refers to a specific period of time as "when [his family] had just returned home from Syria at the end of the Big War," demonstrating that like those before him, he still adheres to his notion of time. The narrator then proceeds to recount a discussion with his grandmother in which she speaks of a moment in time as "shortly after the big snow" and "about the time [they] had the big earthquake." This referral to time in terms of events emphasizes the fact that occurrences influence a person's life. It demonstrates the significance that memories have in people's lives. There exists this repetition of the past in every new occurrence, every word spoken, as the past influences the future. While the concept of time attempts to label specific moments, it is impossible to differentiate the present, past, and future because they are all intertwined in each moment.

The excerpt from "The Telephone" emphasizes the impact of the past, present, and future. Accawi demonstrates that the manmade notion of time is an imposed invention, able to categorize events but unable to decipher their spiritual, emotional significance.

Analysis of the High-Scoring Essay

This excellent essay indeed demonstrates clear understanding of Accawi's multifaceted attitude toward time, comprehending that it is composed of spiritual, cultural, and individual perceptions. The introduction is specifically on topic, and, although it presents a somewhat formulaic three-part thesis statement, it is accurate and it lets the reader know what to expect: a discussion of "contrasting imagery, forceful connotation, and the repetition of ideas."

The first body paragraph examines the juxtaposition of manmade and natural imagery, amply backing up the concept with a sufficient number of relevant examples. Instead of simply walking through the essay chronologically, the student is able to pair examples from the excerpt's early paragraphs and later portions. This demonstrates that the student has an excellent grasp of detail and can gracefully articulate ideas about the particulars. The student's idea about the "old sock stuffed with other, much older socks" is an unusual one, a concept that most test takers will not observe. This kind of tangible perception separates the high-scoring essays from the medium, especially when presented with panache.

The middle body paragraph presents the force of the spiritual connotations in the passage and the direct references to God and Allah. The writer explains how Accawi's divine language takes on a mystic quality, giving time an even more elevated association than mankind's time-keeping devices. This idea unmistakably parallels Accawi's attitude and demonstrates how a strong writer combines analytical ideas with textual evidence.

The final body paragraph examines Accawi's use of repetition. This paragraph's wording may need some refinement, however. Notice how the writer claims Accawi repeats "phrases" but offers no specific examples from the passage. It appears that the writer meant that Accawi repeats *concepts and ideas,* not actual phrases. Still, the essay is executed well, and it sticks to the topic of how Accawi's attitude is developed through his language and style. An AP reader will be generous enough not to penalize the writer for this wording mishap that was likely due to the pressure of time.

Even though this is a high-scoring essay, the conclusion can be viewed as a mere summary of the essay; it offers no new food for thought. However, it does finish with an important statement about time that is true to Accawi's message. Overall, this essay is a very good one; it stays on topic throughout, it is clearly organized and well developed, and it uses language with a flair. It has very few flaws, something any AP reader will immediately excuse. The student's ideas are both articulate and sensitive to Accawi's subtleties. These qualities distinguish the essay and ensure its high score.

Medium-Scoring Essay

In the excerpt from *The Telephone*, Anwar Accawi uses imagery, anecdotes, and simile to show the author's discouragement towards measuring time with instruments such as watches and calendars and his preference towards remembering more emotional past events.

To lesson the relative importance of measured time, the narrator asserts that the sun is his timepiece and God is his calendar. This image of the sun evokes a sense of vague time, which contrasts the exactness of a ticking watch. This precision strips time of the emotion, memories, and feelings. In addition, the image of God, as a supreme omniscient being knowledgeable of both past and future, overshadows the need for the accuracy of calendars by which to remember things. The watch and calendar lack the emotions evoked by the powerful images of the sun and God.

Accawi also uses anecdotes to display the narrator's dissatisfaction with measuring time. The narrator's conversation with his grandmother expresses the idea that time should be expressed in terms of events. Events should therefore be emphasized instead of dates, hours, and minutes, which are too precise and unemotional. The narrator's story of oranges and fish covering the ground shows also that there are events that become a part of society, of memory, and which must be acknowledged as contributing to the present and future through their being mentioned in relation to the present.

Simile is similarly used to depict the importance of expressing the passage of time in terms of events. The author uses the simile of kissing the elderly woman, Im Khalil, as being "like kissing a soft suede glove that had been soaked with sweat and then left in a dark closet for a season." This usage represents the fact that time is found in the feeling of objects, the remembrance of events, not in intangible concepts. It is found in nostalgic memories and the passing of seasons, not in the ticking of clocks or in the boxes of a calendar.

Anwar Accawi, through imagery, anecdotes, and simile, expresses the beauty in life's events and the relative unimportance of the precise measurement of time. Simply because it is possible to measure the passage of time does not mean that it is personally fulfilling to do so.

Analysis for the Medium-Scoring Essay

Frequently, an average essay shows that although the writer may be able to read a passage accurately, he or she fails to delve deeper than the obvious; this essay demonstrates just that trait. It is on topic, but it proceeds in such a simplistic fashion that the reader keeps wanting to say, "Yeah, but so what?" while reading the essay. The introduction is brief and one-dimensional; whereas a more sophisticated writer will notice that Accawi's attitude is complex, this writer merely points out that Accawi prefers remembering emotionally tinged events instead of using watches to measure time. To prove this simple concept, the essay will examine "imagery, anecdotes, and simile."

The body paragraphs all briefly explore these three devices, but they offer very few examples from the text, and they develop no more than surface-level analysis in the process. The first body paragraph simply points out that the sun is an image Accawi uses that is more imprecise than a watch, and that the image of God "overshadows the need for . . . calendars." While this paragraph has two examples, it merely paraphrases Accawi's idea without analyzing *how* his language creates attitude. The writer's concept about Accawi's attitude is essentially accurate, but simultaneously simplistic and undeveloped.

The second body paragraph follows the same format as the first and reproduces the same problems. Two examples of anecdote, the conversation with the narrator's grandmother and the story of the oranges and fish, are retold, but to no great end; just like the first body paragraph, the writer has nothing more significant to say than that Accawi has "dissatisfaction with measuring time."

The last body paragraph is the weakest of all; it shows that the writer noticed one simile while reading and not much more. The writer's reason for using this one simile is the same as in the previous paragraphs; by this point the technique produces boredom in the reader.

Ultimately, an AP reader can reward this essay for essentially being organized and remaining on topic. However, working against a higher score is the fact that it does not see the complexity of Accawi's attitude, nor does it develop paragraphs with analytical integrity. It uses no quotations from the excerpt, which makes it much harder to examine how Accawi's language works. The essay also suffers from simplicity in the writer's own diction; the minimalist presentation mirrors the minimal idea. If the essay were to develop the ideas more deeply and then support them with stronger examples, while showing more sophistication in presentation, it would receive a much higher score.

Answer Sheet for Practice Test 6

Remove this sheet and use it to mark your answers.
Answer sheets for "Section II: Essays" can be found at the end of the book.

Section I
Multiple-Choice Questions

First Passage

1 Ⓐ Ⓑ Ⓒ Ⓓ Ⓔ
2 Ⓐ Ⓑ Ⓒ Ⓓ Ⓔ
3 Ⓐ Ⓑ Ⓒ Ⓓ Ⓔ
4 Ⓐ Ⓑ Ⓒ Ⓓ Ⓔ
5 Ⓐ Ⓑ Ⓒ Ⓓ Ⓔ
6 Ⓐ Ⓑ Ⓒ Ⓓ Ⓔ
7 Ⓐ Ⓑ Ⓒ Ⓓ Ⓔ
8 Ⓐ Ⓑ Ⓒ Ⓓ Ⓔ
9 Ⓐ Ⓑ Ⓒ Ⓓ Ⓔ
10 Ⓐ Ⓑ Ⓒ Ⓓ Ⓔ
11 Ⓐ Ⓑ Ⓒ Ⓓ Ⓔ
12 Ⓐ Ⓑ Ⓒ Ⓓ Ⓔ
13 Ⓐ Ⓑ Ⓒ Ⓓ Ⓔ
14 Ⓐ Ⓑ Ⓒ Ⓓ Ⓔ

Second Passage

15 Ⓐ Ⓑ Ⓒ Ⓓ Ⓔ
16 Ⓐ Ⓑ Ⓒ Ⓓ Ⓔ
17 Ⓐ Ⓑ Ⓒ Ⓓ Ⓔ
18 Ⓐ Ⓑ Ⓒ Ⓓ Ⓔ
19 Ⓐ Ⓑ Ⓒ Ⓓ Ⓔ
20 Ⓐ Ⓑ Ⓒ Ⓓ Ⓔ
21 Ⓐ Ⓑ Ⓒ Ⓓ Ⓔ
22 Ⓐ Ⓑ Ⓒ Ⓓ Ⓔ
23 Ⓐ Ⓑ Ⓒ Ⓓ Ⓔ
24 Ⓐ Ⓑ Ⓒ Ⓓ Ⓔ
25 Ⓐ Ⓑ Ⓒ Ⓓ Ⓔ
26 Ⓐ Ⓑ Ⓒ Ⓓ Ⓔ
27 Ⓐ Ⓑ Ⓒ Ⓓ Ⓔ
28 Ⓐ Ⓑ Ⓒ Ⓓ Ⓔ
29 Ⓐ Ⓑ Ⓒ Ⓓ Ⓔ

Third Passage

30 Ⓐ Ⓑ Ⓒ Ⓓ Ⓔ
31 Ⓐ Ⓑ Ⓒ Ⓓ Ⓔ
32 Ⓐ Ⓑ Ⓒ Ⓓ Ⓔ
33 Ⓐ Ⓑ Ⓒ Ⓓ Ⓔ
34 Ⓐ Ⓑ Ⓒ Ⓓ Ⓔ
35 Ⓐ Ⓑ Ⓒ Ⓓ Ⓔ
36 Ⓐ Ⓑ Ⓒ Ⓓ Ⓔ
37 Ⓐ Ⓑ Ⓒ Ⓓ Ⓔ
38 Ⓐ Ⓑ Ⓒ Ⓓ Ⓔ
39 Ⓐ Ⓑ Ⓒ Ⓓ Ⓔ
40 Ⓐ Ⓑ Ⓒ Ⓓ Ⓔ
41 Ⓐ Ⓑ Ⓒ Ⓓ Ⓔ

Fourth Passage

42 Ⓐ Ⓑ Ⓒ Ⓓ Ⓔ
43 Ⓐ Ⓑ Ⓒ Ⓓ Ⓔ
44 Ⓐ Ⓑ Ⓒ Ⓓ Ⓔ
45 Ⓐ Ⓑ Ⓒ Ⓓ Ⓔ
46 Ⓐ Ⓑ Ⓒ Ⓓ Ⓔ
47 Ⓐ Ⓑ Ⓒ Ⓓ Ⓔ
48 Ⓐ Ⓑ Ⓒ Ⓓ Ⓔ
49 Ⓐ Ⓑ Ⓒ Ⓓ Ⓔ
50 Ⓐ Ⓑ Ⓒ Ⓓ Ⓔ
51 Ⓐ Ⓑ Ⓒ Ⓓ Ⓔ
52 Ⓐ Ⓑ Ⓒ Ⓓ Ⓔ
53 Ⓐ Ⓑ Ⓒ Ⓓ Ⓔ
54 Ⓐ Ⓑ Ⓒ Ⓓ Ⓔ
55 Ⓐ Ⓑ Ⓒ Ⓓ Ⓔ

CUT HERE

Practice Test 6

Section I: Multiple-Choice Questions

Time: 60 minutes

55 questions

Directions: This section consists of selections from prose works and questions on their content, style, and form. Read each selection carefully. Choose the best answer of the five choices.

Questions 1–14. Read the following passage carefully before you begin to answer the questions.

First Passage

We have met here today to discuss our rights and wrongs, civil and political, and not, as some have supposed, to go into the detail of social life alone. We do not propose to petition the legislature to make
(5) our husbands just, generous, and courteous, to seat every man at the head of a cradle, and to clothe every woman in male attire. None of these points, however important they may be considered by leading men, will be touched in this convention. As to their cos-
(10) tume, the gentlemen need feel no fear of our imitating that, for we think it in violation of every principle of taste, beauty, and dignity; notwithstanding all the contempt cast upon our loose, flowing garments, we still admire the graceful folds and con-
(15) sider our costume far more artistic than theirs. Many of the nobler sex seem to agree with us in this opin- ion, for the bishops, priests, judges, barristers, and lord mayors of the first nation on the globe, and the Pope of Rome, with his cardinals, too, all wear the
(20) loose flowing robes, thus tacitly acknowledging that the male attire is neither dignified nor imposing. No, we shall not molest you in your philosophical exper- iments with stocks,[1] pants, high-heeled boots, and Russian belts. Yours be the glory to discover, by per-
(25) sonal experience, how long the kneepan can resist the terrible strapping down which you impose, in how short time the well-developed muscles of the throat can be reduced to mere threads by the con- stant pressure of the stock,[2] how high the heel of a
(30) boot must be to make a short man tall, and how tight the Russian belt may be drawn and yet have wind enough left to sustain life.

But we are assembled to protest against a form of government existing without the consent of the
(35) governed—to declare our right to be free as man is free, to be represented in the government which we are taxed to support, to have such disgraceful laws as give man the power to chastise and imprison his wife, to take the wages which she earns, the property
(40) which she inherits, and, in case of separation, the children of her love; laws which make her the mere dependent on his bounty. It is to protest against such unjust laws as these that we are assembled today, and to have them, if possible, forever erased from
(45) our statute books, deeming them a shame and a dis- grace to a Christian republic in the nineteenth cen- tury. We have met

> *To uplift woman's fallen divinity*
> *Upon an even pedestal with man's.*

(50) And strange as it may seem to many, we now de- mand our right to vote according to the declaration of the government under which we live. This right no one pretends to deny. We need not prove ourselves equal to Daniel Webster to enjoy this privilege, for
(55) the ignorant Irishman in the ditch has all the civil rights he has. We need not prove our muscular power equal to this same Irishman to enjoy this privilege, for the most tiny, weak, ill-shaped stripling of twenty-one has all the civil rights of the Irishman.
(60) We have no objections to discuss the question of equality, for we feel that the weight of argument lies wholly with us, but we wish the question of equality kept distinct from the question of rights, for the proof of the one does not determine the truth of the other.
(65) All white men in this country have the same rights, however they may differ in mind, body, or estate.

---

[1] stocks, line 23; 2. stock, line 29: a stock is a wide, stiff, necktie worn by men in the mid-nineteenth century.

GO ON TO THE NEXT PAGE

1. Which of the following words is used with two meanings?

   A. "rights" (line 1)
   B. "wrongs" (line 2)
   C. "seat" (line 5)
   D. "head" (line 6)
   E. "attire" (line 7)

2. The details of lines 5–7 ("to seat every man at the head of a cradle, and to clothe every woman in male attire") probably derive from

   A. the agenda of feminists seeking the franchise
   B. the arguments of men who oppose women's suffrage
   C. the creative imagination of the speaker
   D. the historically observed results of granting women the vote
   E. the classical ideal of society in which men and women are equal

3. Lines 17–21 advance the argument that

   A. the sexes achieve greater dignity by cross-dressing
   B. judges and clergymen wear flowing robes because this form of dress is traditional
   C. American lawyers and clergymen, as well as members of the Roman Catholic hierarchy, regard women's dress as dignified
   D. human value should not be judged by manner of dress
   E. women's clothing may be more imposing than men's

4. In the first paragraph, which of the following phrases is used ironically?

   A. "social life" (line 3)
   B. "male attire" (line 7)
   C. "every principle of taste, beauty, and dignity" (lines 11–12)
   D. "nobler sex" (line 16)
   E. "neither dignified nor imposing" (line 21)

5. In which of the following phrases in the first paragraph does the speaker use mock-serious diction for satiric effect?

   A. "with his cardinals, too" (line 19)
   B. "thus tacitly acknowledging" (line 20)
   C. "philosophical experiments" (lines 22–23)
   D. "well-developed muscles of the throat" (lines 27–28)
   E. "the constant pressure of the stock" (lines 28–29)

6. In lines 29–31, part of the comedy in the references to the "heel of a boot" and "the Russian belt" is due to the fact that

   A. they are worn by men to appear taller and thinner
   B. both men and women wear boots and belts
   C. women are more likely to dress to impress other women than to impress men
   D. men's clothes are, in fact, more comfortable to wear than women's
   E. the heels of women's shoes are usually higher than those of men's

7. The rhetorical purpose of the first paragraph of the passage is to

   A. introduce with examples the issues to be discussed in the second paragraph
   B. introduce lightly issues that will be seriously developed in the second paragraph
   C. comically present issues with which the serious second paragraph will not be concerned
   D. raise questions to which the second paragraph will give answers
   E. grant concessions to the opponents that the second paragraph will retract

8. In line 54 of the third paragraph, the author refers to Daniel Webster as

   A. a representative of American patriotism
   B. an example of a great orator
   C. a representative of the injustice of the American voting system
   D. an example of the male's superiority to the female
   E. a representative of intelligence

9. Together with lines 53–54 ("We need not prove ourselves . . ."), the argument in lines 56–59 ("We need not prove our . . .")

    A. repeats the idea of the sentence that precedes it

    B. raises possible objections to the idea of the sentence that precedes it

    C. appears to concede a point, but, in fact, does not

    D. demonstrates that the weak as well as the ignorant may vote

    E. is concerned with the question of rights rather than with the question of equality

10. The speaker wishes to keep "the question of equality distinct from the question of rights" (lines 62–63) because

    A. women cannot be equal to men until their rights are equal to men's

    B. though their equality may be doubted, there can be no doubt about women's being denied their rights

    C. the question of the equality of men and women must determine whether or not their civil rights should be the same

    D. she believes the question of equality has already been settled, but the question of rights has not

    E. she can see no real distinction between the two

11. The tone of the second paragraph can best be described as

    A. reasonable and disinterested

    B. soft spoken and confident

    C. dry and ironical

    D. angry and authoritative

    E. tactful and firm

12. Which of the following best describes the relationship between lines 33–49 (paragraph two) and lines 1–32 (paragraph one)?

    A. Lines 33–49 intensify the irony of lines 1–32.

    B. Lines 33–49 mark an important shift in the tone of the passage.

    C. Lines 33–49 introduce a prose style more dependent on concrete details.

    D. Lines 33–49 echo the tone of lines 1–32 but with greater restraint.

    E. Lines 33–49 present a more personal point of view than lines 1–32.

13. Which of the following rhetorical devices are used most frequently in the second paragraph?

    A. *ad hominem* arguments

    B. specialized legal diction

    C. simile and metaphor

    D. ironic understatements

    E. parallel constructions

14. The primary rhetorical purpose of the speaker of the passage is to

    A. reveal the injustice to women in the present laws

    B. report events as objectively as possible

    C. introduce and explain a complex issue

    D. discuss the common humanity of both men and women

    E. appeal to the gender prejudices of the audience

GO ON TO THE NEXT PAGE

Questions 15–29. Read the following passage carefully before you begin to answer the questions.

Second Passage

Everyone knows the popular conception of Florence Nightingale. The saintly, self-sacrificing woman, the delicate maiden of high degree who threw aside the pleasures of a life of ease to suc-
(5) cour the afflicted, the Lady with the Lamp, gliding through the horrors of the hospital at Scutari, and consecrating with the radiance of her goodness the dying soldier's couch—the vision is familiar to all. But the truth was different. The Miss Nightingale of
(10) fact was not as facile fancy painted her. She worked in another fashion, and toward another end; she moved under the stress of an impetus which finds no place in the popular imagination. A Demon possessed her. Now demons, whatever else they may be,
(15) are full of interest. And so it happens that in the real Miss Nightingale there was more that was interesting than in the legendary one; there was also less that was agreeable.

What was the secret voice in her ear, if it was not
(20) a call? Why had she felt from her earliest years, those mysterious promptings towards . . . she hardly knew what but certainly towards something very different from anything around her? Why, as a child in the nursery, when her sister had shown a healthy
(25) pleasure in tearing her dolls to pieces, had she shown an almost morbid one in sewing them up again? Why was she driven now to minister to the poor in their cottages, to watch by sick-beds, to put her dog's wounded paw into elaborate splints as if it was
(30) a human being? Why was her head filled with the queer imaginations of the country house at Embley turned, by some enchantment, into a hospital, with herself as matron moving among the beds? Why was even her vision of heaven itself filled with suffering
(35) patients to whom she was being useful? So she dreamed and wondered, and taking out her diary, she poured into it the agitations of her soul.

A weaker spirit would have been overwhelmed by the load of such distress—would have yielded or
(40) snapped. But this extraordinary young woman held firm, and fought her way to victory. With an amazing persistency, during the eight years that followed her rebuff over Salisbury Hospital, she struggled and worked and planned. While superficially she was
(45) carrying on the life of a brilliant girl in high society, while internally she was a prey to the tortures of regret and remorse, she yet possessed the energy to collect the knowledge and to undergo the experience which alone could enable her to do what she had
(50) determined she would do in the end. In secret she devoured the reports of medical commissions, the pamphlets of sanitary authorities, the histories of hospitals and homes. She spent the intervals of the London season in ragged schools and workhouses.
(55) When she went abroad with her family, she used her spare time so well that there was hardly a great hospital in Europe with which she was not acquainted, hardly a great city whose slums she had not passed through.

(60) Three more years passed, and then at last the pressure of time told; her family seemed to realise that she was old enough and strong enough to have her way; and she became superintendent of a charitable nursing home in Harley Street. She had gained
(65) her independence, though it was in a meagre sphere enough; and her mother was still not quite resigned: surely Florence might at least spend the summer in the country. At times, indeed, among her intimates, Mrs. Nightingale almost wept. "We are ducks," she
(70) said with tears in her eyes, "who have hatched a wild swan." But the poor lady was wrong; it was not a swan that they had hatched; it was an eagle.

15. Which of the following best describes the structure of the first paragraph?

   A. It is divided into two parts, beginning with general statements, and moving to specific commentary.
   B. It is divided into two contrasting parts, with the division coming in line 9.
   C. It alternates a short sentence followed by a long sentence throughout.
   D. It moves from the presentation of Florence Nightingale's strengths (lines 1–8) to the presentation of her weaknesses (lines 9–18).
   E. It presents Florence Nightingale first in figurative language (lines 1–8) and then in literal language (lines 9–18).

16. Which of the following best defines the word "succour" of lines 4–5?

   A. oversee
   B. treat with medicines
   C. relieve
   D. rally
   E. convert

17. In the first paragraph, all of the following words and phrases are used to present the popular conception of Florence Nightingale EXCEPT

   A. "saintly" (line 2)
   B. "self-sacrificing" (line 2)
   C. "the Lady with the Lamp" (line 5)
   D. "interesting" (lines 16–17)
   E. "legendary" (line 17)

18. The first paragraph of the passage employs all of the following contrasts EXCEPT

   A. "the vision" and "the truth" (lines 8–9)
   B. "fact" and "fancy" (line 10)
   C. "another fashion" and "no place in the popular imagination" (lines 11–13)
   D. "the real" and "the legendary" (lines 15–17)
   E. "more interesting" and "less agreeable" (lines 16–18)

19. In the first paragraph, all of the following words have specific religious meanings EXCEPT

   A. "saintly" (line 2)
   B. "maiden" (line 3)
   C. "consecrating" (line 7)
   D. "Demon" (line 13)
   E. "possessed" (lines 13–14)

20. In which of the following sentences is the use of parallel structure most important?

   A. the first ("Everyone knows . . .", lines 1–2)
   B. the third ("But the . . .", line 9)
   C. the fourth ("The Miss . . .", lines 9–10)
   D. the seventh ("Now demons . . .", lines 14–15)
   E. the eighth ("And so . . .", lines 15–18)

21. All of the following words and phrases serve a similar purpose EXCEPT

   A. "popular conception" (line 1)
   B. "vision" (line 8)
   C. "as facile fancy painted" (line 10)
   D. "demons" (line 14)
   E. "the legendary one" (line 17)

22. In which sentence in the first paragraph does the author use archaic diction and clichés?

   A. the first ("Everyone knows . . .", lines 1–2)
   B. the second ("The saintly . . .", lines 2–8)
   C. the third ("But the . . .", line 9)
   D. the sixth ("A Demon . . .", lines 13–14)
   E. the eighth ("And so . . .", lines 15–18)

23. Which of the following phrases in the first paragraph employs BOTH hyperbole and metaphor?

   A. "the Lady with the Lamp" (line 5)
   B. "the horrors of the hospital at Scutari" (line 6)
   C. "consecrating with the radiance of her goodness" (line 7)
   D. "as facile fancy painted her" (line 10)
   E. "no place in the popular imagination" (lines 12–13)

GO ON TO THE NEXT PAGE

24. The words "call" (line 20) and "mysterious" (line 21) in the second paragraph are related to the diction of the first paragraph because their meanings are associated with

    A. medicine
    B. religion
    C. social position
    D. psychology
    E. feminism

25. In the second paragraph, the sentence that is most likely to surprise the conventional expectations of a reader is the

    A. first ("What was . . .", lines 19–20).
    B. second ("Why had she . . .", lines 20–23).
    C. third ("Why, as a . . .", lines 23–26).
    D. fourth ("Why was she . . .", lines 27–30).
    E. fifth ("Why was her . . .", lines 30–33).

26. The significant difference of the syntax of the second paragraph from the rest of the passage is its use of

    A. both loose and periodic sentences
    B. parallel structure
    C. sentence fragments
    D. interrogative sentences
    E. connotative diction

27. The third paragraph implies a contrast between all of the following EXCEPT

    A. "weaker spirit . . . extraordinary young woman" (lines 38–40)
    B. "superficially . . . internally" (lines 44–46)
    C. "reports of the medical commissions . . . histories of hospitals" (lines 51–53)
    D. "the London season . . . ragged school and workhouses" (lines 53–54)
    E. "abroad with her family . . . slums" (lines 55–58)

28. Which of the following best describes the structure of the passage as a whole?

    A. The entire passage is developed chronologically.
    B. The first paragraph gives an overview, and the second, third, and fourth paragraphs develop chronologically.
    C. The first paragraph uses only the point of view of the author, the second and third paragraphs only that of Florence Nightingale, and the fourth paragraph only that of her mother.
    D. The first and second paragraphs generalize about Florence Nightingale, while the third and fourth paragraphs use specific detail.
    E. The first three paragraphs use a first-person narrator, while the fourth paragraph employs direct and indirect discourse.

29. Which of the following is the climactic contrast of the passage?

    A. "three more years . . . the pressure of time" (lines 60–61)
    B. "independence . . . meagre sphere" (line 65)
    C. "Harley Street . . . the country" (lines 64–68)
    D. "ducks . . . wild swan" (lines 69–71)
    E. "swan . . . eagle" (line 72)

Questions 30–41. Read the following passage carefully before you begin to answer the questions.

Third Passage

Once, but only once, does Socrates advise a disciple to enter politics. The unusual advice was given, oddly enough, to Charmides, Plato's uncle, who became the chief lieutenant of Critias in the regime of
(5) the Thirty. In Xenophon's *Memorabilia* Charmides, then a promising young man, is urged by Socrates to enter public life by joining in the debates of the assembly.

Charmides is reluctant to do so. Socrates then puts
(10) to Charmides the same question that might well have been addressed to Socrates. "If a man were to shrink from state business, though capable of discharging it with advantage to the state and honor himself," Socrates argues, "wouldn't it be reasonable to think
(15) him a coward?"

Charmides confesses that he is shy about appearing in public. Socrates says he has often heard Charmides give excellent advice to public leaders in private conversation. Charmides replies that "a pri-
(20) vate conversation is a very different thing from a crowded debate."

Socrates, chiding him, then discloses the depth of his own contempt for the Athenian assembly. "The wisest do not make you bashful," he says to
(25) Charmides, "yet you are ashamed to address an audience of mere dunces and weaklings."

An unmistakable social snobbery lurked behind Socrates' scornful dismissal of Athenian democracy. Who are these people, he asks Charmides, who
(30) make you feel too bashful to address them? Then he calls the roll of the common and—in his view—vulgar occupations represented in the assembly.

"The fullers or the cobblers or the builders or the smiths or the farmers or the merchants," Socrates
(35) ticks them off disdainfully, "or the traffickers in the market-place who think of nothing but buying cheap and selling dear? . . . You are shy of addressing men who never gave a thought to public affairs."[1] Why then did they take time off from their occupations to

(40) show up in the assembly at all? This is the kind of social prejudice—and of mere ranting—one would not expect from a philosopher. It is made all the stranger by his own class background.[2]

Socrates was not a wealthy aristocrat. He was of
(45) the middle class. His mother was a midwife. His father was a stone-cutter, perhaps also a sculptor—the distinction between craftsman and artist was blurred in antiquity. Even the most distinguished artist was still a man who worked with his hands
(50) and depended on his earnings.

How did Socrates earn his bread? He had a wife and three sons to support. He lived to the age of seventy. But he never seems to have had a job or practiced a trade. His days were spent in leisure,
(55) talking. Socrates derided the Sophists for taking payment from their pupils. He prided himself on never asking a fee from his own disciples. How did he support his family? This natural question is never answered in the Platonic dialogues. In the
(60) *Apology*, Socrates describes himself as a poor man, and he certainly was poor by comparison with wealthy aristocrats like Plato so prominent in his adoring entourage. But he was never so poor that he had to take a job or practice a trade.

[1] Memorabilia, 3.7.2–7 (Loeb 4:215–217).

[2] Of course the worst example of snobbery in the Platonic cannon is Plato's supercilious description of rival upstart philosophers in the Republic—"that multitude of pretenders unfit by nature, whose souls are bowed and mutilated by their vulgar occupations even as their bodies are marred by their arts and crafts," whose picture is "precisely that of a little bald-headed tinker who has made money and has just been freed from bonds [i.e., the bonds of servitude, having just purchased his freedom] and has a bath and is wearing a new garment and has got himself up like a bridegroom and is about to marry his master's daughter who has fallen into poverty." (Republic, 4:295E [Loeb 2:47–49]). But Plato put this into the mouth of Socrates many years after the latter's death. There is no evidence that the historical Socrates ever spoke so unkindly and pretentiously. . . . The "little tinker" passage in the Republic was a curious way for Plato to demonstrate his own superiority as a philosopher and a gentleman.

GO ON TO THE NEXT PAGE

30. The author's repetition of the word "once" in the first sentence serves the rhetorical purpose of

    A. providing a transition to Socrates's ideas about politicians
    B. clarifying that Socrates felt some conditions warranted entering politics
    C. adding emphasis to Socrates's ideas about politicians
    D. showing Socrates's many inconsistencies as a philosopher
    E. reinforcing the atypical nature of Socrates's suggestion

31. In stating that "the same question might well have been addressed to Socrates" (lines 10–11), the author implies that

    A. Socrates was already a politician
    B. Socrates never considered entering politics himself
    C. Socrates was hypocritical; he never listened to his own advice
    D. Socrates should have questioned his own refusal to enter politics
    E. Socrates was good at asking questions, but weak with providing answers

32. The rhetorical effect of using direct quotations from Socrates is that they

    A. document the actual words from the philosopher
    B. reveal the humanity of the ancient philosopher
    C. show how Socrates manipulated his disciples
    D. demonstrate how Socrates developed an argument
    E. prove the author's research is valid

33. Socrates cites all of the following stereotypes about public servants EXCEPT

    A. They are not trained to be politicians.
    B. They are incompetent for public office.
    C. Their "vulgar occupations" make them unfit for public service.
    D. They could become competent given the correct training.
    E. Their own self-interests dominate their political decisions.

34. The alliteration in the opening of the fifth paragraph (lines 27–28) has the effect of

    A. adding a sinister "hissing" sound that emphasizes Socrates's disdain
    B. distracting the reader from the content of Socrates's ideas
    C. creating a tone of vulgar roughness in the piece that is consistent with Socrates's emotions
    D. making the prose read like poetry
    E. speeding up the pace of the passage

35. The list of professions which Socrates claims are representative of the men in the assembly implies that

    A. men who participate in the assembly also have successful careers
    B. men in the assembly have strong incentives to maintain their other careers
    C. men in the assembly have neither the training nor the aptitude for politics
    D. the assembly faithfully represents all of the finest professions in Athens
    E. the assembly's diverse representation of talent is its best feature

36. The speaker is surprised to see Socrates display "the kind of social prejudice—and of mere ranting—one would not expect" (lines 40–42) for all of the following reasons EXCEPT that

    A. one would not expect such prejudice in a true philosopher
    B. Socrates was not a wealthy aristocrat
    C. Socrates's mother was a midwife
    D. Socrates's father was a stonecutter
    E. the differentiation between craftsmen and artists was vague in Socrates's time

37. How does the speaker answer the question of how Socrates supported himself and his family?

    A. He worked as a stonecutter, following in his father's trade.
    B. Although untrained, he practiced as a physician.
    C. The author does not resolve this question.
    D. He worked as a tradesman, toiling for long hours on the road.
    E. His wide variety of odd jobs provided literary and philosophical ideas.

38. In note #2, the speaker's rhetorical purpose in quoting Socrates's description of rival upstart philosophers from the *Republic* is to

    A. show that Socrates really was socially prejudiced

    B. imply that Plato faithfully reported Socrates's words

    C. show that this is part of a pattern of Socrates speaking unkindly and pretentiously

    D. dismiss the supposed quote from Socrates, because Plato had put the words into Socrates's mouth years later

    E. suggest that this is an excellent way for Plato to demonstrate his own superiority as a philosopher and a gentleman

39. The cumulative effect of the repetition of short sentences in the opening of paragraphs 7 and 8 is to

    A. emphasize the glowing highlights of Socrates's background

    B. provide a matter-of-fact description of Socrates's middle-class upbringing

    C. satirize the penury of Socrates's parents

    D. engender empathy for Socrates, due to the many hardships that he overcame

    E. provide a hagiography listing Socrates's many virtues

40. Socrates's purpose in referring to the Athenian assembly as "mere dunces and weaklings" (line 26) is to

    A. encourage Charmides to get over his intimidation and to join in the public debates

    B. discourage Charmides from joining these deplorable people

    C. emphasize Socrates's own self-importance

    D. differentiate the assemblymen from men who labor in honest trades

    E. compare the assemblymen favorably with other leaders, with whom Charmides had given private advice

41. The primary purpose of the story of the "little bald-headed tinker" (note #2) is to demonstrate

    A. that an awful fate awaited Charmides if he joined the assembly

    B. that even a lowly tinker could become a fine gentleman

    C. that Socrates's rivals were unfit by nature to be philosophers

    D. that Socrates's highest esteem was reserved for honest tradesmen

    E. that a true philosopher views an honest day's work as the greatest good

GO ON TO THE NEXT PAGE

Questions 42–55. Read the following passage carefully before you begin to answer the questions.

Fourth Passage

The object of this essay is to assert one very simple principle, as entitled to govern absolutely the dealings of society with the individual in the way of compulsion and control, whether the means
(5) used be physical force in the form of legal penalties or the moral coercion of public opinion. That principle is that the sole end for which mankind are warranted, individually or collectively, in interfering with the liberty of action of any of their number
(10) is self-protection. That the only purpose for which power can be rightfully exercised over any member of civilized community, against his will, is to prevent harm to others. His own good, either physical or moral, is not sufficient warrant. He cannot right-
(15) fully be compelled to do or forbear because it will be better for him to do so, because it will make him happier, because, in the opinions of others, to do so would be wise or even right. These are good reasons for remonstrating with him, or reasoning with
(20) him, or persuading him, or entreating him, but not for compelling him or visiting him with any evil in case he do otherwise. To justify that, the conduct from which it is desired to deter him must be calculated to produce evil to someone else. The only part
(25) of the conduct of anyone for which he is amenable to society is that which concerns others. In the part which merely concerns himself, his independence is, of right, absolute. Over himself, over his own body and mind, the individual is sovereign.
(30)   It is, perhaps, hardly necessary to say that this doctrine is meant to apply only to human beings in the maturity of their faculties. We are not speaking of children or of young persons below the age which the law may fix as that of manhood or womanhood.
(35) Those who are still in a state to require being taken care of by others must be protected against their own actions as well as against external injury. For the same reason we may leave out of consideration those backward states of society in which the race it-
(40) self may be considered as in its nonage. The early difficulties in the way of spontaneous progress are so great that there is seldom any choice of means for overcoming them; and a ruler full of the spirit of improvement is warranted in the use of any expedients
(45) that will attain an end perhaps otherwise unattainable. Despotism is a legitimate mode of government in dealing with barbarians, provided the end be their improvement and the means justified by actually effecting that end. Liberty, as a principle, has no appli-
(50) cation to any state of things anterior to the time when mankind have become capable of being improved by free and equal discussion. Until then, there is nothing for them but implicit obedience to an Akbar or a Charlemagne, if they are so fortunate as to find one.
(55) But as soon as mankind have attained the capacity of being guided to their own improvement by conviction or persuasion (a period long since reached in all nations with whom we need here concern ourselves), compulsion, either in the direct form or in
(60) that of pains and penalties for noncompliance, is no longer admissible as a means to their own good, and justifiable only for the security of others.

42. The "one very simple principle" (lines 1–2) is that

  A. the individual should comply with the government's principles under all conditions
  B. a domineering government is an effective government
  C. the government should coerce an individual only when that individual's actions will harm others
  D. individuals have the right to ignore the government's wishes
  E. children do not have sovereignty

43. The predicate nominative that complements "That principle," the subject of the second sentence (lines 6–10), is

  A. "sole end"
  B. "warranted"
  C. "liberty of action"
  D. "self-protection"
  E. "that the sole end . . . self-protection"

44. According to the passage, who of the following may society compel to act correctly?

   A. those who act selfishly
   B. those who harm only themselves
   C. those who demonstrate personal corruption
   D. those who harm others
   E. those who protect against despotism

45. The sentence "These are good reasons . . . otherwise" (lines 18–22) is effective because of its

   A. abstract meaning
   B. parallel syntax
   C. metaphorical references
   D. ironic understatement
   E. personification of government

46. The principle embodied in the phrase "the individual is sovereign" (line 29) is limited to actions that

   A. adversely affect all society
   B. are legal
   C. affect only the individual
   D. society generally ignores
   E. are directed at political enemies

47. According to the passage, which of the following groups may be forced to act in a particular way?

   I. children
   II. adults
   III. immature societies

   A. I only
   B. II only
   C. I and II only
   D. I and III only
   E. I, II, and III

48. It can be inferred from the passage that despotism is NOT acceptable when

   A. the government's actions do not produce the necessary improvement in its citizens
   B. barbarians are allowed to do as they wish
   C. the government's actions harm children
   D. society in general is insecure and unsafe
   E. the people voice opinions against the despot

49. Which of the following are given as allowable methods for preventing a member of society from harming other individuals?

   I. physical force
   II. moral coercion of public opinion
   III. legal penalties

   A. I only
   B. II only
   C. I and II only
   D. II and III only
   E. I, II, and III

50. Which of the following does the passage imply the speaker values most highly?

   A. unlimited individual freedom
   B. protection of the members of society
   C. law and order in society
   D. despotism by the leaders
   E. the sovereignty of children

51. The second paragraph relates to the first paragraph in that it

   A. gives exceptions to the principle of individual sovereignty discussed in the first paragraph
   B. illustrates the actions a government can take in controlling its citizens
   C. lists evidence supporting the assertions made in the first paragraph
   D. gives concrete examples of effective governments
   E. provides anecdotal evidence of individuals acting in self-protection

52. With which of the following would the speaker most likely agree?

   A. Children should be allowed sovereignty.
   B. Charlemagne would make a good ruler in a society able to be "guided" to its "own improvement."
   C. Forced obedience will always be necessary for mankind.
   D. The only appropriate reason to inhibit a citizen having mature faculties is to prevent harm to others.
   E. Despots will always exist.

GO ON TO THE NEXT PAGE

53. Which term best describes the tone of the essay?

    A. sarcastic

    B. cynical

    C. optimistic

    D. matter of fact

    E. pessimistic

54. Which of the following would the speaker be LEAST likely to encourage?

    A. despotism for barbarians

    B. control over children

    C. absolute freedom of action

    D. reasoning and persuasion

    E. self-destructive actions

55. Which of the following rhetorical devices can be found in the essay?

    A. metaphor

    B. personification

    C. syllogistic reasoning

    D. simile

    E. historical allusion

IF YOU FINISH BEFORE TIME IS CALLED, CHECK YOUR WORK ON THIS SECTION ONLY. DO NOT WORK ON ANY OTHER SECTION IN THE TEST.

Section II: Essay Questions

Time: 2 hours, 15 minutes

3 questions

Question 1

(Reading time—15 minutes. Suggested writing time—40 minutes. This question counts one-third of the total essay-section score.)

Directions: The prompt that follows is based on six accompanying sources. This essay requires you to integrate a variety of sources into a coherent, well written essay. Refer to the sources, both directly and indirectly, to support your position. Avoid mere paraphrasing or summarizing. Your argument should be the central focus; the use of the sources should support your argument.

Introduction

In the United States, the African-American community has always had a distinctive culture all its own. However, this unique subculture has managed to influence many aspects of mainstream American culture, most notably, American music. Analyze the degree to which African-American culture has influenced popular American music. Has it made a universal impact on all genres or has it lingered in the background of American society, flourishing only amongst certain racial and socioeconomic groups?

Assignment

Read the following sources carefully. **Then, in an essay that synthesizes at least three of the sources for support, take a position that defends, challenges, or qualifies the claim that the African-American culture has influenced popular American music and culture.**

Refer to the sources as Source A, Source B, and so on; authors' names and titles are included for your convenience.

Source A (Kohl)

Source B (Best and Kellner)

Source C (Hansen)

Source D (Spiegler)

Source E (Why Whites Embrace . . .")

Source F ("The Recording Industry . . .")

GO ON TO THE NEXT PAGE

Source A

Kohl, Paul R. "The Lyrics in African American Pop Culture Music." *Popular Music and Society* October 2004: 1.

The following excerpt briefly examines the public's awareness of the history of rap and hip-hop music.

Casual followers of popular culture are generally unfamiliar with the works and traditions that have influenced modern cultural forms. One of the best examples lies in the area of African-American music. While the music of black America has always had a profound influence on mainstream American culture, much of it has remained underground, invisible to the general public until it bursts into the light, seemingly full grown with no visible past. Thus rap and hip hop are generally seen as reaching back as far as the mid-'70s and the work of DJs like Kool Herc in the South Bronx, but its earlier history, embracing such figures as the Last Poets, Muhammad Ali, and the black American traditions of the dozens, is known only to the historian and true aficionado.

Source B

Best, Steven and Douglas Kellner. "Rap, Black Rage, and Racial Difference." *Enculturation* Spring 1999: 1.

The following is an excerpt that explores the cultural importance of rap music.

Rap music has emerged as one of the most distinctive and controversial music genres of the past decade. A significant part of hip hop culture, rap articulates the experiences and conditions of African-Americans living in a spectrum of marginalized situations ranging from racial stereotyping and stigmatizing to struggle for survival in violent ghetto conditions. In this cultural context, rap provides a voice to the voiceless, a form of protest to the oppressed, and a mode of alternative cultural style and identity to the marginalized. Rap is thus not only music to dance and party to, but a potent form of cultural identity. It has become a powerful vehicle for cultural political expression, serving as the "CNN of black people" (Chuck D), or upping the high-tech ante, as their "satellite communication system" (Heavy D). It is an informational medium to tune into, one that describes the rage of African-Americans facing growing oppression, declining opportunities for advancement, changing moods on the streets, and everyday life as a matter of sheer survival. In turn, it has become a cultural virus, circulating its images, sounds, and attitude throughout the culture and body politic.

GO ON TO THE NEXT PAGE

Source C

Hansen, Suzy. "Hip-Hop Nation." *Salon* 19 July, 2002: 1.

The following excerpt analyzes the impact of hip-hop and its future in the African-American community.

Some young black activists complain that the media marginalizes the good things about hip-hop, choosing to focus on the often misogynistic lyrics, flashy and violent music videos and gangsta image of its stars rather than its more socially conscious messages. But when Russell Simmons' Hip-Hop Summit Action Network helped the United Federation of Teachers and the Alliance for Quality Education draw thousands of people (the estimates range between 50,000 and 100,000) to a recent protest against New York Mayor Mike Bloomberg's $358 million cut in education funding, the press took notice. Stars such as Sean "P. Diddy" Combs, Alicia Keys and LL Cool J showed up to support the cause. A couple of weeks later, a *Washington Post* headline declared: "We the Peeps: After Three Decades Chillin' in the Hood, Hip Hop Is Finding Its Voice Politically."

Mayor Bloomberg took notice, too; shortly after the demonstration, he restored $298 million to his budget proposal. The Hip-Hop Summit Action Network declared victory. Has a hip-hop power movement arrived?

Not quite, says Bakari Kitwana, author of "The Hip Hop Generation: Young Blacks and the Crisis in African-American Culture." A former editor at *The Source,* Kitwana argues that although the hip-hop industry has created a far-reaching constituency, and local and student activist hip-hop groups have emerged across the country, there's still a lot of work to do. Kitwana believes that what he calls the hip-hop generation—made up of African-Americans born between the years 1965 and 1984—desperately needs a national organization, and not necessarily one that's spearheaded by rap stars or entertainment moguls. According to Kitwana, such a national group, one that taps into the vast economic power of the hip-hop industry and that focuses on education, employment and incarceration, could be more influential than the '60s civil rights movement.

Salon spoke to Kitwana from his home in Ohio about the tensions between the civil rights generation and the hip-hop generation, why hip-hop stars need to take responsibility for the content of their lyrics and what kind of leader the hip-hop generation needs.

Source D

Spiegler, Marc. "Marketing Street Culture; Bringing Hip-Hop Style to the Mainstream." *American Demographics* November, 1996: 1.

The following excerpt examines the role rap has played in mainstream American culture.

The Scene: Martha's Vineyard, Massachusetts, a bastion of the white East Coast establishment. A teenaged boy saunters down the street, his gait and attitude embodying adolescent rebellion. Baggy jeans sag atop over-designed sneakers, gold hoops adorn both ears, and a baseball cap shields his eyes. On his chest, a Tommy Hilfiger shirt sports the designer's distinctive pairing of blue, red, and white rectangles.

Four years ago, this outfit would have been unimaginable to this cool teen; only his clean-cut, country-club peers sported Hilfiger clothes. What linked the previously preppy Hilfiger to jeans so low-slung they seem to defy gravity? To a large extent, the answer lies 200 miles southwest, in the oversized personage of Brooklyn's Biggie Smalls, an admitted ex–drug dealer turned rapper.

Over the past few years, Smalls and other hip-hop stars have become a crucial part of Hilfiger's open attempt to tap into the urban youth market. In exchange for giving artists free wardrobes, Hilfiger found its name mentioned in both the rhyming verses of rap songs and their "shout-out" lyrics, in which rap artists chant out thanks to friends and sponsors for their support.

GO ON TO THE NEXT PAGE

Source E

"Why Whites Embrace Black Culture: The Appeal of African-American Culture." *JET* 25 June, 2001: 1.

The following excerpt addresses the appeal of African-American culture.

Blacks' contribution to American culture is so rich and vibrant that everyone wants to benefit from it. Black culture—from the style of dress to music—has such a pervasive influence on all races that *JET* sought to find out why Whites embrace Black culture.

Dr. Michael Eric Dyson, noted professor of religious studies at DePaul University in Chicago, says he knows exactly why so many Whites embrace Black culture.

"Whites are drawn to Black culture because of the extraordinary quality of it, our aesthetic, our style," explained Dyson. "We set the styles. We are the trendsetters of America. America is known globally for its culture, which is Black. When you look at basketball, people love Michael Jordan, Allen Iverson and Kobe Bryant."

Dyson finds it interesting how poor Black people continue to determine the taste of richer White people. "They want to look like us, but they don't want to be us," he noted. "They don't want to live in our skin. It's kind of a cultural voyeurism. It allows White people to safely tour Blackness without being subjected to the reality of being Black. By taking in our Black culture, they are also taking in some of our political and social ideas."

Dr. Cynthia Neal Spence, academic dean at Spelman College, says that it shouldn't come as a surprise that Whites embrace Black culture.

"It is not a new phenomenon," Spence said. "White America has always found Black culture to be exciting, exotic and perhaps more expressive and less restrained than what they identify as their culture. They find our culture to be very exciting and attractive. If you look at music, historically they have attempted to mimic our musical expression in terms of our pop artists and our dance. Elvis Presley admitted that much of his music and movement were patterned after Blacks."

Source F

"The Recording Industry Association of America 2004 Consumer Profile." Recording Industry Association of America. 29 September 2005. Available at www.riaa.com/news/marketingdata/pdf/2004consumerprofile.pdf.

THE RECORDING INDUSTRY ASSOCIATION OF AMERICA

2004 Consumer Profile

Phone: 202/775-0101 Web: www.riaa.com

	1995	1996	1997	1998	1999	2000	2001	2002	2003	2004		
Rock	33.5	32.6	32.5	25.7	25.2	24.8	24.4	24.7	25.2	23.9	%	Total U.S. Dollar Value
Rap/Hip-hop [2]	6.7	8.9	10.1	9.7	10.8	12.9	11.4	13.8	13.3	12.1		The figures below (in millions) indicate the overall size of the
R&B/Urban [3]	11.3	12.1	11.2	12.8	10.5	9.7	10.6	11.2	10.6	11.3		U.S. sound recording industry
Country	16.7	14.7	14.4	14.1	10.8	10.7	10.5	10.7	10.4	13.0		based on manufacturers'
Pop	10.1	9.3	9.4	10.0	10.3	11.0	12.1	9.0	8.9	10.0		shipments at suggested list prices.
Religious [4]	3.1	4.3	4.5	6.3	5.1	4.8	6.7	6.7	5.8	6.0		
Classical	2.9	3.4	2.8	3.3	3.5	2.7	3.2	3.1	3.0	2.0		1995 $12,320.30
Jazz	3.0	3.3	2.8	1.9	3.0	2.9	3.4	3.2	2.9	2.7		1996 $12,533.80
Soundtracks	0.9	0.8	1.2	1.7	0.8	0.7	1.4	1.1	1.4	1.1		1997 $12,236.80
Oldies	1.0	0.8	0.8	0.7	0.7	0.9	0.8	0.9	1.3	1.4		1998 $13,723.50
New Age	0.7	0.7	0.8	0.6	0.5	0.5	1.0	0.5	0.5	1.0		1999 $14,584.50
Children's	0.5	0.7	0.9	0.4	0.4	0.6	0.5	0.4	0.6	2.8		2000 $14,323.00
Other [5]	7.0	5.2	5.7	7.9	9.1	8.3	7.9	8.1	7.6	8.9		2001 $13,740.89
												2002 $12,614.21
												2003 $11,854.40
Full-length CDs	65.0	68.4	70.2	74.8	83.2	89.3	89.2	90.5	87.8	90.3	%	2004 $12,154.70
Full-length cassettes	25.1	19.3	18.2	14.8	8.0	4.9	3.4	2.4	2.2	1.7		
Singles (all types)	7.5	9.3	9.3	6.8	5.4	2.5	2.4	1.9	2.4	2.4		
Music videos/Video DVDs	0.9	1.0	0.6	1.0	0.9	0.8	1.1	0.7	0.6	1.0		Methodology
DVD audio	NA	NA	NA	NA	NA	NA	1.1	1.3	2.7	1.7		This profile represents a combination of
Digital Download	NA	NA	NA	NA	NA	NA	0.2	0.5	1.3	0.9		music-consumption data collected by Peter
SACD	NA	NA	NA	NA	NA	NA	NA	NA	0.5	0.8		Hart Research and The Taylor Research &
Vinyl LPs	0.5	0.6	0.7	0.7	0.5	0.5	0.6	0.7	0.5	0.9		Consulting Group, Inc., during calendar year
												2004. The data for the period from the
												beginning of 2004 through the end of July
												2004 were collected by Peter Hart Research,
10-14 Years	8.0	7.9	8.9	9.1	8.5	8.9	8.5	8.9	8.6	9.4	%	while the data from August through the end
15-19 Years	17.1	17.2	16.8	15.8	12.6	12.9	13.0	13.3	11.4	11.9		of December were gathered by The Taylor
20-24 Years	15.3	15.0	13.8	12.2	12.6	12.5	12.2	11.5	10.0	9.2		Research & Consulting Group.[1]
25-29 Years	12.3	12.5	11.7	11.4	10.5	10.6	10.9	9.4	10.9	10.0		
30-34 Years	12.1	11.4	11.0	11.4	10.1	9.8	10.3	10.8	10.1	10.4		
35-39 Years	10.8	11.1	11.6	12.6	10.4	10.6	10.2	9.8	11.2	10.7		
40-44 Years	7.5	9.1	8.8	8.3	9.3	9.6	10.3	9.9	10.0	10.9		Data based on telephone survey of past
45+	16.1	15.1	16.5	18.1	24.7	23.8	23.7	25.5	26.6	26.4		month music buyers (over 2,000 per year).
												The reliability of the data is +/- 2.2% at a
												95% confidence level. With respect to
Record Store	52.0	49.9	51.8	50.8	44.5	42.4	42.5	36.8	33.2	32.5		genre, consumers were asked to classify
Other Store	28.2	31.5	31.9	34.4	38.3	40.8	42.4	50.7	52.8	53.8	%	their music purchases.
Tape/Record Club	14.3	14.3	11.6	9.0	7.9	7.6	6.1	4.0	4.1	4.4		
TV, Newspaper, Magazine Ad Or 800 Number	4.0	2.9	2.7	2.9	2.5	2.4	3.0	2.0	1.5	1.7		
Internet [6]	NA	NA	0.3	1.1	2.4	3.2	2.9	3.4	5.0	5.9		
Concert	NA	NA	NA	NA	NA	NA	NA	NA	NA	1.6		Permission to cite or copy these statistics is
												hereby granted as long as proper attribution
												is given to the Recording Industry
Female	47.0	49.1	51.4	51.3	49.7	49.4	51.2	50.6	50.9	50.5	%	Association of America.
Male	53.0	50.9	48.6	48.7	50.3	50.6	48.8	49.4	49.1	49.5		

[1] Calendar year 2004 data based upon a combination of survey data collected by Peter Hart Research and The Taylor Research & Consulting Group, Inc. Includes only partial-year data, as Hart did not interview during the months of March, April, June, and July of 2004. Channel data derived solely from Taylor August-December interviews.

[2] "Rap": Includes Rap and Hip-Hop.

[3] "R&B": Includes R&B, Blues, Dance, Disco, Funk, Fusion, Motown, Reggae, Soul.

[4] "Religious": Includes Christian, Gospel, Inspirational, Religious, and Spiritual.

[5] "Other": Includes Big Band, Broadway Shows, Comedy, Contemporary, Electronic, EMO, Ethnic, Exercise, Folk, Gothic, Grunge, Holiday Music House Music, Humor, Instrumental, Language, Latin, Love Songs, Mix, Mellow, Modern, Ska, Spoken word, Standards, Swing, Top-40 Trip-hop.

[6] Internet does not include record club purchases made over the Internet.

GO ON TO THE NEXT PAGE

Question 2

(Suggested time—40 minutes. This question counts one-third of the total essay-section score.)

Directions: The following excerpt is taken from Benjamin Franklin's *Autobiography*. Read the passage carefully and develop an essay that evaluates the validity of Franklin's assertions about the ability to justify one's actions through reasoning. Use appropriate evidence to make your argument convincing.

I believe I have omitted mentioning that in my first voyage from Boston, being becalmed off Block Island, our people set about catching cod and hauled up a great many. Hitherto I had stuck to my resolution of not eating animal food; and on this occasion I considered with my Master Tryon, the taking of every fish as a kind of unprovoked murder, since none of them had or ever could do us any injury that might justify the slaughter. All this seemed very reasonable. But I had formerly been a great lover of fish, and when this came hot out of the frying pan, it smelled admirably well. I balanced some time between principle and inclination: till I recollected, that when fish were opened, I saw smaller fish taken out of their stomachs: Then, thought I, if you eat one another, I don't see why we mayn't eat you. So I dined upon cod very heartily and continued to eat with other people, returning only now and then occasionally to a vegetable diet. So convenient a thing it is to be a *reasonable creature*, since it enables one to find or make a reason for everything one has a mind to do.

Question 3

(Suggested time—40 minutes. This question counts one-third of the total essay-section score.)

Samuel Johnson wrote, "Our desires increase with our possessions. The knowledge that something remains yet unenjoyed impairs our enjoyment of the good before us."

Directions: Write a persuasive essay that qualifies, agrees with, or disagrees with Johnson's assertion. Use appropriate examples to develop your ideas.

IF YOU FINISH BEFORE TIME IS CALLED, CHECK YOUR WORK ON THIS SECTION ONLY. DO NOT WORK ON ANY OTHER SECTION IN THE TEST.

Answer Key for Practice Test 6

Section I: Multiple-Choice Questions

First Passage

1. A
2. B
3. E
4. D
5. C
6. A
7. C
8. E
9. D
10. B
11. D
12. B
13. E
14. A

Second Passage

15. B
16. C
17. D
18. C
19. B
20. E
21. D
22. B
23. C
24. B
25. C
26. D
27. C
28. B
29. E

Third Passage

30. E
31. D
32. B
33. D
34. A
35. C
36. E
37. C
38. D
39. B
40. A
41. C

Fourth Passage

42. C
43. E
44. D
45. B
46. C
47. D
48. A
49. E
50. B
51. A
52. D
53. D
54. C
55. E

Section II: Essay Questions

Essay scoring guides, student essays, and analysis appear beginning on page 323.

Practice Test 6 Scoring Worksheet

Use the following worksheet to arrive at a probable final AP grade on Practice Test 6. Because being objective enough to estimate your own essay score is sometimes difficult, you might give your essays (along with the sample essays) to a teacher, friend, or relative to score if you feel confident that the individual has the knowledge necessary to make such a judgment and that he or she will feel comfortable doing so.

Section I: Multiple-Choice Questions

$$\underset{\substack{\text{right} \\ \text{answers}}}{\underline{\hspace{3cm}}} - (\text{¼ or } .25 \times \underset{\substack{\text{wrong} \\ \text{answers}}}{\underline{\hspace{2cm}}}) = \underset{\substack{\text{multiple-choice} \\ \text{raw score}}}{\underline{\hspace{3cm}}}$$

$$\underset{\substack{\text{multiple-choice} \\ \text{raw score}}}{\underline{\hspace{3cm}}} \times 1.2272 = \underset{\substack{\text{multiple-choice} \\ \text{converted score}}}{\underline{\hspace{3cm}}} \text{ (of possible 67.5)}$$

Section II: Essay Questions

$$\underset{\substack{\text{question 1} \\ \text{raw score}}}{\underline{\hspace{2cm}}} + \underset{\substack{\text{question 2} \\ \text{raw score}}}{\underline{\hspace{2cm}}} + \underset{\substack{\text{question 3} \\ \text{raw score}}}{\underline{\hspace{2cm}}} = \underset{\substack{\text{essay} \\ \text{raw score}}}{\underline{\hspace{2cm}}}$$

$$\underset{\substack{\text{essay} \\ \text{raw score}}}{\underline{\hspace{3cm}}} \times 3.0556 = \underset{\substack{\text{essay} \\ \text{converted score}}}{\underline{\hspace{3cm}}} \text{ (of possible 82.5)}$$

Final Score

$$\underset{\substack{\text{multiple-choice} \\ \text{converted score}}}{\underline{\hspace{3cm}}} + \underset{\substack{\text{essay} \\ \text{converted score}}}{\underline{\hspace{3cm}}} = \underset{\substack{\text{final} \\ \text{converted score}}}{\underline{\hspace{3cm}}} \text{(of possible 150)}$$

Probable Final AP Score

Final Converted Score	Probable AP Score
150–104	5
103–92	4
91–76	3
75–50	2
49–0	1

Answers and Explanations for Practice Test 6

Section I: Multiple-Choice Questions

First Passage

The passage is taken from an address delivered by Elizabeth Cady Stanton to the women's rights convention at Seneca Falls in 1848.

1. **A.** Used as it is in the phrase "rights and wrongs," "rights" means that which is morally good or proper. Modified by "civil and political," "rights" also means privileges.

2. **B.** Stanton here is almost certainly taking up the points repeatedly made by the opponents of women's suffrage (the same kind of objections are currently raised by opponents of women's rights advocates) and using them to provide a comic opening for her address.

3. **E.** Stanton states that clergymen and men in the legal profession in England ("the first nation on the globe") wear flowing robes and so they must agree with women that this attire is more "dignified and imposing" than men's clothing.

4. **D.** The words and phrases in choices A, B, C, and E mean what they say, but the phrase "nobler sex," used here to refer to men, is ironic. The passage makes clear that Stanton does not believe men are "nobler" than women.

5. **C.** The question asks about the use of mock-serious diction for satiric effect. Choices D and E are satiric, but the language here is not inflated. The correct answer is C, which grants pompous dignity to men's fashions by calling them "philosophical experiments." Stanton achieves a similar comic effect with the phrase "yours be the glory."

6. **A.** An audience (then or now) accustomed to hear of women over-concerned for their clothes and appearance should be amused by this pointing of the finger at men. Modern readers may be surprised to learn of elevator shoes in the mid-19th century, or the Russian belt which, like a corset, would make the waist appear smaller.

7. **C.** The first paragraph here is a comic turn, but it is not about the real issues of the address. In fact, the whole paragraph is a good example of the rhetorical technique in which the speaker, by saying she will not talk about something, does indeed talk about it. ("I will not mention that my opponent in this election has served eight years in jail for mail fraud.")

8. **E.** Stanton refers to Daniel Webster to show that males may vote regardless of their education or intelligence. As males, both Daniel Webster and the ignorant ditch-digger have the vote.

9. **D.** The two parallel sentences make the argument that males may vote regardless of their education and regardless of their strength. The vote cannot be given to males because they are stronger physically than females, since gender alone, not physical strength, determines who may vote.

10. **B.** Stanton wants the question of women's rights kept separate from the question of their equality (that is, are females the mental and physical equals of males?) because there can be no doubt about the fact that women are denied rights that the Constitution guarantees.

11. **D.** All of the choices except D use words that are not appropriate here. Stanton is not "disinterested," not "soft-spoken," not "dry or ironical" (although the first paragraph is), not "tactful." The word "angry" may seem strong here, but of the five choices, this is the best. Stanton's use of words and phrases like "disgraceful," "unjust," "a shame and disgrace," support the choice.

12. **B.** The tone of the second paragraph is totally unlike that of the first. The first paragraph is witty and ironic; the second is dead serious. Both use concrete details (C) and both present the author's point of view (E).

13. **E.** The second paragraph uses parallel constructions in lines 33–42 (the series of infinitives) and lines 33–47, in which the two sentences are parallel. An *ad hominem*, Choice A, argument is one that attacks the opponent rather than dealing with the subject ("Can you believe my opponent will raise income taxes when you know he earns $10 million a year?")

14. **A.** Though E is the next-best choice (B, C, and D are simply untrue), the real point here is the injustice to women, which is itemized in the second paragraph.

Second Passage

From Lytton Strachey's *Eminent Victorians* (1918)

15. **B.** The first paragraph has two distinct parts. The first eight lines present the "popular" idealized notion of Florence Nightingale. The division is clearly marked by the sentence "But the truth was different." The rest of the paragraph begins the presentation of what the author claims is the "real Miss Nightingale." Though the paragraph uses both long and short sentences, the alternation is not consistent. Both the third and fourth sentences are short, and the fifth is long only because it uses semicolons in place of periods. The contrast is not between Nightingale's strength and weakness, but between a romantic conception of her and a realistic account.

16. **C.** To succour (the American spelling is succor) is to relieve, to ameliorate at a time of distress.

17. **D.** All but "interesting" are used to present the popular idea of Florence Nightingale. The author argues the *real* woman was "more . . . interesting" though less saintly than the woman of the legend.

18. **C.** Four of these pairs are part of the legendary versus real contrast in the paragraph. "Another fashion" and "no place in the popular imagination," however, are both part of a sentence describing the "real" woman and are not contrasts.

19. **B.** Though "maiden" might be used in a religious context, of itself it is simply the word for a virgin or an unmarried girl or woman. The four other words have specific religious denotations. As it appears here, "possessed" is used (metaphorically) to mean controlled by a spirit.

20. **E.** None of the first four options uses parallel structure. The eighth sentence, however, plays "in the real" against "in the legendary" and "there was more that was interesting" against "there was less that was agreeable."

21. **D.** Four of these words or phrases refer to the popular concept of the sainted Florence Nightingale. "Demons" does not.

22. **B.** The second sentence employs both archaisms like "maiden of high degree" or "couch" and clichés like "saintly, self-sacrificing," "delicate maiden of high degree," and "to succour the afflicted," as the author mocks the sentimental idea of Florence Nightingale. The other sentences avoid these excesses.

23. **C.** The "horrors of the hospital" is not hyperbolic or figurative, and "facile fancy" is not hyperbole, though it is metaphoric. The overstatement is the claim that the "radiance" (a metaphor) of Nightingale's goodness "consecrated" the dying soldiers' deathbeds. She may have made the dying more comfortable, but she did not make them sacred.

24. **B.** Though "call" and "mysterious" can be used without any religious reference, both have specific religious meanings. The word "call" can mean a religious vocation regarded as divinely inspired, and "mysterious" has several different religious meanings, for example, pertaining to that which only faith can explain.

25. **C.** Most modern readers are unlikely to expect the sister's pleasure in "tearing her dolls to pieces" to be described as "healthy," while Florence Nightingale's repairing the victims is "morbid."

26. **D.** Unlike the rest of the passage, the second paragraph depends almost entirely on the use of questions. Six of its seven sentences are interrogative. All of the paragraphs employ connotative diction.

27. **C.** The contrast of choices A and B is clear. In D and E, "the London season" and "abroad with her family" suggest situations associated with the high social position of Florence's well-to-do family, but Florence's concern on these occasions is the world of poverty, of "workhouses" and "slums." The "reports" and "histories" are alike, not contrasted; they are both the subjects of Florence Nightingale's studies.

28. B. The first paragraph establishes the basic contrast of the passage, that of the conventional view of Florence Nightingale with the realistic view that this passage will present. The second, third and fourth paragraphs move chronologically from Florence Nightingale's youth, to her preparation, to her first success.

29. E. This final metaphor is the climax of the passage. The author has emphasized the contrast by the parallel construction of the sentence ("it was not a swan . . . it was an eagle.") The sentence is a final instance of the more genteel notion of Florence Nightingale ("a swan") and the author's vision of her strength and power ("an eagle").

Third Passage

From *The Trial of Socrates* by I. F. Stone

30. E. The author's repetition of the word "once" emphasizes the singularity of the advice; never before and never again would Socrates advise anyone to join the assembly. Choice **C** also has merit; however, while the repetition may add emphasis to Socrates's feelings about politicians, it is not the rhetorical purpose.

31. D. It appears that Socrates needs to do some self-examination of his own refusal. He makes a blanket dismissal of all capable men who shrink from state business, calling them "cowards," yet he himself is included in this group.

32. B. The rhetorical effect of the direct quotations is to help bring Socrates "alive"; they offer modern readers the opportunity to feel an emotional reaction to the ancient philosopher. Choices A and D are partially correct; the quotations do give the actual words and they do demonstrate Socrates's arguments, but these are not the author's intended rhetorical effect.

33. D. Socrates does seem to believe all of these negative stereotypes. The exception is Choice D, which is actually a positive statement (that public servants could be made competent through proper training).

34. A. The author's representation of Socrates's disdain comes through clearly with phrasing that emphasizes an "s" sound, such as "social snobbery," and "Socrates's scornful." This auditory repetition hisses out Socrates's ideas in a snarling fashion. Choice C is not correct because of the phrase "vulgar roughness." The repeated "s" sound is neither vulgar nor rough.

35. C. The speaker includes the quotation ". . . men who never gave a thought to public affairs" to emphasize Socrates's belief that politicians had no training or aptitude for their task. Although Choice E may be technically true, it is not the best response, because Socrates never acknowledged that diversity of talent may be the best feature of the assembly. Choices A and B are incorrect, because Socrates never refers to the tradesmen as "successful," nor does he think that business savvy translates into political success. Choice D contradicts the passage; Socrates does not think these are the "finest" professions.

36. E. While all of the answer choices are cited in the passage, only Choice E is not listed as one of the reasons for the speaker's surprise.

37. C. The speaker states "This natural question is never answered . . ." and he states further ". . . he was never so poor that he had to take a job or practice a trade." Thus, choices A, B, D, and E all contradict the passage.

38. D. In note #2 the speaker wishes to rebut Plato's supposed quote, stating, "There is no evidence that the historical Socrates ever spoke so unkindly and pretentiously. . . ." Choices A and C both mischaracterize the speaker's position on the overly-negative characterization of Socrates. Choices B and E are incorrect; the speaker is challenging both Plato's accuracy and his false superiority.

39. B. The staccato tempo of the sentences brings home the speaker's feelings that Socrates's upbringing and family life were very matter-of-fact and unremarkable; he experienced no glowing highlights, nor extreme penury, nor many hardships to overcome.

40. A. Socrates scoffs at the alleged "dunces and weaklings" in the assembly to persuade Charmides that he should not be shy, but rather, to proceed with his "excellent advice," which he has already offered in private. Choice E is incorrect, but only for the lack of a prefix; the speaker compares the assemblymen *un*favorably with other leaders.

41. **C.** The overt point of the "little bald-headed tinker" is to emphasize Socrates's disdain for his "unfit rivals." Choice A is incorrect; Charmides is not involved. Choices B, D, and E all reverse the speaker's interpretation of the story.

Fourth Passage

From *On Liberty* by John Stuart Mill

42. **C.** The author makes this clear distinction in lines 10–13: The "only purpose for which power can be rightfully exercised over any member . . . is to prevent harm to others." Choices A and B are inaccurate statements of Mill's ideas, and Choice D is not addressed. Mill does contend that children do not have sovereignty (E), but that contention is not the "one very simple principle."

43. **E.** The predicate nominative is the entire clause "that the sole end . . . self-protection." The clause states precisely what "That principle" is.

44. **D.** Mill insists that the only justification for controlling the acts of an individual is to prevent harm to others. No other answer choice names such individuals.

45. **B.** Parallel syntax is evident in the repetition of "or" plus a gerund: "or reasoning . . . or persuading . . . or entreating." None of the other answer choices can be found in this sentence.

46. **C.** Individuals have complete freedom in actions that affect only themselves—as Mill puts it, "Over himself, over his own body and mind." Choice A contradicts the passage, and B, D, and E are not addressed.

47. **D.** Children and "those backward states of society in which the race itself may be considered as in its nonage" (immaturity) may be forced to behave in a particular way by parent or government.

48. **A.** Despotism is acceptable "when dealing with barbarians" and when that form of government produces the improvement of its citizens. If this end is not achieved, despotism is unacceptable.

49. **E.** All of the choices, according to Mill, are allowable.

50. **B.** It can be inferred that, of the choices given, the author values the protection of society most highly. The essay deals primarily with the sovereignty of the individual except in matters of self-protection. But sovereignty of the individual is not among the answer choices. Choice A is incorrect because of the word "unlimited." Mill places restriction on individual freedom; it is not absolute.

51. **A.** The second paragraph gives exceptions to the general principle of individual sovereignty—in the case of children and of "backward states of society." The second paragraph does none of the things listed in choices B through E.

52. **D.** This is the major thrust of the essay. Choice A contradicts the passage. We have no way to determine Mill's opinion on whether Charlemagne would rule a mature society well (B); he is mentioned only as ruling a "backward society." Choices C and E can be eliminated because the word "always" is too extreme, too absolute.

53. **D.** The passage is presented in a matter-of-fact, analytical tone, without emotional wording. There is no evidence of sarcasm, cynicism, or pessimism. Nor is there any evidence of optimism; by acknowledging that it is at times necessary for a government to interfere in citizens' lives, Mill is more realistic than optimistic.

54. **C.** As we've seen, Mill does not encourage "absolute" freedom of action. He does not encourage behavior that harms others. While it is unlikely that Mill would strongly encourage people to indulge in "self-destructive" actions, he does assert that an individual should be free to do so, leaving C as the best answer.

55. **E.** Historical allusions are made to the governments of Akbar and Charlemagne. None of the other rhetorical devices is present in the essay.

Section II: Essay Questions

Question 1

Scoring Guide for Question 1 (African-American Music Influence)

9 Essays that earn a score of 9 meet the criteria for essays that receive a score of 8. In addition, they are especially sophisticated in the use of language, explanation, and argument.

8 Successful

These essays respond to the prompt **successfully,** employing ideas from at least three of the sources from the prompt. They take a position that defends, challenges, or qualifies the claim that African-American culture has influenced popular American music. They effectively argue the position and support the argument with appropriate evidence. The control of language is extensive and the writing errors are minimal.

7 These essays meet the criteria for essays that receive a score a 6 but provide more depth and strength to the argument and evidence. The prose style is mature and shows a wide control over language.

6 Satisfactory

These essays respond to the prompt **satisfactorily.** Using at least three of the sources from the prompt, these essays take a position that defends, challenges, or qualifies the claim that African-American culture has influenced popular American music. The position is adequately argued with support from appropriate evidence, although without the precision and depth of top-scoring essays. The writing may contain minor errors in diction or in syntax, but the prose is generally clear.

5 These essays take a position that defends, challenges, or qualifies the claim that African-American culture has influenced popular American music. It supports the position with generally appropriate evidence but may not adequately quote, either directly or indirectly, from three sources in the prompt. These essays may be inconsistent, uneven, or limited in the development of their argument. While the writing usually conveys the writer's ideas and perspectives, it may demonstrate lapses in diction or syntax or an overly-simplistic style.

4 Inadequate

These essays respond to the prompt **inadequately.** They have difficulty taking a clear position that defends, challenges, or qualifies the claim that African-American culture has influenced popular American music. The evidence may be insufficient or may not utilize enough sources from the prompt. The prose conveys the writer's ideas but suggests immature control over the elements of effective writing.

3 These essays meet the criteria for a score of 4 but reveal less success in taking a position that defends, challenges, or qualifies the claim that African-American culture has influenced popular American music. The presentation of evidence and arguments is unconvincing. These writers show little or no control over the elements of effective writing.

2 Little Success

These essays demonstrate **little success** at taking a position that defends, challenges, or qualifies the claim that African-American culture has influenced popular American music and show little success in presenting it clearly and with appropriate evidence from the sources in the prompt. These essays may misunderstand the prompt, may fail to establish a position with supporting evidence, or may substitute a simpler task by replying tangentially with unrelated, erroneous, or unsuitable explanation, argument, and/or evidence. The prose frequently demonstrates consistent weaknesses in the conventions of effective writing.

1 These essays meet the criteria for a score of 2 but are undeveloped, especially simplistic in their explanation, argument, and/or evidence, or weak in their control of writing.

High-Scoring Essay

The African-American community has long established a unique culture all its own; however, in the past decades African-American music, specifically, has greatly influenced the realm of American music, affecting all social-economic groups. This is largely due to the voice that African-Americans have offered to other individuals through finding a unique cultural identity and the general ability of the African-American community to serve as trend-setters that other cultures follow.

As rap is one of the forms of music created by African-Americans, it has essentially "emerged as one of the distinctive music genres of the past decade" in "articulating the experiences and conditions of African-Americans in a spectrum of marginalized situations," (Source B). Music has historically been a powerful force in the Black oppressed community. From living as objects of forced slavery in their homeland of Africa, to similar horrendous conditions in the United States, and even beyond the abolishment of slavery, many Blacks have expressed the importance of resonating their ancestors' anguish and their present pain through music. The gospel-slave chants gave way to the Blues and Jazz, and modern society has discovered rap as a new voice of the Black community. Many other minority races have endured similar experiences of racial injustice, but have yet to express their personal pains as collectively and uniquely as the African-American community. Because African-Americans have been able to verbalize and transfer their struggles into the public spectrum, other minority races have been able to find refuge in a genre of music that offers healing for their past grief. Like other Black musical genres that came before, rap, in representing the African-American community, has created versatile output. "[It] is thus not only music to dance and party to, but a potent form of cultural identity," for people to share their pain in a familiar ground of music, (Source B). This kind of force cannot but influence all areas of American culture. Just as jazz, blues and other African-American music forms gained acceptance in American culture in the past, so has rap become part of the mainstream of American music, seen through artists such as Eminem. Dr. Spence from Spelman College clarifies the appeal of Black culture as she explains that ". . . White America has always found Black culture to be exciting, exotic and perhaps more expressive and less restrained than what they identify as their culture. They find our culture to be very exciting and attractive. If you look at music, historically they have attempted to mimic our musical expression in terms of our pop artists and our dance. Elvis Presley admitted that much of his music and movement were patterned after Blacks" (Source E). Clearly African-American music has influenced mainstream American music to a strong degree.

Although one might infer that African-American influences only seem to affect those who have endured racial injustice, the reality is that this influence has steadily grown even in the Caucasian community. For example, even in locations known as "white East Coast establishments" such as Martha's Vineyard, Massachusetts, teenagers have embraced the look of "baggy jeans" with "Tommy Hilfiger shirts" that once was associated with rappers such as Biggie Smalls. While White Americans have not necessarily shared the racial struggles that African-Americans have endured, the fact that the Black community remains a dynamic innovator in fashion and attire has allowed the African-American community to assert its culture in a society that embraces new ideas and fresh trends. Ultimately, "Blacks' contribution to American culture is so rich and vibrant that everyone wants to benefit from it," (Source E). Americans are naturally drawn into the aesthetic and extraordinary quality of Black culture. The fact is, Blacks have "created a far-reaching constituency," in blending "gangsta images" with "powerful vehicles for cultural political expression," (Sources B and C). In terms of today's popular music and style trends, no group is more influential than artists in the African-American community. Moreover, mainstream society has embraced this style and accepted it as its own.

Its widespread effects, which impact all socioeconomic groups, prove that the African-American community has firmly established itself in American society, from clothing to music and to the language itself. Ultimately, the exotic and expressive nature of Black culture has manifested itself as an influential community that has affected all of American culture, which thrives on the vitality and nuances that Black individuals have explored in their music and lifestyles.

Analysis of the High-Scoring Essay

This essay earns a high score because of its intelligent presentation and its thorough grasp of American culture. The writer demonstrates a strong understanding of the influences of African-American music and culture in American society. The essay's introduction is concise, claiming that the influence of African-American music is directly linked to the strong voice of the African-American community.

The first body paragraph is exceptionally strong and it helps ensure that this essay earns its high score. Organized around a historical approach, the essay displays the writer's knowledge of the varied influences that have shaped African-American music for centuries. The essay does not overlook the important point that the Black community has traditionally used its music to give voice to ideas that otherwise could not be uttered safely. To hide "their ancestors' anguish and their present pain" (nice alliteration!), African-American musicians and minstrels have created a unique music that has morphed from gospel to blues to jazz to rap. The writer's grasp of this history is admirable and adds to the persuasive power of the essay. The writer also makes the interesting point that no other minority in American culture has achieved the status that the African-American culture has, none other has found such a strong voice. The writer also uses the sources in the prompt effectively, especially the quotation from Source E that helps to explain why greater American culture has embraced African-American music. The notion that African-American music is "exciting, exotic and perhaps more expressive and less restrained" clearly articulates the allure of African-American culture. Overall, this paragraph comes across forcefully because of its logic, its appreciation of history, and its integration of the sources.

Next, the writer explores the effect of the African-American community on realms that are related to but separate from the music genre. Establishing, via examples from the sources, that "white, East Coast establishments" have embraced African-American nuances in dress and in music, the writer makes a strong case that African-American culture does indeed have the power to influence mainstream American society.

The conclusion is not a tremendous addition to the essay, as it basically summarizes the content without adding any new ideas or insights. However, a reader must still give high praise to the essay as a whole. Its clear organization and well-developed ideas combine to create a logical progression through its stand on the topic. It utilizes the sources well and integrates them fluidly; this is the work of a writer who takes time to think carefully before putting pen to paper.

Medium-Scoring Essay

American culture has embraced African-American culture. The music which Americans listen to has been influenced greatly by the greater African American populous. Although African-American culture has maintained a secluded community throughout much of history, its influential abilities have opened up new styles of music in American music today.

African-American music is most notably distinctive for its "articulation of the experiences and conditions of African-Americans living in a spectrum of marginalized situations ranging from racial stereotyping and stigmatizing to struggle for survival in violent ghetto conditions," (Source B). The difficulties which African-Americans endured in the past have essentially become the source of musical inspiration. This in turn has given other Americans a refuge from their own personal struggles and given them a comfortable setting in which music has been revolutionized. Most minority cultures have faced discriminatory hardships. Yet, ultimately, the African-American culture has offered hope to all people. And while, the Caucasian population, as a majority race, may not have much in common with African-American culture on the surface level, the turmoil turned success of African-American culture embodies a universal American tradition.

Americans tend to embrace those who have come out of unfortunate circumstances and ultimately created a lavish lifestyle for themselves; the way in which African Americans have reflected this plight has accounted for some of its impact on the American culture. African-Americans, who grew up in impoverished neighborhoods but were still able to find success out of relative nothingness, exemplify a general perseverance. This perseverance has been accepted as a standard for American culture and given individuals of all cultures something to identify with. The "oversized personage of Brooklyn's Biggie Smalls, an admitted ex-drug dealer turned rapper" is essentially the picture depicted by the African-American culture, (Source D). For Americans, the paramount focus has been the ability of individuals to succeed in extenuating conditions.

In retrospect, the message of perseverance amidst the universal struggles that all cultures endure has made African-American culture alter the ways of American individuals and in turn, American music. Ultimately, it is the type of music which individuals listen to that shows their character and this is the main reason for of the influential abilities of African-American culture.

Analysis of the Medium-Scoring Essay

This writer presents an adequate essay that basically succeeds in addressing the prompt, albeit with very few references from the sources. The essay makes the mistake of beginning with a questionable assertion, that "American culture has embraced African-American culture." Making a global claim such as this is typical of immature writing; avoid presenting ideas in absolute terms that are unlikely to be completely accurate. Such overarching claims are usually only partially correct; surely they cannot be entirely true. If this writer were to carefully qualify the ideas in the first sentence, the reader would be more impressed with the essay's opening. It isn't wise to begin with a sentence that puts off the reader because of its perceived inaccuracy. The second sentence with its awkward phrasing also dims the reader's first impression of the essay. However, the writer does present a thesis that agrees with the notion that African-American culture has made major contributions to American music. Unfortunately, the balance of the essay does not fulfill this promise.

The second paragraph focuses on the idea that African-American music articulates the struggles of the African-American community. It makes an interesting point that most Americans can relate on some level with those who have suffered and survived, those who have risen to success against the odds. The writer does quote a relevant portion of Source B, but this paragraph would be stronger with additional discussion and more examples from the sources. For instance, Source E has an interesting comment about the "cultural voyeurism" that allows White Americans to vicariously relate to the Black community without actually experiencing their hardships. If the writer had included a discussion of an idea like this, the second paragraph would have demonstrated stronger development of its ideas.

The third paragraph discusses how Americans tend to embrace individuals who have overcome adversity and managed to reach a "lavish lifestyle." Unfortunately, this paragraph wanders somewhat off topic as it fails to relate the discussion to music. The paragraph tries to examine how African-American culture has influenced mainstream American culture, but it has little to say other than that Americans admire those who have risen above "unfortunate circumstances." Since this idea is already commonly accepted in American culture, this comment does not add much analytical depth to the essay. Unfortunately, this paragraph, like the others, is also marred with several grammatical and diction errors. The glaring sentence fragments (second sentence) and unnecessary repetition (". . . perseverance. This perseverance . . .") distract a reader from the writer's ideas. Additionally, the writer's stated points are oversimplified, once again claiming that perseverance is a "standard for American culture," and that the example of Biggie Smalls is "essentially the picture depicted by the African-American culture." Understandably, many knowledgeable people might disagree with these overly-broad assertions. Essay writers should avoid such naïve presentation and instead strive to demonstrate intellectual sophistication and factual accuracy in their diction.

The concluding paragraph repeats once again the same idea, that African-American culture has affected American society, and then blends in the concept of music; however, this position is not supported in the essay. In retrospect, the writer needs to focus more clearly on the initial thesis about music and then plan the essay more carefully to support it, or, conversely, revise the thesis to correspond to the ideas the essay actually discusses. Overall, this essay suffers from weak organization and inadequate paragraph development that explores too few of the ideas and information in the sources. The essay tries, but never manages, to rise above an average score.

Question 2

Scoring Guide for Question 2 (Benjamin Franklin)

9 Essays earning a score of 9 meet the criteria for essays that are scored an 8 and, in addition, are especially full or apt in their analysis. They frequently reveal particularly remarkable control of language.

8 Successful

These well-written essays demonstrate clear ideas **successfully** supported by thoughtful, relevant evidence. They illustrate a sound awareness of the logical requirements of an argumentative essay. Stylistically, these essays are mature, using sophisticated sentence structure and diction. The writing need not be error-free, but it clearly shows the ability to construct an effective essay through a combined command of language and logic.

7 Essays earning a score of 7 fit the description of essays that are scored a 6 but provide more complete analysis, and a more mature prose style.

6 Satisfactory

These essays advance a thesis but may provide weaker evidence for it, although the assertions are **satisfactory** and well presented. These essays' style is appropriate to the task, but perhaps with less maturity than that of the top-scoring papers. Some errors in diction or syntax may be present, but the writing demonstrates satisfactory control over the conventions of writing and presents ideas clearly.

5 These essays may be tentative in their assertion of a thesis and may not provide sufficient evidence or discussion to thoroughly convince. They may be adequately written but without control of the full range of elements of composition. Organization may be evident but not entirely effective.

4 Inadequate

Lower-scoring essays **inadequately** respond to the topic. These essays take the initial steps toward a thesis but fall short in the details necessary to convince. They attempt to convey a point of view but demonstrate weak control over diction, syntax, development, or organization. The prose may convey ideas, but may hint at immaturity in control of written English. Simplistic ideas coupled with a simplistic style may characterize low-scoring essays.

3 Essays earning a score of 3 meet the criteria for a score of 4 but demonstrate less ability to respond to the prompt. These essays may show less control over the elements of writing.

2 Little Success

These essays lack the clarity and persuasive force required for effective presentation of an argument. Some attempt may be made to address the issue, but with little or no evidence, the paper shows **little success** at responding to the prompt. They may be exceptionally short and poorly written on several counts. Organization and paragraph development may be particularly weak. Persistent weaknesses in grammar and mechanics may distract the reader.

1 These poorly written essays meet the criteria for a score of 2 but are undeveloped, especially simplistic in their analysis, weak in their control of language.

High-Scoring Essay

It is his reason that separates man from the creatures of the wild. Reason also fathers conscience, to act as a counterweight to the volatile animal passions of which his sentience has suddenly made him aware. If this were the only function of reason, to launch conscience, the world could theoretically be a better place. Imagine a society where a criminal, about to rob a hapless victim, stops as his mind reasons out the consequences. Reaching the reasonable conclusion that any punishment would be longer lasting and worse than the immediate benefits of his crime, the robber stops. Unfortunately, in reality, the human mind just does not work this way. Reason is not entirely an agent of good, of conscience. Reason can enter Promethean combat with the conscience it creates and shrewdly invent a means for its owner to justify some of his baser impulses.

Ben Franklin addresses man's propensity to justify and explain away his actions through reasoning, to allow caprices and animal impulses to persist. His *Autobiography* makes the valid point that once someone has his mind set on doing something, reason frequently acts as a tool to circumvent conscience rather than as an agent of that conscience.

Indeed, virtually any action can be justified through some semblance of reason, no matter how faulty the logic, how heinous the crime. For every violence, for every deceit, a dozen specious premises rise to the task of denying any wrongdoing by the criminal. For example, study the logic which convinced looters during any recent riots in American inner cities that they were justified in robbing innocent storekeepers. This kind of reasoning, sadly, occurs daily in the minds of humanity.

Empirical approaches to life, from the Socratic Method to Hegelian philosophy, have relied on reason to explain both the natural world and the human response to that world. Moral relativism and "situational ethics" depend on reason of a sort. Proponents of such philosophies insist that man must abandon preconceptions, that he must judge each situation as it happens, and use reason to determine what is morally correct under each set of specific circumstances which arise. But it is not only relativists who look to reason as a means of understanding and reacting to the world. Strict, Draconian moral codes find their justification in reason as well. Man's actions, whether representing the "rule of law," or the most liberal definitions of right and wrong, are always defended with arguments paying homage to Reason. This holds as true for the Supreme Court justice as for the urban pickpocket . . . whether the subject feels he is doing the will of God and country, or knows he is shrewdly evading responsibility. Reason is the tool of man's shell game with his conscience.

Franklin, then, is essentially correct. After a moment of balancing "between principle and inclination," man seizes upon the "convenience" of being a "reasonable creature, since it enables one to find or make a reason for everything one has a mind to do." What one has a mind to do may be quixotic or craven, vainglorious or altruistic, but whatever the case man can use reason to nullify the conscience that is its offspring.

Analysis of the High-Scoring Essay

This high-scoring essay begins with a relevant discussion of reason and its function. Introducing the idea that "reason fathers conscience," the writer provides a hypothetical example of a robber who stops mid-crime because his reason has convinced him the punishment would exceed the gain. The thesis follows, with the interesting concept that reason can engage in "Promethean combat" with the conscience to justify any human action. The writer is obviously linguistically talented; the sophisticated diction and syntax are impressive and set the reader's expectations high for the remainder of the essay.

The next paragraph acknowledges Ben Franklin as the inspiration for this topic and capsulizes Franklin's remarks about reason. This paragraph serves as a direct tie to the essay question, but it does not move the essay forward. Fortunately, the next paragraphs are much more impressive.

The third paragraph suggests that humans use reason to justify any kind of action, even immoral ones, and provides another relevant example, looters during recent riots who feel justified in their unlawful actions. The parallel structure in the phrase "no matter how faulty the logic, how heinous the crime" is pleasing to the ear and is another sign of the writer's sophistication.

The fourth paragraph includes a pertinent review of several philosophies and "empirical approaches" that use reason as a way of determining one's actions. This paragraph notes that all those taking positions, from Supreme Court justices to common thieves, use reason to justify actions. The paragraph ends with a somewhat mixed but still effective metaphor— "reason is the tool of man's shell game with his conscience." This writer continues to impress with stylistic sophistication and intellectual panache. High-scoring essays demonstrate the ability to think analytically and deeply, avoiding a surface-level presentation, and communicate ideas with mature techniques just as this essay does.

The concluding paragraph returns to Franklin's insight, that humans will always find a reasonable way to explain any action. The student once more uses sophisticated style and diction with phrasing like "quixotic or craven, vainglorious or altruistic." This writer possesses the command of language evidenced only in top-scoring essays. This essay might be improved if it recognized Franklin's obviously playful tone and responded in kind, at least to some extent. But, overall, the paper is on topic, philosophically insightful, and intelligently presented and provides sufficient convincing examples from real-life situations. It definitely deserves a high score.

Low-Scoring Essay

Ben Franklin is one of our most important Founding Fourfathers. Like Alexander Hamilton and others who never achieved the presidency, he still had a profound impact on the U.S. His importance is shown in his autobiography, where he discusses vegetarianism and the morality of eating fish among other topics.

Ben Franklin contemplates how people can change their mind about things, such as whether it's O.K. to eat animals that have been alive (like fish). He acknowledges that sometimes people are tempted to do something they might think wrong, just as he was tempted by the delightful smell of fish cooking when he was on a boat trip. Franklin also explains that people use reason to approve their actions. His ideas about reason are right. Man frequently employs reason to back up his deeds, whether they are right or wrong. It seems that everyone can find a way to defend their actions. I have personally seen this trait at work, both in myself and my friends.

By using reason, Franklin proved that eating the fish, even though he believed in vegetarianism before, wasn't wrong after all. In the end, Ben Franklin says that it is a good thing that he is a reasonable creature. He means that he was reasonable enough to be open-minded about eating fish; he changed his mind accordingly after listening to his reason. I think Franklin was correct in this point too. It's important to be open-minded about things and not to eliminate what you're willing to try. Like Franklin, we shouldn't be scared to try something new if our reason can explain it to us.

Thus, Ben Franklin shows that reason is a valid tool in helping man to defend his actions, because without reason his actions might be stuck in the same old ways He would never try some thing new. And Benjamin Franklin, as he was a great man of our country, is someone to whom that was important.

Analysis of the Low-Scoring Essay

This poorly written essay would score in the low range. The first paragraph is ineffective. It fails to address the question of the validity of Franklin's assertions on justifying one's actions through reasoning. The paragraph lacks a thesis and includes such irrelevant information as the reference to Alexander Hamilton. The student also demonstrates weak command of language, misusing words such as "Founding Fourfathers."

The second paragraph improves a bit and approaches the topic. Beginning with a paraphrase of Franklin's fish-eating experience, the student gives an opinion on the validity of using reason. But this thesis is especially weak, merely claiming that Franklin was "right." The writer offers no evidence to convince the reader, but rather claims only to have personally seen some examples.

The next paragraph discusses the need for one to be reasonable in order to try new things. The writer is on shaky ground once again, exhibiting simplistic ideas with no support.

The conclusion merely summarizes the essay and still avoids the topic. This essay deserves a low score because it offers no proof for its assertions, its treatment of the topic is superficial, and its presentation is riddled with errors and unsophisticated diction.

Question 3

Scoring Guide for Question 3 (Samuel Johnson)

9 These essays meet the criteria for essays that receive a score of an 8 and, in addition, they are deeper in their understanding of Johnson's ideas. These essays frequently reveal an exquisite use of language.

8 Successful

These well-written essays **successfully** take a stand concerning Johnson's ideas on possessions and substantially support it. The thesis is articulate and relevant to the topic. These essays provide strong and relevant evidence that is intelligently connected to the thesis and demonstrate an understanding of the needs of the essay. Although they need not be without errors, these essays show mature command of style and language.

7 These essays meet the requirements for essays that score a 6 and, in addition, demonstrate a thorough understanding of the author's ideas, while providing stronger and more relevant evidence. The prose style is generally more mature.

6 Satisfactory

These essays **satisfactorily** contemplate Johnson's ideas on possessions but produce a less explicit thesis. Perhaps less relevant or insufficient evidence is offered, and these essays may not be as thoroughly convincing as top-scoring essays. Although well-written, these essays may demonstrate some errors while still showing satisfactory control over diction and the essay requirements.

5 The adequate presentation in these essays includes a thesis but one that is perhaps not as well thought-out as in higher-scoring essays. The ideas may be too hastily conceived. Overall, the argument may not be as strong or convincing as in higher-scoring essays. These essays may appear more opinionated without sufficient evidence to support the opinions. Acceptable organization may be evident, but the style may not be as sophisticated as that in higher-scoring papers.

4 Inadequate

These low-scoring essays fail to convince and therefore **inadequately** address the prompt. The weak presentation may include an unsupported or unsubstantiated thesis, weak paragraph development, and/or poor organization. Confusion may be present in the essay's ideas. Superficial thinking and evidence may be present. Frequent mechanical errors may persist.

3 Essays earning a score of 3 meet the criteria for a score of 4 but demonstrate little understanding of the ideas and a lack of evidence to support the arguments made. These essays may show little control over the elements of writing.

2 Little Success

These poorly written essays lack clarity and coherence. They may have an overly obvious thesis or no thesis at all. Little or no evidence may be a problem, and the connection between the evidence and the thesis may be shallow or nonexistent. These essays may be unusually short and exhibit poor fundamental essay skills. Weak sentence construction may persist, and consistent weaknesses in command of the language may be present. There is **little success** in persuading the reader.

1 These poorly written essays meet the criteria for a score of 2 but are undeveloped, especially simplistic in their analysis, and weak in their control of language.

High-Scoring Essay

There are as many different motivations and convictions which serve to "make people tick" as there are people to experience such impulses. Beyond the broad abstractions, each of us may have a unique force driving us toward happiness—toward the degree of success or self-fulfillment we desire. Nevertheless, the American Dream of financial security and independence, of building a comfortable life, is widespread if not universal.

The poor must struggle for the rudimentary elements of sustenance. The rich are at times perceived as avaricious, striving continually like Philistines for material rewards. Yet such characteristics tend to oversimplify the issues. The truth of the inverse relation Samuel Johnson describes—"Our desires increase with our possessions"—depends closely on his wording.

Desires may increase with our possessions, in the sense that they will numerically increase. Desire, however, the drive and will to succeed, tends to stay constant with each individual, whether poor or wealthy. A person who has worked relentlessly from humble beginnings will likely not abandon that work ethic simply because he has reached some nebulous, ill-defined level of attainment that others term "success." Conversely, Johnson's statement may not apply to the stereotypical "happy-go-lucky" person who desires nothing more than an average home and job, and who may be completely satisfied with his life, once having attained these possessions. Some people simply do not want to improve their place in society, nor do they want to increase their possessions.

Johnson's second statement is more unequivocally true. He writes, "The knowledge that something remains yet unenjoyed impairs our enjoyment of the good before us." Consistent with many a common aphorism—a bird in the hand is worth two in the bush, the grass is always greener on the other side, ad infinitum—Johnson is correctly attesting that many possessions and concrete rewards tend to numb and dull our perceptions, to make us less cognizant of the simple things which enrich our lives more than any amount of gold or stock certificates ever can.

The trick to correctly evaluating the veracity of Johnson's assertion is to avoid blanket generalizations, i.e. "all rich are greedy" or "all poor people are easily pleased." Discerning readers will be able to point to instances in which Johnson is proved correct, and others which contradict his thesis. Nevertheless, it would not be unfair to say that he makes a reasonable statement.

Analysis of the High-Scoring Essay

The first paragraph, although it doesn't directly address Samuel Johnson's concepts, indirectly qualifies them. The writer seems to feel that Johnson's remarks don't universally apply, that people have "different motivations." Although it is refreshing to find a student who does not reach a blanket assertion too quickly, this introduction would improve with more precise diction.

The second paragraph deals with Johnson's ideas more overtly and states the writer's opinion more clearly—that to accept Johnson's generalities is to "oversimplify" the issues. Interestingly, this is exactly what colleges do *not* want students to do; oversimplification in essays demonstrates a simple mind.

The third paragraph offers a more philosophical discussion of Johnson's notion regarding desire. The student makes a distinction between "desires" and "desire," defining "desire" as the "drive and will to succeed" and asserting that people possess this quality in varying degrees. The writer provides hypothetical examples: the person who has a diligent work ethic and doesn't abandon it, even after achieving success, and one who has earned some possessions, such as a home, and desires no more. These examples provide support for the writer's opinion that the first half of Johnson's statement should be qualified.

The fourth paragraph examines Johnson's second assertion and agrees that humans are not always happy with what they have, an idea the writer supports by citing two aphorisms, although the first incorrectly suggests a point of view opposite to that of Johnson and the student writer. The writer asserts that we are "less cognizant" of the simple pleasures of life which "enrich our lives more" than material objects ever can. While this paragraph shows some flaws in thinking, they are not severe enough to lower the score. If the writer were to have time to polish the essay, it appears that these flaws would vanish. In other words, the writer seems to be one who would recognize and repair the essay's minor mistakes, given more time.

The writer's conclusion restates his or her opinion that Johnson's statement, although partially true, cannot be universally applied. The essay, on the whole, is well-written and insightful.

Medium-Scoring Essay

Most people want to have money and attain success. But then what happens when you achieve that goal, and move from poor to rich? Many Americans just become greedy. They already have a lot, but they just want more. Their thirst for money cannot be satisfied, like a man in the desert.

Samuel Johnson addressed this problem. He wrote, "Our desires increase with our possessions. The knowledge that something remains yet unenjoyed impairs our enjoyment of the good before us." I agree that this usually true, and it can be seen in all classes of society. Even poor people prove this point, because they need to first get a house and food for their family. Once they do that, they can feel that the house is no longer good enough and they want to move up. So this family works harder to get a newer house and more possessions, but they forget to appreciate what they have at the time, always thinking that they need more. It's like the unsatisfied family in D. H. Lawrence's "Rocking Horse Winner" that knows "there must be more money!"

This is also the usual attitude that rich people have about money. They are usually less humble about money because they are rich. It is like a game to these rich people, to see how much more money they can get. They are usually more likely to be greedy than the poor or middle class people who just want food, a place to live, and maybe an entertaining evening on occasion; these people think like the lead actor in the movie "Wall Street" who said that "Greed is good."

Rich people are greedier. They usually want to have yachts and fly all over the world to visit ancient ruins or walk the streets of Paris. But poor and middle class people, whether they admit it or not, would probably like the same things, or at least they would like the opportunity for the same things. People just forget to enjoy what they have and always think of what else they need, what else they can buy. Samuel Johnson was correct years ago; his ideas are even more true in modern times.

Analysis of the Medium-Scoring Essay

This essay would likely receive a score near the lower end of the medium range. The introductory paragraph seems to agree with Johnson but is not clear on the agreement.

The second paragraph states the writer's opinion—that he or she does agree with Johnson—and continues with the theoretical example of a poor family that wants more possessions even after basic needs have been met. The student includes a pertinent quotation from D. H. Lawrence, but the presentation is not sophisticated, with the quotation seemingly added as an afterthought.

The third paragraph addresses the rich and their attitudes toward money. As in previous paragraphs, the writer doesn't substantiate opinions with convincing discussion or specific evidence. The quotation from the movie *Wall Street,* while superficially related to the subject, provides no strong evidence.

The conclusion restates the writer's opinion once again and continues to make generalities about human nature that need additional support in order to convince a reader. The student *is* to be commended for integrating Johnson's ideas throughout the essay and for good organization. However, these positive points are offset by the negative: an overly opinionated tone, a lack of both adequate discussion and convincing examples, and faults in style and command of language.

PART VII

SUGGESTED READING LIST

Suggested Reading List

Following is a list of important authors and some of their works that are similar to those used on the AP English Language and Composition Exam. The list is not meant to be all-inclusive or required reading for every student, but reading these works extensively and analyzing the authors' use of language will give you excellent preparation for the exam.

Autobiography, Biography, Journal, and History

Maya Angelou

Gather Together in My Name
The Heart of a Woman
I Know Why the Caged Bird Sings
Singin' and Swingin' and Gettin' Merry Like Christmas

Walter Jackson Bate

John Keats
Samuel Johnson

Charles A. Beard

An Economic Interpretation of the Constitution
The Rise of American Civilization (with Mary R. Beard)

James Boswell

The Life of Samuel Johnson, LL.D.

Van Wyck Brooks

An Autobiography
Days of Phoenix
From a Writer's Notebook

Thomas Carlyle

The French Revolution
Past and Present

Bruce Catton

Mr. Lincoln's Army
A Stillness at Appomattox

Sir Winston Churchill

Blood, Sweat, and Tears
Europe Unite: Speeches 1947 and 1948
A History of the English-Speaking Peoples
In the Balance: Speeches 1949 and 1950
Marlborough
My Early Life
Their Finest Hour

Charles Dana

Any of his nonfiction

Thomas De Quincey

Confessions of an English Opium Eater

Frederick Douglass

The Life and Times of Frederick Douglass
My Bondage and My Freedom
Narrative of the Life of Frederick Douglass

Leon Edel

Bloomsbury: A House of Lions
Henry James, A Life
The Stuff of Sleep and Dreams
Telling Lives

Richard Ellmann

Eminent Domain: Yeats among Wilde, Joyce, Pound, Eliot, and Auden
James Joyce

Antonia Fraser

King James I of England
Mary, Queen of Scots
Oliver Cromwell
The Warrior Queens
The Weaker Vessel: Women's Lot in Seventeenth-Century England

Edward Gibbon

The History of the Decline and Fall of the Roman Empire

Lillian Hellman

Scoundrel Time
An Unfinished Woman

William Dean Howells

Years of My Youth

Alfred Kazin

New York Jew

Starting Out in the Thirties

A Walker in the City

Helen Keller

The Story of My Life

Ross King

Brunelleschi's Dream: How a Renaissance Genius Reinvented Architecture

The Judgment of Paris

Michelangelo and The Pope's Ceiling

Maxine Hong Kingston

China Men

The Woman Warrior

T. E. Lawrence

The Revolt in the Desert

Seven Pillars of Wisdom

Gerda Lerner

The Creation of Patriarchy

The Female Experience: An American Documentary

The Majority Finds Its Past: Placing Women in History

Thomas Macaulay

Critical and Historical Essays

History of England from the Accession of James II

Malcolm X

The Autobiography of Malcolm X

Samuel Eliot Morison

Christopher Columbus, Admiral of the Ocean Sea

The Growth of the American Republic

Harrison Gray Otis: Urbane Federalist

John Henry Newman

Any of his nonfiction

Francis Parkman

The Oregon Trail
Pioneers of France in the New World

Samuel Pepys

Diary

Richard Rodriguez

Days of Obligation
Hunger of Memory

Mari Sandoz

The Battle of the Little Big Horn
Old Jules

Arthur M. Schlesinger, Jr.

The Age of Jackson
The Age of Roosevelt
The Bitter Heritage
Robert Kennedy and His Times
A Thousand Days

George Trevelyan

English Social History

Barbara Tuchman

Bible and Sword
A Distant Mirror
The Guns of August
The Proud Tower
The March of Folly

Richard Wright

American Hunger
Black Boy

Anzia Yezierska

Bread and Givers
The Open Cage
Red Ribbon on a White Horse

Essay, Fiction, and Criticism

Joseph Addison

Selections from *The Tatler* and *The Spectator*

James Agee

Collected Short Prose

A Death in a Family

Michael Arlen

An American Verdict

The Camera Age: Essays on Television

Exiles

Matthew Arnold

Any of his criticism

Margaret Atwood

Cat's Eye

The Handmaid's Tale

Sir Francis Bacon

The Advancement of Learning

The New Atlantis

James Baldwin

Another Country

The Devil Finds Work

The Evidence of Things Not Seen

The First Next Time

Go Tell It on the Mountain

If Beale Street Could Talk

Notes of a Native Son

G. K. Chesterton

Heretics

St. Francis of Assisi

St. Thomas Aquinas

The Victorian Age in Literature

Kenneth Clark

Another Part of the Wood

Civilization

The Other Half

Samuel Taylor Coleridge

Any of his criticism

Arlene Croce

Any of her criticism

Joan Didion

A Book of Common Prayer

Salvador

Slouching Towards Bethlehem

The Year of Magical Thinking

Any of her essays

Ralph Waldo Emerson

The Journals and Miscellaneous Notebooks

Any of his essays

Northrop Frye

Anatomy of Criticism

Fearful Symmetry

Fools of Time

Paul Fussell

Bad, or the Dumbing of America

The Great War and Modern Memory

"Thank God for the Atom Bomb" and Other Essays

Nadine Gordimer

Face to Face

My Son's Story

Not for Publication

Any of her essays

William Hazlitt

Any of his criticism

Zora Neale Hurston

Dust Tracks on a Road

Jonah's Gourd Vine

Their Eyes Were Watching God

Ruth Prawer Jhabvala

Heart and Dust

In Search of Love and Beauty

Samuel Johnson

The Lives of the Poets

Selections from *The Idler* and *The Rambler*

Pauline Kael

5001 Nights at the Movies

I Lost It at the Movies

State of the Art

William Hugh Kenner

A Colder Eye

Charles Lamb

Tales from Shakespeare

Any of his essays

Stephen Leacock

Last Leaves

Winnowed Wisdom

Norman Mailer

Ancient Evenings

The Armies of the Night

The Naked and the Dead

Pieces and Pontifications

Mary McCarthy

Cannibals and Missionaries

Memories of a Catholic Girlhood

The Writing on the Wall

Scott Momaday

The Names: A Memoir

The Way to Rainy Mountain

Montaigne

Any of his essays

Vladimir Nabokov

Lectures on Literature
Pnin
Speak, Memory

V. S. Naipaul

Among the Believers: An Islamic Journey
The Returns of Eva Peron

Joyce Carol Oates

Contraries: Essays
The Edge of Impossibility
First Person Singular
New Haven, New Earth
On Boxing
Woman Writer

Tillie Olsen

Mother to Daughter, Daughter to Mother
Silences
Tell Me a Riddle
Yonnonida

George Orwell

Down and Out in Paris and London
Shooting an Elephant

Cynthia Ozick

Art and Ardor
The Cannibal Galaxy

Walter Pater

Any of his criticism

Adrienne Rich

Of Woman Born
On Lies, Secrets, and Silence

John Ruskin

Modern Painters
Praeterita
Any other criticism

George Santayana

The Life of Reason, or, The Phases of Human Progress
The Sense of Beauty

George Bernard Shaw

The Intelligent Woman's Guide to Socialism and Capitalism
Any of his criticism

Susan Sontag

Against Interpretation
Aids and Its Metaphors
Illness as Metaphor
Styles of Radical Will
Regarding the Pain of Others

Richard Steele

Selections from *The Spectator* and *The Tatler*

John Updike

Assorted Prose
Hugging the Shore: Essays and Criticism
Self Consciousness

Gore Vidal

Matters of Fact and Fiction
Reflections upon a Sinking Ship
View from a Window

Alice Walker

In Love and Trouble
You Can't Keep a Good Woman Down

Eudora Welty

The Eye of the Story: Selected Essays and Reviews
The Golden Apples
Losing Battles
One Writer's Beginnings

E. B. White

The Essays of E. B. White
One Man's Meat

Oscar Wilde

Any of his criticism

Edmund Wilson

Axle's Castle: A Study in the Imaginative Literature of 1870 to 1930
The Devils and Canon Barham: Ten Essays on Poets, Novelists, and Monsters
Letters on Literature and Politics`
Patriotric Gore: Studies in the Literature of the American Civil War
The Shores of Light

Virginia Woolf

The Common Reader
The Death of a Moth
The Moment
Roger Fry
A Room of One's Own
Three Guineas
A Writer's Diary

Political Writing and Journalism

Roger Angell

Five Seasons: A Baseball Companion
Late Innings
Once More Around the Park

Hannah Arendy

Between Past and Future
The Human Condition
On Revolution
The Origins of Totalitarianism

Simone de Beauvoir

The Coming of Age
The Prime of Life
The Second Sex

William F. Buckley

God and Man at Yale
The Governor Listeth
On the Firing Line

Michel-Guillaume Jean de Crèvecoeur

Letters from an American Farmer

Elizabeth Drew

American Journal: The Events of 1976
Washington Journal: The Events of 1973–1974

W. E. B. Du Bois

Autobiography
The Philadelphia Negro
The Souls of Black Folk
Worlds of Color

Nora Ephron

Crazy Salad: Some Things About Women
Wallflower at the Orgy

Frances Fitzgerald

America Revisited
Cities on Hill
Fire in the Lake

Janet Flanner

Janet Flanner's World: Uncollected Writings, 1932–1975
Men and Monuments
Paris Was Yesterday: 1925–1939

John Kenneth Galbraith

The Affluent Society
Ambassador's Journal
The Anatomy of Power
The Nature of Mass Poverty

Charlotte Perkins Gilman

The Charlotte Perkins Gilman Reader
Herland

Ellen Goodman

At Large
Close to Home
Keeping in Touch
Making Sense

Thomas Hobbes

Leviathan

Philosophical Rudiments

Thomas Jefferson

Any of his writings

George Kennan

American Diplomacy 1900–1950

Democracy and the Student Left

Sketches from a Life

Martin Luther King, Jr.

Stride Toward Freedom

A Testament of Hope

The Trumpet of Conscience

John Locke

An Essay Concerning Human Understanding

Two Treatises on Government

Andy Logan

The Man Who Robbed the Robber Barons

Machiavelli

The Prince

John McPhee

Headmaster

A Sense of Who You Are

H. L. Mencken

The Bathtub Hoax and Other Blasts and Bravos from the Chicago Tribune

A Choice of Days

H. L. Mencken's Smart Set Criticism

In Defense of Women

Selected Prejudices

John Stuart Mill

On Liberty

The Subjection of Women

Utilitarianism

Sir Thomas More

Utopia

Jan Morris

Destinations: Essays from Rolling Stone

Olive Schreiner

The Story of an African Farm

William L. Shirer

Berlin Diary
The Nightmare Years
20th Century Journey

Red Smith

The Red Smith Reader
To Absent Friends

Lincoln Steffens

Autobiography
The Shame of the Cities
The Upbuilders

Jonathan Swift

Democracy in America
The Old Regime and the Revolution

Calvin Trillin

American Fried
An Education in Georgia
Third Helpings
Uncivil Liberties

T. H. White

Breach of Faith
Fire in the Ashes
In Search of History
The Making of the President: 1960

Tom Wolfe

Any of his essays

Science and Nature Writing

Isaac Asimov

The Exploding Suns
In Joy Still Felt (autobiography)
In Memory Yet Green (autobiography)
Until the Sun Dies

Jacob Bronowski

The Origins of Knowledge and Imagination
A Sense of the Future

Annie Dillard

An America Childhood
Holy the Firm
Living by Fiction
Pilgrim at Tinker Creek
Teaching a Stone to Talk: Expeditions and Encounters
The Writing Life

Gretel Ehrlich

The Solace of Open Spaces
The Future of Ice: A Journey into Cold

Stephen Jay Gould

Ever Since Darwin
Hen's Teeth and Horse's Toes
The Mismeasure of Man
Time's Arrow, Time's Cycle
An Urchin in the Storm

Richard P. Hallion

On the Frontier: Experimental Flight at NASA Dryden
Taking Flight: Inventing the Aerial Age from Antiquity through the First World War
The Wright Brothers: Heirs to Prometheus
Storm Over Iraq: Air Power and the Gulf War

Peter Matthiessen

At Play in the Fields of the Lord

Far Tortuga

In the Spirit of Crazy Horse

The Snow Leopard

The Tree Where Man Was Born

Margaret Mead

And Keep Your Powder Dry: An Anthropologist Looks at America

Blackberry Winter

Coming of Age in Samoa

Carl Sagan

The Dragons of Eden

A Path Where No Man Thought

Lewis Thomas

The Fragile Species

Late-Night Thoughts on Listening to Mahler's 9th Symphony

The Lives of a Cell: The Notes of a Biology Watcher

The Medusa and the Snail

Final Preparation: "The Final Touches"

1. Spend your last week of preparation on general review of key concepts, test-taking strategies, and techniques.

2. Don't cram the night before the test! It's a waste of time.

3. Remember to bring the proper materials: three or four sharpened No. 2 pencils, an eraser, several ballpoint pens, and a watch.

4. Start off crisply, answering the questions you know first and then coming back to the harder ones.

5. If you can eliminate one or more of the answer choices, make an educated guess.

6. Mark in the reading passages, underline key words, and jot down important information. Take advantage of being permitted to write in the test booklet.

7. Make sure that you're answering what is being asked and that your answer is reasonable.

8. Cross out incorrect choices immediately in the test booklet in order to avoid reconsidering a choice you've already eliminated.

9. Plan your essays carefully and monitor your timing.

Section II: Essays

Section II: Essays

CUT HERE

Section II: Essays

CUT HERE

Section II: Essays

CUT HERE

Section II: Essays

CUT HERE

CUT HERE

Section II: Essays

CUT HERE

Section II: Essays

Section II: Essays

CUT HERE

Section II: Essays

Section II: Essays

CUT HERE